Exploring Security in Software Architecture and Design

Michael Felderer
University of Innsbruck, Austria

Riccardo Scandariato
Chalmers University of Technology, Sweden & University of Gothenburg, Sweden

A volume in the Advances in
Information Security, Privacy, and
Ethics (AISPE) Book Series

Published in the United States of America by
    IGI Global
    Information Science Reference (an imprint of IGI Global)
    701 E. Chocolate Avenue
    Hershey PA, USA 17033
    Tel: 717-533-8845
    Fax: 717-533-8661
    E-mail: cust@igi-global.com
    Web site: http://www.igi-global.com

Library of Congress Cataloging-in-Publication Data

Names: Felderer, Michael, editor. | Scandariato, Riccardo, editor.
Title: Exploring security in software architecture and design / Michael
  Felderer and Riccardo Scandariato, editor.
Description: Hershey, PA : Information Science Reference, [2018] | Includes
  bibliographical references.
Identifiers: LCCN 2018008109| ISBN 9781522563136 (h/c) | ISBN 9781522563143
  (eISBN)
Subjects: LCSH: Computer security. | Software architecture--Security
  measures. | Software engineering--Security measures.
Classification: LCC QA76.9.A25 E996 2018 | DDC 005.8--dc23 LC record available at https://lccn.
loc.gov/2018008109

This book is published in the IGI Global book series Advances in Information Security, Privacy, and Ethics (AISPE) (ISSN: 1948-9730; eISSN: 1948-9749)

British Cataloguing in Publication Data
A Cataloguing in Publication record for this book is available from the British Library.

All work contributed to this book is new, previously-unpublished material.
The views expressed in this book are those of the authors, but not necessarily of the publisher.

For electronic access to this publication, please contact: eresources@igi-global.com.

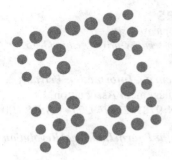

Advances in Information Security, Privacy, and Ethics (AISPE) Book Series

ISSN:1948-9730
EISSN:1948-9749

Editor-in-Chief: Manish Gupta, State University of New York, USA

MISSION

As digital technologies become more pervasive in everyday life and the Internet is utilized in ever increasing ways by both private and public entities, concern over digital threats becomes more prevalent.

The **Advances in Information Security, Privacy, & Ethics (AISPE) Book Series** provides cutting-edge research on the protection and misuse of information and technology across various industries and settings. Comprised of scholarly research on topics such as identity management, cryptography, system security, authentication, and data protection, this book series is ideal for reference by IT professionals, academicians, and upper-level students.

COVERAGE

- Technoethics
- Privacy-Enhancing Technologies
- IT Risk
- Security Information Management
- Information Security Standards
- Privacy Issues of Social Networking
- Device Fingerprinting
- CIA Triad of Information Security
- Cyberethics
- Computer ethics

IGI Global is currently accepting manuscripts for publication within this series. To submit a proposal for a volume in this series, please contact our Acquisition Editors at Acquisitions@igi-global.com or visit: http://www.igi-global.com/publish/.

Titles in this Series

For a list of additional titles in this series, please visit:
https://www.igi-global.com/book-series/advances-information-security-privacy-ethics/37157

Advanced Methodologies and Technologies in System Security, Information Privacy, ...
Mehdi Khosrow-Pour, D.B.A. (Information Resources Management Association, USA)
Information Science Reference • ©2019 • 417pp • H/C (ISBN: 9781522574927) • US $285.00

Handbook of Research on Information and Cyber Security in the Fourth Industrial Revolution
Ziska Fields (University of KwaZulu-Natal, South Africa)
Information Science Reference • ©2018 • 647pp • H/C (ISBN: 9781522547631) • US $345.00

Security and Privacy in Smart Sensor Networks
Yassine Maleh (University Hassan I, Morocco) Abdellah Ezzati (University Hassan I,
Morocco) and Mustapha Belaissaoui (University Hassan I, Morocco)
Information Science Reference • ©2018 • 441pp • H/C (ISBN: 9781522557364) • US $215.00

The Changing Scope of Technoethics in Contemporary Society
Rocci Luppicini (University of Ottawa, Canada)
Information Science Reference • ©2018 • 403pp • H/C (ISBN: 9781522550945) • US $225.00

Handbook of Research on Information Security in Biomedical Signal Processing
Chittaranjan Pradhan (KIIT University, India) Himansu Das (KIIT University, India)
Bighnaraj Naik (Veer Surendra Sai University of Technology (VSSUT), India) and Nilanjan
Dey (Techno India College of Technology, India)
Information Science Reference • ©2018 • 414pp • H/C (ISBN: 9781522551522) • US $325.00

Handbook of Research on Network Forensics and Analysis Techniques
Gulshan Shrivastava (National Institute of Technology Patna, India) Prabhat Kumar
(National Institute of Technology Patna, India) B. B. Gupta (National Institute of Technology
Kurukshetra, India) Suman Bala (Orange Labs, France) and Nilanjan Dey (Techno India
College of Technology, India)
Information Science Reference • ©2018 • 509pp • H/C (ISBN: 9781522541004) • US $335.00

For an entire list of titles in this series, please visit:
https://www.igi-global.com/book-series/advances-information-security-privacy-ethics/37157

701 East Chocolate Avenue, Hershey, PA 17033, USA
Tel: 717-533-8845 x100 • Fax: 717-533-8661
E-Mail: cust@igi-global.com • www.igi-global.com

Table of Contents

Detailed Table of Contents

Chapter 1

    Martin Gilje Jaatun, SINTEF Digital, Norway
    Karin Bernsmed, SINTEF Digital, Norway
    Daniela Soares Cruzes, SINTEF Digital, Norway
    Inger Anne Tøndel, SINTEF Digital, Norway

Threat modeling is a way to get an overview of possible attacks against your systems. The advantages of threat modeling include tackling security problems early, improved risk assessments, and more effective security testing. There will always be limited resources available for security, and threat modeling will allow you to focus on the most important areas first. There is no one single "correct" way of doing threat modeling, and "agile" is no excuse for not doing it. This chapter describes the authors' experiences with doing threat modeling with agile development organizations, outlining challenges to be faced and pitfalls to be avoided.

Chapter 2

    Basel Katt, Norwegian University of Science and Technology, Norway
    Nishu Prasher, Statistics Norway, Norway

Security assurance is the confidence that a system meets its security requirements and is resilient against security vulnerabilities and failures. Existing approaches can be characterized as (1) qualitative in nature, (2) tend to achieve their goals manually to a large extent, (3) very costly, (4) development-process oriented, and finally, (3) treat all security requirements within one domain equally for all applications regardless of the context. In this chapter, the authors propose a security assurance framework and its assurance evaluation process. The framework and process depend on a quantitative security assurance metrics that were developed too. The proposed metric considers both the security requirements and vulnerability. Weight has been introduced to the security requirement metric to measure the importance of security requirements that need to be fulfilled. The framework with the proposed quantitative assurance metrics are evaluated and validated using two field case studies related to two operational REST APIs that belong to and are used by Statistics Norway.

Chapter 3
Kalle Rindell, University of Turku, Finland
Sami Hyrynsalmi, Tampere University of Technology, Finland
Ville Leppänen, University of Turku, Finland

Agile software development was introduced in the beginning of the 2000s to increase the visibility and efficiency software projects. Since then it has become as an industry standard. However, fitting sequential security engineering development models into iterative and incremental development practices in agile methods has caused difficulties in defining, implementing, and verifying the security properties of software. In addition, agile methods have also been criticized for decreased quality of documentation, resulting in decreased security assurance necessary for regulative purposes and security measurement. As a consequence, lack of security assurance can complicate security incident management, thus increasing the software's potential lifetime cost. This chapter clarifies the requirements for software security assurance by using an evaluation framework to analyze the compatibility of established agile security development methods: XP, Scrum, and Kanban. The results show that the agile methods are not inherently incompatible with security engineering requirements.

Chapter 4
Gencer Erdogan, SINTEF Digital, Norway
Phu H. Nguyen, SINTEF Digital, Norway
Fredrik Seehusen, SINTEF Digital, Norway
Ketil Stølen, SINTEF Digital, Norway
Jon Hofstad, PWC, Norway
Jan Øyvind Aagedal, Equatex, Norway

Risk-driven testing and test-driven risk assessment are two strongly related approaches, though the latter is less explored. This chapter presents an evaluation of a test-driven security risk assessment approach to assess how useful testing is for validating and correcting security risk models. Based on the guidelines for case study research, two industrial case studies were analyzed: a multilingual financial web application and a mobile financial application. In both case studies, the testing yielded new information, which was not found in the risk assessment phase. In the first case study, new vulnerabilities were found that resulted in an update of the likelihood values of threat scenarios and risks in the risk model. New vulnerabilities were also identified and added to the risk model in the second case study. These updates led to more accurate risk models, which indicate that the testing was indeed useful for validating and correcting the risk models.

Chapter 5

    Nasser Al-Mur Al-Hadhrami, Ministry of Education, Oman

Incremental software development through the addition of new features and access rules potentially creates security flaws due to inconsistent access control models. Discovering such flaws in software architectures is commonly performed with formal techniques that allow the verification of the correctness of a system and its compliance with applicable policies. In this chapter, the authors propose the use of the B method to formally, and incrementally, design and evaluate the security of systems running under role-based access control (RBAC) policies. They use an electronic marking system (EMS) as a case study to demonstrate the iterative development of RBAC models and the role of the B language in exploring and re-evaluating the security of the system as well as addressing inconsistencies caused by incremental software development. Two formal approaches of model checking and proof obligations are used to verify the correctness of the RBAC specification.

Chapter 6

    Takanori Kobashi, Waseda University, Japan
    Hironori Washizaki, Waseda University, Japan & National Institute of
        Informatics, Japan & SYSTEM INFORMATION Co Ltd, Japan &
        eXmotion, Japan
    Nobukazu Yoshioka, National Institute of Informatics, Japan
    Haruhiko Kaiya, Kanagawa University, Japan
    Takao Okubo, Institute of Information Security, Japan
    Yoshiaki Fukazawa, Waseda University, Japan

Simply confirming potential threats and vulnerabilities in an early stage of the development process (e.g., the requirement or design phase) is insufficient because software developers are not necessarily security experts. Additionally, even if the software design considers security at an early stage, whether the software actually satisfies the security requirements must be confirmed. To realize secure design, the authors propose an application to design software systems with verification of security patterns using model testing. The method provides extended security patterns, which include requirement- and design-level patterns as well as a new designing and model testing process that uses these patterns. Once developers specify threats and vulnerabilities in the target system in an early stage of development, the method can verify whether the security patterns are properly applied and assess if the vulnerabilities are resolved.

Chapter 7

Yun Shu, Auckland University of Technology, New Zealand
Jian Yu, Auckland University of Technology, New Zealand
Wei Qi Yan, Auckland University of Technology, New Zealand

In recent decades, internet auctions have become the most significant e-commerce business model worldwide. With the rapid rise of cloud computing over the last few years, the legacy online auction platform is gradually being replaced using service-oriented cloud computing in real time. This chapter describes the design and implementation of a state and high-performance online auction system over cloud and proposes the methodology to provide persistent state records during the auction process so that we are able to ensure the reliability of submitted bid price and guarantee the security of price message in the delivery process. The authors employ actor-based applications to achieve stateful, parallel, and distributed architecture. Meanwhile, utilizing distributed databases provides secure and efficient data storage. To the best of the authors' knowledge, this is the first time that the actor framework has been applied to the online auction. The preliminary result is for implementation of high-performance and real-time bidding online auction.

Chapter 8

Yun Shu, Auckland University of Technology, New Zealand
Jian Yu, Auckland University of Technology, New Zealand
Wei Qi Yan, Auckland University of Technology, New Zealand

Online auction is one of the most successful internet business models. However, auction fraud has become the highest threat and hazard to the future of this business model. The blockchain provides a new perspective to resolve this problem. It can be used for current financial services, certificates, remittances, and online payments; meanwhile it also provides several crucial services such as smart contract, smart property, trust system, and security services. This chapter discusses how to apply blockchain to a cloud-based online auction and the principle of operation. The purpose is to fundamentally solve the problem of online fraud caused by information asymmetry of electronic transactions. To the best of the authors' knowledge, this is the first time that the blockchain has been applied to authentication of online auction. The preliminary contribution is for preventing auction fraud from the aspects of smart properties and smart contract.

    Abdallah Soualmi, Ferhat Abbas University, Algeria
    Lamri Laouamer, Qassim University, Saudi Arabia
    Adel Alti, Ferhat Abbas University, Algeria

In image watermarking, information is embedded in the original image for many reasons, such as ownership proofing, alteration detection, and/or fingerprinting, but it can also be used for real-time services such as e-payment, broadcast monitoring, and surveillance systems. For these, the data embedded must be extractable even if the image is manipulated intentionally or unintentionally. In contrast, robust techniques are the kind of watermarking that could assure the authenticity and protect the copyright. Many robust image watermarking approaches have been proposed in the last few years, and the purpose of this chapter is to provide a survey about recent relevant robust image watermarking methods existing in the literature.

    Zhe Liu, Auckland University of Technology, New Zealand
    Mee Loong Yang, Auckland University of Technology, New Zealand
    Wei Qi Yan, Auckland University of Technology, New Zealand

In this chapter, the authors propose an improved image encryption algorithm based on digital watermarking. The algorithm combines discrete wavelet transform (DWT), discrete cosine transform (DCT), and singular value decomposition (SVD) together in a DWT-DCT-SVD framework to improve the robust watermarking technique. The secret image is embedded into both high-frequency and low-frequency sub-bands of the host image; this makes it difficult to be attacked in all the sub-bands. To reduce the size of a secret key, the authors use a logistic map to generate random images so as to replace the host images. They tested the algorithm by using five types of attacks and the results indicate that the proposed algorithm has higher robustness than traditional chaotic scrambling method and the DRPE method. It shows strong resilience against the five types of attacks as well as statistical attacks.

    Tosin Daniel Oyetoyan, Western Norway University of Applied Sciences,
       Norway
    Martin Gilje Gilje Jaatun, SINTEF Digital, Norway
    Daniela Soares Cruzes, SINTEF Digital, Norway

Software security does not emerge fully formed by divine intervention in deserving software development organizations; it requires that developers have the required theoretical background and practical skills to enable them to write secure software, and that the software security activities are actually performed, not just documented procedures that sit gathering dust on a shelf. In this chapter, the authors present a survey instrument that can be used to investigate software security usage, competence, and training needs in agile organizations. They present results of using this instrument in two organizations. They find that regardless of cost or benefit, skill drives the kind of activities that are performed, and secure design may be the most important training need.

Chapter 12

Kalle Rindell, University of Turku, Finland
Sami Hyrynsalmi, Tampere University of Technology, Finland
Ville Leppänen, University of Turku, Finland

This chapter describes a case of a large ICT service provider building a secure identity management system for a government customer. Security concerns are a guiding factor in the design of software-intensive products and services. They also affect the processes of their development. In regulated environments, development of products requires special security for the development processes, product release, maintenance and hosting, and also require security-oriented management and governance. Integrating the security engineering processes into an agile development model is argued to have the effect of mitigating the agile methods' intended benefits. The project case was an effort of multi-team, multi-site, security engineering, and development work, executed using the Scrum framework and regulated by governmental security standards and guidelines. In this case research, the experiences in combining security engineering with agile development are reported, challenges discussed, and certain security enhancements to Scrum are proposed.

Preface

Security in architecture and design of modern software system development is driven by two main paradigm shifts, i.e. the transition from functionality-centric to data-centric systems as well as the transition from closed to open systems.

FROM FUNCTIONALITY-CENTRIC TO DATA-CENTRIC SYSTEMS

The world of information technology is evolving towards a kind of software-intensive systems that, more and more extensively, integrate, aggregate and analyze large amounts of data coming from a number of diverse data sources. In this respect, we often hear the adage that "data is the new oil of digital economy". However, this metaphor is quite imprecise. Data sources are easy to obtain on the Internet, e.g., by accessing social media platforms. Hence, differently from crude oil, "drilling" for data is quite inexpensive. Consequently, there is a reduced economic barrier to entry for companies and institutions that want to enter the market of data-intensive software systems.

The rapid growth of such systems is generating a paradigm shift in the field of software development. Traditionally, software systems have been dealing, to a large extent, with the digitalization and automation of human activities. In such systems, the added value consisted primarily of the functionality provided to the users (consulting a medical record, preparing invoices for customers, sending emails, and so on) and to the software qualities attached to such functionality, like usability, performance, and security.

Modern systems collect raw data from the users and their personal devices (like health trackers), raw data from the environment and its smart objects (smart thermostats, home automation devices), as well as higher-level data coming from information providers like social platforms, open-data sites (e.g., OpenStreetMap), and other silos of information. Also different types of data like image, sound or textual data have to be taken into account. Beyond functionality, the success (and added value) of such systems is tied to the availability of the information that is processed as well as its quality. Functionality is often centred around the analysis of data to extract useful information (e.g. make user-specific recommendations, adapt to user habits to make an application more ergonomic, etc.).

In a nutshell, we are moving from traditional software engineering, which is functionality- and software-centric, towards modern software and data engineering, which is data-centric and where the functionality is driven by the availability of data. The success of data-driven functionality (e.g., business intelligence) is therefore measured as the accuracy and trust of the extracted information in terms of its correspondence to reality and ultimately of the veracity of the conclusions drawn from the data analysis process.

FROM CLOSED TO OPEN SYSTEMS

The second aspect of the paradigm shift pertains to the increased openness of modern systems. In the last decade, the major computer science trends of Internet of Things (referring to the objects of the physical world gaining connectivity and intelligence), System of Systems (referring to several systems collaborating and producing emergent behavior) and Big Data (referring to the ability of storing and analyzing large volumes of data) have led to the development of both research and technology in the area of connectivity, storage and computation. These achievements acted as enablers for the development of systems that are characterized by an ultra-wide scale (w.r.t. size and complexity) and openness (e.g., multi-party integration, loosely coupled collaboration, and so on). While ultra-wide scale poses a number of key challenges for both software engineering (think of reliability and performance, for instance) as well as security (think of access control, for instance), openness is the major conundrum.

In fact, the boundary of a modern system is more and more going to resemble a faint line that expands and contracts continuously, with no clear-cut divide between the inside and the outside of a system. In a word, the architects and developers of a system are not in control of all the "moving parts", but, rather, they heavily rely on external dependencies (e.g., external data sources, 3rd-party micro-services, etc.).

THE CHALLENGES

The trends and paradigm shifts mentioned above pose direct challenges to the way we think about software security, in general, and secure design, in particular. The main challenges we identified are:

- Security requirements and secure design need to address both functionality and data like text or image data, jointly;
- Secure design principles need to be reconsidered, in light of open systems and systems-of-systems;
- Secure design should address fast-paced change in systems, be compatible with respective agile and continuous processes and support the involved stakeholders;
- Secure design requires new risk-based quality assurance and testing approaches that are able to cope with complexity due to openness and data-centricity;
- Secure design for large systems should employ AI and automation to a greater extent.

Traditionally, there has been a divide between secure software engineering and secure system engineering. Secure system engineering has been concerned with securing the data and the communication channels (e.g., by means of encryption protocols), while secure software engineering has been concerned with avoiding design and coding flaws in the system functionality. In the era of data-centric systems, these two perspectives have to come together as one.

The increased openness of modern systems represents a challenge for traditional secure software engineering practices. Several secure design tactics (like using a single access point, or reducing the attack surface) rely on the assumption that a clear line could be identified to demark the inside and the outside of the system. Possibly, such principles need to be re-thought and adapted to cope with highly interconnected software systems.

Another consequence of such openness is change. The elements integrated into a system are subject to continuous change. Modern systems need to be able to adapt rapidly in order to be opportunistic and exploit new sources of data as they become available, as this could grant a competitive advantage. Therefore, modern systems have to put up an increased ability to adapt to the changing operating conditions, end-user needs and requirements. Most secure design techniques rely on a stable set of security assumptions, which is not realistic anymore.

The increased complexity and ultra-wide scale of modern systems represent a challenge for security experts. Many of the security-related activities performed during the architectural design of systems are based on human-intensive and expert-based activities. For instance, threat analysis and design reviews are not automated. However, it is increasingly difficult for secure designers to grasp how all the system parts work together and what security assumptions could be safely made about the deployment environment. In this respect, there is a need for smarter tools that can support software designers and security experts in their activities. Such tools should incorporate the development of AI in order to become adaptive to the changing needs of security experts.

ORGANIZATION OF THE BOOK

The chapters in this book attempt to provide an answer to some of the challenges discussed above. The book is organized into twelve chapters. A brief description of each of the chapters follows:

Chapter 1 presents the fundamentals of threat modeling and their application in modern software development with a focus on issues in agile and continuous software development and how to overcome them.

Chapter 2 presents a quantitative security assurance framework for security requirements and vulnerabilities as well as its assurance evaluation process.

Chapter 3 clarifies the requirements for software security assurance by using an evaluation framework to analyze the compatibility of established agile security development methods.

Chapter 4 presents an evaluation of a test-driven security risk assessment approach to assess how useful testing is for validating and correcting security risk models.

Chapter 5 presents an approach to use the B method to formally, and incrementally, design and evaluate the security of systems using role-based access control policies.

Chapter 6 presents an approach to design secure software based on requirements and design level patterns that are used for model testing.

Chapter 7 describes the design and implementation of a state and high-performance online auction system based on cloud technology.

Chapter 8 discusses how to apply blockchain technology to a cloud-based online auction system.

Chapter 9 provides an overview of recent robust image watermarking methods to support the design of systems architectures using that technology.

Chapter 10 presents an improved image encryption algorithm based on digital watermarking to support the design of respective systems.

Chapter 11 presents an evidence-based survey instrument that can be used to investigate software security usage, competence, and training needs in agile organizations to support secure design and respective training needs.

Chapter 12 presents challenges of combining security engineering with agile development and derives security enhancements for Scrum to improve secure design and development in that context.

Michael Felderer
University of Innsbruck, Austria

Riccardo Scandariato
Chalmers University of Technology, Sweden & University of Gothenburg, Sweden

Chapter 1
Threat Modeling in Agile Software Development

Martin Gilje Jaatun
SINTEF Digital, Norway

Karin Bernsmed
SINTEF Digital, Norway

Daniela Soares Cruzes
SINTEF Digital, Norway

Inger Anne Tøndel
SINTEF Digital, Norway

ABSTRACT

Threat modeling is a way to get an overview of possible attacks against your systems. The advantages of threat modeling include tackling security problems early, improved risk assessments, and more effective security testing. There will always be limited resources available for security, and threat modeling will allow you to focus on the most important areas first. There is no one single "correct" way of doing threat modeling, and "agile" is no excuse for not doing it. This chapter describes the authors' experiences with doing threat modeling with agile development organizations, outlining challenges to be faced and pitfalls to be avoided.

DOI: 10.4018/978-1-5225-6313-6.ch001

1. INTRODUCTION

Threat modeling has been identified as one of the most important activities in the Security Development Lifecycle (SDL) (Howard & Lipner, 2006). According to Jeffries (Jeffries, 2012), Microsoft SDL author Michael Howard states: "If you're only going to do one activity from the SDL, it should be threat modeling". The main idea behind threat modeling is to *think like an attacker*. A well-defined threat model helps to identify threats to the different assets of a system by utilizing well-grounded assumptions on the capabilities of any attacker interested in attacking such a system. It enables the teams to identify critical areas of design, which need to be protected. Over time, various threat modeling approaches and methodologies have been developed, and are being used in the process of designing secure applications (Cruzes, Jaatun, Bernsmed, & Tøndel, 2018). The approaches vary from conceptual frameworks to practical methodologies. To speed up software delivery, many organizations have adopted an agile software development approach, in which development teams produce code in shorter iterations with frequent feedback loops. In agile software development, however, threat modeling is not widespread, and the practitioners have few sources of recommendations on how to proceed to adopt the practice in their process. In addition, in agile software development, it is often challenging in itself to adopt security practices, either because security practices are not prioritized, or because the practitioners are not able to see the relevance and importance of the activities to the improvement of the security in the project (Cruzes et al., 2018). Studies in software security usually focus on software security activities in general, and there are few empirical studies focusing on specific practices in agile software development. The threat modeling activity is particularly important in software security, since many security vulnerabilities are caused due to architectural design flaws (McGraw, 2004). Furthermore, fixing such vulnerabilities after implementation may be very costly, requiring workarounds which sometimes increase the attack surface. A well-defined threat model helps to identify threats to different assets of a system by utilizing well-grounded assumptions on the capabilities of any attacker interested in exploiting such a system. It also enables the development teams to identify critical areas of the design which need to be protected, as well as mitigation strategies. However, threat modeling can also be challenging to perform for developers, and even more so in agile software development.

This chapter is based on results from the ongoing *SoS-Agile - Science of Security for Agile Software Development* research project (https://www.sintef.no/en/digital/sos-agile/) which investigates how to meaningfully integrate software security into agile software development activities. The project started in October 2015 and will end in October 2020, and involves many software development companies in Norway. The method of choice for the project is Action Research, which is an appropriate research methodology for this investigation because of the combination of scientific and practical objectives that aligns with the basic tenet of action research, which is to merge theory and practice in a way such that real-world problems are solved by theoretically informed actions in collaboration between researchers and practitioners (Greenwood & Levin, 1998), (Davison, Martinsons, & Kock, 2004).

The remainder of this chapter is structured as follows: Section 2 outlines our approach to threat modeling in broad strokes. In Section 3 we explore some particular challenges associated with agile software development, which influence how we think about threat modeling. Section 4 offers additional recommendations on how to successfully perform threat modeling in agile software development. We conclude in Section 5.

2. FUNDAMENTAL THREAT MODELING ACTIVITIES

Threat modeling is a wide concept that encompasses a broad range of techniques that can be utilized to make a system more secure. Threat modeling usually employs two types of models; one that represents the system that is to be built and another one that represents the actual threats to the system (Shostack, 2014b). In the context of software development, what is being built can be almost anything that will use the developed software, for example a website, a mobile application or a distributed system. The threats will then represent what can go wrong with the system, which includes all the potential reasons why the software may not function as intended. Depending on the scope of the analysis, one may choose to consider not only threats that are due to malicious intervention, i.e., all the different types of attacks that may occur, but also unintentional events, which are caused by legitimate users that make mistakes. In some cases, random failures are also included as potential threats.

Our approach to threat modeling in agile software development organizations consists of a visual representation of three main elements:

- Assets that are essential or critical for the system;
- An overview over how assets are stored, processed or otherwise interact with the system, which includes systems interfaces and potential attack surfaces;
- Threats to the system, which will affect one or more of the identified assets.

These elements can be found, to a greater or lesser extent, in many threat modeling approaches (Dhillon, 2011). In the following we will briefly describe each in turn.

2.1 Asset Identification

In the organizations where we have applied threat modeling, the first step has been asset identification. An *asset* is something that needs to be protected within the system. Usually, assets are the information or services that are vital for the business operation and success, however, the concept of "assets" can also comprise other parts of the system, such as hardware, network components, domains or even people. Although Shostak (Shostack, 2014b) presents this step as optional, and Dhillon (Dhillon, 2011) does not mention the concept explicitly at all, we always perform this activity. In our experience, it creates awareness about security in the organization, it helps the developers understand which components in their systems that need to be protected, and it makes it easier to focus the discussion on relevant threats later on during the threat modeling activities. Asset identification is also included as a compulsory step in most of the existing standards for risk assessments, including ISO/IEC 27005 (ISO, 2011). Even Dhillon (Dhillon, 2011) does this implicitly, e.g., by mentioning annotations of "processes that perform critical security functions" and "encrypted or signed data flows and data stores".

Asset identification, when performed at all, is often done from the top of one's head, with the results documented in a simple list. However, we have found it useful to employ the explicit method formulated by Jaatun & Tøndel (Jaatun & Tøndel, 2008), which we have since evolved: Briefly, the developers, together with the most important stakeholders in the project, participate in a semi-structured brainstorming session, where the first step is to get all possible assets on the table. As a second step, we then engage the participants in an interactive classification session where we try to determine the assets' relative importance or value (referring to Figure 1, we don't worry about the absolute value of "sprockets", but we want to know if they are worth more or less than "sockets", etc.). Based on the developers' knowledge of the system, we finally try to determine the assets' relative ease of exploitation, and end up with a grid as exemplified in Figure 1.

In our experience, many agile teams seem to think that asset identification is a waste of time; spending too much time on documenting something that is often perceived to be obvious. However, we still believe this is a useful exercise that should be performed at least once in each project. Even if the architecture changes, it is unlikely that the assets change - and if there are fundamental changes in the system that introduce new assets, that is a natural trigger for re-doing the asset analysis.

2.2 Data Flow Diagram

The second step in the threat modeling exercise is to get an overview over where the identified assets are stored, processed or otherwise interact with the system. As

Figure 1. Identification and classification of assets

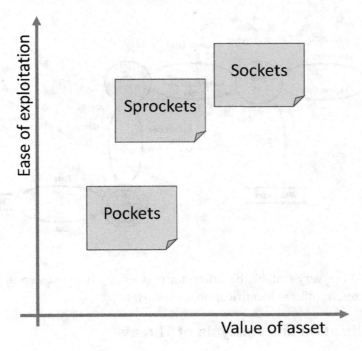

part of this step, it is also useful to define the interfaces of the system that is being analyzed and to identify potential attack surfaces.

As a means to get an overview of the system to be analyzed, we recommend making a Data Flow Diagram (DFD). A DFD is a graphical representation of the most important actors, processes, services, components and data stored in the system, and it highlights how information flows between each of them. An example of a DFD is shown in Figure 2, based on an OWASP threat modeling tutorial (Conklin, 2014). This example shows a simple university library system, with a web front end for access by students and staff, a login process to authenticate users, and a database system (which can be decomposed further). Users are represented by squares, and processes by circles (complex processes that can be decomposed into more detailed data flow diagrams are represented by double circles). Data flows are represented by curved arrows, and data stores are represented by two parallel lines. Finally, trust boundaries are indicated by dashed curved lines.

Drawing the DFD is usually perceived by the team to be worth it, but strictly speaking it takes too long to draw. Participating in a session where the DFD is created is good for newcomers; can be a good onboarding exercise giving new team members a useful overview of the system. The agile culture of no documentation is a detriment to gaining such an overview.

Figure 2. Example data flow diagram (redrawn from example at http://owasp.org)

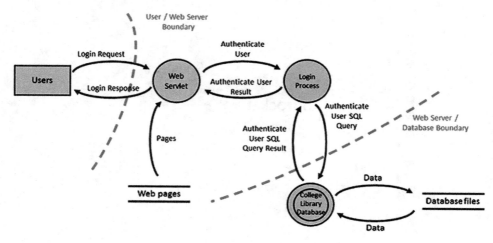

The DFD is a very suitable backdrop for performing the next step in the threat modeling exercise: threat identification and analysis.

2.3 Identification and Analysis of Threats

The last step in the threat modeling exercise is to identify and analyze all relevant threats to the system. This can be done in several ways. Here we present the approach that we have applied, using the STRIDE framework.

Back in the day, Microsoft employees Loren Kohnfelder and Praerit Garg created the STRIDE mnemonic for typical attacks (Shostack, 2014b), based on the first letter of each of the attack types:

- **Spoofing:** An attacker can pretend to be another user, component or system.
- **Tampering:** An attacker can modify data.
- **Repudiation:** An attacker (or other actor) can deny having performed an action or having sent a message if the system has insufficient mechanisms or evidence.
- **Information Disclosure:** An attacker can get read access to protected data.
- **Denial of Service (DoS):** An attacker can prevent legitimate users from using the normal functionality of the system.
- **Elevation of Privilege:** An attacker uses illegitimate means to reach an access level with other privileges than [s]he is supposed to have.

STRIDE can be used to identify threats by analyzing each of the interfaces defined in the DFD, and assess whether any of the attack types are relevant and how they could be executed. STRIDE can also be applied directly on the identified assets, to see whether they are vulnerable to spoofing, tampering, repudiation, etc. attacks.

As stated by Adam Shostak, "STRIDE is a good framework, bad taxonomy" (Shostack, 2014a). This implies that it would be dangerous to consider STRIDE an exhaustive list of threats; there could be other threat types that are relevant for the system. Privacy could be an example; even though some privacy breaks are simply information disclosure, there are more subtle issues that may need to be addressed. An obvious example is when personal data is used for other purposes than the users have consented to. Such a threat will not be identified by the sole use of STRIDE.

To drill down on selected attacks, and explore the attacker's goals and strategies, an attack tree (Schneier, 1999) can be constructed. In this way we can detail all the elements required in order to succeed with the attack, and also explore any alternatives that are available to the attacker. This will also be a good starting point for identifying security tests and possible countermeasures.

In the next section, we discuss the challenges we have experienced when applying these threat modeling activities in agile software development projects.

3. CHALLENGES IN AGILE SOFTWARE DEVELOPMENT PROJECTS

As shown by Camacho et al. (Camacho, Marczak, & Cruzes, 2016), adoption of security practices pose challenges in agile, either because security activities are not prioritized or because the developers do not see the importance of security activities in their projects. In a recent case study (Cruzes et al., 2018), in which we observed eight threat modeling sessions performed by agile software development teams, we identified a number of challenges to applying threat modeling in agile development practices. Here we report the most prominent.

Because of the lack of focus on documentation in agile teams, the teams had very little material to use as a starting point for the meetings. Further, the teams did not take the time to properly document the results from the asset identification activity, mainly because (at this point) they did not see why it would be useful. Also, even though the identification of assets naturally led to a discussion of whether they had the necessary mechanisms to protect those assets, such input was not documented during this phase and was hence not brought forward to the next phases.

Regarding the Data Flow Diagram, it was challenging both to motivate the teams to draw them, and to decide on the right level of abstraction. Some teams spent very long time on this activity. It also turned out to be challenging to map the interfaces of the system that they were modeling with the parts of the systems that other teams were responsible for. Some of the teams mentioned that they actually did not know how the system was really implemented, and the DFDs did not provide confidence that the system was actually implemented that way, especially where there was a lot of legacy code.

The study also revealed the need for better guidelines on how to organize the threat modeling activities, and the need to involve security experts in these activities. To agile teams, 1-2 hour meetings means a long time taken from the sprint hours and the teams sometimes expressed frustration when they did not manage to complete, for example, the DFD during the allocated meeting slot. It was also hard for the teams to say something about how long the models they created would be valid. In our experience, it is highly beneficial to let a security expert lead the threat modeling activities, however, most agile teams do not have such a person.

Threat modeling is a team sport (Jeffries, 2012), and this is also true for agile projects. When drawing a DFD, we like to be in a single room with all team members participating. However, when the software development division consists of distributed teams, which was the case for several of the organizations that we studied, this activity becomes quite challenging (Šmite, Moe, & Torkar, 2008). Even though the teams were used to video conferencing to replace or complement physical meetings, this turned out to be challenging when doing threat modeling. Most of the teams preferred to use the whiteboard when brainstorming around the different models that they created. However, with today's videoconferencing equipment it is generally not possible to see both the people at the other location(s) and their whiteboard at the same time, and often not even the whole whiteboard at a resolution that allows everyone to read everything. We have experimented with different configurations, but the major challenges remain unresolved. We have tried making identical drawings at each participating site, but maintaining consistency of such drawings is hard. Eventually, we expect that technological advances will iron out the kinks in such global collaboration sessions.

One thing we have found is that when threat modeling spans several sessions, it is important to share any diagrams created previously upfront. Since the diagrams may contain company sensitive information, they should be shared in a secure manner, e.g., not sent in regular email.

4. KEY FACTORS FOR SUCCESSFUL THREAT MODELING

The challenges identified in our study (Cruzes et al., 2018), together with challenges previously identified by Tuma et al. (Tuma, Calikli, & Scandariato, 2018), Dhillon (Dhillon, 2011), Assal and Chiasson (Assal & Chiasson, 2018), and Jaatun et al. (Jaatun, Jensen, Meland, & Tøndel, 2011), enabled us to identify a set of key factors for successful threat modeling in agile software development organizations.

4.1 Motivate the Team

Motivating the team is a prerequisite for a successful result! Make sure to explain the purpose of the threat modeling activities up-front and inform the team what they can expect as output of the activity. In particular they need to understand how the outputs can be used in the software development process. Once the purpose has been explained, hopefully the team is already motivated. Further motivation may be provided through educational activities such as short courses, preferably built around previous incidents that were caused by security bugs or flaws in the software of the system that is being developed.

4.2 Invite a Security Expert

Make sure that a security expert participates in all the threat modeling activities. This will help to focus the discussions, leverage relevant results and speed up the work. The security experts should both facilitate the discussions and document the results. He or she does not have to be a member of the development team, in fact, as already stated, most agile teams do not even have a security expert. Engaging someone external to the team has been shown to be a successful approach (Cruzes et al., 2018). However, in the long run it is unrealistic to expect that the software development organization will fund such an external resource. In order to make the security work self-sustainable, the role of the security expert should be eventually assumed by the security champion in the team. What security expertise is needed? Jeffries (Jeffries, 2012) refers to required security training in the SDL guideline (Microsoft, 2012), and states that it is "ideal that team members have an interest in security". The basic concepts in the SDL training include Secure Design, Threat Modeling, Secure Coding, Security Testing, and Privacy. Intriguingly, among the recommended resources are the Bell-LaPadula model and the Biba model – not something we would have thought the average developer would try to tackle!

We have found that teams that had a good architect from the beginning usually have many things covered, so that when threat modeling is performed on an existing system, few new unmitigated threats emerge. In general, this rhymes with results from Oyetoyan et al. (Oyetoyan, Jaatun, & Cruzes, 2017), who found that years of experience correlate with level of software security expertise.

Threat modeling may not be perceived as worthwhile for old systems, particularly for components which are slated for being phased out. Management support for security work is clearly vital (Assal & Chiasson, 2018); lack of such support is detrimental to software security morale, as exemplified by this skeptical quote from a team member at the end of a session: "Will there be hours for implementing security?"

4.3 Manage System Complexity

If threat modeling is performed for the first time with a team, then a good strategy is to limit the scope by zooming in on a selected part of the system. You should also spend some time on understanding the organization's mission and business goals. This will ensure that the asset identification activity includes information and services that are vital to the organization's interest and hence critical to protect. Draw a DFD upfront and decide which part of the system has priority to be analyzed first.

4.4 Short and Efficient Meetings

To agile teams, a 1-2 hour meeting means a long time taken from the sprint hours. Therefore, a thorough preparation of the meetings is crucial for success. The security expert facilitating the meeting needs to make sure that all preparations that could speed up the meeting are done on beforehand. In cases where a team has one or two very strong personalities, the facilitator may have to be active in ensuring that all voices are heard and that the meetings do not exceed the allocated time slot.

4.5 Involve the Remote Team(s)

Whenever the threat modeling activities involve two or more teams connected via videoconferencing, pick one location to be the "main" location, and provide a whiteboard with the data flow diagram here, visible on video to the other locations. Usually, the main location will be the site with the most developers participating. The current technological limitations require that some extra preparations are required for a successful remote session. All groups of remote participants should produce a large printout of

- Asset diagram (placed in value/ease of exploitation grid)

- Data flow diagrams
- STRIDE definition

If the remote participants have access to more display units in addition to those used for the videoconferencing solution, these may be used instead of the printouts; the important thing is to have these items easily available for reference during the discussion. The STRIDE definition may seem superfluous, but we have found that it is a useful reminder for the teams, and even when the definition is well known by the participants it serves as a minimal checklist for guiding the discussion.

4.6 Pick the Best Tool to Solve the Task

Most of the existing tools for threat modeling activities either lack maturity, or they are targeted for security experts (Tuma et al., 2018). These tools may therefore be too complicated for the average developer, and it will be counter-productive to try to force developers to learn a new tool for doing something they already fear is a waste of time. Tools should be chosen carefully, preferably involving security experts, security champions, and representatives from the average developers. It is normally better to err on the side of choosing too few or too simple tools.

4.7 Know the "Definition of Done"

When an organization is just starting out doing threat modeling, knowing when "enough is enough" will be hard. However, instead of letting this cramp the threat modeling initiative into indecision, it is better to simply make some broad requirements that every team can follow, e.g.: "Each team must perform at least one threat modeling session per major system component per quarter." The work will then be "done" (for now) when this session has been completed.

One problem we have experienced is that when a team really gets into the spirit of threat modeling, they sometimes "go wild". How to focus on valid threats? In this case it is particularly useful to have a facilitator (or experienced security champion) to steer the discussion in the right direction.

4.8 Document the Results

All identified assets need to be recorded in central repository, such as the team's issue tracking system (Jira, TFS, or similar). The DFDs should similarly be stored in a central repository. The issue tracking system should also be used to ensure that identified threats are handled in the code (see below).

4.9 Ensure Results Are Propagated to the Code

We have found that the best way of ensuring that threat modeling results end up in the code, is to create a "risk" ticket for each security issue that arises during the modeling sessions. This allows the issue to be handled in a manner that will be familiar to the developers, without introducing any new process elements. Broadly speaking, such tickets will fall into two categories: Either something that needs to be added by the developers, or something that needs to be discussed by other parts of the team. The second type of ticket will then either be closed after discussion (nothing needs to be done), or be transformed into the first type.

5. CONCLUSION

We have studied how threat modeling can be performed in modern software development, and have outlined here a recipe that should work in most agile organizations.

In his keynote at the XP conference in Porto, Portugal on May 23rd 2018, Kent Beck responded to a prioritization question: "If I had to choose, I'd drop security". This reinforces the impression that agile developers are still prone to falling into the trap of "we'll fix security later; we just need to make this work first". It is clear that in some cases, temporarily deprecating security requirements is the right thing to do, but the problem is that most security requirements treated this way end up being simply forgotten. In a previous discussion with another agile developer (Hellesøy, 2017), the point was raised that developers need to start treating technical debt (and thus, security debt) just like financial debt – you may be able to live with some security issues for a limited time, but if you cannot keep up with the down payments, you will eventually be facing bankruptcy.

An important side-effect of involving a development team in threat modeling is a general improvement in security awareness, to the point where the developers potentially become enthusiastic about security (Jeffries, 2012).

Finally, it's not enough to identify threats, management must also prioritize mitigating them!

ACKNOWLEDGMENT

This work was supported by the SoS-Agile project: Science of Security in Agile Software Development, funded by the Research Council of Norway (grant number 247678).

REFERENCES

Assal, H., & Chiasson, S. (2018). Security in the software development lifecycle. In *Fourteenth symposium on usable privacy and security (SOUPS 2018)* (pp. 281-296). Academic Press.

Camacho, C. R., Marczak, S., & Cruzes, D. S. (2016, Aug). Agile team members perceptions on non-functional testing: Influencing factors from an empirical study. In *2016 11th international conference on availability, reliability and security (ARES)* (p. 582-589). Academic Press. doi: 10.1109/ARES.2016.98

Conklin, L. (2014). *CRV2 AppThreatModeling*. Retrieved from https://www.owasp.org/index.php/CRV2AppThreatModeling

Cruzes, D. S., Jaatun, M. G., Bernsmed, K., & Tøndel, I. A. (2018). Challenges and Experiences with Applying Microsoft Threat Modeling in Agile Development Projects. *Proceedings of the 25th Australasian Software Engineering Conference (ASWEC).*

Davison, R., Martinsons, M. G., & Kock, N. (2004). Principles of canonical action research. *Information Systems Journal, 14*(1), 65–86. doi:10.1111/j.1365-2575.2004.00162.x

Dhillon, D. (2011, July). Developer-driven threat modeling: Lessons learned in the trenches. *IEEE Security and Privacy, 9*(4), 41–47. doi:10.1109/MSP.2011.47

Greenwood, D., & Levin, M. (1998). *Introduction to action research: Social research for social change.* SAGE Publications. Retrieved from https://books.google.no/books?id=nipHAAAAMAAJ

Howard, M., & Lipner, S. (2006). *The security development lifecycle.* Microsoft Press.

ISO/IEC 27005:2011 Information technology - Security techniques - Information security risk management. (2011). Retrieved from https://www.iso.org/standard/56742.html

Jaatun, M. G., Jensen, J., Meland, P. H., & Tøndel, I. A. (2011). A Lightweight Approach to Secure Software Engineering. In *A Multidisciplinary Introduction to Information Security* (pp. 183–216). CRC Press.

Jaatun, M. G., & Tøndel, I. A. (2008). Covering your assets in software engineering. In *The third international conference on availability, reliability and security (ARES 2008)* (pp. 1172-1179). Barcelona, Spain: ARES. 10.1109/ARES.2008.8

Jeffries, C. (2012). *Threat modeling and agile development practices*. Retrieved from https://technet.microsoft.com/en-us/security/hh855044.aspx

McGraw, G. (2004). Software security. *Security & Privacy, IEEE, 2*(2), 80–83. doi:10.1109/MSECP.2004.1281254

Microsoft. (2012). *Pre-SDL Requirements: Security Training*. Retrieved from https://msdn.microsoft.com/en-us/library/windows/desktop/cc307407.aspx

Oyetoyan, T. D., Jaatun, M. G., & Cruzes, D. S. (2017). A lightweight measurement of software security skills, usage and training needs in agile teams. *International Journal of Secure Software Engineering, 8*(1), 1–27. doi:10.4018/IJSSE.2017010101

Schneier, B. (1999). Attack trees. *Dr. Dobb's Journal, 24*(12), 21–29.

Shostack, A. (2014a). Elevation of privilege: Drawing developers into threat modeling. *2014 USENIX summit on gaming, games, and gamification in security education (3GSE 14).*

Shostack, A. (2014b). *Threat modeling: Designing for security*. Wiley.

Smite, D., Moe, N. B., & Torkar, R. (2008). Pitfalls in remote team coordination: Lessons learned from a case study. In A. Jedlitschka & O. Salo (Eds.), *Product-focused software process improvement* (pp. 345–359). Berlin: Springer Berlin Heidelberg. doi:10.1007/978-3-540-69566-0_28

Tuma, K., Calikli, G., & Scandariato, R. (2018). Threat analysis of software systems: A systematic literature review. *Journal of Systems and Software, 144.*

Chapter 2
Quantitative Security Assurance

Basel Katt
Norwegian University of Science and Technology, Norway

Nishu Prasher
Statistics Norway, Norway

ABSTRACT

Security assurance is the confidence that a system meets its security requirements and is resilient against security vulnerabilities and failures. Existing approaches can be characterized as (1) qualitative in nature, (2) tend to achieve their goals manually to a large extent, (3) very costly, (4) development-process oriented, and finally, (3) treat all security requirements within one domain equally for all applications regardless of the context. In this chapter, the authors propose a security assurance framework and its assurance evaluation process. The framework and process depend on a quantitative security assurance metrics that were developed too. The proposed metric considers both the security requirements and vulnerability. Weight has been introduced to the security requirement metric to measure the importance of security requirements that need to be fulfilled. The framework with the proposed quantitative assurance metrics are evaluated and validated using two field case studies related to two operational REST APIs that belong to and are used by Statistics Norway.

DOI: 10.4018/978-1-5225-6313-6.ch002

INTRODUCTION AND BACKGROUND

Assurance can be defined as the estimate of the likelihood that a system will not fail in some particular way (Anderson, 2010). Consequently, security assurance can be defined as the estimate that the system will not be compromised in some particular way. According to the National Institute of Standard and Technology (NIST) (Kissel., 2013), assurance is defined as following as the *"Grounds for confidence that the other four security goals (integrity, availability, confidentiality and accountability) have been adequately met by a specific implementation.* "Adequately met" includes (1) functionality that performs correctly, (2) sufficient protection against unintentional errors (by users or software), and (3) sufficient resistance to intentional penetration or bypass.". According to (Ouedraogo, Mouratidis, Khadraoui, Dubois, & Palmer-Brown, 2009) security assurance is defined as the confidence that the system meets its security requirements. Further, authors in (Spears, Barki, & Barton, 2013) define security assurance as the degree of confidence that security needs are satisfied, and it represents the level of trust we give to the system (Bischop, 2002).

We define *security assurance* as the confidence that a system meets its security requirements and is resilient against security vulnerabilities and failures. The confidence indicated by the security assurance represents the level of trust we give to a system that is safe to use. W*e assume that an assurance scheme (will be defined later) contains the set of goals and objectives that need to be achieved to reach a particular level of assurance. Such goals can be defined in terms of requirements that need to be fulfilled, or vulnerabilities and threats that need to be avoided.* Evaluation, on the other hand, can be defined as (Anderson, 2010) (Bischop, 2002) *"the process of gathering and analyzing evidence that a system meets, or fails to meet, a prescribed assurance target".* Assurance technique (Such, Gouglidis, Knowles, Misra, & Rashid, 2016), *or activity, is defined as a method of assessing an assurance target.*

This means that *evaluation* represents the process of evidence assembly and level assessment, while an *assurance technique,* represents the technical method that is used in the evaluation process for assessment. Assurance scheme in some standards, like *the Common Criteria (CC)[1], can be defined in terms of security requirements and assurance requirements.*

Evidence collected in the evaluation process will be defined in terms of measurements associated with a set of defined security metrics. A security metrics can be defined as a measure that depicts the security level, security performance or security strength of a system [5]. Authors in [35] categorize security metrics based on four key dimensions (1) metrics of system vulnerabilities (2) metrics of system defense strength (3) metrics of attack (or threat) severity (4) metrics of system dimension or situations. In the context of security assurance, we define a security assurance metric, shortly assurance metric, as the indicator that provides an evidence that the assurance target meets a particular level of the assurance scheme.

Since the orange book, there has been a plethora of research, industrial and standardization activities in the area of security assurance and evaluation. For example, the state of art review (Goertzel, et al., 2007), the industrial driven assurance initiatives and maturity models like Building Security In Maturity Mode (BSIMM)[2] and OpenSAMM[3], and the evaluation standard CC. The majority of these approaches can be characterized of one or more of the following characteristics. (1) They are qualitative in nature and tend to achieve their goals manually, to a large extend, which lead to a very costly evaluation process (Such, Gouglidis, Knowles, Misra, & Rashid, 2016) and an inaccurate and not repetitive security assurance levels. This prevents Small and medium-sized Enterprises (SMEs) from fully utilizing the current assurance and evaluation standards and are they were left out to deal with the security assurance problem on their own, if at all. (2) They are development-process oriented, in which evaluation criteria covers all phases of the development process and no special treatment is given to the deployed product. This, however, is not well suited for the DevOps practice and methodology for development and operation. Finally, (3) they treat security requirements within one domain equally for all applications regardless of the context. This requires various applications within the same domain and with different security requirements to develop their evaluation profiles, or criteria.

The economic aspects of security assurance and evaluation process has been discussed in (Such, Gouglidis, Knowles, Misra, & Rashid, 2016). Furthermore, the problem of the qualitative nature of security assurance metrics and the need for quantitative indicators has been identified in the literature as well (Ouedraogo, et al., 2014). Recent efforts (Thakurta, 2013) (Yoo, Vaca, & Kim, 2017) (Abdulrazeg, Norwawi, & Basir, 2017) indicate that prioritization of security requirements based on the application context is an important aspect during in the application life cycle. On the other hand, recent research work (Joshi & Singh, 2017) that applied quantitative methods are focusing mainly on vulnerabilities but not security requirements.

We believe that security assurance metrics should be quantitative in nature and include both perspectives, the positive side of security, i.e., security requirement fulfillment, and the negative side of the security, i.e., threat and vulnerability existence. Furthermore, the importance, or relevance, factor of security requirements, alongside the risk factor of security vulnerabilities should be considered. This chapter presents a framework for quantitative security assurance that provides a high-level security assurance evaluation and distinguishes two perspectives: protection and vulnerability. Accordingly, three types of security metrics were developed that can be used in the evaluation process. We adapt a similar evaluation process to the one presented in [6] for the development of the security assurance metrics.

Two case studies were carried out at Statistics Norway to validate the proposed method and verify its results. This include applying the assurance method to evaluate two operational REST APIs that belong and are used by Statistics Norway[4], which is the Norwegian national statistical institute and the main provider of official statistics. The first one, *TS-API*, is an internal private API which will be anonymized due to security reasons. This API does not hold any data and it is used for transformation of the data, and its security concerns are mostly related to integrity of the data, such that the data must not be changed, before it is sent further. The other REST API, *PX-API*[5], is an open API which has a detailed user-documentation available on the report (Statistics-Norway, 2017). This API lets the user create a customized dataset, based on queries made towards over 5000 *StatBank* tables Statistics Norway offer.

Analysis showed that the API with the most security requirements fulfilled got a slightly higher security assurance score. Lower weights for some security requirements in the other open REST API led to minor effects of their absence to the total assurance score.

The rest of the chapter is organized as follows. The next section discusses the related work and the main concepts presented in this paper. Then we present the security assurance process, and the different elements and indicators of our security assurance metrics are defined and discussed. Later we present the case studies and results and finally we analyze the results, conclude and present the plans for the future work.

RELATED WORK

Research on security assurance metrics and evaluation methods is vast. The majority of work focus on software security assurance throughout the software development life cycle process (Agreement, 2009) (Goertzel, et al., 2007). This is a valid approach as dealing with security from the early stages of the development process will end up with more secure system. However, the emphasis on the process vs implementation leads to overlooking the actual practical security posture of the system implementation and its operations (Jansen, 2010).

Various frameworks and standards have been developed for evaluating security assurance of systems, such as for example the BSIMM and OpenSAMM maturity models, the OWASP Application Security Verification Standard (ASVS) (Jim, 2016) and the Common Criteria (CC) (Agreement, 2009). BSIMM is a study of how different organizations deals with software security, which resulted in a software security framework that is organized in 116 activities and 12 practices. Similar to BSIMM, OpenSAMM is an open software security framework developed by OWASP that provides guidelines on which software security practices should be used and how to assess them. Maturity models provide qualitative frameworks to evaluate the security posture of the process and culture practiced in an organization. ASVS, developed by OWASP, provides guidelines for web application security testing and its security controls. It also collects a list of security assurance requirements and an associated qualitative evaluation scheme that consists of three maturity levels. The CC provides a framework that allows specifying security and assurance requirements that need to be evaluated to determine the security, or trust, level of a system. CC distinguishes between a security functional requirement and a security assurance requirement. The first specifies a security requirement, or function, that a system or a product must provide, while the later specifies the assurance techniques that must be taken to assess to which level the security functional requirements are fulfilled. The main criticism against such standards is that (1) they tend to focus on the process more than evaluating the actual system's implementation, (2) they depend on security assurance metrics that are qualitative in nature and (3) they are done manually to a large extend.

Spears et al. (Spears, Barki, & Barton, 2013) examined assurance in a regulatory context. They aim at conceptualizing assurance by applying Capability Maturity Model (CMM) to security processes. CMM is a framework for helping organizations to move their process from being ad-hoc, less organized and less effective to a highly effective state of security. Their work provides the abstract theoretical background of CMM and focuses on processes rather than implementation. Joshi et al. (Joshi & Singh, 2017) proposes a framework that contributes to improvement of the security level of their University campus network. The model is a quantitative information security risk assessment model which uses CVSS. The framework is divided into three main phases, including threat identification (weak points identification), threat prioritization, and mitigation (improving the security position). This approach is based on OCTAVE risk assessment method, is quantitative in nature and results in prioritization of threats, but the main problem is the lack of security requirement verification.

Such et al. (Such, Gouglidis, Knowles, Misra, & Rashid, 2016) provides an economic study of security assurance techniques. It provides a taxonomy and suggests a framework with 20 "assurance techniques". The techniques are split over 5 high-level categories, review, observe, interview, independent validation, and test. The first four techniques are mainly manual measures, and the last one can be automated. Testing includes different verification methods, like formal verification, fuzz testing, static and dynamic analysis, and vulnerability scanning. Our approach's main assurance technique is based on this category. Furthermore Such et al. conducted a survey on 153 industry practitioners where 81% had over 5 years of experience to study the characteristics those assurance techniques, like expertise required, number of people required, time required for completion, effectiveness and cost. The main finding of the work was to compute a measure of cost-effectiveness for each assurance technique, which is not the focus of the current work.

Tung et al. (Tung, Lo, Shih, & Lin, 2016) has proposed a framework where they have applied security activities and practices of secure development life cycle to generate security guidelines and improving software security. This framework is an integrated security testing framework that particularly can be used while developing a software. Other authors applied formal methods for measuring security, e.g., authors in (Port & Wilf, 2017) applied decision-theoretic approach. The approach is based on two options indicating security level, which are "send", which means that the system is secure enough to use, and "hold", which means that the system is not secure enough to use. Further two simple indicators of security sufficiency are made, "Pass"/"Fail". "Pass" means there will be no losses from a security breach, and "Fail" is the opposite. This work's method to "measure" how much security is theoretical and not practical to be used in industrial setting.

Hudic et al. (Hudic, Smith, & Weippl, 2017) offers a security assurance assessment methodology for hybrid clouds. Systems and services in the cloud are multi-layered and multi-tenant environments. Hence, the proposed methodology of Hudic et al. consist of identification and isolation of specific components that are of interest, where the independent assurance level is calculated for each of them. Further, the authors aggregated assessments into assurance levels for various groups. The focus of this work is mainly on security requirements and policy compliance.

Additionally, some initiatives aimed at developing operational methodologies for security assurance of IT infrastructures. Pham et al. (Pham, Baud, Bellot, & Riguidel, 2008) proposes an attack graph-based security assurance method based on multi-agents. The authors defined an "attackability" metric for static evaluation and other metrics for anomaly detection at run time. Pendleton et al. discuss in their survey paper (Pendleton, Garcia-Lebron, Cho, & Xu, 2017) how hard it is to develop security metrics. They used attack surface estimation to detect vulnerabilities within a system. In their study they define security metrics based on four key indicators: system vulnerabilities, the system defense strength, the attack (or threat) severity and (4) the system dimension or situation. Instead of evaluating the security directly, they estimate the number of access points to the subject system by counting available interfaces, supported protocols, open ports, open sockets, installed software, etc. The current work considers these factors through the two-main security assurance metric types, security requirement metrics and vulnerability metrics. Additionally, we consider the security requirement importance, besides the vulnerability risks.

BUGYO (Haddad, et al., 2011) (Bulut, Khadraoui, & Marquet, 2007) can be cited as the first methodology and tool for continuous security assurance evaluation; security assurance evaluation in the context of BUGYO was aimed at probing the security of runtime systems rather than products. This work investigates a quantitative approach for defining security assurance metrics that provides an overall security assurance evaluation of a target of evaluation.

Ouedraogo et al. (Ouedraogo, et al., 2014) also advocate the need for a Security Assurance (SA) system which can be embedded within a current IT system. The purpose of the SA-system is to identify vulnerabilities and mitigate these by a so-called assurance-driven approach. Hence, the output is a set of assurance indicators of the system. Their paper analyzes the practical challenges associated to the assessment of SA and shows when the assurance level eventually drops. The main focus of these work is on run-time monitoring, and not testing, to check the availability of security mechanisms.

Savola (Savola, 2013) explains a security metric as a metric that illustrates the security level, security performance or the security strength of a system. Savola's paper is mainly about identifying quality criteria of security metrics. The result were three foundational quality criteria: correctness, measurability and meaningfulness.

Please note that this work build on the previous research started by the authors in (Katt & Prasher, 2018) (Weldehawaryat & Katt, 2018).

SECURITY ASSURANCE FRAMEWORK

In this section we present a general-purpose assurance framework that defines the basic components of assurance, or an assurance ecosystem (Such, Gouglidis, Knowles, Misra, & Rashid, 2016). Figure 1 shows the basic components in the framework, which are security assurance scheme, security assurance target, security assurance metrics, security assurance technique, evaluation evidence and security assurance level. For the sake of simplicity, we omit "security" from all component names that start with "security assurance". In the following we define and describe the concepts presented in the security assurance framework.

1. **Assurance Profile:** An assurance profile indicates the set of the security objectives, based upon the assurance level for a class of systems will be decided. Additionally, it contains the basic design and components of a system and its environment in that specific class. The security objectives are specified as a set of (1) security requirements and their fulfillment conditions and a set of (2) potential vulnerabilities and threats, and their existence conditions. The concept of an assurance profile can be compared to the concept of protection profiles of Common Criteria. For example, an assurance profile can be defined for the class of office applications. An instance of an assurance profile specified for one system is called an assurance scheme.

Figure 1. Security assurance framework

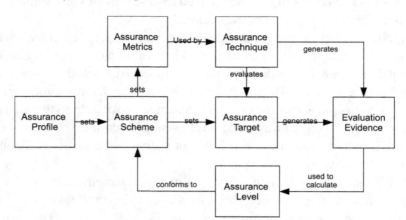

2.   **Assurance Scheme:** An assurance scheme is an instance of an assurance profile defined for a specific system, called an assurance target. It contains the same security objectives taken from the assurance profile it instantiates in terms of security requirements and vulnerabilities, and their fulfillment and existence conditions, respectively. Also, it contains specific details about the system design and its environment. Furthermore, it specifies the weight for each security requirement and the risk for each vulnerability, or threat, specified in the assurance profile. Assurance schemes can also indicate the way the security requirements and vulnerability conditions can be checked. For example, in our test-based methodology, test cases could be specified that check each requirement's condition and each vulnerability's. The assurance scheme will be used to set up the assurance target and the assurance metrics.

3.   **Assurance Target:** An assurance target can be defined as the system under evaluation, for which assurance level will be assessed. In order to prepare the assurance target for evaluation it needs to be deployed in the operational environment. Assurance scheme contains the information and models that can be used to set up the assurance target and its environment.

4.   **Assurance Metrics:** An assurance metric can be defined as a quantitative measure that provides an evidence that the assurance target meets a particular level of the assurance scheme. Thus, it must be derived from the security assurance objective defined in the assurance scheme and the assurance profile. It indicates to which degree the assurance target fulfills the security requirements' conditions and the vulnerabilities' conditions. It can be used by the assurance technique to set up the evaluation process.

5. **Assurance Technique:** An assurance technique can be defined as a method that can be used for evaluating and assessing the assurance target. Such et al. [8] provide a comprehensive classification of assurance techniques, including review, observe, interview, independent validation and testing. The most suitable technique within an automated evaluation process is testing, which will be adapted in this work. This does not close the door to use other techniques too when needed.

6. **Evaluation Evidence:** Evaluation evidence can be defined as a set of measurements that can result from applying the assurance technique on the assurance target.

7. **Assurance Level:** An assurance level can be defined as the level of confidence that we have on the assurance target as defined in the assurance scheme and calculated from the evaluation evidence.

SECURITY ASSURANCE EVALUATION PROCESS

We define a security assurance evaluation process, shortly "evaluation process", as the process of evaluating the security assurance level of the assurance target. The input is an *assurance profile* and information about the assurance target to be evaluated and the output is the assurance level. Our proposed evaluation process considers three main types of metrics: vulnerability metrics, security requirement metrics and security assurance metrics. The different types of assurance metrics will be discussed in the next section. Figure 2 shows the different activities in the evaluation process. Please note that ellipse indicates an activity, while rectangles indicate the output and/or the input artifacts of an activity. The evaluation process consists of six main activities: Modeling and specification, assurance metrics definition, assurance target deployment, Assurance technique execution, evidence processing and assurance level calculation.

Modeling and Specification

This step takes as input an assurance profile (AP) and information about the system (SI), and results in the definition of an assurance scheme (AS) for the assurance target. To get the assurance scheme for the assurance target, this activity performs the following: (1) the application and its environments will be specified, (2) the weight of the security requirements (in the AP) will be estimated, as well as (3) the risk of the vulnerabilities (in the AP) will be assessed.

Figure 2. Security assurance evaluation process. The acronyms used are: SI: System Information. AP: Assurance Profile. AS: Assurance Scheme AM: Assurance Metrics. AT: Assurance Target. E: Evidence. MV: Metrics Values.

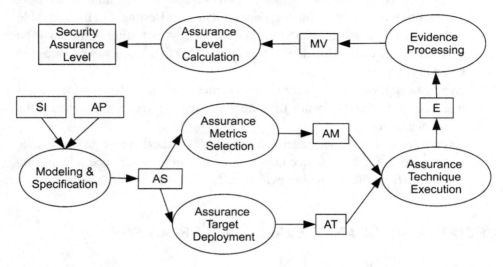

The application modeling allows decomposing the application in order to identify its main components, its environment, its assumptions, and its critical assets. Security functions and vulnerabilities related to the basic security concepts of the application and its environment will be extracted from the assurance profile and analyzed in the context of the assurance target. The resulted assurance scheme includes (1) the specification of the assurance target and its environment, (2) the set of security requirement, their weights, and their fulfillment conditions and (3) a set of vulnerabilities, against which the target needs to be secured, their risk values, and their existence condition.

There has been some confusion when checklists are defined to verify security requirement fulfillment and to verify vulnerability existence. Insufficient TLS/SSL configuration is a vulnerability, while secure communication through HTTPS is a requirement. Ensuring the fulfillment of the requirement does not mean that the vulnerability does not exist. Further, if validation of the HTTP Certificate is deactivated it does not matter that the encryption is enforced, still it is possible to decrypt the information. To capture the whole picture, it is important to not only to focus on security vulnerabilities, but in addition create a checklist for security requirements. By doing this it is easy to get an understanding of what we expect from the API and what we don't expect from it (Felderer, et al., 2016).

Assurance Metric Selection

In this step the set assurance metrics will be extracted from the assurance scheme. They will be used later by the assurance technique for evaluation and assessment. Assurance metrics aim at quantifying the results and measurements from the test cases performed to check to what extend the security requirements' conditions and the vulnerabilities' conditions are true. We use the *GQM* (Goal Question Metric) approach (Caldiera & Rombach, 1994) to link the quantitative measurements to the security goals and objectives, through test cases defined for the conditions of the security requirements and vulnerabilities. Depending on the measurements being performed, assurance metrics in our approach can be classified as follows:

1. **Security Requirement Metrics:** Relate to a measurement that evaluates whether security protection mechanisms exist and fulfill defined security requirements using the GQM method.
2. **Vulnerability Metrics:** Relate to a measurement that evaluates the weaknesses/ severity and vulnerabilities existence in the systems using the CVSS and GQM methods.

Assurance Target Deployment

This step is responsible of deploying the assurance target. The input of this activity is the assurance scheme and the output is the deployed assurance target.

Assurance Technique Execution

Based on the list of assurance metrics specified before, a set of test cases corresponding to the specified assurance metrics will be defined, as well as, a suitable assurance technique(s) will be decided. Furthermore, this step will execute the defined test cases against the assurance target that has been deployed in previous step.

Evidence Processing

The execution of the assurance technique will result in the different types of measurements that correspond to the assurance metric specified before. Evidence processing activity is responsible of processing and aggregating these probes and measurements to calculate the different elements of the assurance metrics.

Assurance Level Calculation

Once the security requirement and vulnerability metrics are determined, this step aims at calculating the overall security assurance level of the assurance target.

SECURITY ASSURANCE METRICS

In this section we define meaningful and measurable metrics that capture the requirements fulfilled and the vulnerabilities existed in the system. We assume that there are a finite set of m security requirements $r_1 \dots r_m$, as well as a finite set of n potential vulnerabilities $v_1 \dots v_n$, defined for the assurance target. We assume that these sets are specified in the assurance scheme.

Requirements and Vulnerabilities

A security metric is often defined as a metric that depicts the security level, security performance or security strength of a system. Based on our following definition of *security assurance: the confidence that a system meets its security requirements and is resilient against security vulnerabilities and failures,* we notice that security assurance consists of two main elements.

We assume that fulfilling a security requirement through a security mechanism and checking its correct functionality will cover the first element. On the other hand, checking the (non-)existence of known potential vulnerabilities in the system gives the resistance assurance to intentional penetration or bypass that constitutes the second element.

Thus, we define the assurance metric of an assurance target, AM as follows[6]

$$AM = RM - VM \tag{1}$$

RM is the requirement metric and *VM* is the vulnerability metric.

The previous discussion suggests that security requirement *fulfillment* and vulnerability *existence* factors are two important indicators that need to be considered when security assurance is evaluated. Additionally, the discussion in section 1 motivates that (1) security requirement importance, relevance, or weight, as we call it, and (2) vulnerability *risk* value should be considered as well. Putting all together we conclude that the security assurance metrics consists of two elements, security requirement metric and vulnerability metric. The first will be defined based on two main factors, fulfillment and weight, while the other will be defined based on two main factors, existence and risk.

Fulfillment and Existence

In order to map the fulfillment of security requirements and existence of security vulnerabilities into measurable evidences, we use the *GQM* approach. It enables deriving measurable metrics from defined conceptual goals by developing questions that cover the goals, for which the answers represent the measurable metrics. It is defined as tree structure consists of three levels (Caldiera & Rombach, 1994).

1. **Conceptual Goal:** A goal in our case models the fulfillment of a particular security requirement or the existence of a particular vulnerability.
2. **Operational Question:** A question is used to define the way the achievement of a particular goal can be performed. A question in our context represents a test case that aims at (1) checking whether a security requirement is fulfilled by a security mechanism(s) or (2) (security)
3. **Quantitative Answers:** An answer represents a metric that is associated with a particular question, i.e., test case, to check it in a measurable way.

If we assume that the overall goal is to check the security assurance level of the assurance target. This main goal can be divided into sub-goals, each of which is associated with the fulfillment of one security requirement or the existence of one security vulnerability. After that we define the *test cases* that check the fulfillment(s) or existence(s).

Finally, we quantify the results of the test cases and associate them to the metrics. For example, table 1 shows applying GQM for checking the fulfillment of the security requirement *user input should be sanitized*. Note that ASVS standard, among others, is used to construct the list of questions and test cases.

Weight and Risk

Weighting is explained as "The process of weighting involves emphasizing the contribution of some aspects of a phenomenon (or of a set of data) to a final effect or result, giving them more weight in the analysis. That is, rather than each variable in the data contributing equally to the final result, some data are adjusted to contribute more than others[7]."

In relation to security, not all security requirements are equally important. That depends on the objectives and functions of the evaluation target and what it does and if it processes sensitive data? The weights will express how important a security requirement is and it must be done according to what we want to protect. A scale from *0-10* will aid to express the levels of importance. Where *0* is assigned to requirements that are meaningless and futile, and *10* is the maximum expressing a vital requirement. The technique used to assign weights to security requirements is out of scope of this work, but it has been assigned manually by domain and security experts.

On the other hand, the term risk can be defined as the probability and the consequence of an unwanted incident. That is, a risk is an impact of uncertainty on systems, organizations etc. Further, risk management is the process of managing of this impact, where the purpose is to protect against the threats. Within the risk management process, risk assessment is the activity in which risks are identified and analyzed. Several frameworks and methods have been developed for risk analysis, and organizations may choose their method depending on the type of risks they encounter, or their business area. In our case study we applied both CVSS (Common Vulnerability Scoring System) and DREAD[8] (Damage, Reproducibility, Exploitability, Affected users, and Discoverability), for calculating risks, while CVSS result were mainly used in metrics calculations. While using DREAD, we noticed that it is difficult to use in the real world, especially for both reproducibility and discoverability factors.

CVSS helps to achieve a score, a decimal number, which reflects the vulnerability's severity, in the range of [0.0, 10.0]. The metrics are calculated in three different groups: base, temporal and environmental. The two latter metrics are optional to use depending on the system and context. Base metrics consist of two metrics, exploitability and impact metrics, which represents the intrinsic and fundamental characteristics of a vulnerability that do not change over time or across user environments. Temporal metrics reflect if the characteristics of the vulnerability changes over time, and environmental metrics reflect characteristics of vulnerabilities that are unique to a particular user's environment.

Requirement and Vulnerability Metrics

Based on the previous discussion, we define a security requirement metric Rm_i for a given security requirement r_i at a specific time instance as:

$$Rmi = \left(w_i \times \sum_{j=1}^{k} f_{ij} \right) \qquad (2)$$

where k represents the number of test cases, or questions, defined for the security requirement r_i, w_i is the weight of the it and f_{ij} is the fulfillment factor of the jth test case of the same i^{th} requirement. Another way to calculate the security requirement metric is to find out the average of all the fulfillment factors of all test cases, instead of taking the sum. The formula will be in this case:

$$Rmi = \left(w_i \times \frac{\left(\sum_{j=1}^{k} f_{ij} \right)}{k} \right) \qquad (3)$$

We used the second form in the calculation of the case studies. The fulfillment factor can have three values, *0*, *1* and *0.5*. A test case that shows that a security requirement is not fulfilled will be assigned a value 0, 1 means that a test case result indicates the fulfillment of a requirement, and 0.5 indicates the partial fulfillment. GQM can be used, as aforementioned, to measure the fulfillment of the security requirements.

As a result, we define the accumulate security requirement metrics of an application at a specific time instance as:

$$RM = \sum_{i=1}^{m} Rm_i \qquad (4)$$

where m represents the total number of security requirement defined for the assurance target. Table 1 shows how to construct the test cases for a security requirement and link it to a measurable fulfillment factors.

Similarly, we define the first form of a vulnerability metric Vm_i for a given security vulnerability at a specific time instance as:

Table 1. Example of applying GQM approach to quantify the fulfillment factor for the security

Sub-goal	Question / Condition	Answer / metric
	Do server side input validation failures result in request rejection and are logged?	1 (Full)
	Do input validation routines are enforced on the server side?	1 (Full)
	Are prepared statements used for protecting SQL queries, and others?	1 (Full)
Use input sanitization	Do security controls preventing LDAP Injection enabled?	0.5 (Avarage)
	Does the AT defend against HTTP parameter pollution attacks?	0 (Weak)
	Is client side validation used?	0 (Weak)
	Is positive validation (whitelisting) used for input data, like REST calls and HTTP headers?	0 (Weak)
	Is JSON.parse used to parse JSON on the client.?	0 (Weak)

$$Vm_i = \left(r_i \times \sum_{j=1}^{p} e_{ij} \right) \tag{5}$$

where, p represents the number of test cases defined for this vulnerability type, r_i is the risk of the ith vulnerability and e_{ij} is the existence factor for j^{th} test case defined for the ith vulnerability.

The existence factor can have three values, 0 means that the test case indicates no vulnerability, 1 indicates the existence of the vulnerability for the test case, and 0.5 indicates the partial existence.

Thus, the vulnerability metric of a system at a specific time instance can be calculated using the risk of vulnerabilities and their existence factor as follows:

$$VM = \sum_{k=1}^{n} Vm_k \tag{6}$$

where n represents the total number of vulnerabilities defined for the assurance target.

Finally, we define the *assurance metric* (AM) as the difference between *security requirement metric* (RM) and *vulnerability metric* (VM). Thus, the assurance metrics can be calculated as follows:

$$AM = RM - VM \tag{7}$$

where, *AM* is the security assurance metric at a given time instance, *RM* is the security requirement metric at that time instance, and *VM* is the vulnerability metric at the same time instance.

From equation 7, it can be noticed that *AM* is *minimum* when the following two conditions are met:

1. All security requirements are not fulfilled (*RM* becomes zero), which causes the value of the first term to be minimum (zero), and
2. All possible vulnerabilities exist, and all have a maximum risk value. This makes the second term to be maximum (*VM*).

AM, on the other hand, can be *maximum* if (i) *VM* is minimum for all vulnerabilities, and (ii) the protection mechanisms have been found to be effective to fulfill the defined security requirements (*RM* is maximum) for all requirements.

Scale Consideration and Optimization

The scale of AM depends on the number of requirements and vulnerabilities.

However, such large variant range is difficult to work with and interpret, so the score must be normalized to a common domain. It is possible to shrink a large scale to fit into a new, smaller scale. The method used here is min-max normalization (Khajvand & Tarokh, 2011) as shown in the following equation.

$$v' = \frac{v - min_A}{max_A - min_A}\left(newmax_A - newmin_A\right) + newmin_A \qquad (8)$$

In which, min_A and max_A are minimum and maximum values of an attribute, A, while $newmin_A$ and $newmax_A$ are the new minimum and new maximum values after normalization. v, is a value in the old scale that will be transformed to the value v'.

CASE STUDIES

This section describes case studies and how the quantification method was applied to two case studies, which are two REST APIs that belong to Statistics Norway, where one of the authors is employed. The first one is an internal API that will be anonymized due to security reasons. The other REST API is an open API, which has a detailed user-documentation available on the website. This API lets the user create a customized dataset, based on queries made towards over 5000 StatBank tables Statistics Norway offer.

The public API is *PX-API*[9], which is the official open API that Statistics Norway offers. Its main URL is composed as follows:

http://data.ssb.no/api-name/api-version/lang/

Further, there are two ways to find tables in the API. One id from the console (http://data.ssb.no/api/v0/en/console/) and the second is the URL itself (http://data.ssb.no/api/v0/en/table/). The data can only be extracted from the console, while from the URL the metadata can be extracted. The URL allows to navigate through the StatBank tables, in which you get the overview of all tables first, and then you can select and move to more specified data/statistics. The structure of the URL is as follow:

http://data.ssb.no/api/v0/no/table/(topic)/(subtopic)/(statistics)/(tablename)

This API is public, and the availability requirement is the one that are weighted most, compared to integrity and confidentiality.

The other API, *TS-API* is a private API, and the name stands for "Top Secret API", which is anonymized in this work. The API does not hold any data, but it is used for data transformation.

Thus, the integrity of data processed in this API is assessed to be the most important security requirement. The integrity requirement stems from the objective that in the transformation activity the data transformed must not change before it is sent further.

We will discuss in this section the different parts of the assurance profile that we created for these case studies, and how the security assurance evaluation process used the developed assurance profile on to evaluate the pubic API case study. In the next section the results will be presented.

Assurance Profile

As defined before, assurance profiles specify the objectives of security assurance as a set of (1) security requirements and their fulfillment conditions and as set of (2) vulnerabilities and their existence conditions. In this section we list the set of security requirements that are specified for REST API applications and their fulfillment conditions. The fulfillment conditions are specified in terms of test cases. Similarly, the set of vulnerabilities and their existence conditions, in terms of test cases, will be specified.

Security Requirements

A total of 10 security requirements were considered as vital for a REST API. OWASP ASVS standard was mainly used to define these lists. In the following is the set of security requirements defined and for each requirement a sample of one conditions (Project, 2016) is mentioned.

1.　Authentication: a total of 7 conditions were specified, e.g., *"Do credentials such as passwords, security tokens and API keys appear in URL."*
2.　JSON Web Tokens (JWT) security: a total of 3 conditions were specified, e.g., *"Are JWT (Json) tokens invalidated after logout"*.
3.　Access Control: a total of 6 conditions were specified, e.g., *"Is Oauth2 protocol present"*.

4. Input Sanitation: a total of 8 conditions were specified, e.g., *"Are that input validation routines enforced on the server Side."*.
5. Error Handling: a total of 4 conditions were specified, e.g., *"Does that error handling logic in security controls deny access by default"*.
6. Data Protection: a total of 6 conditions were specified, e.g., *"Are all sensitive data sent between client and server sent in the HTTP body or header"*.
7. Communication Security: a total of 7 conditions were specified, e.g., *"Are backend TLS connection failures logged"*.
8. HTTP Security: a total of 8 conditions were specified, e.g., *"Do the HTTP headers or any part of its response expose detailed version information of system components"*
9. Web Services: a total of 4 security requirements are specified, e.g., *"Is the same encoding style used between the client and the server."*
10. Cross-site scripting mechanisms. One condition is specified. *"Do the server apply secure mechanisms against cross site scripting"*

Security Vulnerabilities

A total of 9 main vulnerabilities were considered to be crucial for a REST API. This list was gathered mainly from OWASP Top Ten list. For each vulnerability the set of existence conditions were defined too, which ranged from 1 condition, e.g., cross cite request forgery, and 12 conditions defined for broken access control. The list is

1. Injection
2. Broken Authentication
3. Sensitive Data Exposure
4. Broken Access Control
5. Elevation of Privilege
6. Cross-Site Scripting
7. Cross-Site Request Forgery
8. Parameter Tampering
9. Man-in-the-middle-attack

Assurance Evaluation Process

After the assurance profile was defined, evaluation of both case study API was conducted based on the security assurance evaluation process. The following steps have been performed.

Step 1: MODELING and Specification

This activity takes as input both an assurance profile and application information and results in an assurance scheme as output. Based on the application information the assurance target is modeled and the weight and risk values for each requirement and vulnerability, respectively, are calculated.

1. **Modeling:** Figure 3 shows the model of the request and the response classes of the API and all resources associated with them. The main resources are *MainTable, Topic, Sub-Topic, Statistics,* and *Table*.
2. **Weight Estimation:** Weights of security requirements in the range [0-10] were estimated by security and domain expert from Statistics Norway. Authentication is regarded as not relevant and assigned the weight *0*. Similarly, *data protection* and *JWT* security requirements were assigned the weight *0*. On the other hand, input sanitization is regarded as the most important security requirement and assigned the weight *8*. The weights of the rest of the requirements range from 5 to 7.
3. **Risk Assessment:** For each vulnerability stated in the assurance profile, the risk has been assessed by using the CVSS method. All factors in the CVSS score were taken into account, including exploitability, impact, and temporal

Figure 3. PX-API UML modeling

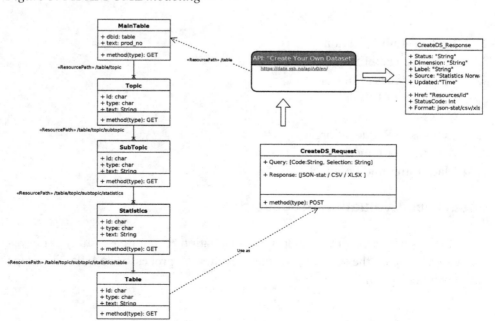

factors. The exploitability factor is assessed based on the following metrics: the attack vector (AC), Attack Complexity (AC), Privileged Required (PR) and User interactions (UI). The impact factor is assessed based on the Scope, Confidentiality Impact (CI), Integrity Impact (II) and Availability Impact (AI). Finally, temporal factor depends on exploit code maturity, remediation level, and report confidence. Table 2 shows the risk calculation for three examples of vulnerabilities.

Step 2: Assurance Metrics Selection

In the second step we derive the assurance metrics components from the assurance scheme that is resulted from the first step. The assurance metric has two main components, requirement metric and vulnerability metric. As mentioned in the "Security Assurance Metrics" section, we use the GQM methodology to derive quantitative metrics for each requirements and vulnerabilities. Sub-goals in this case are to answer to the questions "Is requirement X fulfilled?" or "Does vulnerability Y exist?". Questions, or test cases, are derived from the conditions that were defined for each security requirement and the conditions that were defined for each vulnerability. For example, the condition "Do credentials such as passwords, security

Table 2. Risk calculation for three vulnerabilities in the case studies

Factors		Vulnerability		
		Broken Authentication	Broken Access Control	Elevation of Privilege
Exploitability Metrics	AV	Network	Network	Local
	AC	Low	Low	Low
	PR	None	Low	Low
	UI	None	None	None
Impact Metrics	Scope	Unchanged	Unchanged	Unchanged
	C	None	None	None
	I	High	High	High
	A	None	None	None
Temporal Metrics	E	High	High	Functional Exploit exists
	RL	Official Fix	Official Fix	Official Fix
	RC	Confirmed	Confirmed	Reasonable
Environmental Metrics	IR	High	High	High
CVSS Base Score		7.5	7.5	5.5
CVSS Temporal Score		7.2	7.2	5.1
CVSS Environmental Score		8.9	8.9	6.8
CVSS Overall		8.9	8.9	6.8

tokens and API keys appear in URL." Can be transformed into the test case: "Check if credentials such as passwords, security tokens and API keys appear in URL.". The answer to this question, i.e., the result of the test case is quantified into three values. 0, 0.5 and 1. For example, the use cases defined for fulfillment factor of the security requirement "user input sanitization" are 8 depicted in Table 1

Step 3: Test Case Execution

In this step we executed the test cases stated in the assurance metrics definitions in order to calculate the *fulfillment* factor of requirements and *existence* factor of vulnerabilities. For the 10 security requirements, a total of 53 test cases were defined. Also, a total of 36 test cases were defined to test the existence of the 9 vulnerabilities. The conditions associated with each requirement, or vulnerability, will be mapped to at least one test case (one test case in our case study). For example, *communication security*'s condition *"Are backend TLS connection failures logged"* can be mapped into following one test case: *"Checking if backend TLS connection failures are logged!"*. The same applies for all conditions for security requirements and vulnerabilities.

Some of the test cases will test fulfillment of security requirements, and others the existence of vulnerabilities. The security functional testing is mainly done by checking manually if the security mechanisms exists or not. The security vulnerability testing on the other hand is partially done automatically. The tools that used to execute the test cases were mainly open-standard tools. Examples of some tools used, *SQLmap* is used for detecting and exploiting SQL injection vulnerabilities., *Burp-Suite* was used as a web scanner to find different web related vulnerabilities, and it can be used as proxy to directly interact and manipulate web communication with the server. *Wireshark* was used to sniff traffic and network protocol analyzers. Finally, *python* was used for automated tasks.

Step 4: Evidence Processing

After executing the test cases, *measurements* for calculating the requirement and vulnerability metrices were collected and analyzed, please refer to equations 2 and 5. Please note that values of weight and risk have been estimated in step 1, though, risk values can be re-evaluated after this step (optional). Fulfillment and existence factors are mainly measured based on the results of the test case execution. Table 1 gives an example of how the security requirement *"user input should be sanitized"* is mapped into 8 test cases / conditions and the result of each test case is quantified into the values 0, 0.5, or 1. While step 4 executes these test cases, in this step, the results of execution will be collected and quantified. Table 3 shows how mapping between different security requirements into a set of conditions/test case and consequently the measurement that result from executing the test cases will be quantified into the fulfillment factor. The second column of the table shows how many test cases were defined for each security requirement, e.g., 7 test cases were defined for authentication requirements. The third column, on the other hand, shows how the results of these test cases were quantified in terms of fulfillment score, for which the fulfillment score of all test cases were 0. Similarly, existence scores were calculated for the vulnerabilities.

Step 5: Assurance Level Calculation

In order to calculate the assurance level, we need to calculate first the assurance metric, as stated in Equation 7, and then the final assurance score will be normalized, as in Equation 8. The requirement metric (RM) for example can be calculated based on the weight factor for each requirement and fulfillment factor for each test case. Table 4 shows how RM, which is *19.25* is calculated for the first case study depending on equations 3 and 4. Similarly, VM can be calculated, and the value is *2.93*, and

Table 3. Mapping the measurements of the test cases into fulfillment score

Security Requirement	Condition/Test Case	Fulfillment
Authentication	1.1 -1.7	0
JWT	2.1 -2.3	0
Access Control	3.1-3.5	0
	3.6	1
Input Sanitation	4.1	1
	4.2	1
	4.3	1
	4.4-4.8	0
Error Handling	5.1	1
	5.2	1
	5.3	1
	5.4	0
Data Protection	6.1-6.6	0
Communication Security	7.1	1
	7.2	0.5
	7.3, 7.5 & 7.6	0
	7.4	0.5
HTTP Security	8.1	0.5
	8.2	1
	8.3-8.7	0
	8.8	0.5
Web Services	9.1-9.4	0
Cross Site-Scripting Mech.	10.1	1

Table 4. Calculating the Requirement Metric (RM) for the case study

Security Requirement	Fulfill-ment	Num. of test cases	Average	Weight	Rm_i (Eq. 3)
Authentication	0	7	0.00	0	0.00
JWT	0	3	0.00	0	0.00
Access Control	1	6	0.17	5	0.83
Input Sanitation	3	8	0.38	8	3.00
Error Handling	3	4	0.75	7	5.25
Data Protection	0	6	0.00	0	0.00
Communication Security	2	6	0.33	5	1.67
HTTP Security	2	8	0.25	6	1.50
Web Services	0	4	0.00	0	0.00
Cross Site-Scripting	1	1	1.00	7	7.00
Requirement Metric RM (Eq. 4)					19.25

then the assurance metric will be resulted from subtracting VM from RM, i.e. $AM = 19.25 - 2.93 = 16.32$.

The second step is to normalize the final assurance score (Equation 8). As we discussed before, $newmin_{AM} = 0$ and $newmax_{AM} = 10$. The original min and max value can be calculated as follows. The total number of security requirements in our case is 10 and the total number of vulnerability types is 9. Further, we assumed that the maximum value of the weight/risk a security requirement/vulnerability, respectively, can get is 10. Then, min_{AM} applies when every vulnerability is present, and each of them is assigned the max risk score, while no security requirement is fulfilled, i.e.,

$$newmin_{AM} = 0 - (9 \times 10) = -90.$$

The maximum score can be calculated similarly, and it has the value:

$$newmin_{AM} = (10 \times 10) - 0 = 100.$$

Thus, the scale will range from -90 up to 100. After normalization, the final normalized assurance metric value is

$$AM'_{PX-API} = \frac{AM - min_{AM}}{max_{AM} - min_{AM}} (newmax_{AM} - newmin_{AM}) + newmin_{AM} = 5.59$$

Conducting the same aforementioned steps for the second case study, i.e., TS-API, resulted in an assurance matric $AM'_{TS-API} = 5.64$.

ANALYSIS AND VALIDATION

There has been little research on quantification of security, in which the security of a system is measured, and the work presented in this chapter is an attempt to fill this gap. First, we started with a general taxonomy to clarify the main concepts applied in a security assurance ecosystem. The framework presented is a general-purpose security assurance framework that incorporate two different types of quantitative security metrices, security requirement metric and vulnerability metrics. Each captures a different perspective of the total security posture of the assurance target. The security requirement metric depends on two main factors, which are weight and fulfillment, while the vulnerability metric's factors are risk and existence. In the last chapter we presented the result of applying our framework on the public REST API application offered by Statistics Norway.

One of the main ideas that we introduced into the security requirement metric, comparing to the other literature, is the weight. Both case studies used the same assurance profile, and thus they were evaluated against the same set of security requirements and vulnerabilities. However, due to the different usages and goals of the two REST APIs, the importance of some security requirements is completely different, and thus they were assigned different weights. This has its reflection on the total security assurance score. The main idea is that we do not want to penalize a system for not completely fulfilling a requirement that is not important for that application. For example, authentication for a public API is not important at all, and not fulfilling this security requirement is acceptable, while authentication has an importance for a private secrete API. Regarding these case studies, the weight distribution was different, in which the public API had four security requirements that were weighted 0, while for the private one, three other security requirements were weighted 0.

In order to validate our framework, we conducted interviews with those security and domain experts that had been involved in the case studies. A questionnaire was developed for this purpose, which includes the following questions.

1. Do you think the developed security assurance framework based on quantitative security assurance metrics is helpful, why and when?
2. Do you think that you will use the list of requirement/vulnerability when you security test/develop a REST API in the future? and why?

3.   Do you think that dividing the assurance metrics into requirement and vulnerability elements is sound?
4.   Is it possible that a security requirement can be only partially fulfilled? If yes, which scale can represent the fulfilment confidence, e.g., scale 0..1, 0..2, 0..3? (For this thesis work this scale has been used. 0=not present, 0.5=partly present, 1=present)
5.   Do you have any other feedback to the developed security assurance framework?

The feedback, which was collected from these interviews and non-formal discussions with other was very positive.

Framework

The feedback to the first question is that a framework for security testing, a REST API as an example, is definitely useful for many roles and functions in the organization. For the developer it can help as a guide on how to develop secure applications and provide secure product to the end user. For a security tester, the framework with security profiles that indicate security requirements and potential vulnerabilities, can be used as a reference for what to prioritize and test, and when automated, it can reduce the manual work. Additionally, the organization can use the framework and the security profiles as a refence to follow for everyone. Thus, the different stages of the proposed process can be done separately.

Security Requirements and Vulnerabilities (Security Profiles)

The answers to the second question were very positive, particularly from the management. Actually, the management of Statistics Norway decided that the proposed REST API security profile, i.e., the list of security requirements and vulnerabilities, will be followed and used in the future for any REST API that will be developed. The flexibility of changing the weights and risks when conducting the evaluation process, and not bound them to a security profile is appreciated. An additional feedback was that it was beneficial and agile of checking the requirements during security testing, which has not been common.

Security Assurance Metrics

The feedback about the metrics in questions 3 and 4 was mainly that a metric that is able to measure the security can help the management to make better decisions. Though, difficulties achieving that is recognized. Additionally, there has been a discussion on the values that the fulfillment factor of security requirements can take.

It was noticed that limiting the result to only 0 and 1 was not enough. Adding the score 0.5 was appreciated, because for some security requirements, some control is in place, but they might not be functioning properly, or as expected. Thus neither 0 nor 1 could fit this situation.

Other Feedback

The feedback that was received from the management was that the proposed framework was satisfactory and building similar security profiles for other domains is seen as future work. Further, a discussion by the experts about a possible security assurance level at the beginning revealed that the levels of both API should be close, and the actual results gave very similar security assurance levels for both REST APIs (5.95 vs 5.64).

CONCLUSION AND FUTURE WORK

In this paper, we presented security assurance framework and evaluation process that is based on a quantitative security assurance metrics. The metrics cover both the positive posture of system security, through including the security requirement metric, and the negative posture through the vulnerability metric. The security assurance evaluation process for conducting security assurance evaluation using our metrics was discussed. Finally, two cases studies in the area of REST API were presented and discussed. In the first, two vulnerability test cases indicated the existence of one vulnerability *(sensitive data exposure)*, while 12 security requirement test cases indicated the fulfillment of 6 security requirements. In the second, 4 vulnerability test cases indicated the existence of two vulnerabilities. Regarding security requirements, 17 test cases indicated the fulfillment of 7 requirements. The first API got the assurance metric score 5.59 and the second got the score of 5.64.

The weigh and risk score are necessary contributors to the final security assurance score. Requirement weights that is part of our security assurance metric is one of the new features of our method. The weight assigned indicates how security is emphasized in the assurance target. For example, if authentication is necessary to make a specific API secure, the importance of that security requirement will also be high, hence the weight is also high. For a requirement that does not consolidate the security, or its presence is not vital to the assurance target, it will get a lower weight. Similar to vulnerability risk estimation, security requirement weight is assigned by security experts and is based on the application context.

Considering the public API case study, the *authentication* requirement is estimated not to be important at all, while the importance of the *communication security* requirement is estimated to be medium, and of the *input sanitization* requirement is estimated to be high (according to the security expert). Consequently, (not) fulfilling the first requirement will not have any influence, while fulfilling the last will have a great impact on the total security assurance score.

The framework has been validated through interview to the main security and domain experts from the organization who used and was involved in the process. A very positive feedback has been received and the merits of this approach has been recognized. In particular, the security profiles and security assurance quantification. As indicated also in the feedback, as a future work we plan to work on security profiles in other domains. Additionally, we plan to work on automation. This include test case generation test cases definition based on pre-defined assurance profiles and abstract application and threat models. Thus, making security assurance evaluation easier to use and available to wider range of enterprises that cannot afford the current assurance solutions.

REFERENCES

Abdulrazeg, A. A., Norwawi, N. M., & Basir, N. (2017). RiskSRP: Prioritizing Security Requirements Based on Total Risk Avoidance. *Advanced Science Letters*, *23*(5), 4596–4600. doi:10.1166/asl.2017.8901

Agreement, T. (2009). *Common criteria for information technology security evaluation part 1: Introduction and general model july 2009 revision 3 final foreword*. NIST.

Anderson, R. J. (2010). *Security engineering: a guide to building dependable distributed systems*. John Wiley & Sons.

Bischop, M. (2002). *The Art and Science of Computer Security*. Addison-Wesley Longman Publishing Co., Inc.

Bulut, E., Khadraoui, D., & Marquet, B. (2007). Multi-agent based security assurance monitoring system for telecommunication infrastructures. In *Proceedings of the Fourth IASTED International Conference on Communication, Network and Information Security* (pp. 90-95). ACTA Press.

Caldiera, V. R.-G., & Rombach, H. D. (1994). Goal question metric paradigm. Encyclopedia of software engineering, 528-532.

Felderer, M., Buchler, M., Johns, M., Brucker, A. D., Breu, R., & Pretschner, A. (2016). Security testing: A survey. In *Advances in Computers* (pp. 1–51). Elsevier.

Goertzel, K. M., Winograd, T., McKinley, H. L., Oh, L. J., Colon, M., McGibbon, T., & Vienneau, R. (2007). *Software security assurance: a State-of-Art Report (SAR). In Information Assurance Technology Analysis Center (IATAC)*. Academic Press. doi:10.21236/ADA472363

Haddad, S., Dubus, S., Hecker, A., Kanstren, T., Marquet, B., & Savola, R. (2011). Operational security assurance evaluation in open infrastructures. In *Risk and Security of Internet and Systems (CRiSIS), 2011 6th International Conference on* (pp. 1-6). IEEE.

Hudic, A., Smith, P., & Weippl, E. R. (2017). Security assurance assessment methodology for hybrid clouds. *Computers & Security, 70,* 723–743. doi:10.1016/j. cose.2017.03.009

Jansen, W. (2010). *Directions in security metrics research*. Diane Publishing.

Jim, M. (2016). *Open Web Application Security Project*. OWASP. Retrieved from https://www.owasp.org/images/3/33/OWASP_Application_Security_Verification_Standard_3.0.1.pdf

Joshi, C., & Singh, U. K. (2017). Information security risks management framework--A step towards mitigating security risks in university network. *Journal of Information Security and Applications,* 128-137.

Katt, B., & Prasher, N. (2018). Quantitative security assurance metrics: REST API case studies. In *Proceedings of the 12th European Conference on Software Architecture: Companion Proceedings*. ACM. 10.1145/3241403.3241464

Khajvand, M., & Tarokh, M. J. (2011). Estimating customer future value of different customer segments based on adapted rfm model in retail banking context. *Procedia Computer Science, 3,* 1327–1332. doi:10.1016/j.procs.2011.01.011

Kissel, R. L. (2013). *Glossary of Key Information Security Terms*. NIST Pubs. doi:10.6028/NIST.IR.7298r2

Ouedraogo, M., Kuo, C.-T., Tjoa, S., Preston, D., Dubois, E., Simoes, P., & Cruz, T. (2014). Keeping an eye on your security through assurance indicators. In *Security and Cryptography (SECRYPT), 2014 11th International Conference on* (pp. 1-8). IEEE.

Ouedraogo, M., Mouratidis, H., Khadraoui, D., Dubois, E., & Palmer-Brown, D. (2009). Current trends and advances in IT service infrastructures security assurance evaluation. *The School of Computing, Information Technology and Engineering, 4th Annual Conference,* 132-141.

Pendleton, M., Garcia-Lebron, R., Cho, J.-H., & Xu, S. (2017). *A survey on systems security metrics. In ACM Computing Surveys* (pp. 1–35). CSUR.

Pham, N., Baud, L., Bellot, P., & Riguidel, M. (2008). A near real-time system for security assurance assessment. In *The third International Conference on Internet monitoring and protection* (pp. 152-160). IEEE.

Port, D., & Wilf, J. (2017). A Decision-Theoretic Approach to Measuring Security. *Proceedings of the 50th Hawaii International Conference on System Sciences.* 10.24251/HICSS.2017.737

Project, O. W. (2016). *Application Security Verification Standard 3.0.1.* OWASP.

Savola, R. M. (2013). Quality of security metrics and measurement. *Computers & Security, 37,* 78–90. doi:10.1016/j.cose.2013.05.002

Spears, J. L., Barki, H., & Barton, R. R. (2013). Theorizing the concept and role of assurance in information systems security. *Information & Management, 50*(7), 598–605. doi:10.1016/j.im.2013.08.004

Statistics-Norway. (2017). *StatBank API User Guide. Statistics Norway.* Statistics Norway. Retrieved from http://www.ssb.no/en/omssb/tjenester-og-verktoy/api/px-api/_attachment/248250?_ts=15b48207778

Such, J. M., Gouglidis, A., Knowles, W., Misra, G., & Rashid, A. (2016). Information assurance techniques: Perceived cost effectiveness. *Computers & Security, 60,* 117–133. doi:10.1016/j.cose.2016.03.009

Thakurta, R. (2013). A value-based approach to prioritise non-functional requirements during software project development. *International Journal of Business Information Systems, 12*(4), 363–382. doi:10.1504/IJBIS.2013.053213

Tung, Y.-H., Lo, S.-C., Shih, J.-F., & Lin, H.-F. (2016). An integrated security testing framework for Secure Software Development Life Cycle. In *Network Operations and Management Symposium (APNOMS), 2016 18th Asia-Pacific* (pp. 1-4). IEEE. 10.1109/APNOMS.2016.7737238

Weldehawaryat, G. K., & Katt, B. (2018). Towards a Quantitative Approach for Security Assurance Metrics. In *SECURWARE 2018: The Twelfth International Conference on Emerging Security Information, Systems and Technologies.* IARIA.

Yoo, S. G., Vaca, H. P., & Kim, J. (2017). Enhanced Misuse Cases for Prioritization of Security Requirements. *Proceedings of the 9th International Conference on Information Management and Engineering,* 1-10. 10.1145/3149572.3149580

KEY TERMS AND DEFINITIONS

Assurance Metrics: An assurance metric can be defined as a quantitative measure that provides an evidence that the assurance target meets a particular level of the assurance scheme. It indicates to which degree the assurance target fulfills the security requirements' conditions and the vulnerabilities' conditions.

Assurance Profile: An assurance profile indicates the set of the security objectives, based upon the assurance level for a class of systems will be decided. Additionally, it contains the basic design and components of a system and its environment in that specific class. The security objectives are specified as a set of (1) security requirements and their fulfillment conditions and a set of (2) potential vulnerabilities and threats, and their existence conditions.

Assurance Scheme: An assurance scheme is an instance of an assurance profile defined for a specific system, called an assurance target. It contains the same security objectives taken from the assurance profile it instantiates in terms of security requirements and vulnerabilities, and their fulfillment and existence conditions, respectively. Also, it contains specific details about the system design and its environment. Furthermore, it specifies the weight for each security requirement and the risk for each vulnerability, or threat, specified in the assurance profile.

Assurance Target: An assurance target can be defined as the system under evaluation, for which assurance level will be assessed.

Assurance Technique: An assurance technique can be defined as a method that can be used for evaluating and assessing the assurance target.

Evaluation Evidence: Evaluation evidence can be defined as a set of measurements that can result from applying the assurance technique on the assurance target.

Security Assurance: A security assurance can be defined as the confidence that a system meets its security requirements and is resilient against security vulnerabilities and failures. The confidence indicated by the security assurance represents the level of trust we give to a system that is safe to use.

Security Assurance Evaluation Process: Shortly "evaluation process," can be defined as the process of evaluating the security assurance level of the assurance target. The input is an assurance profile catalog and information about the assurance target to be evaluated and the output is the assurance level.

ENDNOTES

[1]   https://www.commoncriteriaportal.org/

[2]   https://www.bsimm.com/

[3]   https://www.opensamm.org/

[4]   https://www.ssb.no/en/

[5]   http://data.ssb.no/api-name/api-version/lang/

[6]   Another way to define the assurance metric is as a pair <RM, VM> instead of subtracting the vulnerability metric from the requirement metric.

[7]   https://en.wikipedia.org/wiki/Weighting

[8]   https://www.owasp.org/index.php/Threat_Risk_Modeling

[9]   A detailed description of this API can be found in (Statistics-Norway, 2017).

Chapter 3
Security Assurance in Agile Software Development Methods:
An Analysis of Scrum, XP, and Kanban

Kalle Rindell

iD https://orcid.org/0000-0003-3349-5823
University of Turku, Finland

Sami Hyrynsalmi
Tampere University of Technology, Finland

Ville Leppänen
University of Turku, Finland

ABSTRACT

Agile software development was introduced in the beginning of the 2000s to increase the visibility and efficiency software projects. Since then it has become as an industry standard. However, fitting sequential security engineering development models into iterative and incremental development practices in agile methods has caused difficulties in defining, implementing, and verifying the security properties of software. In addition, agile methods have also been criticized for decreased quality of documentation, resulting in decreased security assurance necessary for regulative purposes and security measurement. As a consequence, lack of security assurance can complicate security incident management, thus increasing the software's potential lifetime cost. This chapter clarifies the requirements for software security assurance by using an evaluation framework to analyze the compatibility of established agile security development methods: XP, Scrum, and Kanban. The results show that the agile methods are not inherently incompatible with security engineering requirements.

DOI: 10.4018/978-1-5225-6313-6.ch003

INTRODUCTION

During the last decade, agile software development methods have become an industry *de facto* standard. The aim of these methods has been to improve efficiency as well as transparency of software development (Abrahamsson et al., 2002). The methods promote iterative development and informal interaction, and put a lower or even negative value to strict processes. This is particularly stressed in cases where documentation is used as a means of communication, whether used to convey the customer requirements to the development team, or for communication within the team itself, e.g., in the form of specifications (Beznosov and Kruchten, 2004; Ko et al., 2007; LaToza et al., 2006).

Introducing strict security requirements to the software development process usually results in creation of excess security assurance, such as a formal security architecture, out of necessity to fulfill the strict external security criteria. Integrating the security requirements, such as reviews, security testing, processes and documentation into an agile method, the cost of the development effort is very likely to increase (Beznosov and Kruchten, 2004). The entire extra 'management overhead' is in direct contradiction with agile methods' core philosophy of leanness and informality (Beck et al., 2001). Thus, applying the security processes to the agile or lean development methods has the potential of rendering the methods, by definition, something that is neither agile nor lean.

On the other hand, the need for software security has been always one of the main drivers in software development. While quality assurance remains a key process to ensure software robustness, effectiveness and usability, security assurance provides the means to develop and deploy software components and systems that protect the system's data, their users' privacy and the system resources.

The operating environment of the software products and services has been evolving and changing due to extensive use of the Internet and public services as well as the ever-increasing pervasiveness and ubiquitous characteristic of software solutions. In addition, the software industry itself has gone through an unprecedented shift from sequential development methods (e.g. waterfall-type) towards iterative and incremental software development methods (e.g. agile and lean). In addition, due to the large scale adaptation of agile methods in the industry (Licorish et al. 2016, VersionOne 2018), the new agile development methods seem to be able to reclaim at least some of their claimed benefits.

Furthermore, the need for security has also been realized in the form of several commercial, international and national standards. To comply with these, several security frameworks and security-focused development methods have been presented. However, knitting together strict security engineering practices and adaptable agile software methods is not straightforward and may cause remarkable problems.

Furthermore, the selection of a software development method to be used in a development project has consequences into the software architecture and design. While the manifesto for agile software development states that the best architectures and design emerges from self-organized teams (Beck et al., 2001), this statement has been often criticized. For example, renowned software engineering researcher Philippe Kruchten (2010) has repeatedly questioned whether the concept of 'agile architecture' combines two incompatible approaches. In the context of security sensitive projects, this question is even more topical as it is a hard and arduous task to embed security into a product afterwards.

Therefore, the objective of this chapter is to study how well the selected agile methods are adaptable to security development practices. For the purposes of this study, we have selected three widely-used development methods, Scrum, XP and Kanban. We use Microsoft Secure Development Lifecycle (SDL) model as a benchmark for the evaluation – as the model is designed for high regulation environment and therefore its practices as well as the required frequency of occurrence should define the baseline required for this kind of activities in the industry.

These agile development methods are evaluated against a security requirement framework. The security requirement framework is created with adaption from the Finnish governmental security instructions, named *VAHTI* (VAHTI, 2016). The evaluation framework presented in this study consists of 22 different security requirements, selected from the instructions from software development. The compliance of the selected development methods is then evaluated against the requirements of VAHTI, and the applicability and adaptability of the 'security-enhanced' methods themselves are evaluated. In this analysis, SDL's activities and their properties are used to guide the analysis.

The remaining of this chapter is structured as follows. The next section discusses shortly on different software development methods as well as related work. It is followed by a presentation of the evaluation framework and VAHTI security regulation as defined by Finnish government. After that, the results of applying the presented evaluation framework into XP, Scrum and Kanban are presented. Finally, in the last three sections the findings are discussed, future research avenues presented, and the study summarized.

BACKGROUND

The security claims of a software product or a service need to be backed with evidence; it cannot be declared only by the developer. To verify the security claims stated by the software, evidence is gathered through several activities such as reviewing the software, documentation written during the development, and processes as well as through security testing, and security auditing.

Combined, these requirements create a need for the software developers to be able to choose a development methodology that supports not only the creation of software for the selected software domain, but also satisfies the security requirements (SAFECode 2012). Preferably, this is done in the most efficient way possible, taking into account the organization and the operational environment. In software development, efficiency is gained by close integration to the utilized development methodology.

In the following, we will first take a look on different agile software development methods later studied in this chapter. It is followed by a review of related studies done in examining security engineering in agile software development context.

Software Development Methods

A series of different kinds of software development methods have been presented (Abrahamsson et al., 2002). In our use, a 'software development method' defines how a software development process is divided into different phases, how the phases are arranged, and what kinds of artefacts are produced during the different phases. Instead of more traditional methods, as so-called 'waterfall' and spiral models, our focus turns on modern lightweight development methods labelled as *agile*.

For this study, we have chosen three agile software development methods: E*xtreme Programming* (XP), *Scrum*, and *Kanban*. These methods were selected as they are among the most popular and most used ones in the latest surveys (Licorish et al. 2016) as well as they have been the among the most popular ones during the last decade (cf. VersionOne 2013, 2018). That is, these methods can be interpreted to present the core of agile software development methods. All of these methods can be considered archetypes of agile software development methods, with strong use base in the industry. Thus, they are also eligible candidates for development work carried out in highly regulated environments.

In addition to the selected agile methods, we take a look on Microsoft's SDL model that acts as a reference point for the evaluation. As the SDL model is designed especially for highly regulated information security environments, it should lay the needed level of security engineering activities in software projects.

Extreme Programming. XP is one of the first and most widely used agile development models. The XP method principally consists of a collection of practices and values; that is, it does not define strictly how the actual development process should be carried out (Beck, 1999). In addition, XP promotes a number of techniques, such as 40-hours week, iteration planning game, test-first development and small releases.

However, the guidelines given by the method are quite practical, such as the use of pair programming or continuous integration. Popularity of the XP method, especially in the beginning of the first decade of the 21st century, has spun attempts to bring security elements into the method. Previous work of security enhancements into the XP method consist of security-related user stories and abuser stories in the planning phase (Boström et al., 2006; Ge et al., 2007).

Scrum. Scrum can be considered as the current mainstream of the software industry (see VersionOne, 2018). The method defines certain roles for the team members, their responsibilities as well as certain tools, activities and a loose framework for the development process. The development work is divided into sprints that usually last from two to four weeks. (Schwaber, 1995, 2004)

In the extant literature, earlier examples of security enhancement to Scrum consist of loosely SDL-based security features specifically aimed for regulated environments, such as in a case presented by Fitzgerald et al. (2013). These features and processes include 'hardening sprints', which consist entirely of security-related planning and documentation, and regulation-driven security and quality assurance reviews and checks. This methodology includes new roles that are not included in baseline Scrum. Scrum has been selected due to its overwhelming popularity in the current software development industry (VersionOne, 2013, 2018).

Kanban. Kanban, much like XP, can be understood simply as a set of development concepts, ideas and principles, rather than a tightly-defined set of processes, practices and roles. It therefore provides a rather flexible framework for development, focusing on the work flow: the work flow is visualized, the amount of work in progress is limited, and the development lead time is measured. This helps the developers to stay informed of the work backlog, aims to ensure that the team members do not get overloaded, and provides metrics to optimize the development time. Kanban is typically combined with more prescriptive methods, leading into creation of e.g. Scrumban (Nikitina et al., 2012) and other hybrid methods.

Security Development Lifecycle. Microsoft's effort to improve the security of their software has led them to develop their own security framework, the Security Development Lifecycle process. SDL is based on iterative spiral model borrowed from and adaptable to agile methodologies (Microsoft, 2012; Baca and Carlsson, 2011).

The approach selected in the SDL, when adapted without modification, is quite heavy on processes, documentation and organization – a contrast to the agile methods discussed above. This forms part of the motivation of this study, aiming to identify the minimal set of SDL elements required to fulfill the security requirements. SDL divides activities into three categories: *one-time* requirements, *bucket* requirements and *every-sprint* requirement. The naming of the categories appears to suggest that SDL for Agile is meant for Scrum or Scrum-like methods. SDL emphasizes the use source code static analysis tools as the principal security activity, followed by threat modeling and security testing.

Related Work

A starting point for the research was formal categorization of security aspects for software development, and conducting a feature analysis using DESMET (Kitchenham et al., 1997). DESMET framework was presented in the 1990s for evaluation of software development methods. The evaluation may be quantitative or qualitative, and based on experiments, case studies, screenings, effect analyses, feature analyses or surveys. The nature of this study suggested a screening feature analysis, with easily quantitative results: the requirement is either fulfilled or not, and each method and security process is analyzed as a simulated case study, based on expert opinions and without instantiation.

Beznosov and Kruchten (2004) earlier used a similar approach; however, they did not use established security criteria or framework, nor an external evaluation criteria. In addition, there exists a number of studies concerning secure software development concept in general, also covering the topic of security-focused testing (Fitzgerald and Stol, 2014). Furthermore, Abrahamsson et al. (2003) made an early contribution comparing agile software development methods by their suitability for different stages of development life cycle, and their support for project management — both important aspects from the security point of view. In their study, security engineering was not considered *per se*, as they focused more on general issues in different agile software development methods.

Regarding more specifically literature on security engineering in agile software development, a series of work has been presented (cf. Rindell et al., 2017b). A common nominator for the earlier literature seems to be an approach of documenting a proprietary corporate software development method, or even specify own development method (e.g., Baca and Carlsson, 2011; Boström et al., 2006; Rindell et al., 2015). For example, Baca and Carlsson (2011) also compare existing software methodologies, including SDL, with a proprietary method, and claim also a new proprietary method of their own. In addition, for instance Vuori (2011) discusses how IEC 61508 standard can be used to improve agile software development methods' suitability for a safety-critical development environment.

Furthermore, Wäyrynen et al. (2004) discusses whether security engineering approach can be implemented into XP development method at all. They also discussed certain activities – e.g., static code reviews, security policies –that might need to be included into XP to make it more security engineering friendly. Boström et al. (2006) continued this topic and proposed the use of abuser stories and security-related user stories as a part of XP to make it more suitable for security engineering.

Similar approach has been utilized by Köngsli et al. (2006), who notes the mismatch between requirements for security engineering projects and agile software development. Yet, the study does not specifically discuss on the claimed shortcomings. Nevertheless, the study reviews a bulk of literature and lists several different security activities that should be taken into account. Chivers et al. (2005) also note the mismatch between XP and security engineering. Their proposal is iterative security architecting to maintain a 'good enough' (from a security point-of-view) architecture during iterative and incremental development work. Also Ge et al. (2007) aim to improve security engineering in XP through security training and security architecture. Their security activities include, e.g., security stories.

Adelyar and Norta (2016) and Adelyar (2018) adopted a different approach and studied what kind of security challenges there are in agile methods. Their results show that there are certain developer and customer activities that might enable the presence of security flaws in the software product.

De Win et al. (2009) used an alternative approach and focused on three security engineering standard processes in the field: CLASP, SDL and Touchpoints. Their focus is on these practices and whereas they acknowledge, e.g., XP, it is not clear how well the studied cases are suitable for mainstream software security engineering projects with an agile approach. Ayalew et al. (2013) continue this work and focus on cost-benefit analysis. However, their work produces also a list of comparable agile security activities.

Sonia et al. (2014) assigns an agility value to different security engineering activities. In their analysis, all security activities studied are seem to be incompatible with at least one modern agile activity. Thus, their work further emphasizes the difference and incompatibility of security engineering and agile software development methods.

Othmane et al. (2014) propose their own secure agile development method for *continuous security*. Their approach is to adapt different security engineering activities in each development sprint in order to guarantee that the software produced in each iteration is secured.

In addition, empiric research has been conducted on the impact of agile methods on software security (Alnatheer et al., 2010). There also exists case studies in adapting Scrum-based methods in an environment with strict formal security regulations (Fitzgerald et al., 2013; Rindell et al., 2016, Oyetoyan et al., 2016).

The study by Fitzgerald et al. (2013) discusses security regulations and Scrum in considerable depth, yet only within the scope of a single company and a single development method. The case study by Rindell et al. (2016, 2017a) focuses also on a case using Scrum-based method but it is as well restricted by the scope of a single project. Oyetoyan et al. (2016) studied two organizations using Scrum in their development work. The focus of the study is on the skills, trainings and experience of the development teams. The study shows that security awareness improves the use of security activities in the development work.

To summarize the review of related work, it can be noted that there are a series of work devoted for improving different aspects of security engineering in agile software development methods. However, a common claim seems to be that agile methods are inherently insecure and inapplicable for security engineering (Rindell et al., 2017b). Yet, there is a lack of work addressing whether this can be considered to be true or just a myth.

This study takes an alternative approach and aims to evaluate the vanilla versions of different agile software development methods against a security engineering framework. To depart from the previous work, that have assumed the insecurity of these methods, we instead use an industry standard (i.e., VAHTI regulation) as a baseline for defining security activities needed.

EVALUATION FRAMEWORK

This chapter aims to assess how well agile software development methods are suitable for security engineering projects by using a nationwide criteria and new development methods, and the SDL security framework as a benchmark. In contrast to most of the previous approaches, security is in this chapter considered to be an *absolute* requirement for software. In the agile method terminology, security is considered an essential part of the customer satisfaction, which the agile methods aim to promote (Beznosov and Kruchten, 2004).

We concentrate on the challenges this brings into the development process and the quality assurance closely associated with security controls. This study also makes the security requirement more specific by using a well-established security criteria, VAHTI, and inspecting the applicability of the selected software methodologies to comply with this criteria. The term 'security assurance' is used to describe the drive to mitigate security vulnerabilities in a measurable and evidence-backed way, comparable to the term 'quality assurance', which aims to mitigate software discrepancies in general. In a regulatory context, security assurance conveys also the meaning of security proof, referring to written security documentation and e.g. logs.

The specific set of security requirements used in this chapter is based on VAHTI (literally translated *'Guard'*, a mnemonic acronym in Finnish for 'Government Information Security') security regulation. VAHTI is one of the earliest and most comprehensive sets of open and public information system security regulations. The instructions consist of 51 documents, published since 2001, aiming at covering the whole life cycle of the governmental information systems. The guideline covers also various aspects of information systems management, governance, use, and, ultimately aid implementing Finland's national information security strategy, published in 2009.

VAHTI instructions specify three security levels ('basic', 'increased' and 'high'). The instructions were originally targeted only for government's internal information systems work; due to public sector's integral part in the Finnish society, VAHTI is in the process of becoming a de facto security standard in any information system that interacts with a governmental system. VAHTI exists to harmonize the security requirements among the public institutions, a set of national standards has been developed, based on standards such as ISO/IEC 27002 (ISO/IEC, 2013), and derived from Systems Security Engineering – Capability Maturity Model (ISO/IEC standard 21827, 2008). These requirements aim to cover the life cycle and various use cases of the public information systems, and span over several dozen public documents.

VAHTI was selected due to two main reasons. First, the selection of a governmental regulation that is in active use in Finland allows us to focus on aspects and activities that are actively used in the industry. That is, instead of developing an own evaluation framework from the scratch, we depart from the previous work by using an existing and widely-used instruction set in our analysis. Second, VAHTI allows us to focus on a more comprehensive picture of a security engineering instead of a single standard. While this also forces us to select the suitable criteria for the evaluation of the software development methods, the evaluation framework based on this kind of an instruction set should be more general than one based on a more narrow standard.

For developing the evaluation framework for this study, we focused on all VAHTI criteria in different phases and regulation levels. VAHTI security criteria for application development comprises the whole life cycle of software. The complete list of security requirements in VAHTI includes 118 activities (FMoF, 2013). This list was analyzed through by the authors and relevant criteria for the software development methods were selected. The selection was made based on the relevance of the requirements to the software development method: the selected criteria are either requirements for the documentation, reviews or the development process itself.

We excluded requirements that did not directly relate to the software development method or approach used. For example, requirements for handling data storage as well as physical access to the server room are not relevant for the software development method's point-of-view. That is, those can be handled regardless of the development method used.

The only selected organizational requirement, the one for security training, was included due to the fact that SDL as well as previous work (e.g., Ge et al., 2007 and Oyetoyan et al., 2016) emphasizes this as a security-enhancing mechanism. Furthermore, it may affect the development roles in the software development method.

From the complete list of VAHTI's security requirements, 22 activities directly concerning the software development methods were selected. The selected security requirements are presented in Table 1. The table also links each requirement back to the respective VAHTI security level.

We evaluate each criteria through four dimensions: i) requirements *integrality* in a development method, ii) requirement's *frequency* of occurrence in the development work, iii) level of *automation* and iv) *cost* of performing or carrying out the requirement. Each of these dimensions are clarified more in the latter.

In the evaluation, we study whether each requirement is i) an integral part of the method; ii) the method can be adjusted to support the requirement; or iii) the method is incompatible with the requirement or there are needs for improvement in the method. This evaluation was done by the authors discussing and analyzing how well the requirement can be implemented in each of the selected software development methods. All authors are expert in software engineering and it was required that a mutual agreement needed to be reached before continuing.

The other assessment criteria of the frequency requirement for each technique is defined as it is by SDL. That is, the analysis of these requirements needed frequency is based on how often SDL requires them to be used. The frequency is encoded into three values: i) one-time requirements; ii) bucket requirements and iii) every-sprint requirements.

Each task is further ranked to either Automated, Semi-automated or Manual. Semi-automated means the bulk of the work is done by automated tools, which in turn may require a considerable amount of manual configuration. This analysis is based on the description in the VAHTI instruction set and it is subjectively evaluated by the authors. However, the authors mutually agreed on the level of the automation during the analysis.

Cost is calculated by multiplying the level of automation with the frequency of the task. The cost of security requirement's, that has to be carried out only one-time during the project and which can be easily automated, would be considered as a very low. Similarly, manual requirement that has to be carried out in each sprint would be considered as a very high in its cost. The remaining combinations are similarly categorized into the following scale: Very Low, Low, Medium, High, and Very High.

RESULTS

Table 2 summarizes the Scrum's, XP's and Kanban's compliance with each security requirement in the evaluation framework. In addition, Table 3 reports each criterion's level of automation and estimated cost as this was found an important factor. In the following, we will discuss on the central observations based on these analyses.

Table 1. The evaluation framework's criteria

No.	Criterion	VAHTI level
1	Application Risk Analysis	Basic
2	Test Plan Review	Basic
3	Threat Modeling	Basic
4	Goal and criticality	Increased
5	Business Impact Analysis	Increased
6	Documentation of Security Solutions	Increased
7	Application Security Requirements	Increased
8	Application Security Settings Definition	Increased
9	Security Testing	Increased
10	Security Auditing	Increased
11	Architecture guidelines	High
12	External Interface Review	High
13	Use of Secure Design Patterns	High
14	Attack Surface Reduction	High
15	Architectural Security Requirements	High
16	Internal Communication Security	High
17	Security Test Cases Definition	High
18	Test Phase Code Review	High
19	Use of Automated Testing Tools	High
20	Security Mechanism Review	High
21	Application Development-time Auditing	High
22	Security training	High

The three first criteria (*Application Risk Analysis*, *Test Plan Review* and *Threat Modeling*) of the framework can be considered as a basic requirement for all kinds of application development projects. That is, *Application Risk Analysis* is an essential security element and it has been or it can be well integrated into all methods. Yet, it can be done only manually as SDL requires it to be carried out in each iteration. Therefore, it is costly.

Test Plan Review is an internal security activity in which the personnel reviews the test plan. All of the studied development methods support this integrally while its cost is high. *Threat Modeling* consists of compiling the list of the threats and keeping that up to date during every sprint. This is a cornerstone activity of SDL and essential to any security related development project. The activity provides a baseline for risk analysis and guides architectural choices, among other things. The

Table 2. Compliance of XP, Scrum and Kanban with different security requirements presented in the evaluation framework

No.	Requirement	XP	Scrum.	Kanban
1	Application Risk Analysis	Integral	Integral	Integral
2	Test Plan Review	Adaptable	Adaptable	Adaptable
3	Threat Modeling	Integral	Integral	Integral
4	Goal and Criticality	Adaptable	Adaptable	Adaptable
5	Business Impact Analysis	Adaptable	Adaptable	Adaptable
6	Documentation of Security Solutions	Adaptable	Adaptable	Adaptable
7	Application Security Requirements	Integral	Integral	Integral
8	Application Security Settings Definition	Adaptable	Adaptable	Adaptable
9	Security Testing	Integral	Integral	Integral
10	Security Auditing	Adaptable	Adaptable	Adaptable
11	Architecture guidelines	Adaptable	Adaptable	Adaptable
12	External Interface Review	Integral	Integral	Integral
13	Use of Secure Design Patterns	Integral	Integral	Integral
14	Attack Surface Reduction	Integral	Integral	Integral
15	Architectural Security Requirements	Integral	Integral	Integral
16	Internal Communication Security	Integral	Integral	Integral
17	Security Test Cases Definition	Adaptable	Adaptable	Adaptable
18	Test Phase Code Review	Integral	Integral	Integral
19	Use of Automated Testing Tools	Integral	Integral	Integral
20	Security Mechanism Review	Adaptable	Adaptable	Adaptable
21	Application Development-time Auditing	Incompatible	Incompatible	Incompatible
22	Security training	Adaptable	Adaptable	Adaptable

threat 'landscape' is dependent on the software's intended users and use environment. This is essential to all methods and easily integrated to them. This requirement was not mandatory even at VAHTI's highest level, which can be considered as a clear omission to the instruction set. A potential explanation to this could be the restrictions in the availability of threat modeling tools. Alternatively threat modeling can be performed as a manual task using e.g. Microsoft's STRIDE mnemonics for component analysis. In this approach, the system and its components are reviewed for security threats in the categories of Spoofing, Tampering, Repudiation, Information disclosure, Denial of Service, and Elevation of Privilege.

Table 3. The level of automation, frequency of occurrence and relative cost of the evaluation framework's security requirements

No.	Requirement	Level of automation	Frequency	Cost
1	Application Risk Analysis	Manual	Every sprint	Very high
2	Test Plan Review	Manual	Bucket	High
3	Threat Modeling	Manual	Every sprint	High
4	Goal and Criticality	Manual	One-time	Low
5	Business Impact Analysis	Manual	Bucket	Low
6	Documentation of Security Solutions	Manual	Bucket	Low
7	Application Security Requirements	Manual	Bucket	High
8	Application Security Settings Definition	Manual	Bucket	High
9	Security Testing	Automated	Every sprint	Medium
10	Security Auditing	Manual	One-time	Low
11	Architecture guidelines	Manual	One-time	Low
12	External Interface Review	Manual	Bucket	High
13	Use of Secure Design Patterns	Manual	One-time	Low
14	Attack Surface Reduction	Manual	Every sprint	Very high
15	Architectural Security Requirements	Manual	One-time	Low
16	Internal Communication Security	Semi-automated	Every sprint	Medium
17	Security Test Cases Definition	Manual	Every sprint	Very high
18	Test Phase Code Review	Manual	Every sprint	Very high
19	Use of Automated Testing Tools	Automated	Every sprint	Very low
20	Security Mechanism Review	Manual	One-time	Low
21	Application Development-time Auditing	Manual	One-time	Low
22	Security training	Manual	Every sprint	Very high

The following six criteria (i.e., the requirements from number 4 to 10 in Table 1) can be considered to be essential to all security engineering projects with increased information security alertness. With the notable exceptions of *Application Security Requirements* and *Application Security Settings Definition,* the cost of these requirements is estimated to be low in a development project.

The *Goal and Criticality* requirement means classification of the software and documentation of its purpose. Both XP and Scrum were found lacking in this respect while the Scrum-based methods are more readily adaptable to produce planning phase documentation. Kanban-based methods are also considered adaptable.

Business Impact Analysis is basically method independent requirement, and as such, considered adaptable to all methods. This document should be produced in the planning phase, and updated during the implementation when the application's incremental threat analyses implicate further threats to the business environment.

Documentation of Security Solutions is a direct requirement to communicate the security requirements to the developers through documentation. All agile methods are fundamentally against this approach, and will need improvement to be able to take into efficient use.

Document on *Application Security Requirements* is a high-level description, covering the criticality of the information handled by the software, threat analysis, and other functional security requirements. All security related development methods were deemed to support creation of this document in the planning phase. Similarly, *Application Security Settings Definition* is an extensive documentation step, where all the software settings, interfaces, administration steps, test data, encryption details etc. are listed and thoroughly documented. A suggested action would be a separate documentation sprint, to be added into the agile methods.

On one hand, *Security Testing* states that security testing should be incorporated into the standard testing procedure. This requirement is supported by all methods. On the other hand, *Security Auditing* is a requirement for Increased and High VAHTI levels. Furthermore, it requires an external auditor. This requirement was included due to its strain on the development process, mainly through architecture auditing. Also this requirement is supported by all selected methods.

The remaining twelve criteria can be considered to be essential for a software development project where information security requirements are extremely high. As the VAHTI instruction set is defined by a governmental agency, it is not a surprise that special emphasizes has been put on these requirements. Furthermore, on average these requirements are more costly to carry out than the ones belonging essentially in the increased security category.

Architecture guidelines define the principles guiding the application development, in this context especially from the security point of view. This requirement is adaptable to all development methods. *External Interface Review* is an analysis of the software's external interfaces and comparison to architectural and application level principles. All methods support the performance of this action. *Use of Secure Design Patterns* mandates classifying the software due to its architecture type, such as client-server, mobile, web or embedded application. The design pattern is then selected based on the architectural type. All of the studied methods support this requirement.

Attack Surface Reduction includes identifying and analyzing all software functionality where the participants cannot completely trust each other, such as open services, user or administrator actions or database connections. All methods support this step. *Architectural Security Requirements* mean analysis of the application's architecture against known or anticipated threats. All methods support this requirement. *Internal Communication Security* concerns especially applications utilizing multi-tier architecture and ties the deployment of the application into the development phase. Largely method independent planning-phase activity, but still supported by each method.

Security Test Cases Definition is an absolute requirement for almost all security-related development, and VAHTI gives here specific instructions how the test cases should be defined, such as use of empiric evidence, known issues and several sources. This requirement is adaptable to all methods. *Test Phase Code Review* is informally performed by the internal security personnel, and documented either separately or even straight into the source code. This requirement is also supported by all of the studied methods.

Use of Automated Testing Tools is more or less standard practice for all agile software development, regardless of the used methodology. On the security side, the tools include fuzz testing tools, vulnerability scanners, code analyzers and continuous integration tools. This requirement is quite naturally supported by all three included agile methods.

Security Mechanism Review is a code-level review of how security components are implemented. Basically it is method independent, but may be difficult to implement in iterative methods as after changes this review has to be done again. As such, this activity might require a specific hardening sprint, as a time-consuming activity like this may be difficult to fit into the work flow.

Application Development-time Auditing is a high-level security audition at various points of application development. Intrinsically a waterfall-type approach, causing difficulties with iterative methods. *Security training* means organizing purpose-oriented and role-based training for the personnel responsible for the application development, such as the product owner, developers and testers. This requirement is adaptable to all of the studied methods.

DISCUSSION

The three agile methods (Scrum, XP and Kanban) studied in this chapter were found to have certain issues with adaptability of security tasks. Repetitive (i.e., multi-sprint or every-sprint) documentation and review tasks were found specifically incompatible with these methods. While a theoretical examination cannot establish concrete benefits gained from the use of agile methods, it was deemed unjustifiable to claim that their use would have an adverse effect on security assurance. Instead, use of agile prompts including security items e.g. in the user stories and integrating them into the backlog as a part of regular conduct of an agile development project. All three methods were found inherently compatible with or adaptable to all planning and implementation phase activities. Incorporating security reviews and auditing into the iterative development processes proved to be a tougher issue. The SDL prompts these activities to be completed in "each and every sprint", or "the sprint is deemed incomplete". However, the wording of the SDL has since 2015 been altered, and the word *sprint* is no longer used as a synonym for *release*, which is the current term. It appears that Microsoft, too, has awoken to the reality in which not every agile sprint produces a released version of software.

When compared to the previous work in the field, this study is produces somewhat different results, explained by the different research approach. Whereas the previous work has been focused on defining more or less a 'perfect' method for agile security engineering and underlining all possible obstacles, we adapted a different route for our analysis. Instead of a rigid model, this study concentrated on the aspects that are needed to be changed in order to use a popular agile method in a development project that needs to fulfill governmental security development instructions. That is, we were looking for a 'good enough' solution and the result shows that mismatch between agile methods and security engineering might be too harshly reported. Especially the concerns of agile methods' compatibility with formal requirements can be quite readily dismissed based on a theoretical analysis only.

Nevertheless, the use of studied agile methods clearly requires quite heavy process customization, in order for them to be applicable to projects with formal security requirements. The key findings were that *continuous security planning*, in the form of iterative design and architecture activities, has the most potential to improve the security of the finalized product. On other hand, at the higher security levels, incorporating every-sprint security reviews make it difficult to retain the 'agility' of a method – and formal auditing requirements worsen this situation altogether. Incorporating the 'hardening sprints', suggested by e.g. Fitzgerald et al., (2013), or focusing on security only in the planning phase of the project (Boström et al., 2006; Ge et al., 2007), may simply lead to superficial fulfillment of the requirements, potentially leading to security issues afterwards. Methodology-based evaluation suggests that security assurance is best achieved through investing in both planning and implementation tasks.

Scrum is the only one of the methods that include any kind of role definitions. Security methodologies, on the other hand, tend to have specific role definitions and push for strict separation of duties. Table 4 presents a summary of key tasks and properties required from a security assured software development method. The table states whether the selected methods have the roles defined (Yes or No), or support the extension of existing roles to cover the more security-specific one. This

Table 4. Security task role definition

No	Task	XP	Scrum	Kanban
1	Security specialist roles defined	No	Yes	No
2	Documentation and guidelines produced	Yes	Yes	Yes
3	Support for development time security reviews	No	Yes	No
4	Support for delivery time security reviews	No	Yes	No
5	Compliant development process roles defined	No	No	No

comparison reveals a more worrying side of the secure agile methods, especially regarding role definition.

SDL defines several security roles for the development team, such as reviewer/ advisor, auditor, expert, and team champions. It also promotes strict and vigorous separation of duties, all while the agile methods typically define only a minimum set of roles or none at all. Scrum, in its basic form, defines only the roles of Product Owner, Developers and the Scrum Master. Of these, the Developer is the most appropriate one to assume the responsibilities of a security specialist. This, however, is a clear violation of the industry standard 'separation of duties' rule: the developers themselves are rarely the best persons to break their own code. This approach is anti-agile in two ways: teams not sharing information is a clear violation against the agile philosophy, and having separate teams working in parallel bogs down the development speed while increasing the cost. The same lack of defined security roles also characterizes XP and Kanban, all while giving organizations more freedom in choosing the development tools, mechanisms and processes.

In addition, the message in the studied literature is clear about certain benefit of employing agile methods to develop security-oriented software: developing the software in numerous iterations towards the finalized product may actually improve security assurance, as the product is kept potentially shippable after every sprint – an agile ideal, although rarely achievable. This greatly helps in tracking the changes in security development and detecting possible security threats. In addition, the promoted use of automated testing and other tools is an inherent part of security development, directly applicable also to fuzz testing.

FUTURE RESEARCH DIRECTIONS

This study opens new fruitful research avenues for future development in security regarding software architecture and design fields. While there are different adaptations defined and presented for secure agile software development, there is a lack of empirical evidence and test regarding these adaptations. Future work should be aimed to develop usable agile software development improvements that comply with the requirements of security engineering. Furthermore, this kind of a development work should incorporate the 'good enough' principle in order to keep the benefits achieved with agile methods. If the method aims for too good or too strict security process, it might be that transparency and efficiency of agile methodologies will be lost.

In addition, this chapter calls for a new kind of thinking into the security engineering. While security is and will be a main driver in many, if not in all, software development projects, also other aspects are important. These include, e.g., efficient and fast development. The current development in this field has been based purely on the security engineering perspective and much of the realism in the industry is bypassed. Therefore, especially in the agile security engineering field a new fresh start is needed for defining, e.g., cost-efficient solutions and integrating security engineering practices into other activities. While improving awareness has been showed to have good effect on security engineering, lightweight solutions could also work.

The limitation of this study is a lack of empiric evidence, and the logical next step would be to instantiate the methods and possibly include more of them. While security should be based on 'defined' rather than 'empiric' logic, practice will show not only the applicability of the methods themselves, but also the real cost of security mechanisms to the development process. Security cost is becoming increasingly necessary to pay, as Finland's public sector's software security regulations show. As the cost of development is much smaller than rewriting and refactoring an existing code base, integrating the security processes to the development method is crucial. The ultimate objective should be nothing less than finding a framework for the software developers to choose the correct set of roles, methods and processes for each situation and purpose.

CONCLUSION

This study used established and widely-used Finnish government's security criteria, VAHTI, as a basis for evaluation of three approaches to software development for a regulated environment. Selected security framework was Microsoft SDL and the methods XP, Scrum, and Kanban. Research objective of this study was to use lightweight DESMET evaluation criteria to analyze the adaptability of agile methods to security development, and to estimate the cost of security-related tasks. The study shows that in a theoretical framework the agile methodologies are readily adaptable to even the most strict security requirements. This result departs from the extant literature, which too often presents agile software development methods incompatible with security engineering practices. Therefore, this chapter suggests future activities in developing and using agile methods for the use of security work in software architecture and design.

REFERENCES

Abrahamsson, P., Salo, O., Ronkainen, J., & Warsta, J. (2002). *Agile software development methods.* VTT Publications.

Abrahamsson, P., Warsta, J., Siponen, M. T., & Ronkainen, J. (2003). New directions on agile methods: A comparative analysis. In *Proceedings of the 25th International Conference on Software Engineering* (pp. 244–254). Washington, DC: IEEE Computer Society.

Adelyar, S. H. (2018). *Secure Agile Agent-Oriented Software Development. Tallinna University of Technology, Dissertations in Natural Sciences No. 51.*

Adelyar, S. H., & Horta, A. (2016). Towards a Secure Agile Software Development Process. In *2016 10th International Conference on the Quality of Information and Communications Technology* (pp. 101-106). IEEE. 10.1109/QUATIC.2016.028

Alnatheer, A., Gravell, A., & Argles, D. (2010). Agile security issues: A research study. *Proceedings of the 5th International Doctoral Symposium on Empirical Software Engineering.*

Ayalew, T., Kidane, T., & Carlsson, B. (2013) Identification and Evaluation of Security Activities in Agile Projects. Springer. doi:10.1007/978-3-642-41488-6_10

Baca, D., & Carlsson, B. (2011). Agile development with security engineering activities. In *Proceedings of the 2011 International Conference on Software and Systems Process, ICSSP '11* (pp. 149–158). New York: ACM.

Beck, K. (1999). Embracing change with extreme programming. *IEEE Computer, 32.*

Beck, K., Beedle, M., Van Bennekum, A., Cockburn, A., Cunningham, W., Fowler, M., . . . Thomas, D. (2001). *Manifesto for agile software development.* Retrieved from http://agilemanifesto.org/

Beznosov, K., & Kruchten, P. (2004). Towards agile security assurance. *NSPW '04 Proceedings of the 2004 workshop on New security paradigms, 47–54.*

bin Othmane, L., Angin, P., Weffers, H., & Bhargava, B. (2014). Extending the Agile Development Process to Develop Acceptably Secure Software. *IEEE Transactions on Dependable and Secure Computing, 11*(6), 497-509.

Boström, G., Wäyrynen, J., Bodén, M., Beznosov, K., & Kruchten, P. (2006). Extending XP practices to support security requirements engineering. *Proceedings of the 2006 International Workshop on Software Engineering for Secure Systems, SESS '06*. 10.1145/1137627.1137631

Chivers, H., Paige, R. F., & Ge, X. (2005) Agile security using an incremental security architecture. *Proceedings of the 6th international conference on Extreme Programming and Agile Processes in Software Engineering*. 10.1007/11499053_7

De Win, B., Scandariato, R., Buyens, K., Grégoire, J., & Joosen, W. (2009). On the secure software development process: CLASP, SDL and Touchpoints compared. *Information and Software Technology, 51*(7), 1152–1171. doi:10.1016/j.infsof.2008.01.010

Fitzgerald, B., & Stol, K.-J. (2014). Continuous software engineering and beyond: Trends and challenges. In *Proceedings of the 1st International Workshop on Rapid Continuous Software Engineering* (pp. 1–9). New York: ACM. 10.1145/2593812.2593813

Fitzgerald, B., Stol, K.-J., O'Sullivan, R., & O'Brien, D. (2013). Scaling agile methods to regulated environments: An industry case study. *Proceedings of the 2013 International Conference on Software Engineering, ICSE '13*, 863–872. 10.1109/ICSE.2013.6606635

FMoF (2013). *Sovelluskehityksen tietoturvaohje*. FMoF.

Ge, X., Paige, R., Polack, F., & Brooke, P. (2007). Extreme programming security practices. In Agile Processes in Software Engineering and Extreme Programming, volume 4536 of Lecture Notes in Computer Science (pp. 226–230). Springer Berlin Heidelberg. doi:10.1007/978-3-540-73101-6_42

ISO/IEC (2013). Information technology - security techniques - code of practice for information security controls iso/IEC 27002:2013.

ISO/IEC standard 21827 (2008). Information Technology – Security Techniques – Systems Security Engineering – Capability Maturity Model (SSE-CMM). ISO/IEC.

Kitchenham, B., Linkman, S., & Law, D. (1997). Desmet: A methodology for evaluating software engineering methods and tools. *Computing & Control Engineering Journal, 8*(3), 120–126. doi:10.1049/cce:19970304

Ko, A. J., DeLine, R., & Venolia, G. (2007). Information needs in collocated software development teams. In *Proceedings of the 29th International Conference on Software Engineering, ICSE '07*. IEEE Computer Society. 10.1109/ICSE.2007.45

Kongsli, V. (2006). Towards agile security in web applications. In *Companion to the 21st ACM SIGPLAN symposium on Object-oriented programming systems, languages, and applications (OOPSLA'06)* (pp. 805-808). ACM.

Kruchten, P. (2010) Software Architecture and Agile Software Development – A Clash of Two Cultures? In *Proceedings of the International Conference on Software Engineering, ICSE'10* (pp. 497-498). ACM.

LaToza, T. D., Venolia, G., & DeLine, R. (2006). Maintaining mental models: A study of developer work habits. In *Proceedings of the 28th International Conference on Software Engineering, ICSE '06* (pp. 492–501). New York: ACM. 10.1145/1134285.1134355

Licorish, S. A., Holvitie, J., Hyrynsalmi, S., Leppänen, V., Spínola, R. O., Mendes, T. S., ... Buchan, J. (2016). Adoption and suitability of software development methods and practices. In *23rd Asia-Pacific Software Engineering Conference, APSEC 2016* (pp. 369–372). IEEE Computer Society. 10.1109/APSEC.2016.062

Microsoft. (2012). *Microsoft security development lifecycle (SDL) process guidance - version 5.2*. Microsoft.

Nikitina, N., Kajko-Mattsson, M., & Stråle, M. (2012). From Scrum to Scrumban: A case study of a process transition. In *Proceedings of the International Conference on Software and System Process, ICSSP '12* (pp. 140–149). IEEE Press. 10.1109/ICSSP.2012.6225959

Oyetoyan, T. D., Cruzes, D. S., & Jaatun, M. G. (2016). An Empirical Study on the Relationship between Software Security Skills, Usage and Training Needs in Agile Settings. In *2016 11th International Conference on Availability, Reliability and Security* (pp. 548—555). ACM.

Rindell, K., Hyrynsalmi, S., & Leppänen, V. (2015) Securing Scrum for VAHTI. In *Proceedings of 14th Symposium on Programming Languages and Software Tools (SPLST)* (pp. 236-250). University of Tampere.

Rindell, K., Hyrynsalmi, S., & Leppänen, V. (2016). Case study of security development in an agile environment: building identity management for a government agency. In *Proceedings of 2016 11th International Conference on Availability, Reliability and Security (ARES)* (pp. 556-593). IEEE. 10.1109/ARES.2016.45

Rindell, K., Hyrynsalmi, S., & Leppänen, V. (2017a). Case Study of Agile Security Engineering: Building Identity Management for a Government Agency. *International Journal of Secure Software Engineering, 8*(1), 43–57. doi:10.4018/IJSSE.2017010103

Rindell, K., Hyrynsalmi, S., & Leppänen, V. (2017b). Busting a Myth: Review of Agile Security Engineering Methods. In *Proceedings of the 12th International Conference on Availability, Reliability and Security (ARES'17)* (pp. 74:1-74:10). ACM. 10.1145/3098954.3103170

SAFECode. (2012). *Practical security stories and security tasks for agile development environments*. Retrieved from http://www.safecode.org/publication/SAFECode_ Agile_Dev_Security0712.pdf

Schwaber, K. (1995). Scrum development process. *Proceedings of the 10th Annual ACM Conference on Object Oriented Programming Systems, Languages, and Applications (OOPSLA)*, 117–134.

Schwaber, K. (2004). *Agile Project Management with Scrum*. Redmond, WA: Microsoft Press.

Sonia, S. A., & Banati, H. (2014). FISA-XP: An agile-based integration of security activities with extreme programming. *Software Engineering Notes*, *39*(3), 1–14. doi:10.1145/2597716.2597728

VAHTI. (2001-2016). *VAHTI instructions*. Retrieved from https://www.vahtiohje. fi/web/guest/home

VersionOne. (2013). *8th Annual State of Agile Survey*. Retrieved from http://www. versionone.com/pdf/2013-state-of-agile-survey.pdf

VersionOne, C. (2018). *12th Annual State of the Agile Survey*. Author.

Vuori, M. (2011). *Agile Development of Safety-Critical Software*. Tampere: Tampere University of Technology.

Wäyrynen, J., Bodén, M., & Boström, G. (2004). Security Engineering and eXtreme Programming: An Impossible Marriage? Springer Berlin Heidelberg.

Chapter 4
An Evaluation of a Test–Driven Security Risk Analysis Approach Based on Two Industrial Case Studies

Gencer Erdogan
SINTEF Digital, Norway

Ketil Stølen
SINTEF Digital, Norway

Phu H. Nguyen
SINTEF Digital, Norway

Jon Hofstad
PWC, Norway

Fredrik Seehusen
SINTEF Digital, Norway

Jan Øyvind Aagedal
Equatex, Norway

ABSTRACT

Risk-driven testing and test-driven risk assessment are two strongly related approaches, though the latter is less explored. This chapter presents an evaluation of a test-driven security risk assessment approach to assess how useful testing is for validating and correcting security risk models. Based on the guidelines for case study research, two industrial case studies were analyzed: a multilingual financial web application and a mobile financial application. In both case studies, the testing yielded new information, which was not found in the risk assessment phase. In the first case study, new vulnerabilities were found that resulted in an update of the likelihood values of threat scenarios and risks in the risk model. New vulnerabilities were also identified and added to the risk model in the second case study. These updates led to more accurate risk models, which indicate that the testing was indeed useful for validating and correcting the risk models.

DOI: 10.4018/978-1-5225-6313-6.ch004

INTRODUCTION

Security risk analysis is carried out in order to identify and assess security specific risks. Traditional risk analyses often rely on expert judgment for the identification of risks, their causes, as well as risk estimation in terms of likelihood and consequence. The outcome of these kinds of risk analyses is therefore dependent on the background, experience, and knowledge of the participants, which in turn reflects uncertainty regarding the validity of the results.

In order to mitigate this uncertainty, security risk analysis can be complemented by other ways of gathering information of relevance. One such approach is to combine security risk analysis with security testing, in which the testing is used to validate and correct the risk analysis results. This is referred to as test-driven security risk analysis.

The authors have developed an approach to test-driven security risk analysis, and as depicted in Figure 1, the approach is divided into three phases. Phase 1 expects a description of the target of evaluation. Then, based on this description, the security risk assessment is planned and carried out. The output of Phase 1 is security risk models, which is used as input to Phase 2. In Phase 2, security tests are identified based on the risk models and executed. The output of Phase 2 is security test results, which is used as input to the third and final phase. In the third phase, the risk models are validated and corrected with respect to the security test results.

Although strongly related, it is important to note that test-driven risk analysis is different from the more common combination of risk analysis and testing, which is referred to as risk-driven (or risk-based) testing. The purpose of risk-driven testing is to makes use of risk assessment within the testing process to support risk-driven test planning, risk-driven test design and implementation, and risk-driven test reporting. Großmann and Seehusen (2015) provide a detailed explanation of these two approaches by combining the well-known and widely used standards ISO 31000 (ISO, 2009) and ISO/IEC/IEEE 29119 (ISO, 2013a), with a focus on security.

Figure 1. Overview of the test-driven security risk analysis approach
Source: Authors' work

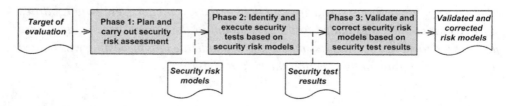

In this chapter, the authors present an evaluation of the test-driven security risk analysis approach based on two industrial case studies. The objective of the case studies was to assess how useful testing is for validating and correcting security risk models. The basis of the evaluation is to compare the risk models produced before and after testing. That is, the authors compare the difference in risk models produced in Phase 1 with the updated risk models produced in Phase 3.

The first case study was carried out between March 2011 and July 2011, while the second case study was carried out between June 2012 and January 2013. In the first case study the authors analyzed a multilingual financial Web application, and in the second case study the authors analyzed a mobile financial application. The systems analyzed in both case studies serve as the backbone for the system owner's business goals and are used by many users every day. The system owners, which are also the customers that commissioned the case studies, required full confidentiality. The results presented in this chapter are therefore limited to the experiences from applying the test-driven security risk analysis approach.

The reminder of the chapter is structured as follows. First, the chapter describes the background concepts relevant for this chapter and then describes the test-driven security risk analysis approach, followed by a description of the research method. Then, the chapter gives an overview of the two case studies as well as the results obtained which are the basis of the evaluation. Then, the chapter provides a discussion of the results with respect to three research questions and an overall hypothesis defined as part of the research method. Finally, the chapter discusses related work and highlights the key findings before providing the conclusion.

BACKGROUND

This section provides the main background concepts in security risk assessment, security testing, and their combination. The key terms and definitions are summarized at the end of this chapter.

Security Risk Assessment

The most relevant part of a general risk management process within the context of this chapter is risk assessment. That is, the steps related to risk identification, risk estimation, and risk evaluation. The following provides a high-level explanation of these steps. Risk assessment is explained in detail in the next section. The reader is referred to ISO 31000 (ISO, 2009) for a detailed explanation of the complete risk management process.

Risk identification is the process of finding, recognizing and describing risks. This involves identifying sources of risk, areas of impact, events (including changes in circumstances), their causes and their potential consequences. Risk identification can involve historical data, theoretical analysis, informed and expert opinions, and stakeholder's needs (ISO, 2009). Risk estimation is the process of comprehending the nature of risk and determining the level of risk. Risk estimation provides the basis for risk evaluation and decisions on whether risks need to be treated, and on the most appropriate risk treatment strategies and methods (ISO, 2009). Risk evaluation is the process of comparing the results of risk estimation with risk criteria to determine whether the risk and/or its magnitude is acceptable or tolerable. Risk evaluation assists in the decision about risk treatment (ISO, 2009).

There exist many risk analysis methods, for example, OCTAVE (Alberts, Dorofee, Stevens, & Woody, 2003), CRAMM (Barber & Davey, 1992) and NIST SP800-30 (NIST, 2012), to mention a few. It is beyond the scope of this chapter to provide a detailed explanation of the various risk analysis method, but it is necessary to introduce CORAS, which is the risk analysis method applied in the approach explained in this chapter.

CORAS is a model-based approach to risk analysis (Lund, Solhaug, & Stølen, 2010) and ranked as one of the 10 popular risk assessment methods together with OCTAVE, CRAMM and NIST SP800-30 (Gritzalis, Iseppi, Mylonas, & Stavrou, 2018). The CORAS method is an asset-driven defensive risk analysis approach divided into eight steps. The method is asset-driven in the sense that the assets to be protected are identified early on as part of the characterization of the system, service, business or process to be analyzed, that is, the target of analysis. The first four steps of the CORAS method are introductory and used to establish a common understanding of the target of the analysis, and to make the target description that will serve as a basis for the subsequent risk identification. The introductory steps include documenting all assumptions about the environment or setting in which the target is supposed to work, as well as making a complete list of constraints regarding which aspects of the target should receive special attention, which aspects can be ignored, and so forth. The remaining four steps are devoted to the actual detailed analysis. This includes identifying concrete risks and their risk level as well as identifying and assessing potential treatments for unacceptable risks. The CORAS method and its concepts are explained in detail in the next section.

Security Testing

Security testing is a type of testing conducted to evaluate the degree to which a test item, and associated data and information, are protected so that unauthorized persons or systems cannot use, read, or modify them, and authorized persons or systems are not denied access to them (ISO, 2013a). Model-based testing (MBT) is a variant of testing that relies on the behavior models of a system under test (SUT) and/or its environment to (automatically) derive test cases for the system (Utting, Pretschner, & Legeard, 2012). Based on models, MBT allows the tests derivation process to be structured, reproducible, programmable, and documented. An MBT approach in which the security requirements of a SUT are the main focus for testing is called model-based security testing (MBST) (Felderer, Zech, Breu, Büchler, & Pretschner, 2016). The model of a SUT dedicated to test generation is often called test model. In practice, limited testing resource such as time makes test selection and prioritization criteria vital to guide the selection and execution of tests generated from test model. Among many possible criteria, security risks driven by threats (e.g., specified in CORAS models) are important in MBST. The use of security risk assessment to drive the test selection and prioritization is key in any (model-based) risk-driven security testing approach.

The Combinations of Security Risk Assessment and Security Testing

It is necessary to distinguish between the two strategies for the combined use of security risk assessment and security testing: *risk-driven security testing* and *test-driven security risk analysis*. In risk-driven security testing the objective is to use security risk assessment to support security testing. This involves risk-driven test planning, risk-driven test design and implementation, and risk-driven test reporting. However, we may also use security testing to support the security risk analysis process. This is referred to as test-driven security risk analysis in which the objective is to make use of security testing to validate and correct the risk assessment results.

Security risk assessment can complement and improve security testing because the high-level perspective of the security risk assessment can provide guidance for focusing on the most relevant risks to the activities carried out during security testing. Risk-driven security testing is the most popular way of combining security risk assessment and security testing as we discuss later in the related work section. In test-driven security risk analysis, security test results are used to provide valuable feedback for improving the security risk assessment process. The next section presents the details of test-driven security risk analysis, which is the focus of this chapter. Integrating and interweaving the activities from both risk-driven security testing and test-driven security risk analysis would be beneficial for both sides of an overall assessment of the security of a system on different levels (Großmann & Seehusen, 2015).

TEST-DRIVEN SECURITY RISK ANALYSIS

As already illustrated in Figure 1, the test-driven security risk analysis process is divided into three phases. Each phase is further divided into various steps. Figure 2 shows the steps within each phase. In the following, we give a more detailed description of each phase.

Security Risk Assessment (Phase 1)

The security risk assessment phase consists of four steps corresponding to the steps of the CORAS method, which is a model-driven approach to risk analysis (Lund et al., 2010). The purpose of the first step is to prepare the security risk assessment. The first step is carried out together with the customer and involves defining a precise scope and focus of the target of evaluation, defining security assets that needs to be taken into consideration during the risk assessment, defining likelihood and consequence scales necessary for risk estimation, as well as defining risk evaluation matrices based on the likelihood and consequence scales for evaluating risks.

Table 1 shows an example of a likelihood scale. In this approach to test-driven security risk analysis, the term likelihood is a general description of the frequency for incidents to occur, and the likelihood scale defines the values that will be used when assigning likelihood estimates to unwanted incidents in the risk model. Because incidents may have different impact depending on which security asset is harmed, a separate consequence scale is defined for each security asset taken into consideration. Let us assume that we have defined a security asset named *availability of service*. Table 2 shows an example consequence scale defined for this security asset, in which the consequence values are defined in terms of downtime. Another security asset could for example be *confidentiality of user data*. This security asset would have a different consequence scale concerning the disclosure of confidential user data such as login credentials, credit card information, and privacy-related data.

Figure 2. The steps in test-driven security risk analysis
Source: Authors' work

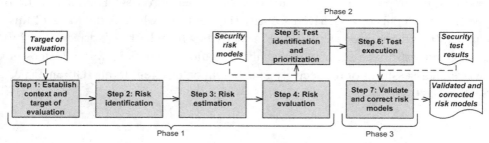

Table 1. Likelihood scale

Likelihood value	Description	Definition
Rare	Less than once per year	[0, 1): 1y
Unlikely	One to five times per year	[1, 5): 1y
Possible	Five to twenty times per year	[5, 20): 1y
Likely	Twenty to fifty times per year	[20, 50): 1y
Certain	Fifty times or more per year	[50, ∞): 1y

Source: Authors' work

Table 2. Consequence scale for asset: Availability of service

Consequence value	Description
Insignificant	Downtime in range [0, 1 minute)
Minor	Downtime in range [1 minute, 1 hour)
Moderate	Downtime in range [1 hour, 1 day)
Major	Downtime in range [1 day, 1 week)
Catastrophic	Downtime in range [1 week, ∞)

Source: Authors' work

Having made the necessary preparations, the next step is to carry out security risk assessment. That is, risk identification, risk estimation, and risk evaluation. The risk models are constructed on-the-fly during the risk assessment process which is carried out in a series of workshops. The information obtained in these workshops is usually based on expert judgment, mostly from representatives of the customer on whose behalf the analysis is conducted.

During risk identification (Step 2), risks are identified by analyzing the target of evaluation and identifying potential unwanted incidents that may harm certain security assets. In addition, threat scenarios causing the unwanted incidents, as well as threats initiating the threat scenarios are identified. The process of risk identification is carried out by creating risk models using the CORAS modeling language. The constructed risk models are referred to as CORAS risk models. Figure 3 shows an example of a CORAS risk model, and as illustrated, a CORAS risk model is a directed acyclic graph where every node is of one of the following kinds.

- **Threat:** A potential cause of an unwanted incident.
- **Threat Scenario:** A chain or series of events that is initiated by a threat and that may lead to an unwanted incident.
- **Unwanted Incident:** An event that harms or reduces the value of an asset.

- **Asset:** Something to which a party assigns value and hence for which the party requires protection.

Risks can also be represented in a CORAS risk model. These correspond to pairs of unwanted incidents and assets. If an unwanted incident harms exactly one asset, as illustrated in Figure 3, then the unwanted incident will represent a single risk. If an unwanted incident harms two assets, then the unwanted incident represents two risks, etc. As illustrated in Figure 3, a security aspect of certain information can be regarded as an asset. For example, the confidentiality of user data may be an important asset for a banking company.

Vulnerabilities that may be exploited by a threat to cause security risks are also identified as part of risk identification. Vulnerabilities are illustrated as open locks and are attached on relations in a CORAS risk model. A relation in a CORAS risk model may be one of the following kinds.

- **Initiates Relation:** A relation that goes from a threat *A* to a threat scenario or an unwanted incident B, meaning that *A* initiates *B*.
- **Leads to Relation:** A relation that goes from a threat scenario or an unwanted incident *A* to a threat scenario or an unwanted incident *B*, meaning that *A* leads to *B*.

Figure 3. Example of a CORAS risk model
Source: Authors' work

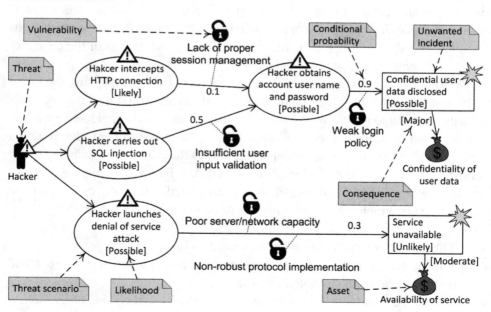

- **Harms Relation:** A relation that goes from an unwanted incident A to an asset B, meaning that A harms B.

Vulnerabilities may be assigned on the initiates relations or the leads-to relations going from A to B, describing a weakness, flaw or deficiency that opens for A leading to B.

Having identified risks, the next step is to estimate the likelihood of risks occurring, as well as the consequence of risks (Step 3). This step makes use of the predefined likelihood and consequence scales (Table 1 and Table 2 in this example). The likelihood estimation is carried out by first estimating the likelihood of threat scenarios causing the risks, which also includes the estimation of conditional probabilities. Then, based on these estimates, the likelihood of unwanted incidents is calculated. During the calculation it is important to consider whether the threat scenarios are mutually exclusive or independent, and make sure that the calculations are carried out in a consistent manner. However, it is beyond the scope of this chapter to explain the rules for calculating likelihood values using CORAS risk models. The reader is referred to the CORAS approach (Lund et al., 2010) for a precise explanation of the calculation rules. Finally, to complete risk estimation, the consequence for each risk is estimated by making use of the predefined consequence scale. Thus, relations and nodes may have the following risk-measure annotations.

- **Likelihood Values:** May be assigned to a threat scenario or an unwanted incident A, estimating the likelihood of A occurring.
- **Conditional Probabilities:** May be assigned on the leads to relations going from A to B, estimating the probability that B occurs given that A has occurred.
- **Consequence Values:** May be assigned on the harms relations going from A to B, estimating the consequence that the occurrence of A has on B.

Having estimated risks, the next step is to evaluate the risks with respect to their likelihood and consequence values to determine a *risk level* for each identified risk (Step 4). The risk level is calculated by plotting a risk into a *risk matrix* with respect to its likelihood and consequence value. Risk evaluation matrices are constructed with respect to predefined likelihood and consequence scales and are typically divided into three risk levels: Low, medium, and high, which is commonly used as a basis to decide whether to accept, monitor, or treat risks, respectively. Such risk acceptance criteria are typically associated with security requirements or goals. Figure 4 shows an example of a risk evaluation matrix constructed with respect to the likelihood scale in Table 1, and the consequence scale in Table 2. That is, Figure 4 shows a risk evaluation matrix constructed for evaluating risks that impact the security asset *availability of service*. As shown in Figure 4, the cells of the matrix are divided into three groups to represent *low, medium,* and *high* risks. For example, by mapping the risk *service unavailable* captured in Figure 3 to the risk evaluation matrix, we see that the risk is assigned a *low* risk level. Similarly, if we map the risk *confidential user data disclosed* to a similar risk matrix, then it is assigned a *high* risk level.

In traditional risk analysis, the next step is to decide which risks to treat, based on the risk evaluation matrix, and then suggest treatments for those risks. In other words, the risk evaluation matrix is used as a basis to prioritize risks to be treated and typically the prioritization is based on the risk levels. Intuitively, *high* risks are selected to be treated first, *medium* risks are selected to be treated second or monitored, and *low* risks are either acceptable or treated last. The process of risk treatment is also carried out in the approach presented in this chapter. However, before risks treatment, the obtained risk models are tested to check their validity. This is explained in detail in the next two sections, but the main idea is as follows. In case the test results do not match the information conveyed by the risk models, the risk models are corrected according to the test results. In case the test results match the information conveyed by the risk models, no changes are made to the risk models. Either way, the testing increases the confidence in the validity of the risk models, which in turn increases the confidence of the decisions made related to risk treatment.

The reader is referred to (Lund et al., 2010) for further explanation on the steps of Phase 1. Throughout the chapter, we use the term *risk model element*, or just *element* for short, to mean a node, a relation, or an assignment, and we will sometimes use the terms unwanted incident and risk interchangeably when the distinction is not important.

Figure 4. Risk evaluation matrix
Source: Authors' work

		Consequence				
		Insignificant	Minor	Moderate	Major	Catastrophic
Likelihood	**Rare**	*low*				
	Unlikely			**Service unavailable**		
	Possible				**confidential user data disclosed**	
	Likely					
	Certain	*medium*				*high*

Security Testing (Phase 2)

The security testing phase consists of two steps, test identification and prioritization (Step 5), and test execution (Step 6). In Step 5, test cases are designed by first identifying high-level test procedures based on CORAS risk models. Then, the test procedures are prioritized and manually refined into concrete test cases.

A CORAS risk model can be seen as a set of statements about the world. One way of identifying test procedures based on a CORAS risk model is to derive statements with respect to the threat scenarios in the risk model. CORAS provides algorithms that may be used to translate a risk model into English prose (Lund et al., 2010), and these algorithms are used in the approach described in this chapter to construct test procedures. Typically, a threat scenario corresponds to a particular type of attack, and the purpose of testing a threat scenario is to find vulnerabilities that may be exploited by the attack. Based on the risk model in Figure 3, the following test procedures may be identified.

- Check that Hacker initiates Hacker intercepts HTTP connection with likelihood Likely.
- Check that Hacker initiates Hacker carries out SQL injection with likelihood Possible.
- Check that Hacker initiates Hacker launches denial of service attack with likelihood Possible.
- Check that Hacker intercepts HTTP connection leads to Hacker obtains account user name and password with conditional probability 0.1, due to vulnerability Lack of proper session management.
- Check that Hacker carries out SQL injection leads to Hacker obtains account user name and password with conditional probability 0.5, due to vulnerability Insufficient user input validation.
- Check that Hacker launches denial of service attack leads to Service unavailable with conditional probability 0.3, due to vulnerabilities Poor server/network capacity and Non-robust protocol implementation.
- Check that Hacker obtains account user name and password leads to Confidential user data disclosed with conditional probability 0.9, due to vulnerability Weak login policy.

Having identified test procedures as described above, those that are considered most important to test are prioritized and selected (that is, not all threat scenarios of the risk model are tested). The priority of a threat scenario, and thereby the priority of its corresponding test procedure is assessed by estimating its severity, as well as the required effort to implement and carry out the test procedures in terms of time.

Note that this effort estimate is not related to effort estimates for risk treatment, which may be related to security requirements or goals. The focus here is to estimate the effort required for test procedures as described above, which in turn is used as a basis to create test cases to validate and correct the risk picture.

Severity is an estimate of the impact that a threat scenario has on the identified risks. The intuition is that a high degree of impact should result in a high priority. In the extreme case, if the threat scenario has zero impact on a risk, then there is no point in testing it. The severity is also affected by the risk analyst's confidence in the correctness of the threat scenario. Intuitively, the less confident we are about the correctness of the threat scenario, the more it makes sense to test it. If we, however, are completely confident in the correctness of the threat scenario, then there is no point in testing it because then we strongly believe that this will not give us any new information.

The severity estimation is carried out as follows. First, the conditional probabilities are expressed as conditional probability intervals to reflect the confidence in the correctness of the threat scenarios. For example, considering the example in Figure 3, threat scenario *Hacker carries out SQL injection* leads to threat scenario *Hacker obtains account user name and password* with conditional probability *0.5*. If we are completely certain that the conditional ratio is *0.5*, for example based on historical data that shows that account credentials have been compromised in half of the successful code injections, then we express this as an interval in terms of *[0.5, 0.5]* representing the presumed minimum and maximum probability, respectively. As mentioned above, in this case there is no point in testing the threat scenario because we are certain about its correctness. However, if we are uncertain about the correctness of the threat scenario, for example due to the lack of documentation of the target of analysis and would like to express an interval considering probabilities between *0.4* and *0.6*, we write *[0.4, 0.6]*. The width of the interval expresses the uncertainty. That is, the wider the width between the minimum probability and the maximum probability, the less confident we are about the estimate. Second, for each probability interval, we recalculate the severity of the threat scenario in question with respect to the minimum probability, and then with respect to the maximum probability. In the former we obtain minimum severity for the threat scenario in question, while in the latter we obtain the maximum severity. Third, we subtract the maximum severity from the minimum severity and obtain a value which is used as the priority of the threat scenario in question. We do this for all threat scenarios in the risk model and obtain a prioritized list of threat scenarios, that is, a prioritized list of test procedures.

Having prioritized the test procedures using the severity score, we select those procedures that will be implemented by also taking effort into account. Effort is an estimate of the time it will take to implement and carry out the corresponding test procedure. It is important to consider effort, because in some situations the effort required to carry out certain test procedures may be outside the boundaries of available time and budget. In such cases, the customer must make a cost-benefit analysis and decide whether to carry out the test procedures. Moreover, it is often very difficult to test whether a threat will carry out an attack in the first place; at least this is difficult to test using conventional testing techniques. The first three test procedures listed above are examples of such test procedures, and in this case, we would exclude them from the test selection.

The priority of a test procedure is carried out as described above. It is beyond the scope of this chapter to give a detailed explanation of this process, and the reader is therefore referred to earlier work for a more detailed explanation (Seehusen, 2014). After selecting the test procedures with the highest priority, they are refined into concrete test cases by making a detailed description of how they should be tested. Inspired by the guidelines provided by ISO/IEC/IEEE 29119 (ISO, 2013b), the test cases are specified based on the test procedures in the following way. First, test objectives are defined for each test procedure. This includes defining test objectives addressing the threat scenarios captured by the test procedures. Second, preconditions for each test case are documented in terms of threat profile (what kind of profile may initiate the threat scenario represented by the test procedure?) and technicality (what kind of technical preconditions must be considered and be in place to carry out the test case?). Third, the test case process is documented in terms of tools (what tools are to be used to carry out the test case?) and procedure (how shall the test case be executed?). Fourth, the vulnerabilities addressed by the test case are documented. Finally, a description of verdict assignment is provided (in what situations has the test case passed, failed or is inconclusive? – additional verdicts may be used). Step 6, test execution, is the activity of executing the tests identified in Step 5, as well as recording the test results. The test cases are typically executed on a test environment provided by the customer.

Validation and Correction of Risk Models (Phase 3)

The validation and correction phase consists of one step (Step 7), which has two main purposes. The first is to validate and correct the risk models (output of Phase 1) with respect to the test results (output of Phase 2). The second is to identify treatments for the updated risk models. This step is based on the corresponding step of the CORAS method. However, most of the reminder of this chapter will be devoted to explaining the degree to which the risk models had to be updated by taking the test results into consideration.

Based on the test results, we may validate the risk models by checking whether the test results correspond to the information conveyed by the risk models. If the test results do not correspond to the information conveyed by the risk models, then we may correct the risk models with respect to the test results in terms of *adding*, *deleting* or *editing* risk model elements. Let RM_B be the risk model before testing, and RM_A be the risk model after testing. The following points describe what we mean by adding, deleting and editing risk model elements based on the test results.

- **Add:** An element in RM_A has been added if it is not in RM_B.
- **Delete:** An element in RM_B has been deleted if it is not in RM_A.
- **Edit:** A node or relation in both RM_B and RM_A has been edited if its assignment in RM_B or RM_A is different.

RESEARCH METHOD

The case study research was conducted in four main steps. First, the case study was designed, which includes defining the objective, the units of analysis, as well as the research questions. Second, the test-driven security risk analysis approach was carried out within an industrial setting. Third, the relevant data produced in the test-driven security risk analysis was collected. Fourth, the collected data was analyzed with respect to predefined research questions. Figure 5 gives an overview of the main activities of the research method. The research method is inspired by the guidelines for case study research in software engineering provided by (Runeson, Host, Rainer, & Regnell, 2012). This research approach was applied in both case studies.

As mentioned in the introduction, the objective of the case studies was to assess the usefulness of testing for validating and correcting the risk models. Although the authors carried out the complete test-driven security risk analysis approach in both case studies, they specifically focused on the degree to which the test results yielded information that caused an update of the risk models. That is, the units of analysis are the risk models produced in Phase 1, and the validated and corrected risk models produced in Phase 3. Thus, the data that were collected and analyzed in the case studies were mainly the risk models produced in Phase 1 and Phase 3.

Figure 5. The main activities of the research method
Source: Authors' work

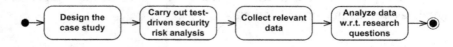

The authors' hypothesis is that security testing is useful for validating and correcting the security risk models. As already explained, the test results may be used to validate the risk models. However, if the test results do not correspond to the information conveyed by the risk models, then we may use the test results to correct the risk models in terms of adding, deleting, and editing risk model elements. Thus, the following research questions are defined.

RQ1: To what extent are the test results useful for correcting the risk model by adding elements?

RQ2: To what extent are the test results useful for correcting the risk model by deleting elements?

RQ3: To what extent are the test results useful for correcting the risk model by editing elements?

OVERVIEW OF THE TWO CASE STUDIES

Both case studies were carried out in an industrial setting, and the analyzed systems were already deployed in production and used by many users every day. As described above, the authors carried out workshops together with the representatives of the customers as part of the approach. However, the time devoted to the workshops was limited and mainly used to gather the necessary information, as well as to communicate findings. Most of the time in the case studies was devoted to carry out the steps before and after the workshops.

Case Study 1: Test-Driven Security Risk Analysis of a Financial Web Application

In the first case study, the authors analyzed a multilingual web application which is designed to deliver streamlined administration and reporting of all forms of equity-based compensation plans. The web application was deployed on the servers of a third-party service provider, as well as maintained by the same service provider with respect to infrastructure. However, the web application was completely administrated by the client commissioning the case study for business purposes, such as customizing the web application for each customer, as well as patching and updating features of the web application. The focus of this case study was to analyze the system to identify security risks that may be introduced internally by the client when administrating the application, as well as security risks that may be introduced externally via features available to customers. In this case study, it was decided not to consider security risks related to infrastructure because this was a contractual responsibility of the service provider.

Table 3 gives an overview of the workshops in the first case study in terms of time spent in each step of the approach before, during, and after the workshops. The table reflects the size of the case study in terms of number of participants, as well as the invested time in carrying out the approach in an industrial setting. The column *step* shows the steps of test-driven security risk analysis that were carried out in the corresponding workshop. In the *participant* column, the denotations C:*n* and A:*m* represent *n* participants from the customer side and *m* participants from the risk analysis team. The column *duration during workshop* shows the time spent in each workshop. The columns *duration before workshop* and *duration after workshop* give the approximate time spent before and after each workshop, respectively. Notice that there was no workshop addressing Step 6 (test execution). This is because test execution was entirely conducted between the fifth and the sixth workshop, which is why the duration after Workshop 5 is approximately 100 hours. The total time spent in the first case study was approximately 293 hours.

During the case study, the authors made use of the CORAS tool (CORAS, 2018) to create CORAS risk models as well as to identify test procedures. Based on the test procedures, the authors designed the test cases and executed them automatically, semi-automatically and manually using the following tools.

- **Automated Testing:** IBM Rational Software Architect (IBM, 2018), Smartesting CertifyIt (Smartesting, 2018), Selenium (Selenium, 2018), Eclipse (Eclipse, 2018).
- **Semi-Automated Testing:** OWASP Zed Attack Proxy (OWASP, 2018).
- **Manual Testing:** Wireshark (Wireshark, 2018).

Table 3. Overview of the workshops in the first case study

Workshop	Date	Step	Participant	≈ Duration Before Workshop	Duration During Workshop	≈ Duration After Workshop
1	28.03.2011	Step 1	C:1, A:3	≈ 8 hours	2 hours	≈ 10 hours
2	12.04.2011	Step 1	C:3, A:4	≈ 8 hours	3 hours	≈ 10 hours
3	09.05.2011	Step 1	C:2, A:3	≈ 10 hours	3 hours	≈ 10 hours
4	20.05.2011	Step 2 and 3	C:1, A:2	≈ 15 hours	6 hours	≈ 45 hours
5	27.05.2011	Step 4 and 5	C:1, A:2	≈ 15 hours	6 hours	≈ 100 hours
6	07.07.2011	Step 7	P:2, A:2	≈ 10 hours	2 hours	≈ 30 hours

Source: Authors' work

All the tests were executed at the level of the HTTP protocol, that is, at the application level, and from a black-box perspective of the system that was analyzed. The automated process was as follows. First the authors specified a model of the system under test using IBM RSA (IBM, 2018) together with the CertifyIt plugin (Smartesting, 2018), then they used CertifyIt to generate abstract Java tests, then they concretized these in Java using Eclipse, and finally the authors executed them using the Selenium plugin (Selenium, 2018) on the Firefox Web browser (Mozilla, 2018).

The semi-automated process was carried out using the OWASP Zed Attack Proxy tool (OWASP, 2018) to intercept the HTTP requests and responses. The authors manually altered the information in the requests and responses and used Wireshark (Wireshark, 2018) to analyze the communication between the client and the server at the IP level.

Case Study 2: Test-Driven Security Risk Analysis of a Mobile Financial Application

In the second case study, the authors analyzed a mobile application designed to provide various online financial services to the users on their mobile devices. In contrast to the first case study, this application was deployed on the local servers of the client commissioning the case study. The online financial services were accessible only via a dedicated mobile application installed on a mobile device. Moreover, all aspects related to maintenance and administration was the responsibility of the client. However, some few aspects related to content displayed to the user were directly handled by a third party. The focus of this case study was to analyze the mobile application to identify security risks that may be introduced from an external point of view. That is, the authors identified security risks that may be introduced by the third party when administrating the few aspects of the mobile application, as well as security risks that may be introduced via features available to customers.

Table 4 gives an overview of the workshops in the second case study, as well as the approximate time spent before and after each workshop. Like the first case study, there was no workshop addressing Step 6 (test execution), which was conducted between the fifth and sixth workshop. Notice that in the first case study, the three first workshops were dedicated to Step 1 (establish context and target of evaluation), while in the second case study the authors only needed one workshop for the same step. This is because in the first case study, the context and target of evaluation was not entirely clear in the beginning and needed to be concretized over several iterations. In the second case study, the context and target of evaluation were somewhat concretized by the customer prior to the first workshop, and it was therefore sufficient with one workshop for Step 1. In addition, the authors got access to the system documentation prior to the first workshop, which was useful to get a good understanding of the target of evaluation before the workshop. The total time spent in the second case study was approximately 322 hours. Moreover, the fact that the authors spent approximately 293 hours in the first case study and 322 hours in the second case study, in which the analyzed systems were different in terms of architecture and complexity, shows that the approach is applicable in industrial settings within reasonable time. This also gives an indication of how much time and effort may be required by the participants involved in the test-driven security risk analysis process in an industrial setting.

Risk modeling, test procedure generation, test case design and the execution of the test cases were carried out in a similar manner as in the first case study. In addition to the tools used in the first case study, the authors made use of the tool Burp Suite Free Edition (Portswigger, 2018) for automatic analysis purposes, and Google Chrome (Google, 2018) for manual tests.

RESULTS

This section presents the results obtained in both case studies and describes the difference between the risk models before and after testing for each case study.

Results Obtained in Case Study 1

After testing, no nodes or relations were added to or deleted from the risk model. The only risk model elements that were added and deleted were vulnerabilities (recall that vulnerabilities are not classified as nodes, but as assignments to relations). More precisely, one vulnerability was deleted, and four vulnerabilities were added after testing. However, it is important to note that the deletion of vulnerabilities was not

Table 4. Overview of the workshops in the second case study

Workshop	Date	Step	Participant	≈ Duration Before Workshop	Duration During Workshop	≈ Duration After Workshop
1	19.06.2012	Step 1	C:7, A:4	≈ 20 hours	5 hours	≈ 25 hours
2	23.08.2012	Step 2	C:5, A:3	≈ 8 hours	6 hours	≈ 35 hours
3	21.09.2012	Step 3	C:4, A:3	≈ 8 hours	6 hours	≈ 35 hours
4	01.10.2012	Step 4	C:3, A:3	≈ 8 hours	2.5 hours	≈ 25 hours
5	16.11.2012	Step 5	C:6, A:3	≈ 10 hours	3 hours	≈ 85 hours
6	24.01.2013	Step 7	C:4, A:3	≈ 8 hours	2 hours	≈ 30 hours

Source: Authors' work

only based on the test results. In the case studies, the analyst removed vulnerabilities by taking the test results into consideration, as well as own experience and knowledge from conducting previous security tests. That is, the vulnerabilities were removed from the risk models based on expert judgement, and not purely based on the test results. Figure 6 illustrates the number of risk model nodes, the number of vulnerabilities, and the number of relations before and after testing.

The only risk model elements that were tested in the case study were threat scenarios. The aim of testing a threat scenario was to discover whether the target of evaluation had vulnerabilities that could be exploited by the attack described by the threat scenario. Figure 7 shows the total number of threat scenarios and risks that were identified, the total number of tested threat scenarios, and the total number of unwanted incidents and threat scenarios *potentially affected* by the tested threat scenarios. All threat scenarios or unwanted incidents that a tested threat scenario *T* can lead up to are potentially affected by the testing. For example, if the likelihood value of *T* is edited after testing, then this may have a rippling effect on the likelihood values of all threat scenarios or unwanted incidents caused by *T*. It is therefore, in principle, possible that the complete risk model is affected by testing. However, this depends on which threat scenarios are selected for testing in the testing phase. As can be deduced from Figure 7, six out of 43 threat scenarios were tested, 14 out of 43 threat scenarios were potentially affected by the testing (this includes the six threat scenarios selected for testing), and 13 out of 31 risks were potentially affected by the testing. In CORAS, an unwanted incident may also lead to other threat scenarios or unwanted incidents. This means that there may be situations where it is possible to test risks. However, such situations were not encountered neither in the first nor the second case study, which is why Figure 7 reports zero risks tested.

Figure 6. The number of risk model nodes, vulnerabilities, and relations before and after testing
Source: Authors' work

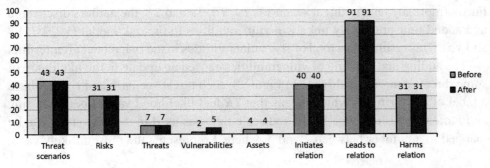

Figure 7. The number of risks and threat scenarios tested and potentially affected by the testing
Source: Authors' work

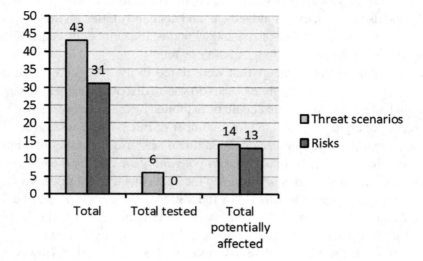

The risk model in Figure 8 represents an anonymized excerpt of the risk model identified in the case study. Furthermore, it shows all risk model elements that were tested and potentially affected by the testing, as well as the difference between the threat scenarios, risks, and vulnerabilities before and after testing. The threat scenarios that were tested are represented by ellipses with a dotted outline. All the other elements of the diagram are potentially affected by the tested threat scenarios. It can be noted that the level of indirection from the tested threat scenarios to the risks is quite large.

The vulnerabilities *V1* and *V6* were identified as potential vulnerabilities during the risk assessment, that is, prior to the testing. By testing threat scenario *T1*, the authors discovered that vulnerability *V1* did not exist and it was therefore removed from the risk model. The testing of threat scenario *T22*, however, revealed that vulnerability *V6* did in fact exist and therefore remained in the risk model after testing. Furthermore, by testing threat scenarios *T4*, *T6*, *T7* and *T8*, the authors discovered and added four previously unknown vulnerabilities to the risk model (*V2*, *V3*, *V4* and *V5*). This resulted in a total of five vulnerabilities in the risk model after testing.

The adding and deleting of vulnerabilities caused an update in the likelihood of some threat scenarios and risks. In Figure 8, each threat scenario and risk *TR* have a label of the form *i / j* which means that *TR* had likelihood value *i* before testing and *j* after the testing. The likelihood scale that was used in the case study can be mapped to a number between *1* and *5*, where *1* represents the most unlikely value and *5* represents the most likely value. All the threat scenarios and risks whose likelihood values were edited after testing are in Figure 8 represented with a darker color than the threat scenarios and risks that were not edited. Note that all except one risk model element (threat scenario *T1*) whose likelihood values were edited after testing were estimated to be more likely after testing than before testing. Threat scenario *T1* was estimated to be less likely after testing due to the absence of vulnerability *V1*.

Recall that risks may have risk levels which are calculated based on likelihood and consequence values. The change in likelihood values resulted in the risk levels of four risks being changed after testing; the risk level of risks *C2*, *I1*, *I2*, and *I3* were changed because of the increase in likelihood, while the risk level of risks *C1* and *C3* did not change although their likelihood increased after testing. More specifically, the risks *C2* and *I2* changed from *low* to *medium* with respect to risk level, while the risks *I1* and *I3* changed from *low* to *high*. The risk *C1* remained at risk level *low* after testing, while the risk *C3* remained at risk level *medium* after testing. The reason why the risk level of risks *C1* and *C3* did not increase was because the increase of their likelihood did not have sufficiently high impact to increase their risk level. The possible risk levels in the case studies were low, medium, and high.

Results Obtained in Case Study 2

Like the first case study, no nodes were added to or deleted from the risk model after testing. One vulnerability was added to the risk model, while four vulnerabilities were deleted from the risk model after testing. In addition, one leads-to relation was added *as part of* the one vulnerability added to the risk model. Figure 9 illustrates the number of risk model nodes, the number of vulnerabilities, and the number of relations before and after testing.

The only risk model elements that were tested in the second case study were, as in the first case study, threat scenarios. The chart in Figure 10 shows the total number of threat scenarios and risks that were identified, the total number of tested threat scenarios, and the total number of unwanted incidents and threat scenarios potentially affected by the tested threat scenarios. Furthermore, the chart shows that 8 out of 24 threat scenarios were tested, 13 out of 24 threat scenarios were potentially affected by the testing (this includes the 8 threat scenarios selected for testing), and 14 out of 26 risks were potentially affected by the testing.

Like Figure 8, Figure 11 represents an anonymized excerpt of the risk model identified in the case study. The graphical notation of Figure 11 is equivalent to the notation used in Figure 8.

Figure 8. Difference between risk models before and after testing
Source: Authors' work

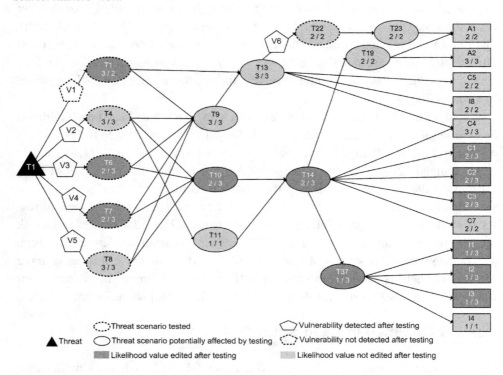

Figure 9. The number of risk model nodes, vulnerabilities, and relations before and after testing
Source: Authors' work

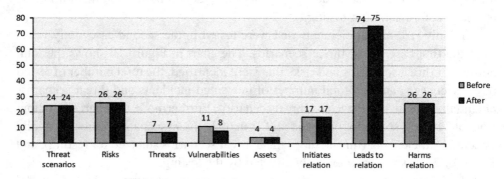

Figure 10. The number of risks and threat scenarios tested and potentially affected by the testing
Source: Authors' work

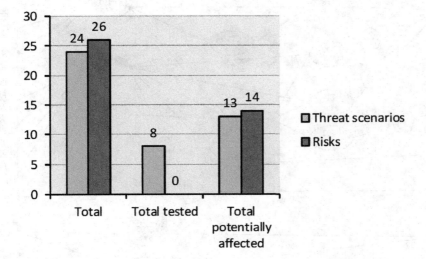

In the second case study, all vulnerabilities except one (*V11*) were modeled as potential vulnerabilities during the risk assessment. By testing the threat scenarios selected for testing, the authors discovered that the vulnerabilities *V1*, *V2*, *V8* and *V10* did not exist. These vulnerabilities were therefore removed from the risk model after testing. The testing revealed that the other seven presumed vulnerabilities did exist and therefore remained in the risk model after testing. In addition, by testing threat scenario *FT06* the authors discovered that *FT06* may also lead to risk *RT2* by exploiting a previously unknown vulnerability *V11*. Thus, the authors added vulnerability *V11* to the risk model. This resulted in a total of eight vulnerabilities in the risk model after testing.

However, the adding and deleting of vulnerabilities did not cause an update of the likelihood values. This is because the vulnerabilities were not sufficiently severe to affect the likelihood of the tested threat scenarios. As a result, none of the tested threat scenarios changed likelihood value after testing. Hence, none of the threat scenarios and risks potentially affected by the testing changed likelihood value.

Figure 11. Difference between risk models before and after testing
Source: Authors' work

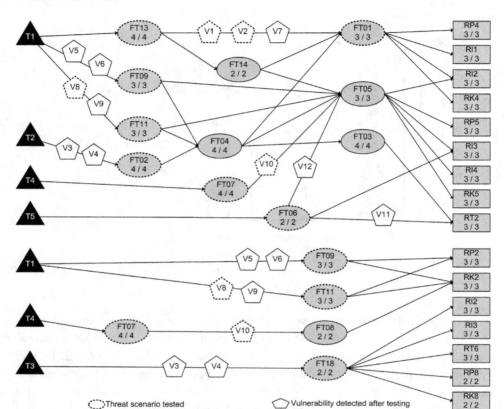

DISCUSSION

This section discusses the results obtained in the case studies with respect to the research questions.

To What Extent Are the Test Results Useful for Correcting the Risk Model by Adding Elements (RQ1)?

Based on the results discussed above and the numbers in Figure 6 and Figure 9, we know that new vulnerabilities were added to the risk models after testing. In addition, we see from Figure 9 that one new relation was added to the risk model after testing. However, this relation was added as part of a vulnerability. The relation would not been added if the vulnerability had not been discovered. No other kinds of risk model elements were added.

Why did the testing only yield new information about the vulnerabilities? The main reason for this is that the tests were designed with respect to the threat scenarios, and the purpose of the tests was to identify vulnerabilities that could be exploited by the threat scenarios. In other words, the tests were designed to uncover vulnerabilities; not unknown assets, threats, threat scenarios, or risks. These elements were instead part of the context in which the testing was performed.

Recall that an asset is something that is of value for the party, and that can be harmed by a risk. If a party has no assets, then there is no reason to conduct a risk analysis. For this reason, assets are always identified in the beginning of the risk analysis, before the risks are identified. In our experience, the process of identifying the risks has never led to the identification of new assets because the assets are then part of the context of the risk identification. The same is also true for the testing.

The argument is similar regarding threats. A threat is a potential cause of an unwanted incident such as a hacker, an insider or a virus, and the testing is performed with regards to the identified threats. It therefore seems unlikely that the testing would uncover additional threats.

In principle, we cannot rule out that testing could yield information that would lead to the identification of new threat scenarios or risks. For instance, it might be the case that a threat scenario may be refined (that is, split up into more than one threat scenario) after testing, or lead to the identification of an unwanted incident that had not been previously thought of. However, as long as the tests are designed to uncover vulnerabilities, we believe that this would be unlikely.

As mentioned in the results section, some vulnerabilities in the case studies were only discovered by testing and were not known prior to the testing. That is, they were not identified during the risk assessment phase, but only during the testing phase. It is worth noticing that these vulnerabilities could never have been uncovered if the authors had performed risk analysis alone (without doing the testing), regardless of how much effort the authors would have spent. This is because of the limited amount of information that was available to the authors in the target description on which the risk assessment was based.

To What Extent Are the Test Results Useful for Correcting the Risk Model by Deleting Elements (RQ2)?

Based on the results, we know that the test results led to the deletion of exactly one kind of risk model element, namely vulnerabilities. In the first case study, the test results led to the deletion of one vulnerability, while in the second case study four vulnerabilities were deleted after testing. The authors believe that this result is generalizable. That is, in general, threats, threat scenarios, risks and assets are unlikely to be deleted after testing, whereas vulnerabilities may be deleted.

The reason why we deleted the vulnerabilities after testing was that the testing provided evidence that a potential vulnerability identified in the risk assessment phase was not present in the system. Based on this, as well as expert judgement, the authors removed the vulnerabilities from the risk models. The authors also believe that in general, testing can support the deletion of vulnerabilities, since the tests can be designed to check whether a specific vulnerability is present in the system or not.

The reason why threats and assets are unlikely to be deleted after testing is the same as for why they are unlikely to be added after testing. That is, the assets and threats are part of the context in which the testing is performed, and the testing is therefore unlikely to yield information about this context.

As for threat scenarios and unwanted incidents, these are risk model elements that contain assigned likelihood values. Therefore, there will never be a need to delete these from the risk model after testing. Instead of deleting them from the risk model, we would assign a low likelihood value on these risk model elements.

To What Extent Are the Test Results Useful for Correcting the Risk Model by Editing Elements (RQ3)?

The results obtained for the first case study show that 6 out of 43 threat scenarios and 6 out of 31 risks were edited with respect to likelihood values. The six threat scenarios and the six risks are illustrated with darker color in Figure 8. Moreover, 4 out of the 6 risks that were edited with respect to likelihood values were assigned a higher risk level because of the new likelihood values. The results obtained for the second case study show that there was no change in the likelihood values, because the identified vulnerabilities in the second case study were not sufficiently severe to have an influence on the likelihood values.

For all risk model elements that were edited in the first case study (except for one), the likelihood value was increased after testing, that is, they were believed to be more likely after testing than before testing. The reason for this was that the testing uncovered vulnerabilities that were previously unknown, which led to the belief that certain threat scenarios and risks were more likely to occur than believed before testing.

In one of the threat scenarios in the first case study, the likelihood value was decreased after testing because of the deletion of one vulnerability. Although four vulnerabilities were removed after testing in the second case study, they were not sufficiently severe to decrease the likelihood values of the threat scenarios.

In general, the authors believe that testing will uncover information that may cause the likelihood values of threat scenarios and unwanted incidents to be edited after testing. The testing did not result in editing the consequence values that unwanted incidents have on assets. The reason for this is that all the tests were designed to uncover information about vulnerabilities that would increase or decrease the likelihood of a successful attack. The consequence of a successful attack was already known in advance. The authors believe this result is generalizable. As long as all risks have been identified before testing, their consequences can be estimated before testing, and it is unlikely that the testing will uncover information which will cause the consequence values to change.

Summary and Lessons Learned

The authors overall hypothesis is that security testing is useful for validating and correcting the security risk models. Based on the authors' experience, the test results are useful for *correcting* the risk models in terms of *adding* or *deleting* vulnerabilities, as well as *editing* likelihood values.

Vulnerabilities are either added to or deleted from the risk models because the test cases are designed to discover vulnerabilities. However, even if it is unlikely, the possibility of identifying new threat scenarios or risks based on the test results cannot be completely ruled out. Furthermore, the test cases are designed with respect to threat scenarios which contain likelihood values. The adding or deleting of vulnerabilities may therefore have an influence on the likelihood of the corresponding threat scenarios. Thus, adding or deleting vulnerabilities may result in editing likelihood values.

The test results are also useful for *validating* the risk models in terms of discovering the presence or absence of presumed vulnerabilities, and thereby increasing the trust in the risk models. Even if the testing does not identify new vulnerabilities, or lead to an update of likelihood values, it is still useful for validating the correctness of the risk models. For example, in the second case study, the testing did not lead to any update of the likelihood values, and it confirmed the presence of 7 out of 11 presumed vulnerabilities. This indicates that the risk assessment was of high quality.

Based on the authors' experience, an industrial security risk analysis without testing is typically carried out between 250 and 300 hours. In the first case study, the authors spent approximately 293 hours, and in the second case study the authors spent approximately 322 hours. Furthermore, in both case studies, approximately 25% of the total time was devoted to the testing phase. The authors believe that the return of investment in testing outweighs the alternative, which is carrying out the risk analysis without testing. The authors believe this because, in both case studies, testing was useful to validate and correct the risk models as described above, and thereby mitigated the uncertainty in the risk models. In both case studies, it would not have been possible to validate or correct the risk picture without test execution.

This is due to the limited amount of information that was available to the authors in the target description, and because the testing uncovered issues which only appeared in extremely specific circumstances which could not have been reproduced without executing the system under analysis.

RELATED WORK

This chapter has presented an evaluation of a test-driven risk analysis approach specialized on security. Test-driven risk analysis is the process of using testing to improve the risk analysis results. The authors distinguish this from the notion of risk-driven (or risk-based) testing which is the process of using risk analysis to improve the test process. This distinction is usually unclear in the literature as argued by Erdogan, Li, Runde, Seehusen, and Stølen (2014). However, most of the literature on combining risk analysis and testing fits into the latter category (risk-driven testing). Indeed, the idea of combining risk analysis and testing first originated from the testing community, and this integration is also reflected in the recent software testing standard ISO/IEC/IEEE 29119 (ISO, 2013a). Several risk-driven testing approaches have been proposed over the years. These approaches have in common that the identified risks become the driving factor for one or more of the activities within a testing process: Test planning, test design, test implementation, test execution, and test evaluation (Felderer & Schieferdecker, 2014); (Felderer, Grossmann, & Schieferdecker, 2018). In a systematic literature review on approaches for the combined use of risk analysis and testing Erdogan et al. (2014) identify three other approaches that address test-driven risk analysis. The first two approaches described below do not address security. Nevertheless, they suggest techniques in which testing is used to improve the risk analysis results.

Wong, Qi, and Cooper (2005) suggest a test-driven risk analysis approach in which risk of code is described as the likelihood that a given function or block within source code contains a fault. Their mathematical risk model is updated based on metrics related to both the static structure of code as well as dynamic test coverage. A more complex static structure leads to higher risk, while more thoroughly tested code has less risk. The approach is evaluated on an industrial software used for configuring antennas. The approach is supported by a tool in which the only feedback to the risk analyst or developer is a categorization of risky source code.

Schneidewind (2007) proposes an approach that supports both risk-driven testing and test-driven risk analysis. With a focus on reliability, the approach suggests a risk-driven reliability model and testing process where the risk of software failure is used to drive test scenarios and reliability predictions. Both consumer and producer risks are considered. In addition to comparing empirical values of risk and reliability to specified threshold values, emphasis is placed on evaluating the mathematical model that predicts risk and reliability. The evaluation is carried out in terms of a hypothetical example problem applied on the NASA shuttle flight software.

Großmann, Berger, and Viehmann (2014); Großmann, Schneider, Viehmann, and Wendland (2014) suggest an approach that supports both risk-driven security testing and test-driven security risk analysis. Their approach is somewhat similar to the approach described in this chapter in the sense that it makes use of threat scenarios to identify security tests. This is the risk-driven testing part of their approach. Then, based on the test results, they update the risk models. This is the test-driven risk analysis part of their approach. However, although it is mentioned that the test results may lead to the identification of additional vulnerabilities, threat scenarios, and unwanted incidents, it is not explained exactly how this may be achieved. In particular, as discussed, it is not obvious how additional threat scenarios or unwanted incidents can be identified by testing threat scenarios. Moreover, they mention that based on the test results, the likelihood values may become more precise. Again, it is not clear how this is achieved, and this is also not a straight forward process. For example, in the approach described in this chapter, a level of severity is assigned to the identified vulnerabilities. Then, based on the severity level, it is assessed whether the likelihood value of the relevant threat scenario should be increased, decreased or remain unchanged. The approach by Großmann, Schneider, et al. (2014) is supported by a tool and they give an analytical evaluation of the tool and mention that the approach will be evaluated in future case studies.

Großmann and Seehusen (2015) show how to combine the existing standards ISO 31000 (ISO, 2009) for risk assessment, and ISO/IEC/IEEE 29119 (ISO, 2013a) for testing into an approach that supports both security risk assessment and security testing. This approach integrates two different workstreams of the two standards in such a way that security risk assessment activities and security testing activities complement each other, especially in the overall combined security assessment process. The test-based risk assessment workstream describes how testing activities can support risk identification and risk estimation. The approach in this chapter is in line with the test-based risk assessment workstream, covering all three activities: risk identification, risk estimation, and risk evaluation. Moreover, this chapter provided an evaluation, based on two industrial case studies, of the test-based risk assessment workstream described by Großmann and Seehusen (2015). Risk-based security testing is not the focus of this chapter, even though it is closely related. It is fair to say that the approach presented by Großmann and Seehusen (2015) is a continuation in the same line of the approach presented in this chapter. As a continuation, Großmann and Seehusen (2015) give a systematic integration of both workstreams: risk-based testing and test-based risk assessment. So far, the former seems more popular than the latter as the literature consists of more approaches focusing on risk-driven testing as discussed by Felderer and Schieferdecker (2014) and Felderer et al. (2018) compared to the few test-based risk assessment approaches discussed in this section. It is worth to explore more of the latter as reported in this chapter. Indeed, the industry-based evaluation in this chapter focuses on examining the usefulness of testing for validating and correcting the risk models produced in the security risk assessment phase, which to the best of our knowledge, has not been done previously.

Felderer and Ramler (2016) conducted a thorough empirical study of how risk-based testing is applied in small and medium size enterprises (SMEs) for reducing testing cost and time. Using qualitative methods, the authors conducted analyses across five case studies. Besides the research questions on how software testing is organized in SMEs, or the difference in risk-based testing conducted in SMEs compared to large enterprises, their focus on the role of risk in software testing of SME is highly relevant to our study, even though our focus is more specifically on security risk. They found that even though risk was mainly considered implicitly, and sensitive to subjective perception, risk was involved in all the surveyed testing activities and was used to make testing more effective and efficient. This study is a good complementation in terms of scope to our evaluation in this chapter, which focuses on how useful test-based risk assessment is for validating and correcting the risk models in industrial settings.

The risk models presented in this chapter are based on the CORAS method (Lund et al., 2010), which is one of the recognized techniques systematically reviewed by Tuma, Calikli, and Scandariato (2018). The systematic review conducted by Tuma et al. (2018) discusses 26 threat analysis approaches for secure software design, including CORAS classified in the risk-centric category. For an overview of threat analysis techniques the readers are referred to Tuma et al. (2018).

CONCLUSION

This chapter has described an evaluation of a process for test-driven security risk analysis based on experiences from applying this process in two industrial case studies. The objective of the evaluation was to evaluate how useful testing is for validating and correcting the risk models produced in the security risk assessment phase. To make the evaluation precise, the authors analyzed the difference between the risk models produced before and after the testing.

The process of testing yielded useful information, which led to an update of the risk models created before testing. Specifically, in the first case study, four vulnerabilities were added to the risk model, and one vulnerability was deleted from the risk model. This resulted in a corrected risk model containing five vulnerabilities instead of two vulnerabilities. In the second case study, one vulnerability was added to the risk model, while four vulnerabilities were deleted. This resulted in a corrected risk model containing eight vulnerabilities instead of 11 vulnerabilities.

Furthermore, in the first case study, six out of 43 threat scenarios and six out of 31 risks were edited with respect to likelihood values. Moreover, four out of the six risks that were edited with respect to likelihood values were assigned a higher risk level because of the new likelihood values. In the second case study, on the other hand, there were no editing in terms of updating the likelihood values of the threat scenarios and unwanted incidents. The reason to this is that the vulnerabilities in the second case study were not sufficiently severe to affect the likelihood values. However, the fact that seven out of 11 presumed vulnerabilities were confirmed present, and that there was no need in updating the likelihood values, suggests that the risk assessment was of high quality.

The testing was useful in the sense that it yielded more accurate risk models, which indicates that testing is indeed useful for validating and correcting risk models. Another important point is that the testing uncovered vulnerabilities that would never have been uncovered in the risk analysis phase, regardless of how much effort the authors would have spent in the risk analysis phase. This is because of the limited amount of information that was available to the authors in the target description on which the risk assessment was based. In other words, if the risk analysis phase had been extended with the effort spent on testing, we would not have uncovered the vulnerabilities that were uncovered in the testing phase.

ACKNOWLEDGMENT

This work has been conducted as a part of the DIAMONDS project (201579/S10) and the AGRA project (236657) funded by the Research Council of Norway, as well as the RASEN project (316853) and the NESSoS network of excellence (256980) funded by the European Commission within the 7th Framework Programme. The first article version of this chapter was presented in the International Workshop on Quantitative Aspects in Security Assurance (QASA 2012).

REFERENCES

Alberts, C., Dorofee, A., Stevens, J., & Woody, C. (2003). *Introduction to the OCTAVE Approach.* Retrieved from http://www.dtic.mil/docs/citations/ADA634134

Barber, B., & Davey, J. (1992). The use of the CCTA risk analysis and management methodology CRAMM in health information systems. In *7th International Congress on Medical Informatics.* (pp. 1589-1593). North-Holland.

CORAS. (2018). *The CORAS Tool.* Retrieved from http://coras.sourceforge.net/coras_tool.html

Eclipse. (2018). Retrieved from https://www.eclipse.org/

Erdogan, G., Li, Y., Runde, R. K., Seehusen, F., & Stølen, K. (2014). Approaches for the combined use of risk analysis and testing: A systematic literature review. *International Journal of Software Tools for Technology Transfer, 16*(5), 627–642. doi:10.100710009-014-0330-5

Felderer, M., Grossmann, J., & Schieferdecker, I. (2018). *Recent Results on Classifying Risk-Based Testing Approaches.* Computing Research Repository, arXiv:1801.06812

Felderer, M., & Ramler, R. (2016). Risk orientation in software testing processes of small and medium enterprises: An exploratory and comparative study. *Software Quality Journal, 24*(3), 519–548. doi:10.100711219-015-9289-z

Felderer, M., & Schieferdecker, I. (2014). A taxonomy of risk-based testing. *International Journal of Software Tools for Technology Transfer, 16*(5), 559–568. doi:10.100710009-014-0332-3

Felderer, M., Zech, P., Breu, R., Büchler, M., & Pretschner, A. (2016). Model-based security testing: A taxonomy and systematic classification. *Software Testing, Verification & Reliability, 26*(2), 119–148. doi:10.1002tvr.1580

Google. (2018). *Chrome.* Retrieved from http://www.google.com/chrome/

Gritzalis, D., Iseppi, G., Mylonas, A., & Stavrou, V. (2018). Exiting the Risk Assessment Maze: A Meta-Survey. *ACM Computing Surveys, 51*(1), 1–30. doi:10.1145/3145905

Großmann, J., Berger, M., & Viehmann, J. (2014). A trace management platform for risk-based security testing. In *Proceedings of the International Workshop on Risk Assessment and Risk-driven Testing* (pp. 120-135): Springer.

Großmann, J., Schneider, M., Viehmann, J., & Wendland, M.-F. (2014). Combining risk analysis and security testing. In *Proceedings of the International Symposium On Leveraging Applications of Formal Methods, Verification and Validation* (pp. 322-336). Springer.

Großmann, J., & Seehusen, F. (2015). Combining Security Risk Assessment and Security Testing Based on Standards. In *Proceedings of the International Workshop on Risk Assessment and Risk-driven Testing* (pp. 18-33). Springer. 10.1007/978-3-319-26416-5_2

IBM. (2018). *IBM Rational Software Architect*. Retrieved from http://www.ibm.com/developerworks/downloads/r/architect/index.html

ISO. (2009). *ISO 31000: Risk Management - Principles and Guidelines*. Geneva: International Organization for Standardization.

ISO. (2013a). *ISO/IEC/IEEE 29119-1: 2013 (E) Software and systems engineering - Software testing - Part 1: Concepts and definitions*. Geneva: International Organization for Standardization.

ISO. (2013b). *ISO/IEC/IEEE 29119-2: 2013 (E) Software and systems engineering - Software testing - Part 2: Test process*. Geneva: International Organization for Standardization.

Lund, M. S., Solhaug, B., & Stølen, K. (2010). *Model-driven risk analysis: the CORAS approach*. Springer.

Mozilla. (2018). *Firefox Web browser*. Retrieved from https://www.mozilla.org/en-US/firefox/desktop/

NIST. (2012). *NIST SP 800-30, Revision 1, Guide for Conducting Risk Assessments*. National Institute of Standards and Technology.

OWASP. (2018). *OWASP Zed Attack Proxy Project*. Retrieved from https://www.owasp.org/index.php/OWASP_Zed_Attack_Proxy_Project

Portswigger. (2018). *Portswigger Burp Suite Free Edition*. Retrieved from http://portswigger.net/burp/download.html

Runeson, P., Host, M., Rainer, A., & Regnell, B. (2012). *Case study research in software engineering: Guidelines and examples*. John Wiley & Sons. doi:10.1002/9781118181034

Schneidewind, N. F. (2007). Risk-driven software testing and reliability. *International Journal of Reliability Quality and Safety Engineering, 14*(02), 99–132. doi:10.1142/S0218539307002532

Seehusen, F. (2014). A technique for risk-based test procedure identification, prioritization and selection. In *Proceedings of the International Symposium On Leveraging Applications of Formal Methods, Verification and Validation* (pp. 277-291). Springer. 10.1007/978-3-662-45231-8_20

Selenium. (2018). *SeleniumHQ*. Retrieved from http://www.seleniumhq.org/

Smartesting. (2018). *Smartesting CertifyIt*. Retrieved from http://www.smartesting.com/en/certifyit/

Tuma, K., Calikli, G., & Scandariato, R. (2018). Threat analysis of software systems: A systematic literature review. *Journal of Systems and Software, 144*, 275–294. doi:10.1016/j.jss.2018.06.073

Utting, M., Pretschner, A., & Legeard, B. (2012). A taxonomy of model-based testing approaches. *Software Testing, Verification & Reliability, 22*(5), 297–312. doi:10.1002tvr.456

Wireshark. (2018). Retrieved from https://www.wireshark.org/

Wong, W. E., Qi, Y., & Cooper, K. (2005). Source code-based software risk assessing. In *Proceedings of the 2005 ACM symposium on Applied computing* (pp. 1485-1490). ACM. 10.1145/1066677.1067014

KEY TERMS AND DEFINITIONS

Risk-Driven Security Testing: Security testing that makes use of security risk assessment within the security testing process to support risk-driven test planning, risk-driven test design and implementation, and risk-driven test reporting.

Security: The preservation of confidentiality, integrity, and availability of information.

Security Risk Assessment: The process of risk identification, risk estimation, and risk evaluation specialized towards security.

Security Testing: The process of software testing to check whether a system meets its specified security requirements.

Test Case: A set of preconditions, inputs (including actions, where applicable), and expected results, developed to drive the execution of a test item to meet test objectives, including correct implementation, error identification, checking quality, and other valued information. The terms test case and test are sometimes used interchangeably.

Test Procedure: A sequence of test cases in execution order, and any associated actions that may be required to set up the initial preconditions and any wrap up activities post execution.

Test-Driven Security Risk Analysis: Security risk analysis that makes use of security testing within the security risk analysis to validate and correct risk models.

Chapter 5
Modeling and Re–Evaluating Security in an Incremental Development of RBAC–Based Systems Using B Method

Nasser Al-Mur Al-Hadhrami
Ministry of Education, Oman

ABSTRACT

Incremental software development through the addition of new features and access rules potentially creates security flaws due to inconsistent access control models. Discovering such flaws in software architectures is commonly performed with formal techniques that allow the verification of the correctness of a system and its compliance with applicable policies. In this chapter, the authors propose the use of the B method to formally, and incrementally, design and evaluate the security of systems running under role-based access control (RBAC) policies. They use an electronic marking system (EMS) as a case study to demonstrate the iterative development of RBAC models and the role of the B language in exploring and re-evaluating the security of the system as well as addressing inconsistencies caused by incremental software development. Two formal approaches of model checking and proof obligations are used to verify the correctness of the RBAC specification.

DOI: 10.4018/978-1-5225-6313-6.ch005

INTRODUCTION

Critical systems, including e-commerce, enforce security policies that preserve the availability, integrity, and secrecy of data. Defects in applied security policies for a given system, e.g., ambiguous properties or inconsistent access control models, result in unreliable security of the system. Furthermore, from the process of incremental software development, the addition of new features and insertion of new access rules may render the access control models inconsistent and create security flaws. Therefore, exploring and addressing such flaws in software architectures is required to preserve the reliability of a system. A common approach to study and analyse security is to formally specify the system and its properties in models that allow for the verification of their correctness and compliance to applicable policies, such as Role-based Access Control (RBAC) policies (Ferraiolo & Kuhn, 1995).

RBAC is one of the most effective security models adopted in recent years that facilitates the administration of security in large organisations. The principal motivation behind RBAC models is that users are not directly granted access to an enterprise's objects. Instead, access permissions are administratively associated with roles, and users are administratively assigned to appropriate roles. This mechanism simplifies the management of authorisations and provides flexibility in specifying and enforcing security policies, particularly in dynamic systems (Ferraiolo & Kuhn, 1995). Evaluation of the correctness and consistency of such policies is essential to ensure the reliability and robustness of dynamic systems.

We discuss the application of the B language (Abrial, 1996) to incrementally develop and re-evaluate the security of an Electronic Marking System (EMS) running under RBAC policies. With B specifications, we study the impact of iterative development on the system's specification of access rights for subjects to resources modelled as an RBAC. The access rights include, for example, that teachers can access the system to add, edit or delete marks, and students have the authorisation to submit reports and view their grades. Such a system requires reliable assurances that the RBAC model is consistent and complies with a set of security policies.

The B language is a formal method based on *set theory* and *first-order logic* used to model and refine a system's specification (Schneider, 2001) using a special notation, i.e., language, called Abstract Machine Notation (AMN). The model development process creates multiple proof obligations that guarantee the correctness of the model and the desired properties (invariants) that the model must preserve. Proving the obligations, verifying the properties, and simulating the model are functions commonly supported by tools such as ProB (Leuschel & Butler, 2003).

This chapter is organised as follows. In Section 2, we provide overviews of the RBAC model, its properties, and refer to related work on applying formal specifications to implement RBAC policies. In Section 3, we overview the B method used to formally model and evaluate our EMS system's specification running under RBAC policies. In Section 4, we introduce the EMS system without policies. In Section 5, we augment the system with basic RBAC policies, namely $RBAC_0$. We show how the policy is implemented in the model and discuss its weaknesses and inconsistencies. In Section 6, we further develop the model to run under $RBAC_2$ policy constraints focusing on the types of such constraints, separation of duties, and cardinality constraints. In Section 7, we model the EMS under role hierarchies (i.e., $RBAC_1$). To evaluate the correctness of our RBAC model running under these properties, we leverage, in Section 8, the B specification to model operations that allow the system's administrator to perform user assignments and revoke existing assignments. Section 9 discusses the formal verification of the model using the two approaches of model checking and theorem proving. Finally, in Section 10, we conclude the chapter with a discussion of future work.

BACKGROUND

Role-Based Access Control

RBAC is an efficient access control model used to facilitate the administration of security in large organisations with hundreds of users and thousands of permissions (Sandhu et al., 1996). Beginning in the 1970s with multi-user applications, the RBAC model rapidly evolved over the next three decades as a technology for applying high-level security to large-scale systems. The pivotal idea behind the RBAC model is that permissions are associated with roles to which users are administratively assigned. Users are not directly mapped into permissions for accessing system resources but to specific roles previously assigned to those permissions. This mechanism ensures that only authorised users can perform functions on specified data or resources (Ferraiolo & Kuhn, 1995).

Unlike traditional lattice-based access control policies, such as Discretionary Access Control (DAC) and Mandatory Access Control (MAC), security administration for RBAC models is simply implemented through specifying roles to organise access privileges. This process offers multiple benefits including the ease of managing and controlling the dynamic nature of organisations, such as registering new users (i.e., hiring new employees) and changing work positions and responsibilities of users. For example, it is easy to reconfigure a user into a new functional role within an organisation by removing the association with a current role and assigning to a new one without the need to manipulate or change the permissions associated to the previous role. Another benefit for applying RBAC models is that they implement the principle of *least privilege*, which states that users should have only the minimum privileges required to accomplish their tasks (Yu & Brewster, 2012).

Various dimensions of RBAC define properties and uses of the model. The relation between four models is shown in Figure 1 with their essential characteristics described in Table 1. $RBAC_0$, the base model, is the core version defining the minimum requirement for a system. This model contains the basic elements for any RBAC policy, such as the sets of users (U), Roles (R), Permissions (P), and Sessions (S). $RBAC_1$, $RBAC_2$, and $RBAC_3$ are advanced models each adding features or properties to the base model. For example, $RBAC_1$ incorporates the concept of role hierarchy, and $RBAC_2$ restricts the relations between the elements in the other models through providing constraints in the form of conditions (Sandhu et al., 1996).

Formal Specifications of RBAC Models

In computer science, formal specifications are notation-based languages that use mathematical techniques to model systems and software, which typically describe a system, analyse its behaviour, and verify its properties through rigorous and effective reasoning tools (Fraser et al., 1994). Given their power of discovering software bugs during early stages of the development lifecycle, modelling a system and designing security policies using formal techniques significantly strengthen the reliability of the system (Lockhart et al., 2017).

Recently, formal specifications have been widely adopted in modelling and proofs of correctness for many critical systems as well as evaluating security policies, including RBAC models (Drouineaud et al., 2004). Yu and Brewster (2012) propose a formal specification for formalising RBAC constraints that includes the separation

Figure 1. The elements of RBAC security policy

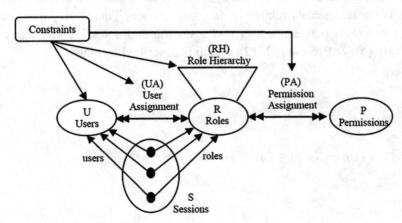

Table 1. Description of RBAC elements

Code	Description
Users (U)	Persons who interact with a system.
Roles (R)	Prescribed behaviours describing positions or functions within an organisation.
Permissions (P)	Descriptions of the type of interaction a user may have with a data or resource object.
Object (O)	A passive entity that represents information and can receive new information.
User Assignment (UA)	A many-to-many relationship between users and roles.
Permission Assignment (PA)	A many-to-many relationship between permissions and roles.
Session (S)	A mapping between a user and activated roles to which the user is assigned.
Role Hierarchy (RH)	A partial order relationship on roles.
Constraints (C)	Restrictions on any of the above relationships or assignments.

of duties. Formal verification of RBAC policies also received attention from many researchers, such as Yuan et al. (2006) and Jha et al. (2008).

To formalize RBAC models, it is essential to understand the components and properties, such as sets, relations, and constraints. From the basic elements of the RBAC model listed in Table 1, the first four elements of U, R, P, and S can be mathematically described as *sets*, while UA and PA are *relationships* between these sets (Hu & Ahn, 2008). Since UA and PA are many-to-many relations, they can be formally expressed as (Yuan et al. 2006)

$$UA \subseteq U \times R \ \& \ PA \subseteq R \times P$$

Regarding the S set, a user can be activated for many sessions, but a session is related to only one user. In addition, any session can be assigned to many roles, and that role is not necessarily related to only one session. Therefore, *users* and *roles* represent *functions* between a user and a session and a session and many roles, respectively (Yu & Brewster, 2012), which is described formally as

users: S→U

roles: S→2R

$roles(S_i) \subseteq \{ r \mid (user(S_i), r) \in UA \}$, *for activating roles by a user*

The RBAC$_1$ model has the same elements as the base model, RBAC$_0$, except that it defines the concept of Role Hierarchy (RH), which describes a partial order relation on the roles (formally, $RH \subseteq R \times R$). The partial order may also be written with '$\geq$', such as *role1* $\geq$ *role2*, which means that *role1* is the parent and *role2* is the child (Chae & Shiri, 2007).

To formalise RBAC constraints (i.e., the RBAC$_2$ model), the type of constraints must be specified, such as cardinality constraints or separation of duties. For separation of duties (SoD), there must be a definition of the SoD type along with the element of the RBAC model to which this type is applied (e.g., UA, PA or RH*)* (Strembeck & Neumann, 2004). Cardinality constraints are simply formalised by specifying the maximum number of elements (or relations), such as

card $(R) \leq 8$, *to specify the maximum number of roles for set R.*

card $(user \mapsto R) \leq 3$, *to specify the maximum number of assignments for user to set R.*

The Static Separation of Duties (SSD) and Dynamic Separation of Duties (DSD) are two types of separation of duties. SSD is used when a user cannot be mapped into two conflicting roles simultaneously. For example, given two mutually exclusive roles, *ra* and *rb*, a user *u* can be assigned to only one of these roles and not both at the same time (Yu & Brewster, 2012). This condition is formally expressed as

$\forall$ *ra, rb* $\in$ *Roles, a* $\neq$ *b,* $\forall$ *u* $\in$ *Users,* $(ra, r_b) \in SSD$

$\Rightarrow (u, ra) \notin UA$ *or* $(u, rb) \notin UA$

DSD, on the other hand, is used when it is acceptable to assign a user to two conflicting roles statically. However, these roles cannot be activated for the same user in the same session (Yuan et al., 2006). For example, if *ra* and *rb* are conflicting roles, then a user *u* can have a session with both roles valid, but only one session may be activated to the user, such that

$\forall ra, rb \in$ *Roles, a* $\neq$ *b,* $\forall u \in$ *Users,* $(ra, rb) \in DSD$,

$(u, ra) \in$ *Session_UA,* $(u, rb) \in$ *Session_UA,*

$\Rightarrow (u, ra) \notin$ *Session_UA or* $(u, rb) \notin$ *Session_UA*

THE B METHOD

Formal methods, in the context of software engineering, are mathematical techniques and tools used to develop and analyse software systems (Clarke et al., 1996). The methods can be applied to model and verify various types of systems, including safety-critical systems, for the purpose of obtaining a correct product. The main purpose of formal methods is to develop a precise statement of *what* the software is to do instead of *how* it is to be achieved. Several examples of such methods exist, such as ASM, VDM, Z, and the B method (Clarke et al., 1996).

The B method (Abrial, 1996) is a formal method based on *set theory* and *first-order logic* used to specify, refine, and implement software, and it uses a language called an Abstract Machine Notation (AMN) (Schneider, 2001) to develop an abstract specification and its refinement. Figure 2 shows the primary building block (i.e., clauses) of AMN. This language enables the developer to start with an abstract model of the system and refine it until obtaining a final implementable version (Cansell & Méry, 2012).

The process of developing B specifications for a system and its refinement can be formally verified. B Theory specifies the proof obligations to ensure the correctness of a given specification (Hallerstede, 2008). Moreover, B supports tools specifically designed to validate the specification and generate theorem proofs, such as B-toolkit, Atelier B, and proB tools. In this work, we use the proB tool (Leuschel & Butler, 2003) as a model checker for evaluating the security of the EMS specification, and additional details are discussed in Section 9.

Figure 2. The general template for Abstract Machine Notation (AMN)

```
MACHINE          machine_name
SETS             sets
CONSTANTS        machine_constants
PROPERTIES       prop
VARIABLES        variables
INVARIANT        inv
INITILISATION    variables_initialisations
OPERATIONS
     result ← operation (x) ≙
             PRE    P
             THEN   S
             END;
       ...
END
```

Due to the simplicity of its notation, the capability of modelling and refining specifications, and generating proof obligations, we propose the use of B specifications to model the RBAC-based system and re-evaluate its security following the model changes resulting from incremental development. The re-evaluation of the specification may suggest an enhancement of the basic RBAC model by adding new properties or incorporating new access control models to the current version of the software.

CASE STUDY: THE ELECTRONIC MARKING SYSTEM

The Electronic Marking System (EMS) assesses students in Oman's schools and provides an integrated assessment environment allowing users to access the system within their authorisations to fulfil the evaluation system's requirements within the educational institutions. For example, students can electronically submit papers for a unit to be graded by the corresponding teacher. Then, teachers can establish, edit, and delete their students' marks. In addition, headmasters and students' guardians can also access the system for viewing the students' marks and signing final reports.

The EMS system can be accessed by a variety of users, including the system admin (responsible for controlling and managing the entities and resources of the system), students, teachers, headmasters, and guardians. Therefore, users are classified into the three entities (i.e., database's tables) of staff, students, and guardians where the staff entity represents teachers and headmasters as well as the system's admin. The other entities of the system as well as the relationships between these entities are briefly demonstrated in table 2 and table 3, respectively.

In the following sections, we model role-based access policies for the EMS system based on the system's specifications and requirements. We develop these policies incrementally using the B language. In other words, we initiate our software development, i.e., version 1, by modelling the basics of the RBAC policies as the $RBAC_0$ model. We next evaluate the version's security and, if needed, propose

Table 2. Entities of the EMS system

Entity Name	Description
UNITS	To represent all units taught at a given school.
SUBMISSIONS	To store the submitted reports by students.
FINAL_REPORTS	Contains final reports for all students.
MARKS	Its contents are natural numbers, representing the students' marks.
ROLES	Represents the various roles in the EMS, i.e., admin, teacher, student, etc.

Table 3. Relations between the EMS entities

Relation Name	Description
Studies	A relation between a student and a unit, where each student studies more than one unit, and that unit can be registered for many students.
taughtBy	A relation between a unit and a teacher, where each unit must be taught by at least one teacher, and that teacher can be registered for more than one unit.
hisGuardian	A relation between a student and a guardian. A student may have more than one guardian allowing them to track the student's educational level. In addition, a guardian can be registered for more than one student.
Submits	A relation between a student and a submission, where any student can submit any number of reports (depending on the unit and the academic level of the student).
reportFor	A relation between a submitted report and a unit. Here, all submitted reports are mapped to the corresponding units, and each unit may accept more than one report as submissions.
submissionMark	A relation between a submitted report and a mark (i.e., a natural number). Intuitively, it is not possible to map two different marks to the same report, but the same mark can be found in many reports.
InClassMark	A relation between a unit and a mark representing the student's mark of their participations and activities inside the class during the year.
examMark	A relation between a unit and a mark to specify the student's exam mark.
studentReport	A relation between a student and a final report, where each student must receive a final report for each unit showing their final marks. However, it is not possible to assign two final reports to the same student.
hasTheRole	Maps a user to a set of roles (e.g., student, teacher, headmaster or student's guardian), where by default each user is assigned to only one role (except in certain circumstances, as we discuss later on).

appropriate solutions to update the flawed version. Updating a version may include the addition of new security policies or the incorporation of new RBAC models. This process of updating and evaluating the system is repeated until proof obligations are created that guarantee the correctness of the model and the desired properties that the model shall preserve. Finally, we discuss how, with the B method, such proof obligations are generated and how the model consistency is verified.

EMS VERSION 1 AND THE BASIC RBAC MODEL

This section discusses the construction of the basic RBAC policy for the EMS system through the definition of the following elements (see Figure 3):

- Sets of *USERS*, *ROLES*, and *PERMISSIONS*.
- Relationships between these three sets.

Figure 3. Elements of the basic RBAC model

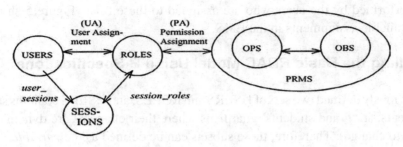

These elements form the $RBAC_0$ model, which is one of the four conceptual models for the RBAC security policy, as discussed above. This model is the basic pattern as it represents the minimum requirements needed for a system, and the other three models are built from this model (Ahn & Hu, 2007). For the EMS system, the basic elements required to instantiate an RBAC policy include:

- **U (Users):** According to the database structure, there are three types of users in the system, including students, students' guardians, and staff. The latter contains the system admin, teachers, and headmaster. Thus, each user represents an element in the USERS set.
- **R (Roles):** Six roles describe the primary functionality for the EMS users, which are stored into the ROLES entity of the database and is defined as

ROLES = {admin, student, teacher, headteacher, headmaster, student_guardian}

- **P (Permissions):** Each permission represents a relationship pair of (operation, object). For example, students can perform the *operation* of submitting a report such that each submitted report is stored in the SUBMISSIONS table (the *object*).
- **User Assignment (UA) and Permission Assignment (PA):** User Assignment (UA) is a many-to-many relationship between the system's users *U* and roles *R*. For example, all students should be assigned the role *student*, and teachers are assigned to the role *teacher*. In some cases, it is possible to assign a user to two different roles if required for their responsibilities within the system. For instance, in the case of the absence of the school manager, the deputy headmaster (or any teacher) might be authorised to perform the headmaster's permissions, which is configured through temporarily assigning another individual to the *headmaster* role in addition to their own primary role. Permission Assignment (PA) is also a many-to-many relationship that maps

roles into permissions (e.g., system functions). The functions can only be performed by the users who are assigned to these roles. Figure 5 shows all available assignments in the EMS.

Modelling the Basic RBAC Model Using B Specifications

We previously defined two sets of USERS and ROLES, and USERS contains subsets of students, staff, and students' guardians where their elements are dynamic (i.e., subject to change). Therefore, these subsets can be defined as the *variables*

staff, students, studentGuardian

Similarly, the subset *staff* contains teachers, the school manager, and other staff members. However, since the EMS provides roles to teachers and school managers, we represent only these two subsets as *variables*

teachers, manager

Now, we declare within the INVARIANT clause that each of these variables is a subset of the USERS set, and some are also subsets of the *staff* subset, provided that no element of each subset can be found in two subsets. For example, if a student is a member of the *students* subset, then the student cannot also be a member of the *staff* subset (i.e., *students* ∩ *staff* = { }). This can be expressed using the B specification as

students ⊆ *USERS* ∧

staff ⊆ *USERS* ∧

students ∩ *staff* = { } ∧

studentGuardian ⊆ *USERS* ∧

studentGuardian ∩ *students* = { } ∧

Figure 4. The permission relationship of Adding Submission for students

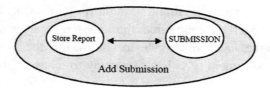

Figure 5. Roles and Permissions of the EMS system

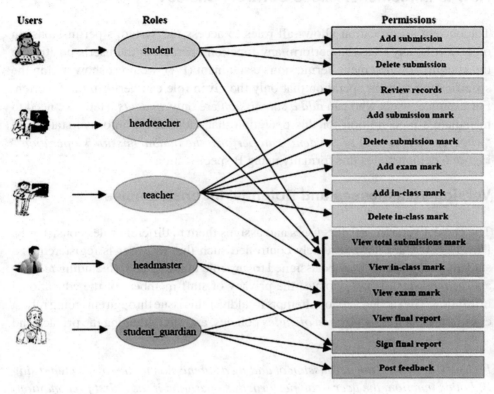

manager ⊆ *staff* ∧

teachers ⊆ *staff* ∧

manager ∩ *teachers* = { }

To model the User Assignment (UA), which assigns each user to a certain role, we need to define a relation between the USERS set and the ROLES set. This relation is, in turn, a set of elements where each is a pair of *user* and *role*. For example, if a user *u* is assigned to the role *r*, then the element for the relation is defined as {(*u*, *r*)}.

Since elements of the relation between USERS and ROLES are subject to change (i.e., assigning new users to roles or revoking existing assignments), we represent this relation as a *variable* named *hasTheRole*. We declare this formally within the INVARIANT clause as

hasTheRole ∈ *USERS* ↔ *ROLES*

How to Implement Access Control Policies?

The current specification allows all roles to access the system's permissions. In other words, any user can perform any function apart from the user's position in the system. To implement Permission Assignment (PA), we must show within the specification of each operation that only the given role can perform the function. For example, users who can *add a submission* are only *students*. Here, we need to formulate a precondition for this operation that satisfies the informal statement, *"whoever has the role of 'student' can perform the addSubmission's operation."* Figure 6 demonstrates this formally using B specifications.

Version Weaknesses and Potential Inconsistencies

The current version registers users and assigns them to different roles consistently. However, UA are not adequately controlled such that if a user is registered as a student, then the user may be assigned to any role in the system (including *teacher* and *headmaster*), which violates the privacy of staff members of the educational institution. The second version attempts to address this issue through enforcing robust constraints, such as *separation of duties* policies, and strengthening the privacy and

Figure 6. Assigning the permission of adding a submission to the role student using B. In this function, the user s can perform this operation if (as a first precondition) s has the role of student.

$$addSubmission \ (s, \ report, \ u) \ \triangleq$$

> **PRE**
>
> > $$hasTheRole[\{s\}] = \{student\} \ \land$$
> >
> > $report \in SUBMISSION \ \land$
> > $report \notin reports \ \land$
> > $u \in studies[\{s\}] \ \land$
> > $card(submit[\{s\}] \cap reportFor^{-1}[\{u\}]) < maxSubmissions$
>
> **THEN**
>
> > $reports \ := reports \cup \{report\} \ ||$
> > $submits \ := submits \cup \{s \mapsto report\} \ ||$
> > $reportFor \ := reportFor \cup \{report \mapsto u\}$
>
> **END;**

confidentiality of school managers by specifying *cardinality* constraints that allow only a specific number of users (e.g., two users of the headmaster and the deputy headmaster) to the role assignment of *headmaster*.

EMS VERSION 2 WITH ENFORCEMENT OF SEPARATION OF DUTIES AND CARDINALITY POLICIES

Separation of Duties (SoD) and cardinality are advanced properties used to form a new pattern for an RBAC model, namely $RBAC_2$ (also called the *constraints pattern*). $RBAC_2$ is regarded as the main motivation behind RBAC policies because it defines a powerful mechanism to force restrictions and establish a high-level security policy (Poniszewska-Maranda, 2005). Constraints can be specified and applied to any relationship or assignment defined in the base model ($RBAC_0$), such as UA, PA, and S.

Many types of applicable constraints exist, such as SoD (mutual exclusiveness of roles) and cardinality constraints (Ray et al., 2004). The most cited in the literature for RBAC is SoD. This type of constraint states that the same user cannot be assigned to two conflicting roles. For example, if there are two conflicting sets of roles S_1 and S_2, then if a user u is assigned to a role in S_1, then this implies that u is not assigned to any role in S_2, and vice versa.

Another example of a user assignment constraint controls the number of users assigned to a role. For example, in the educational system, there is typically a school manager and an assistant, so the role *headmaster* must be associated with only two users. We call this *cardinality constraints*, which can also be applied to other elements such as sessions (S). It might be possible for a user to be mapped into two roles, but the user cannot be active in both roles simultaneously. Constraints on sessions can restrict, for example, the number of sessions in which a user can be active (Sandhu et al., 1996).

Proposed Solution for Version 1 Inconsistency

Role inconsistency occurred in the initial version due to a lack of rules and policies that control assignments of users to roles. This means that any user in the system can be assigned any number of roles and perform any function. This scenario unacceptably grants students the permission of adding marks for their submissions and teachers the authorisation to submit reports for themselves. Another security flaw exists related to the open number of assignments to the role *headmaster*. Due to the absolute powers and privileges assigned to the school manager, it is so important to allow only one user (or two, as a maximum, if we consider the deputy headmaster is also authorised to sign final reports of students) to be assigned the role of *headmaster*.

A proposed solution for addressing the issue of open assignments and ensuring the system users are only authorised to perform the appropriate functions is to separate the users' duties. This is accomplished by splitting the system's roles into two distinct sets such that each is conflict-free and a user cannot be assigned to two roles from both sets. In the EMS system, we define the two conflicting classes (sets) of roles as

$sod_1 = \{teacher, headteacher, headmaster\}$, and

$sod_2 = \{student, student\_guardian\}$

These sets of roles mean that if someone is assigned to a role from sod_1, they may not be assigned to any role from sod_2, and if someone is assigned to a role from sod_2, they must not be assigned to any role from sod_1. It is evident that because of the nature of permissions assigned to the roles in each set, it is impractical for these permissions to be performed by the roles from the other set. For instance, we should not identify a teacher who submits a report on behalf of a student, and it is impossible for students to add marks to their submissions.

On the other hand, and in some circumstances, it may be possible for a user assigned to a role in a set to be assigned to another role within the same set. For example, in case of the absence of the school manager, the deputy headmaster (or any teacher) may be assigned to the role of *headmaster* to sign final reports on the school manager's behalf. As another example, a student can sign their final report if the system has not yet registered a guardian for that student.

Regarding the cardinality constraints in our system, it does not matter how many students are assigned to the *student* role or how many teachers are mapped to the *teacher* role as they depend on the number of students and teachers within an educational institution. However, there must be a specific number of users (e.g., two users) who can be assigned to the role *headmaster*. Therefore, we formulate a 'B' predicate that satisfies this cardinality.

THE USE OF THE B METHOD TO ADDRESS THE INCONSISTENCY

Implementing Separation of Duties

We defined in the previous section the elements of the roles that exist in each set. Since the elements are known for each class, we can specify these within the INITIALISATION clause as

$sod_1 = \{teacher, headteacher, headmaster\}$,

$sod_2 = \{student, student\_guardian\}$

Each of sod_1 and sod_2 is a subset of the ROLES set, and their intersection is an empty set. Therefore, this must be declared within the INVARIANT clause as

$sod_1 \subseteq ROLES \wedge sod_2 \subseteq ROLES \wedge sod_1 \cap sod_2 = \{\ \}$

Next, we formulate the condition of SoD using B specifications as

$\forall(u, role1, role2). (u \in USER \wedge role_1 \in sod_1 \wedge role2 \in sod_2 \wedge$

$role1 \in hasTheRole[\{u\}] \Rightarrow not\ (role2 \in hasTheRole[\{u\}]) \wedge$

$\forall(u, role1, role2). (u \in USER \wedge role1 \in sod_1 \wedge role2 \in sod_2 \wedge$

$role2 \in hasTheRole[\{u\}] \Rightarrow not\ (role1 \in hasTheRole[\{u\}])$

Implementing Cardinality Constraints

As discussed, the number of users who might be assigned to the *headmaster* role must not be greater than two. Hence, we must declare this within the INVARIANT clause by stating that for the role *headmaster*, where *headmaster* $\in sod_1$, the cardinality of users who have the role *headmaster* must be less than or equal to 2.

$\forall(headmaster). (headmaster \in sod_1 \Rightarrow$

$card(hasTheRole^{-1}[\{headmaster\}]) \leq 2$

Version Weaknesses and Potential Inconsistencies

This enhanced version provides a powerful mechanism to increase security through constraints on user assignments. We also notice that if we assign a new user to a role from any set, the user will be available to be assigned to any other role belonging to the same set. This feature resolves the problem of how to grant head teachers the permission of adding marks, for example. We know that head teachers have their tasks and permissions to perform in the system. However, these permissions do not allow them to add or delete marks (review Figure 5). Therefore, this version could be further improved to *automatically* grant head teachers the permissions associated with the role *teacher* as soon as they are assigned to role *headteacher*.

EMS VERSION 3 WITH ENFORCEMENT OF ROLE HIERARCHY POLICIES

Role Hierarchy (RH) is an additional property of the RBAC model represented by $RBAC_1$ to describe the structure of roles that reflects the hierarchal nature of positions and responsibilities in an organisation. In other words, role hierarchy represents the presence of senior roles (more powerful roles) and junior roles (less powerful roles), where senior roles can inherit permissions from the junior roles (Sohr et al., 2008). In educational systems, there are head teachers (seniors) who have more privileges than teachers (juniors) for reviewing and accrediting marks. However, they can also add, edit, and remove marks exactly in the same way as teachers do (typically they are assigned to units with students). Hence, head teachers should inherit these permissions from teachers to execute these same tasks.

Proposed Solution for Version 2 Inconsistency

Since the current version does not allow head teachers to add or delete marks, we must implement a mechanism that associates the *headteacher* role with the *teacher* role without allowing the reverse relationship. With this association established, head teachers may access the teachers' permission levels. Figure 7 shows the concept of RH and illustrates how head teachers can add marks, for instance.

The Use of the B Method to Address the Inconsistency

Head teachers have permissions, such as reviewing records. However, they are also teachers and can perform operations associated with teachers. We must formulate a

Figure 7. Role hierarchy where head teachers inherit permissions of the role teacher

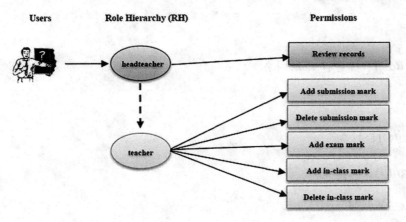

predicate that satisfies the concept of 'inheritance' where head teachers inherit the permissions from the *teacher* role. In B specifications, this is expressed as

$\forall(u, headteacher). (headteacher \in sod_1 \wedge u \mapsto headteacher \in hasTheRole$

$\Rightarrow headteacher \in hasTheRole[\{u\}] \wedge teacher \in hasTheRole[\{u\}])$

representing that for every user *u* and *headteacher* role, where *headteacher* $\in sod_1$ and the user is assigned to the role *headteacher*, then the user *u* has the role *teacher* in addition to the role *headteacher*.

Version Inconsistency and Proposed Solution

To understand the potential weaknesses that may exist in the new version, we consider the scenario of if the system's admin can register as a teacher and add marks? The answer is yes because the system's admin is the only person who performs user-assignments in the system. This allows the admin to potentially create a false teacher, assign themselves to the role *teacher* and benefit from teachers' privileges, such as the permission of *adding marks* to insert marks for students in a corresponding unit.

Nonetheless, this scenario is not straightforward because the function of adding marks is defined with multiple preconditions that must be *conjunctively* fulfilled to perform the operation. For example, not any teacher in the system can add an exam mark for a specific student, but only the teacher who teaches that student within a specified unit, as is expressed in the following B code.

addExamMark (t, m, s, u) $\triangleq$

PRE

hasTheRole[{*t*}] = {*teacher*} $\wedge$

m $\in$ $\mathbb{N}$ $\wedge$

u $\in$ *studies*[{*s*}] $\wedge$

t $\in$ *taughtBy*[{*u*}] $\wedge$

u $\mapsto$ *m* $\notin$ *examMark*

THEN

examMark:= examMark $\cup$ {*u* $\mapsto$ *m*}

END;

Therefore, the teacher (*t*) can add a mark (*m*) for student (*s*) in unit (*u*) if and only if the preconditions above are satisfied.

Still, the admin can create a false teacher through registering a new user, assigning the role *teacher*, and assigning the teacher to a unit. Doing so, however, will lead to eventually exposing the flaw as soon as the legitimately assigned teacher of the student inserts a mark. The last precondition of the above operation (i.e., *u* $\mapsto$ *m* $\notin$ *examMark*) states that for the teacher to grant an exam mark for a unit, the exam must not have been previously marked. Accordingly, an exam would either be marked by the false teacher or the real teacher when the operation is performed. If the false teacher grants the exam mark, then the real teacher would not be allowed to insert a mark, leading to an investigation of the cause of the system's fault.

We resolve this scenario by applying a minor modification to one of the defined relations in the invariant of the machine. Currently, we have a relation, named '*taughtBy*', that assigns units to different teachers in the system through

taughtBy $\in$ *UNITS* $\leftrightarrow$ *teachers*

This relation states that any unit in the UNITS set can be registered to any teacher in *teachers* set and that a teacher can be assigned to any unit from the UNITS set. It is apparent, then, that since one unit can be related to more than one teacher, the version's vulnerability lies in the possibility of assigning many users to the same unit. Therefore, a possible solution is to change the type of the relation (↔) to be the *total function* with the symbol (→) as

taughtBy ∈ *UNITS* → *teachers*

The above function is a special relation representing that every course in the UNITS set must be assigned to **exactly one** teacher in the set *teachers*. This condition guarantees that once the admin completes teacher assignments to their units, they will no longer be allowed to create a false teacher and assign themselves to any registered unit, as in the following example to illustrate the work of the new following relations

studies ∈ *students* ↔ *UNITS* ∧

taughtBy ∈ *UNITS* → *teachers*

Assuming that a student *s* is assigned to the unit '*Math*' (the first relation), and the unit '*Math*' is assigned to a teacher *t* (the second relation), then the teacher *t* is the **only** staff member who can teach the student *s* for the unit '*Math*', and, thus, may access the permission of adding marks.

So far, the updated specification addressed some issues regarding the inconsistencies of access policies caused by our incremental development. To evaluate our final RBAC model under the defined properties of the three versions, we first need to construct operations that allow the system's admin to assign users and revoke assignments. Then, we verify the correctness of the RBAC policies using the two approaches of model checking and proof obligations.

MODELLING OPERATIONS FOR USER ASSIGNMENT (UA) AND REVOKING USER ASSIGNMENT

In this section, we use the B language to model an operation for *user assignment* and another for *revoking user assignment*. The two operations must preserve the invariant clause, i.e., predicates, such as separation of duties, cardinality, and role hierarchy.

Operation for User Assignment (UA)

To assign a user *u* to a role *r*, the following preconditions must be satisfied:

- *u* is a user belonging to the USERS set, **and**

- (r belongs to the first conflict class of roles sod_1 **and** u belongs to *staff*) **or** (r belongs to the second conflict class of roles sod_2 **and** u belongs to either *students* or *studentGuardian*), **and**
- The user cannot be assigned to the same role twice, i.e., there must be no previous relationship between the user u and that role r before the application of this operation.

The second precondition satisfies the concept of mutual exclusiveness of roles (SoD), such that only staff members can be assigned to any role from the sod_1 set, and only students and guardians can be assigned to a role from the sod_2 set. Thus, the preconditions of the operation are formulated as

$u \in USERS \wedge$

$((u \in staff \wedge r \in sod_1) \vee ((u \in studentGuardian \vee u \in students) \wedge r \in sod_2)) \wedge$

$u \mapsto r \notin hasTheRole$

If these preconditions are satisfied, then the performance of the operation depends on special cases of the role's values (e.g., values of r). For example,

- If r belongs to sod_1, and r is *headteacher*, then we apply the role hierarchy (i.e., assign the user u to both the *headteacher* and *teacher* roles).
- If r belongs to sod_1, and r is *headmaster*, and the cardinality constraint (of *headmaster*) is satisfied (i.e., less than two), then we assign the user u to the role *headmaster*.
- Otherwise (i.e., no specific case for r), then we assign the user u to the role r.

The B specification representing this operation's body is then

```
    IF
          (r ∈ sod₁  ∧  r = headteacher)
    THEN
                    hasTheRole:= hasTheRole  ∪  {u ↦
headteacher}  ∪  {u ↦  teacher}
    ELSIF
          (r ∈ sod₁  ∧  r = headmaster  ∧  card(hasTheRole⁻¹[
{headmaster}])  < 2)
    THEN
                    hasTheRole:= hasTheRole  ∪  {u ↦ r}  | |
```

$$card(hasTheRole^{-1}[\{headmaster\}]) := card(hasTheRole^{-1}[\{headmaster\}]) + 1$$

ELSE

$$hasTheRole := hasTheRole \cup \{u \mapsto r\}$$

END

In case of r = *headmaster*, once the user u is assigned to this role, there is another statement that updates the current value of the cardinality constraint of the role *headmaster* to make sure the next assignment to this role, if required, will satisfy the predefined condition (i.e., < 2). As will be seen in the modelling of the *revoking user assignment* operation, this statement does the opposite. In other words, it decreases (by one) the current number of headmaster's assignments when a revocation for an existing assignment is performed. Figure 8 shows the complete B specification for the operation of User Assignment.

Operation for Revoking User Assignment

To revoke an existing assignment between a user u and a role r, three preconditions must be satisfied. First, u is a user (i.e., u belongs to USERS set), second, r is a role (i.e., r belongs to ROLES set), and third, the user u is already assigned to the role r (i.e., u $\mapsto$ r belongs to the relation *hasTheRole*). If these preconditions are satisfied, then the revocation of the assignment depends on special cases (i.e., values) of both *hasTheRole* relation and the role r. For example,

Figure 8. The B specification for the operation of assigning a user to a role

```
assignUserToRole (u, r)  ≜
   PRE
      u ∈ USER ∧
      ((u ∈ staff ∧ r ∈ sod1) ∨ ((u ∈ studentGuardian ∨ u ∈ students) ∧
         r ∈ sod2)) ∧
      u ↦ r ∉ hasTheRole

   THEN
      IF    (r ∈ sod1 ∧ r = headteacher)
      THEN
         hasTheRole := hasTheRole ∪ {u ↦ headteacher} ∪ {u ↦ teacher}
      ELSIF (r ∈ sod1 ∧ r = headmaster ∧
                card(hasTheRole⁻¹[{headmaster}]) < 2)
      THEN
         hasTheRole := hasTheRole ∪ {u ↦ r} ||
         card(hasTheRole⁻¹[{headmaster}]):= card(hasTheRole⁻¹[{headmaster}]) + 1
      ELSE
         hasTheRole := hasTheRole ∪ {u ↦ r}
      END
   END;
```

- If the user *u* is assigned to the roles of *headteacher* and *teacher* (i.e., the case of role hierarchy), then we remove these assignments,
- If the role is *headmaster,* then we remove the link between the user *u* and the role *headmaster* and decrease the current number of headmaster's assignments by one,
- Otherwise (i.e., no special values), then we remove the link between the user *u* and the role *r*.

Figure 9 shows the complete B specification for the operation of revoking user assignment.

EVALUATION AND MODEL TESTING

Validating and verifying software is commonly performed using code inspection and testing (Hansen & Leuschel, 2012). However, discovering bugs becomes more complex when testing large systems with a large number of system executions. Formal specifications and verification enable considering all situations and identifying all possible bugs.

Two key approaches for formal verification exist of model checking and theorem proving (Boulanger, 2012). Model checking is an automated approach for verifying the correctness and consistency of a model. The *proB* tool is a B machines-supported tool that verifies the consistency of B specifications automatically (Hansen & Leuschel, 2012). The core idea of model checking is that all the machine's nodes (states) are

Figure 9. The B specification for the operation of revoking user assignment

```
revokeUserAssignment (u, r) ≜
    PRE
        u ∈ USER ∧
        r ∈ ROLES ∧
        u ↦ r ∈ hasTheRole

    THEN
        IF    hasTheRole[{u}] = {headteacher, teacher}
        THEN
            hasTheRole := hasTheRole - {u ↦ headteacher} - {u ↦ teacher}
        ELSIF  r = headmaster
        THEN
            hasTheRole := hasTheRole - {u ↦ r}  ||
            card(hasTheRole⁻¹[{headmaster}]):= card(hasTheRole⁻¹[{headmaster}]) - 1
        ELSE
            hasTheRole := hasTheRole - {u ↦ r}
        END
    END;
```

visited to examine the existence of potential bugs. The *proB* tool generates and graphically displays, if needed, counter-examples when a violation of the invariant is discovered (Attiogbe, 2009). Theorem proving (or proof obligations), on the other hand, constructs a *mathematical proof* representing that a statement is true (Boulanger, 2012). Since formal proofs do not use natural languages, they are expressed symbolically, such as with a proof language. For abstract machines to be correct and consistent, many proof obligations must be demonstrated, including the four clauses of an abstract machine (i.e., PROPERTIES, INVARIANT, INITIALISATION, and OPERATIONS), whereas there is a separate proof obligation for each operation in a machine (Mentré et al., 2012).

Testing the RBAC Model Using proB Tool

In the following, we use the *proB* tool as a model checker for testing the correctness of our RBAC model and perform the following:

- Test the process of registering users and UA.
- Test cardinality constraints and RH.
- Test the operation of revoking user assignment.

First, we initiate our system by registering users representing one student and one teacher. We see how the defined SoD constraints work when assigning users to roles by monitoring the state of the invariant once an operation is performed. If the performance of any operation results in the invariant state code '*ok*', representing no violation (as appears on the left-hand side of the *proB* tool window), then the machine's state, at least at the current time, is correct. Figures 10 through 13 show the registration of a student 'USER1' and a teacher 'USER2', and the possible roles to be assigned to each. The figures also illustrate the machine's state before and after applying the correct assignments.

To test the cardinality constraints, we register a school manager (e.g., *USER4*) into the system and assign it to the role *headmaster* (see Figure 14). According to the B code of assigning a user to a role outlined in Section 8, the system should accept (at maximum) two assignments to the *headmaster* role, and the role will be still available in the sod_1 set even when two assignments are established. However, the cardinality condition defined in the operation will block additional assignments. This condition represents a significant update to our previous B specification of the *user assignment* operation in Al-hadhrami et al. (2016), wherein we specified only one user for the role *headmaster* after which the role becomes unavailable until the assignment is revoked.

Figure 10. Registering a student and the roles available for assignment

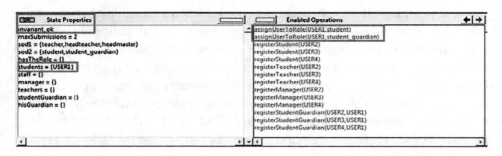

Figure 11. The student is assigned to role 'student'

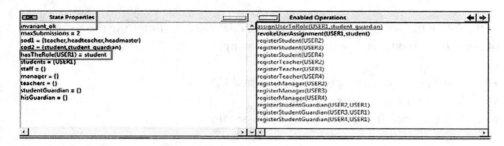

Figure 12. Registering a teacher and the roles available for assignment

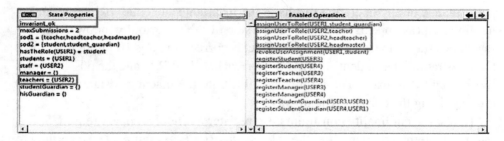

To test the role hierarchy, we register a new teacher (*USER5*) into the system and assign it to the role *headteacher*, instead of the *teacher* role, after which the user automatically inherits the *teacher* role. As a result, the user maintains two roles of *headteacher* and *teacher* (see Figures 15 and 16).

Figure 13. The teacher is assigned to role 'teacher'

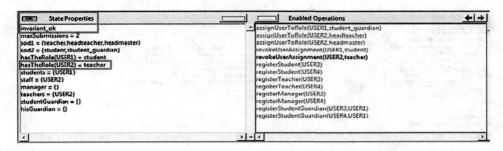

Figure 14. Registering a manager and the roles available for assignment

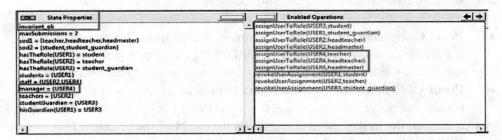

Figure 15. Registering a head teacher and the roles available for assignment

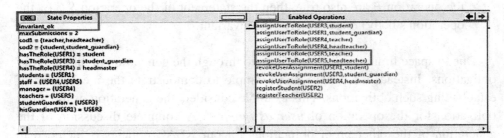

Theorem Proving: Proof Obligations

In addition to the validation process in the previous section, a mathematical proof (i.e., proof obligations) can be constructed to demonstrate the correctness and consistency of the RBAC model. According to the B theory, for the RBAC specifications to be correct and consistent, multiple proof obligations must be satisfied represented by the four clauses of the machine. Since the PROPERTIES clause is not included in the current specification of our RBAC model (although there is a representation

Figure 16. The head teacher inherits the role 'teacher'

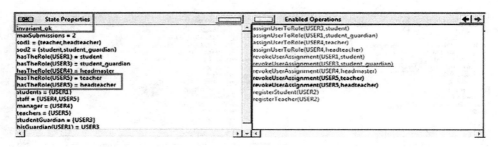

of this clause in the complete specification of the EMS system itself), the proof obligations remain only for the following clauses:

- **Proof Obligation for Invariant:** Expressed as $(Prp \Rightarrow \exists \, v. \, I)$, which means that under the assumption that Prp (PROPERTIES clause, if found[1(1)]) is true, then the invariant I is satisfied by at least one of the machine's variables v.
- **Proof Obligation for Initialisation:** Expressed as $(Prp \Rightarrow [Init] \, I)$, which means that under the assumption that Prp (PROPERTIES clause, if found) is true, then the initialisation clause $Init$ must establish the invariant I.
- **Proof Obligation for Operations:** For each operation in the machine, there is a separate proof obligation expressed as $(I \wedge P \Rightarrow [S] \, I)$, which means that under the assumption that invariant I is true and the preconditions of the operation P are also true, then the statement of the operation S (i.e., the operation's body) must preserve the invariant I.

Due to space limitations, we will not go through the generation of all the proof obligations. Instead, we choose one example to demonstrate the mechanism of establishing such obligations. This example considers the generation of the proof obligation for the operation of *user assignment*. A complete discussion of the generation of the other proof obligations for our RBAC policies is included in previous work (Al-hadhrami et al., 2016), which exhaustively demonstrates and mathematically proves the correctness of these policies.

Proof Obligation for the Operation of User Assignment (UA)

Recalling the *assignUserToRole* operation in Section 8, and the expression $I \wedge P \Rightarrow [S] \, I$ for the proof obligation, the statement S (the operation's body) that must preserve the invariant I has three cases:

- If r belongs to sod_1, and r is *headteacher*, then we apply the role hierarchy (i.e., assign the user u to both the *headteacher* and *teacher* roles).
- If r belongs to sod_1, and r is *headmaster*, and the cardinality constraint (of *headmaster*) is satisfied (i.e., less than two), then we assign the user u to the role *headmaster*.
- Otherwise (i.e., no specific case for r), then we assign the user u to the role r.

We only work on the second case (the cardinality constraint case) as an example to show the obligation of the operation when assigning a user (say, Sarah) to the role *headmaster*. The expression $I \wedge P \Rightarrow [S] I$ is then replaced by the corresponding statements as

$$
\begin{aligned}
&I \ \wedge \\
&\quad u \in USER \ \wedge \\
&\quad ((u \in staff \ \wedge \ r \in sod_1) \ \vee \ ((u \in \\
&studentGuardian \ \vee \ u \in students) \ \wedge \ r \in sod_2)) \ \wedge \\
&\quad u \mapsto r \notin hasTheRole \ \wedge \\
&\quad (r \in sod_1 \ \wedge \ r = headmaster \ \wedge \\
&card(hasTheRole^{-1}[\{headmaster\}]) \ < 2) \ \Rightarrow \\
&\quad [hasTheRole := hasTheRole \ \cup \ \{u \\
&\mapsto r\} \ | \ | \\
&\quad card(hasTheRole^{-1}[\{headmaster\}]) := \\
&card(hasTheRole^{-1}[\{headmaster\}]) \ + \ 1]. \ I
\end{aligned}
$$

Where I represents all the predicates we defined for the INVARIANT clause.

Suppose we have the following information in the database, and the system's administrator wants to assign the user "Sarah" to the role "headmaster" (here, u = Sarah, and r = headmaster):

$sod_1 = \{teacher, headteacher, headmaster\}$

$sod_2 = \{student, student\_guardian\}$

staff = \{*Mary, Sarah, Fatma*\}

hasTheRole = \{(*Mary, headmaster*), (*Fatma, headteacher*), (*Fatma, teacher*)\}

Since all preconditions of the operation are satisfied, including the cardinality constraint of the *headmaster* role (i.e., < 2), it is possible then to assign Sara to the role *headmaster*. Accordingly, we would have the following information updated:

hasTheRole $= \{(Mary, headmaster), (Fatma, headteacher) (Fatma, teacher), (Sarah, headmaster)\}$

card(hasTheRole^{-1}[$\{headmaster\}$]) $= 2$

Obtaining this information clearly preserves the invariant clause. In other words, no violations are made to the following: the relation *hasTheRole*, values of the sod_1 and sod_2 sets, separation of duties policy, cardinality constraint and role hierarchy policy, proving the correctness of our specification for the operation of user assignment.

CONCLUSION

Incremental development of software can create inconsistencies in access control policies and non-compliance with general security policies, such as separation of duties. We proposed the use of the B method to formalise and evaluate the security of an electronic marking system operating under role-based access control policies. The case study demonstrated that this approach enables identification of inconsistencies and weaknesses in role-based access control policies caused by incremental software development suggesting that formal methods can preserve security policies.

Future directions include refining the B specifications of the model towards obtaining an implementable policy, i.e., low-level security rules. We will study the impact of the refinement on maintaining the coherence and consistency of the RBAC policy. We also plan to incorporate other models of access control into the specification of the EMS system to understand their effect and, consequently, if the security of the system improves facilitating its usage under more hostile environments, for example, as a mobile application running over untrusted client devices.

REFERENCES

Abrial, J. R. (1996). *The B Book*. Cambridge University Press. doi:10.1017/CBO9780511624162

Ahn, G. J., & Hu, H. (2007, June). Towards realizing a formal RBAC model in real systems. *Proc. of the 12th ACM symposium on Access control models and technologies*, 215-224. 10.1145/1266840.1266875

Al-Hadhrami, N., Aziz, B., & Othmane, L. (2016). An Incremental B-Model for RBAC-Controlled Electronic Marking System. *International Journal of Secure Software Engineering*, 7(2), 37–64. doi:10.4018/IJSSE.2016040103

Attiogbe, C. (2009). Tool-Assisted Multi-Facet Analysis of Formal Specifications (Using Alelier-B and ProB). *Proc. IASTED Conf. on Software Engineering*, 85-90.

Boulanger, J. (2012). *Industrial Use of Formal Methods: Formal Verification.* London, UK: ISTE Ltd and John Wiley & Sons, Inc. doi:10.1002/9781118561829

Cansell, D., & Méry, D. (2012). Foundations of the B method. Computing and Informatics, 22(3-4), 221-256.

Chae, J. H., & Shiri, N. (2007). Formalization of RBAC policy with object class hierarchy. *Proc. Information Security Practice and Experience*, 162-176.

Clarke, E. M., & Wing, J. M. (1996). Formal methods: State of the art and future directions. *ACM Computing Surveys*, 28(4), 626–643. doi:10.1145/242223.242257

Drouineaud, M., Bortin, M., Torrini, P., & Sohr, K. (Sep. 2004). A First Step Towards Formal Verification of Security Policy Properties for RBAC. *Proc. of the 4th IEEE International Conference on Quality Software*, 60-67. 10.1109/QSIC.2004.1357945

Ferraiolo, D., Cugini, J., & Kuhn, D. R. (1995, December). Role-based access control (RBAC): Features and motivations. *Proceedings of 11th annual computer security application conference*, 241-48.

Fraser, M. D., Kumar, K., & Vaishnavi, V. K. (1994). Strategies for incorporating formal specifications in software development. *Communications of the ACM*, 37(10), 74–87. doi:10.1145/194313.194399

Hallerstede, S. (2008, September). On the purpose of Event-B proof obligations. In *International Conference on Abstract State Machines, B and Z* (pp. 125-138). Springer.10.1007/978-3-540-87603-8_11

Hansen, D., & Leuschel, M. (2012, January). Translating TLA+ to B for Validation with ProB. In Integrated Formal Methods (pp. 24-38). Springer Berlin Heidelberg.

Hu, H., & Ahn, G. (2008, June). Enabling verification and conformance testing for access control model. *Proc. of the 13th ACM symposium on Access control models and technologies*, 195-204. 10.1145/1377836.1377867

Jha, S., Li, N., Tripunitara, M., Wang, Q., & Winsborough, W. (2008). Towards formal verification of role-based access control policies. *IEEE Transactions on Dependable and Secure Computing*, 5(4), 242–255. doi:10.1109/TDSC.2007.70225

Leuschel, M., & Butler, M. J. (2003). ProB: A Model Checker for B. *Lecture Notes in Computer Science, 2805*, 855–874. 10.1007/978-3-540-45236-2_46

Lockhart, J., Purdy, C., & Wilsey, P. A. (2017, June). The use of automated theorem proving for error analysis and removal in safety critical embedded system specifications. In *Aerospace and Electronics Conference (NAECON), 2017 IEEE National* (pp. 358-361). IEEE.10.1109/NAECON.2017.8268802

Mentré, D., Marché, C., Filliâtre, J. C., & Asuka, M. (2012). Discharging proof obligations from Atelier B using multiple automated provers. *Proc. Third International Conference, ABZ*, 238-251. 10.1007/978-3-642-30885-7_17

Poniszewska-Maranda, A. (2005, June). *Role engineering of information system using extended RBAC model. In 14th IEEE International Workshops on Enabling Technologies* (pp. 154–159). Infrastructure for Collaborative Enterprise.

Ray, I., Li, N., France, R., & Kim, D. K. (2004, June). Using UML to visualize role-based access control constraints. In *Proceedings of the ninth ACM symposium on Access control models and technologies* (pp. 115-124). ACM. 10.1145/990036.990054

Sandhu, R. S., Coyne, E. J., Feinstein, H. L., & Youman, C. E. (1996). Role-based access control models. *Computer, 29*(2), 38–47. doi:10.1109/2.485845

Schneider, S. (2001). *The b-method: an Introduction*. Basingstoke, UK: Palgrave.

Sohr, K., Drouineaud, M., Ahn, G. J., & Gogolla, M. (2008). Analyzing and managing role-based access control policies. *Knowledge and Data Engineering. IEEE Transactions on, 20*(7), 924–939.

Strembeck, M., & Neumann, G. (2004). An Integrated Approach to Engineer and Enforce Context Constraints in RBAC Environments. *Proc. of the 8th ACM Symposium on Access Control Models and Technologies (SACMAT 2003), 3*, 392–427. 10.1145/1015040.1015043

Yu, S., & Brewster, J. (2012). Formal specification and implementation of RBAC model with SOD. *Journal of Software, 7*(4), 870–877. doi:10.4304/jsw.7.4.870-877

Yuan, C., He, Y., He, J., & Zhou, Z. (2006). *A Verifiable Formal Specification for RBAC Model with Constraints of Separation of Duty*. Academic Press.

ENDNOTE

[1]   It should be noted here that, while some B machines do not include the properties clause (i.e., no properties are defined), it is still valid to generate proof obligations for the other clauses (i.e., invariant and initialisation) by only proving the satisfaction of the other variables (components) in the given proof formula. For example, the proof obligation for the invariant clause is established when it is provable that the invariant I is satisfied by at least one of the machine's variables v.

Chapter 6
Designing Secure Software by Testing Application of Security Patterns

Takanori Kobashi
Waseda University, Japan

Haruhiko Kaiya
Kanagawa University, Japan

Hironori Washizaki
Waseda University, Japan & National Institute of Informatics, Japan & SYSTEM INFORMATION Co Ltd, Japan & eXmotion, Japan

Takao Okubo
Institute of Information Security, Japan

Yoshiaki Fukazawa
Waseda University, Japan

Nobukazu Yoshioka
National Institute of Informatics, Japan

ABSTRACT

Simply confirming potential threats and vulnerabilities in an early stage of the development process (e.g., the requirement or design phase) is insufficient because software developers are not necessarily security experts. Additionally, even if the software design considers security at an early stage, whether the software actually satisfies the security requirements must be confirmed. To realize secure design, the authors propose an application to design software systems with verification of security patterns using model testing. The method provides extended security patterns, which include requirement- and design-level patterns as well as a new designing and model testing process that uses these patterns. Once developers specify threats and vulnerabilities in the target system in an early stage of development, the method can verify whether the security patterns are properly applied and assess if the vulnerabilities are resolved.

DOI: 10.4018/978-1-5225-6313-6.ch006

INTRODUCTION

Security has become a critical issue as more businesses operate on open networks and distributed platforms. Software must be supported with security measures (Maruyama, Washizaki, & Yoshioka, 2008). Because threats and vulnerabilities within a system cannot be sufficiently identified during the early development stage, security measures must be addressed in every phase of software development from requirements engineering to design, implementation, testing, and deployment. However, creating software with adequate security measures is extremely difficult due not only to the vast number of security concerns, but also the fact that not all software engineers are security specialists.

Patterns, which are reusable packages that incorporate expert knowledge, represent frequently recurring structures, behaviors, activities, processes, or "things" during the software development process. Many security patterns and abstract security patterns have been proposed to resolve security issues (Buschmann, Fernandez-Buglioni, Schumacher, Sommerlad, & Hybertson, 2006) (Lai, Nagappan, & Steel, 2005) (Fernandez, et al., 2018) (Fernandez, et al., 2016) (Fernandez, Washizaki, & Yoshioka, 2016) (Fernandez, Yoshioka, & Washizaki, 2015a) (Fernandez, Yoshioka, & Washizaki, 2015b) (Fernandez, Yoshioka, & Washizaki, 2014) (Fernandez, et al., 2014)(Fernandez, Yoshioka, & Washizaki, 2008). For example, Buschmann et al. (2006) developed 25 design-level security patterns. By referencing these patterns, developers can efficiently realize software with a high security level.

Security patterns, which are a level of abstraction, encapsulate security-related problems and solutions that recur in certain contexts for secure software system development and operations (Maruyama, Washizaki, & Yoshioka, 2008) (Washizaki, 2017) (Fernandez, et al., 2010) (Nhlabatsi, et al., 2010). Since the late 1990's, almost 500 security patterns have been proposed.

Although UML-based models are widely used for design, especially for model-driven software development, whether patterns are applied correctly is often not verified (Maruyama, Washizaki, & Yoshioka, 2008). The lack of systematic guidelines with respect to applications may result in inappropriately applied security patterns. In particular, developers can instantiate security patterns at the wrong places with the incorrect structure. Additionally, properly applying a security pattern does not guarantee that threats and vulnerabilities are resolved. These issues may result in security damage.

To address the aforementioned problems, we propose a method to design and verify security patterns using model testing. Our method extends existing security patterns, formalizes the security and pattern requirements, confirms that the patterns are properly applied, and assesses whether vulnerabilities are actually resolved.

Then we propose a new testing process to verify the applied patterns and a tool to support model testing.

Our method does not fully automate all required steps. For example, pattern selection and combination are not automated. Moreover, our method is not sufficient for secure design since it verifies only that security patterns are applied as formalized in security and pattern requirements. Patterns may be instantiated in different ways, and the presence of threats not addressed by the security patterns cannot be verified. Nevertheless, we believe that our method can mitigate the risk of instantiation of security patterns at inappropriate locations with incorrect structures by guiding and testing security pattern applications to confirm that they are appropriately applied.

Our method employs USE (Büttnera, Gogollaa & Richtersb, 2007), which is a tool in UML-based simulation environments that runs tests to specify and verify information systems based on subsets of UML and OCL (Kleppe & Warmer, 1999). OCL is a semiformal language that can express constraints for various software artifacts as well as specify constraints and other expressions in modeling languages. USE was initially implemented in Java at Bremen University (Germany) to evaluate OCL expressions via simulations. To verify OCL constraints, developers can create an instance of a class in USE and then input the value as a test case.

Our method initially executes test scripts in a design model that does not consider security in USE (Test First). These test scripts are generated automatically. Then vulnerabilities to threats identified in the requirement stage are detected. Next security patterns are applied. Then tests are re-executed to confirm that the vulnerabilities are resolved. In our secure design method, we use OCL expressions as the requirements and verify whether the target model satisfies these requirements.

Our method provides three major contributions:

- Newly extended security patterns using Object Constraint Language (OCL) expressions, which include requirement- and design-level patterns;
- A new model-based design and testing process using Test-Driven Development (TDD) as the foundation to design and verify that patterns are applied correctly and that vulnerabilities are resolved using these extended patterns;
- A tool to support pattern applications by creating a script to execute model testing automatically[1].

This chapter is organized as follows. The background section describes the background and problems with security software development. The design method section details our new method, which integrates security patterns. The design process section uses an example to apply our pattern to an example Web system. The threats to validity section describes internal and external threats. The related works section describes previous studies. Finally, the conclusion and future work section summarizes this chapter.

BACKGROUND

This section overviews security requirement patterns (SRPs) and security design patterns (SDPs). In addition, we describe problems in secure software development with security patterns by showing a motivating example.

SRPs

SRPs identify assets, threats, and countermeasures (Okubo, Kaiya & Yoshioka, 2012). A security pattern is reusable as a security package and includes security knowledge, allowing software developers to design secure systems like security experts. Various types of security patterns exist. For example, SRPs are used at the requirement level, while SDPs are applied at the design stage level. SRPs consist of Context, Problem, Solution, and Structure, which are summarized as follows:

- **Context:** The situation of the pattern and system environments
- **Problem:** The issue that the target function aims to address
- **Solution:** The security goal that the applied pattern should satisfy
- **Structure:** The format to describe the assets, threats and countermeasures.

Our method adopts the Misuse case with the Assets and Security Goal (MASG) model (Okubo, Taguchi & Yoshioka, 2009), which is an extension of the misuse case (Andreas & Sindre, 2000) to provide the structure of assets, threats, and countermeasures at the requirement level. The MASG model can model attackers, attacks, and countermeasures as well as normal users and their requirements (Figure 1). The MASG model consists of the following:

- **Data Assets:** Assets to be protected
- **Use case Assets:** Functions related to assets
- **Security Goals:** Reasons to protect assets

Identifying assets improves threat recognition, while identifying security goals determines what security measures are important in the target system. The MASG model also contains a security requirement analysis process. First, system assets are identified and security goals are defined. Next, threats that may violate the goals are defined and security countermeasures against these threats are determined (Okubo,

Kaiya & Yoshioka, 2012). Finally, security countermeasures that satisfy the security goals are confirmed.

For example, a SRP named "Payment" (Okubo, Kaiya & Yoshioka, 2012) can be described as follows.

- **Context:** It is necessary to provides a function, which provides a payment or makes a purchase by credit card, E-money, and so on.
- **Problem:** For the assets such as "Credit card info.", "Personal info" and "Password", there are various threats and misuse cases such as "Steal info." and "Unintended use".
- **Solution:** The countermeasure for the threats are "Identification and authentication (I&A)" and "Prevent CSRF".
- **Structure:** Figure 1 shows a typical structure of the assets, threats, and countermeasures for the pattern under a context of a shopping website. The function "make a payment" has several assets, which could be threatened. In the model, "Disclosure" is a threat for "make a payment", while "personal information" is an asset. "Spoofing", "Elevation of privilege", and "SQL Injection" enable Disclosure. In addition, countermeasures such as "I&A (Identification and Authentication)", "Authorization", or "Input and Data Validation" are effective to mitigate threats. Although the MASG model helps comprehensively detect security issues at the requirement level, it does not indicate whether the identified threats exist in the software system.

SDPs

An SDP is an established technique to satisfy the security specifications. The pattern descriptions can be reused in multiple systems. An SDP includes Name, Context, Problem, Solution, Structure, Dynamics, Consequences, and See Also. Usually, SDPs provide concrete design-level solutions for the countermeasures stated in the SRPs. Connections with the corresponding SRPs can be established by the descriptions of See Also and other sections such as Context and Problem.

- **Context:** The situation in which the pattern is applied and the functional design specifications that require countermeasures
- **Problem:** The issue that the target function aims to address
- **Solution:** The objectives for security countermeasures
- **Structure:** The framework of the countermeasures
- **Dynamics:** The behavior of the countermeasures
- **Consequences:** How threats are mitigated by countermeasures.

Figure 1. Sample MASG model for a shopping website

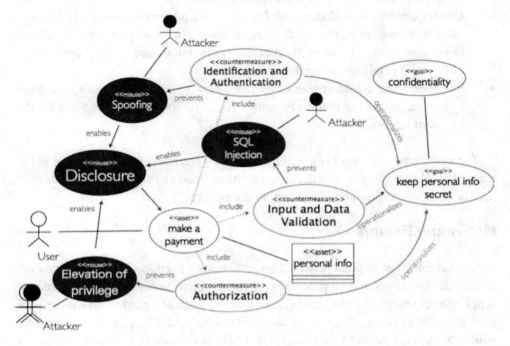

- **See Also:** Related patterns, including corresponding SRPs.

As examples of SDPs, Buschmann et al. (2006) proposed 25 design-level security patterns. One of which is the Role Based Access Control (RBAC) pattern, which is a representative pattern for access control. RBAC demonstrates how to assign precise access rights to roles in an environment where access to computing resources must be controlled to preserve confidentiality and the availability requirements (Buschmann, et al., 2006) (Okubo, Kaiya & Yoshioka, 2012). Below RBAC is used as an example (Priebe, et al., 2004):

- **Context:** Any environment where control access of computing resources is needed and where users can be classified according to their jobs or tasks.
- **Problem:** Permissions for subjects accessing protected objects have to be described in a suitable way. A central authority should be responsible to grant authorization. Furthermore, a convenient administration should be guaranteed for a large number of subjects and objects. The principle of least privilege should be supported.
- **Solution:** Assign users to roles and give rights to these roles so they can perform their tasks.

- **Structure:** Figure 2 shows the structure.
- **Consequences:** Introducing roles reduces the administrative effort because there is no need to assign rights to individuals. The structuring of roles allows larger groups to be handled. By means of the session concept, implementation of the least privilege principle is supported.
- **See Also:** The RBAC pattern describes how to design a security measure to realize one of the countermeasures (i.e., Authorization) identified by the Payment pattern.

Figure 3 shows the process to apply the RBAC pattern to a design model in the form of UML. Developers usually examine items such as Problem and Solution to decide the applicability and how to apply the pattern.

Motivating Example

As an example of an applied pattern, Figure 4 shows a portion of "make a payment" of a UML class diagram that processes payment on the Web. An SDP alone cannot support the development lifecycle because it lacks systematic guidelines with respect to applications (Dong, Peng & Zhao, 2008). Consequently, formally describing which rules must be verified is difficult (Abramov, Shoval & Sturm, 2009). In addition, most SDPs do not specifically mention systematic guidelines until the relations with Security Requirements are defined. Under the present conditions, even if developers intend to apply SDPs such as RBAC (Figure 2) to a structural model (Figure 4), a security measure may not mitigate an identified threat. Additionally, the appropriateness of the applied pattern to the model and the pattern's ability to resolve vulnerabilities are often inadequately verified. Consequently, these situations may lead to inappropriately applying patterns and unresolved vulnerabilities.

Figure 2. Structure of RBAC

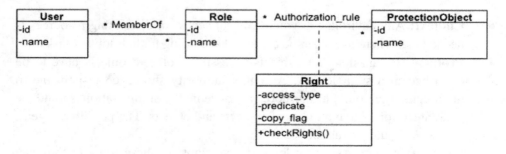

Figure 3. Application of an SDP

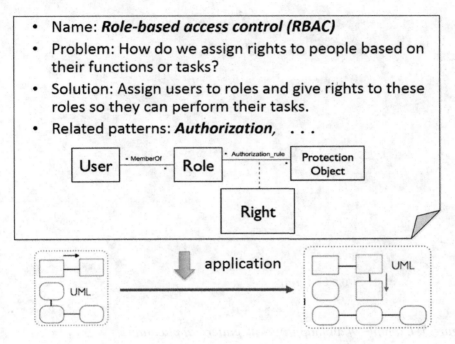

Figures 5 shows an example where RBAC is incorrectly applied to the model shown in Figure 4. The NG design implies that the access right depends on the user instead of the role. Moreover, the appropriate functional behavior of the access control cannot be confirmed until the design model is tested. Thus, the applied measures may not resolve threats and vulnerabilities.

SECURE DESIGN METHOD

In this section, we explain our method. Firstly, we describe the process of our secure design method. Secondly, we show examples of Ex-SRP and Ex-SDP. Finally, we apply our method to a purchasing system on the Web as an example.

Process of Our Design Method

Figure 6 overviews our method. We prepare extended SRPs (Ex-SRPs) and the corresponding extended SDPs (Ex-SDPs) for well-known SRSs and SDPs. If necessary, security experts prepare more Ex-SRPs and their corresponding Ex-SDPs. These new SRPs and SDPs are expansions of existing ones. They can be used to

Figure 4. "Make a payment" portion of a class diagram for payment processing

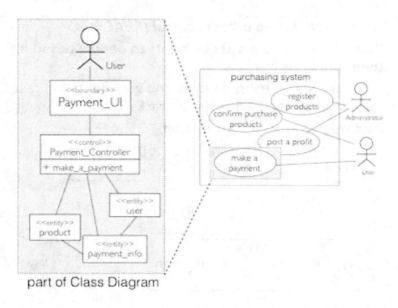

Figure 5. Example of an inappropriate pattern application

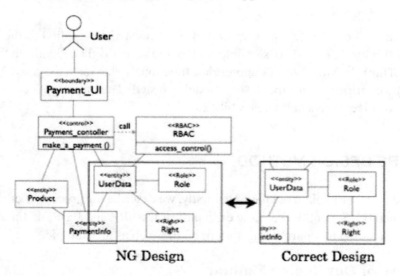

confirm the presence of vulnerabilities in the target model and whether the applied patterns are appropriately applied.

Our method involves six steps (Figure 6):

1. Determine the threats and countermeasures in the system. Ex-SRPs identify the types of assets, threats, and countermeasures present while considering the functional requirements and their associations at the requirement level.
2. Execute a test to verify that the input model satisfies the Security Requirements. A design class diagram, which does not consider security, is used to execute tests to verify whether the Security Requirements (in OCL) are satisfied. Whether the input model satisfies the Security Requirements can be confirmed at this the requirement stage.
3. Select Ex-SDPs. After confirming that the target model does not satisfy the Security Requirements, Ex-SDPs related to countermeasures of Ex-SRP are selected.
4. Set Security Design Requirements using Pattern Requirements. Security Design Requirements, which are combinations of each Pattern Requirement, as requirements that the model must satisfy.
5. Apply Ex-SDPs. Specifically, the structure and behavior of Ex-SDPs are applied to an input model that does not consider security by binding pattern elements to the model based on stereotypes.
6. Execute tests to verify the appropriateness of each Ex-SDP (i.e., confirm whether the Security Design Requirements are satisfied).

In this chapter, we adopt the UML notation (Bondareva & Milutinovich, 2014) to describe the target system because UML-based models are common in system design. For example, the UML notation is typically used to describe the structure and behavior of SDPs. Additionally, the static structure and dynamic behavior the system are represented by a class diagram and communication diagram, respectively. To separate concerns with an application, we describe a system with three types of classes: boundaries, controls, and entities. Boundaries are objects that interface with system actors. Entities are objects representing system data, while controls are objects that mediate between boundaries and entities (Pilgrim, 2013).

Ex-SRPs and Ex-SDPs

Figure 7 shows the overall structures of Ex-SRPs and Ex-SDPs. In addition to existing SRPs and SDPs, extended patterns contain Security Requirements and Pattern Requirements, respectively. Ex-SDP describes how to design security measures to realize countermeasures identified by Ex-SRPs. For example, RBAC, Multilevel

Figure 6. Process of our method

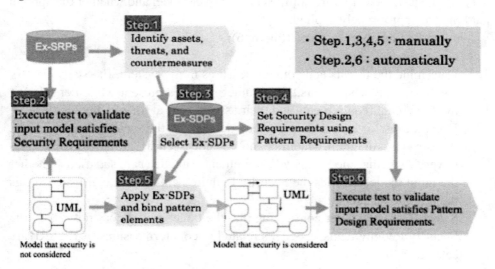

Figure 7. Overall structures of Ex-SRPs and Ex-SDPs

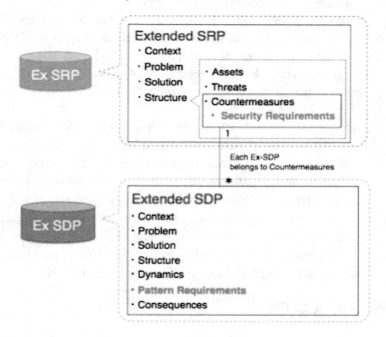

Security, and Reference Monitor (Buschmann et al, 2006) are design patterns related to Authorization. Below we briefly describe Ex-SRPs and Ex-SDPs.

Ex-SRPs are organized by the following items. An example is given in the Example of Design Process section.

- **Context, Problem and Solution:** These are the same as those of SRPs.
- **Structure:** In addition to the assets, threats, and countermeasure, Security Requirements that each countermeasure must satisfy are addressed. Security Requirements are represented in the decision table and the OCL statement form. If a model does not satisfy the Security Requirements, then the measures do not remove vulnerabilities and the system may contain threats. In TDD, these requirements represent test cases that must be satisfied.

Herein we assume that there are nine types of countermeasures: Input and Data Validation, Identification and Authentication, Authorization, Configuration Management, Sensitive Data, Session Management, Cryptography, Exception Management, and Auditing and Logging. These countermeasures can be referenced in the Security Frame Category (Mackman & Maher, 2007), which is Microsoft's systematic categorization of threats and vulnerabilities. We assume these nine categories are typical countermeasures at the requirement level because they represent critical areas where security mistakes are most common. Developers can use these categories to divide the system architecture for further analysis and to help identify application vulnerabilities. Table 1 details each countermeasure.

Ex-SDPs are organized by the following items. Connections with the corresponding Ex-SRPs can be established by the descriptions of See Also and other sections such as Context and Problem.

- **Context, Problem, Solution, Structure, Consequences and See Also:** These are the same as those of SDPs.
- **Pattern Requirements:** To meet the requirements (constraints), the structure and behavior must be satisfied when a pattern is applied. If a model does not satisfy the Pattern Requirements, then the pattern is applied inappropriately.

For example, Figure 8 shows the structure and behavior of RBAC as an example of Ex-SDPs. In our method, stereotypes are used to represent pattern elements. In RBAC, stereotypes, such as <<RBAC>>, <<User Data >>, <<Role>>, and <<Right>>, are pattern elements. When developers apply a pattern, the pattern elements are bound based on stereotypes. In Figure 8, "Subject Controller" using the RBAC controller behaves as access control. To employ RBAC, if rights are not specified in the role that an actor belongs, this system assumes that the actor does

Table 1. Explanation of each countermeasure adopted from (Santos, 2017; Mackman & Maher, 2007)

Countermeasure	Description
Input / Data Validation	How do you know that the input your application receives is valid and safe? Input validation refers to how your application filters, scrubs or rejects input before additional processing.
Identification / Authentication	Who are you? Authentication is the process where an entity proves the identity of another entity, typically through credentials, such as a username and password.
Authorisation	What can you do? Authorisation is how your application provides access controls for resources and operations.
Sensitive Data	Who does your application run as? Which databases does it connect to? How is your application administered? How are these settings secured? Configuration management refers to how your application handles these operational issues.
Session Management	How does your application handle sensitive data? Sensitive data refers to how your application handles any data that must be protected either in memory, over the network or in persistent stores.
Cryptography	How are you keeping secrets (confidentiality)? How are you tamper-proofing your data or libraries (integrity)? How are you providing seeds for random values that must be cryptographically strong? Cryptography refers to how your application enforces confidentiality and integrity.
Exception Management	When a method call in your application fails, what does your application do? How much do you reveal? Do you return friendly error information to end users? Do you pass valuable exception information back to the caller? Does your application fail gracefully?
Auditing and Logging	Who did what and when? Auditing and logging refers to how your application records security-related events.

Figure 8. Structure and behavior of RBAC

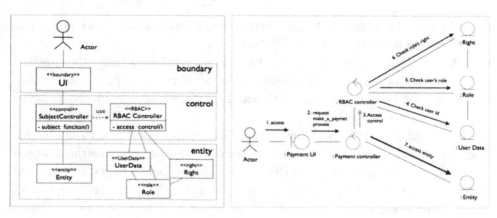

not have permission to access. Hence, the actor cannot execute processes requiring Authorization. This security capability is realized because this pattern satisfies the Pattern Requirements of RBAC.

Table 2 and Figure 9 show the Pattern Requirements of RBAC in the decision table and the OCL statement form, respectively, for "if rights are given in a role that an actor belongs, then the actor has access permission". The actor can access the asset. The decision table (Table 2) is prepared for ease of understanding of the corresponding Pattern Requirements since the OCL expressions can be difficult for developers to comprehend.

Table 2. Pattern Requirements of RBAC (conceptual)

		1	2
Conditions	rights are given in <<Role>> which an <<User_Data>> belongs	Yes	No
Actions	<<Actor>> is considered to have access permission.	×	
	<<Actor>> is not considered to have access permission.		×
	execute process requiring access control.	×	
	not execute process requiring access control.		×

Figure 9. Pattern Requirements of RBAC (OCL)

```
context subject_controller
 inv access_control:
  if self.RBAC.Right->exists(p |
        p.right = true and
        p.role_id = p.Role.id and
        p.role_id = p.Role.User_Data.role_id )
 then
     self.UI.Actor.right = true and self.subject_function = true
 else
     self.UI.Actor.right = false and self.subject_function = false
 endif
```

Figure 10 shows the test script to verify whether the model-applied pattern satisfies the Pattern Requirements. Developers provide concrete test cases to the target model in our tool. Our tool outputs the test script, which is then translated to execute a test in USE. Both the Security and Pattern Requirements can be verified simultaneously using an OCL statement. The former determines the presence of vulnerabilities at the design level, while the latter confirms if the pattern is appropriately applied. In our method, appropriate application means that security patterns are applied as formalized in the security and pattern requirements.

EXAMPLE OF THE DESIGN PROCESS

To confirm that our method realizes secure design, we applied it to a purchasing system on the Web. We assumed that Figure 1 shows the assets, threats, and

Figure 10. Example of a test script

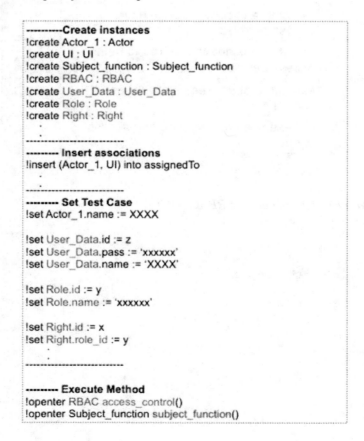

```
----------Create instances
!create Actor_1 : Actor
!create UI : UI
!create Subject_function : Subject_function
!create RBAC : RBAC
!create User_Data : User_Data
!create Role : Role
!create Right : Right


--------------------------
--------- Insert associations
!insert (Actor_1, UI) into assignedTo


--------------------------
--------- Set Test Case
!set Actor_1.name := XXXX

!set User_Data.id := z
!set User_Data.pass := 'xxxxxx'
!set User_Data.name := 'XXXX'

!set Role.id := y
!set Role.name := 'xxxxxx'

!set Right.id := x
!set Right.role_id := y


--------------------------
--------- Execute Method
!openter RBAC access_control()
!openter Subject_function subject_function()
```

countermeasures using the MASG model. We initially identified and modeled the assets, threats, and countermeasures in the system by referring to the Ex-SRPs of the requirement called commercial transaction on the Web. Next, we executed tests of the model that does not consider security (Figure 11) to verify whether the vulnerabilities to threats identified by Ex-SRPs are detected. Table 3 explains each element in this model.

The tests reveal that the system does not have a function to check the condition to execute the "make a payment" process. In other words, even if this user is not a regular user, the process may still be executed.

After confirming that the vulnerabilities exist in the input model, we set the Security Design Requirements and applied Ex-SDPs. Finally, we executed tests to confirm that the Security Design Requirements are satisfied due to an appropriately applied pattern.

Step 1: Identify Threats and Countermeasures in the System

Referring to Figure 1, I&A, Input and Data Validation, and Authorization are countermeasures for Spoofing, Elevation of Privilege, and SQL Injection in the "make a payment" process, respectively. For simplicity, each threat has one countermeasure.

Figure 11. Model that does not consider security

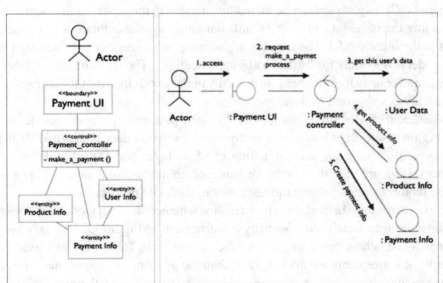

Table 3. Explanation of each element

Element	Stereotype	Description
Payment UI	boundary	Interface that payment informations are input into.
Payment Controller	control	Element that has a "make a payment" method.
User Info	entity	Element that contains user's data such as name and gender.
Product Info	entity	Element that contains product data.
Payment Info	entity	Element that contains payment data. when the actor finishes make a payment process, this instance will be created.

Step 2: Execute a Test to Verify That the Input Model Satisfies the Security Requirements

Then by referencing the Security Requirements used for each Ex-SRP countermeasure, the set for the Security Requirements should be satisfied in the "make a payment" process. Table 4 and Figure 12 show the Security Requirements. If necessary, the prepared OCL expression can be manually adjusted to the input requirement model by adding the necessary properties and changing the element names to the actual ones in the input model. The fact that adjustments are necessary is a clear sign that the model is not ready for further pattern applications. The decision table (Table 4) allows the Security Requirements to be easily understood since the OCL expressions are not always apparent to developers.

The Security Requirements for the "make a payment" process include: actor is a regular user, actor has access permission, and valid data is inputted. If these requirements, which are a combination of I&A, Input and Data Validation, and Authorization are met, then the actor can execute the "make a payment" process. These requirements represent the test cases in the TDD process.

Next, we executed a model test to determine whether the input model that does not consider security satisfies the Security Requirements in Figure 12. That is, whether test cases 1–8 behave according to the expected action in Table 4 are verified. If the Security Requirements are not satisfied, then the appropriate countermeasures are not taken, which means that the threats identified using Ex-SRP may exist.

Table 4. Security Requirements for the "make a payment" process (conceptual)

		1	2	3	4	5	6	7	8
Conditions	<<Actor>> is regular user	Yes	Yes	Yes	Yes	No	No	No	No
	<<Actor>> has access right	Yes	Yes	No	No	Yes	Yes	No	No
	valid data is inputed in <<UI>>	Yes	No	Yes	No	Yes	No	Yes	No
Actions	execute "make a payment" process	✖							
	not execute "make a payment" process		✖	✖	✖	✖	✖	✖	✖

Figure 12. Security Requirements for the "make a payment" process (OCL)

```
context payment_controller
  inv SecurityRequirement :
   if self.payment_UI.User.registered_user = true and
      self.payment_UI.User.right = true and
      self.payment_UI.is_safe_input = true then
    self.make_a_payment = true
  else
    self.make_a_payment = false
  endif
```

Figure 13 shows a case where the regular user, has access permission, and uses valid input data are all false (Table 5, test case 8). Because the input model lacks object constraints, an actor may carry out "make_a_payment = true" (i.e., an actor can execute the "make a payment" process without being a regular user or permission). Hence, the Security Requirements of the "make a payment" process are not satisfied by the input model that does not consider security, and the OCL evaluation in USE becomes false in Figure 16.

Table 6 shows the results of the eight test cases. Only case 1 satisfies the Security Requirements in Table 4 and Figure 12, confirming the necessity of I&A, Input and Data Validation, and Authorization countermeasures.

Figure 13. Conditions of the Security Test in USE

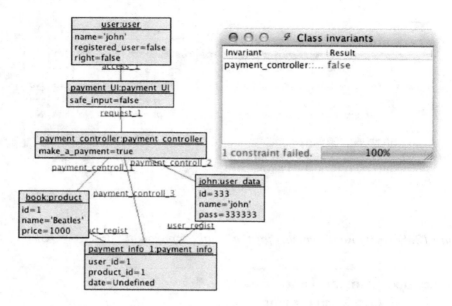

Table 5. Results of the Security Test

		1	2	3	4	5	6	7	8
	<<Actor>> is regular user	Yes	Yes	Yes	Yes	No	No	No	No
Conditions	<<Actor>> has access right	Yes	Yes	No	No	Yes	Yes	No	No
	valid data is inputed in <<UI>>	Yes	No	Yes	No	Yes	No	Yes	No
Actions	execute "make a payment" process	×	×	×	×	×	×	×	×
	not execute "make a payment" process								

Step 3: Select Ex-SDPs

We selected Ex-SDP related to the countermeasures of Ex-SRP. Then we added these to the structure to realize security capabilities. We selected Password Design and Use, RBAC, and Prevent SQL Injection for I&A, Input and Data Validation, and Authorization, respectively[2].

Step 4: Set Security Design Requirements Using the Pattern Requirements

Table 6 and Figure 14 show combinations of each Pattern Requirement necessary for the "make a payment" process, which are referred to as Security Design Requirements. If necessary, the prepared OCL expression of each Pattern Requirement can be adjusted to the input model by adding the properties or changing the element names to the actual ones in the input model. The fact that adjustments are necessary is a clear sign that the model is not ready for further pattern applications.

Step 5: Apply Ex-SDPs and Bind Pattern Elements

We applied these Ex-SDPs. During pattern applications, we bind these pattern elements to a stereotype in our tool. Figure 15 shows the conditions to apply a pattern using our tool. Figures 16 and 17 show the structure and behavior after applying the patterns to a model that does not consider security. In other words, these models consider security. Compared with the model in Figure 11, there are several conditions (Table 7) to execute the "make a payment" process. Table 7 explains the added element.

Table 6. Security Design Requirements of the "make a payment" process (conceptual)

		1	2	3	4	5	6	7	8
Conditions	the same ID and Password that are inputted into <<Login_UI>> exist in <<User_Data>> respectively	Yes	Yes	Yes	Yes	No	No	No	No
	rights are given in <<Role>> which an <<User_Data>> belongs	Yes	Yes	No	No	Yes	Yes	No	No
	valid data is inputed in <<UI>>	Yes	No	Yes	No	Yes	No	Yes	No
Actions	<<Actor>> is considered regular user	×	×	×	×				
	<<Actor>> is consider non-regular user					×	×	×	×
	considers that <<Actor>> have access permission	×	×			×	×		
	consider that <<Actor>> does not have access permission			×	×			×	×
	consider that valid data is inputed	×		×		×		×	
	consider that invalid data is inputed		×		×		×		×
	execute "make a payment" process	×							
	not execute "make a payment" process		×	×	×	×	×	×	×

Figure 14. Security Design Requirements of the "make a payment" process (OCL)

```
context payment_controller
 inv check_id_and_pass:
  if self.password_and_use.User_Data->exists(p |
            p.id = self.password_design_and_use.Login_UI.id and
            p.pass = self.password_design_and_use.Login_UI.pass)
  then
     self.Payment_UI.actor.regular_user = true
  else
     self.Payment_UI.actor.regular_user = false
  endif

context payment_controller
 inv access_control:
  if self.RBAC.Right->exists(p |
         p.right = true and
         p.role_id = p.Role.id and
         p.role_id = p.Role.User_Data.role_id )
  then
     self.Payment_UI.actor.right = true
  else
     self.Payment_UI.actor.right = false
  endif

context payment_controller
 inv sanitize_input_data_payment_UI:
  if self.Payment_UI.Prevent_SQL_Injection.sanitize_input_data = true
  then
     self.Payment_UI.valid_input_data = true
  else
     self.Payment_UI.valid_input_data = false
  endif

context payment_controller
 inv sanitize_input_data_login_UI:
  if self.password_design_and_use.Login_UI.Prevent_SQL_Injection.sanitize_input_data = true
  then
     self.password_design_and_use.Login_UI.valid_input_data = true
  else
     self.password_design_and_use.Login_UI.valid_input_data = false
  endif

context payment_controller
 inv security design requirement:
  if self.Payment_UI.actor.regular_user = true and
     self.Payment_UI.actor.right = true and
     self.Payment_UI.valid_input_data = true and
     self.password_design_and_use.Login_UI.valid_input_data = true
  then
     self.make_a_payment = true
  else
     self.make_a_payment = false
  endif
```

Figure 15. Conditions of pattern application in our tool

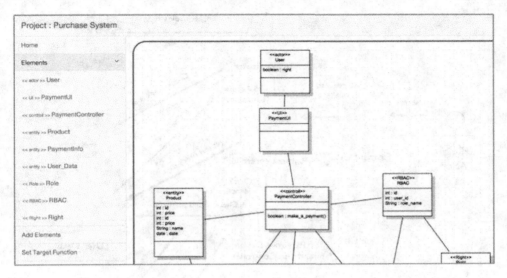

Figure 16. Model that considers security (structure)

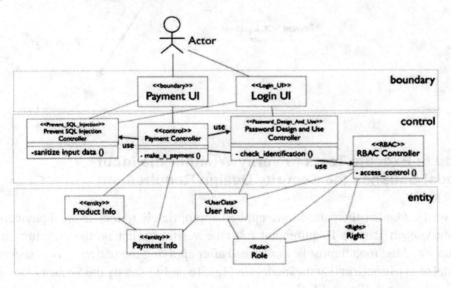

Figure 17. Model that considers security (behavior)

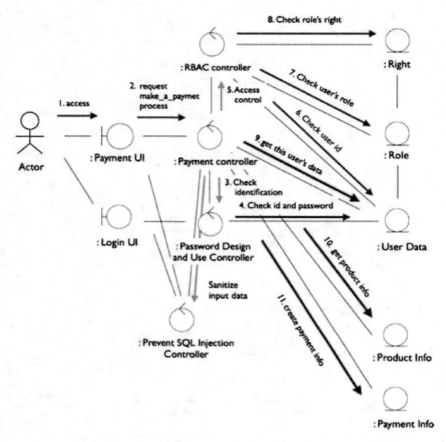

Step 6: Execute Tests to Verify Whether the Input Model Satisfies the Security Design Requirement

To verify whether the patterns are applied appropriately to the "make a payment" process, each Pattern Requirement must be verified. That is, the structure and behavior of the model must be confirmed after applying the patterns. We executed model tests to confirm that the models in Figs. 16 and 17 satisfy the Security Design Requirements in Figure 14. Specifically, we confirmed that test cases 1–8 behave as expected (Table 6). First, concrete test cases are inputted into the model created in Step 4 to generate a test script. Then this script is translated to execute tests in USE. Finally, the OCL statement using this test script in USE is evaluated. Figure 18 shows the conditions of the Security Design Test in USE.

Table 7. Explanation of added element

Element	Stereotype	Description
Login UI	boundary	Interface that ID and PASSWORD are input into.
Password Design and Use Controller	control	Element that has a "check identification" method. This method returns true when ID and PASSWORD match.
RBAC Controller	control	Element that has a "access_control" method. This method returns true when access permission is given in Role that an actor belongs.
Prevent SQL Injection Controller	control	Element that has a "sanitize input data" method. This method returns true when all input data are sanitized in user interface.
Role	entity	Element that contains role informations which user belongs.
Right	entity	Element that contains access permission informations which role has.

Figure 18 shows a case where access permission is denied for the "Role" of the actor, but the system does not sanitize the input data in "Login UI" (Table 6, test case 4). Prior to applying patterns, USE outputs "make_a_payment = true" (i.e., an actor can execute the "make a payment" process, even if the actor does not have permission or inputs invalid data). After the patterns are applied, USE outputs "make a payment = false", and the actor cannot execute the "make_a_payment" process because access permission is not specified in the role and the system assumes invalid data is used in "Login UI". Consequently, the OCL statements in Figure 18 are true. Executing all the test cases validates that the output model after the pattern application satisfies the Security Design Requirements of the "make a payment" process.

To summarize, we applied Ex-SDPs for the "make_a_payment" process, which requires I&A, Input and Data Validation, and Authorization, and then executed a model test. If patterns are applied appropriately, then the output model will satisfy the Security Requirements. The initial input model did not satisfy the Security Requirements of the "make a payment" process, but the output model that applied patterns to satisfy the Security Design Requirements does. The output model is not usually verified directly against the Security Requirements since the output model is extended from the input model. By preparing the Pattern Requirements corresponding to the Security Requirements, the existence of vulnerabilities can be verified by using the Pattern Requirements. In this manner, the appropriate application of SDPs and

Figure 18. Conditions of the Security Design Test in USE

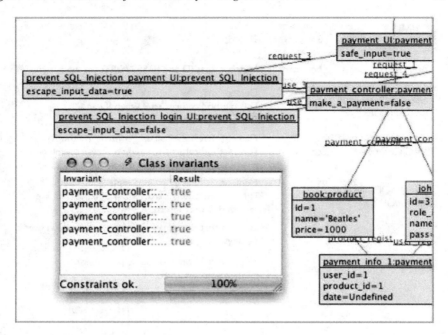

the existence of vulnerabilities to threats identified at the requirements stage can be verified before and after pattern application.

Limitations

Our method has various limitations. First, our method is not sufficient for secure design because it only verifies that security patterns are applied as formalized in the security and pattern requirements and patterns may be instantiated in different ways. Since the final output models after security pattern applications are not usually verified directly against the Security Requirements of Ex-SRPs, Ex-SDPs containing the Pattern Requirements must be carefully prepared to ensure that the Pattern Requirements of Ex-SRPs satisfies the corresponding Security Requirements.

Because test cases are created based on threats and countermeasures identified in the requirement stage, the presence of threats not identified in the requirement stage cannot be verified. In addition, the criteria to select Ex-SDP may be impractical because the range is influenced by the security policy, platform, and risk analysis.

The verification correctness of by preparing the Pattern Requirements corresponding to Security Requirements, the existence of vulnerabilities can be verified by using the Pattern Requirements.

In terms of development processes, we only assume that our method is employed to model-driven or model-centric developments that adopt UML including OCL. Thus, the process can be model-driven agile development as well as traditional plan-driven model-driven development.

In terms of security patterns, our method only addresses concrete security requirement and design patterns that provide concrete structures (in UML) with constraints (in OCL). High-level conceptual security architecture patterns such as the Firewall pattern is hard to be addressed in our method.

THREATS TO VALIDITY

Threats to Internal Validity

In the example, the patterns were applied by one of authors with professional development experience familiar with our method and security patterns. Therefore, it is possible that general developers may apply our process inappropriately. Additionally, our method may be time consuming compared to other approaches as developers may be unfamiliar with our method. Although our tool provides a flow for the design process, it executes test automatically. In the future, we should confirm that the expected outcomes are achieved by developers unfamiliar with our method.

Threats to External Validity

We confirmed the applicability of our method by targeting a Web application. We did not verify whether our method is applicable to other types of systems. Therefore, it is difficult to generalize the results. Moreover, additional security patterns and experiment testers are needed. Hence, it is possible that our method is not applicable to all security patterns. Although we used representative patterns and a typical model for software development to confirm that our method is useful, we should confirm that our method is applicable to more general patterns and large-scale examples.

RELATED WORKS

Security Modeling

Recently, UML-based models have been used for design. Previous research adopted UML-based models to describe security patterns (Jurjens, Popp, & Wimmel, 2002) (Finkelstein, Honiden & Yoshioka, 2004). To model security concerns, modeling techniques such as UMLsec (Jurijens, 2005) and SecureUML (Basin, Doser & Loddersted, 2002) have been proposed. UMLsec is defined in the form of a UML profile using standard UML extension mechanisms. Stereotypes with tagged values are used to formulate the security requirements, while constraints are used to verify whether the security requirements hold during specific types of attacks.

SecureUML focuses on modeling access control policies and how these policies can be integrated into a model-driven software development process. It is based on an extended model of role-based access control (RBAC) and uses RBAC as a meta-model to specify and enforce security. RBAC lacks support to express access control conditions that refer to the state of a system such as the state of a protected resource. In addressing this limitation, SecureUML introduces the concept of authorization constraints. Authorization constraints are preconditions to grant access to an operation.

Although these techniques can support modeling security-related concerns in UML, developers who are not security specialists have some difficulty employing these approaches because they must understand the details of formal semantics. Our method adopts SDPs that support developers who are not security specialists. Additionally, our tool enables design without understanding the details of formal semantics except for standard OCL notations.

Model-Based Security Testing

Model-Based Testing (MBT) is a technique to generate part or all of a test case from a model (Dalal, et al., 1999). A model is an abstract representation expressing an operation, structure, behavior, or any other concern to be realized by or related to the system. In the context of security testing, the process of deriving tests tends to be unstructured, irreproducible, undocumented, lacking detailed rationales for the test design, and dependent on the ingenuity of the tester or hacker. This has motivated the use of explicit models (Felderer, et al., 2016). Tretmans and Brinksma proposed an automated MBT tool (Tretmans & Brinksma, 2003), while Felderer et al. proposed a method of Model-Based Security Testing (MBST) that relies on models to test whether a software system meets its security requirements (Felderer, et al., 2010).

Moreover, there are many other publications on MBST techniques since this is a relatively new research field with potential in industrial applications (Schieferdecker, et al., 2012). Felderer et al. proposed a taxonomy for MBST approaches and used it to systematically classify 119 publications (Felderer, et al., 2016). However, none of these publications focused on security design pattern applications.

We previously proposed a support method for SDPs in the implementation phase of software development (Yoshizawa, et al., 2016) (Yoshizawa, et al., 2014). Since the previous method addresses the implementation phase and our method presented in this chapter addresses the analysis and design phase, they are complementary.

Model Checking

Model checking is a method to verify a formula against a logic model algorithmically (Clarke, Emerson, Edmund & Sistla, 1986). This verification technique can be automated by a model checker. Several articles describe the verification of security specifications using model-checking tools such as SPIN (Josang, 1995) (Jiang & Liu, 2008). However, a specific language, which developers must learn, is necessary to check the model. Additionally, due to the general scale of development, describing security specifications using a specific language is time consuming compared with our method.

Pattern Verification

According to our previous surveys on security pattern research (Ito et al., 2015) (Washizaki et al., 2018), several articles verify security pattern applications. Abramov et al. (2009) have suggested using a stereotype for a database application to verify security patterns. Although their method can confirm the applied patterns structurally, it cannot assess whether the pattern behaviors in the model resolve vulnerabilities to threats.

Dong et al. (2009) have proposed an approach to verify the compositions of security patterns using model checking. They presented a guideline to specify the behavior of security patterns in a model specification language. They defined synchronous messages, asynchronous messages, and alternative flows of a UML sequence diagram and transformed them into CCS specifications. Although this approach formally defines the behavioral aspect of security patterns and provides transformation scripts to confirm the properties of the security patterns by model checking, it does not formally analyze the security requirements of the target system. Therefore, even if the verification of security patterns application is executed appropriately, it does not guarantee that threats and vulnerabilities are resolved. On the other hand, our method sets security requirements and security design requirements prior to verifying that the threats and vulnerabilities are resolved.

Similarly, Hamid et al. proposed a method to verify the application of object-oriented design patterns at the model level using UML and OCL (Hamid, Percebois and Gouteux, 2012). Although the method is similar to our method in terms of utilization of OCL to check the correctness of the application, their method does not address security aspects. In contrast, our method is useful to design and verify the application of security patterns.

Test-Driven Development (TDD) for Security

TDD is a software development technique that uses short development iterations based on prewritten test cases to define the desired improvements or new functions. Our testing process employs TDD. TDD requires that developers generate automated unit tests to define code requirements prior to writing the actual code (Choi, Kim & Yoon, 2009). The test case represents requirements that the program must satisfy (Astels, Beck, Boehm, Fraser McGregor, Newkirk & Poole, 2003).

Although some approaches implement security requirements by adopting TDD (Munetoh & Yoshioka, 2013) (Sonia & Singhal, 2011), they do not specifically handle security design patterns. Consequently, such methods require developers to manually prepare test cases when applying and testing security design patterns. This is highly burdensome.

CONCLUSION AND FUTURE WORK

If software developers are not security experts, patterns may be inappropriately applied. Additionally, threats and vulnerabilities may not be mitigated even if patterns are applied correctly. Herein we propose a secure design method that verifies SDPs using a model test in a UML model simulation environment. Specifically, assets, threats, and countermeasures are identified in the target system during an early stage of development. Both the appropriateness of the applied patterns and the existence of vulnerabilities identified in the first stage of the design model are verified.

This method offers three significant contributions. First, Ex-SRP and Ex-SDP, which are newly extended security patterns using OCL expressions, include requirement- and design-level patterns. Second, a new model-based design and testing process based on TDD designs verifies the patterns are correctly applied and whether vulnerabilities exist using these extended patterns. Finally, a tool to support pattern applications automatically generates a script to test the model. In the future, we intend to conduct experiments using more general and large-scale examples as well as consider applications based on the dependencies among the patterns, which should realize more practical uses.

REFERENCES

Abramov, J., Shoval, P., & Sturm, A. (2009). Validating and Implementing Security Patterns for Database Applications. *Proceedings of the 3rd International Workshop on Software Patterns and Quality (SPAQu'09)*.

Andreas, L., & Sindre, G. (2000). Eliciting Security Requirements by Misuse Cases. In *Proceedings of the 37th International Conference on Technology of Object-Oriented Languages and Systems (TOOLS-Pacific 2000)*. IEEE Computer Society.

Astels, D., Beck, K., Boehm, B., Fraser, S., McGregor, J., Newkirk, J., & Poole, C. (2003). Discipline and Practices of TDD (test driven development). *Companion of the 18th annual ACM SIGPLAN conference on Object-oriented programming, systems, languages, and applications (OOPSLA'03)*.

Basin, D., Doser, J., & Loddersted, T. (2002). SecureUML: A UML-Based Modeling Language for Model-Driven Security. *Proceedings of the 5th International Conference Model Engineering, Concepts, and Tools (UML'02)*.

Bondareva, K., & Milutinovich, J. (2014). *Unified Modeling Language*. Retrieved September 10, 2014, from http://www.omg.org/gettingstarted/what_is_uml.htm

Buschmann, F., Fernandez-Buglioni, E., Schumacher, M., Sommerlad, P., & Hybertson, D. (2006). *Security Patterns: Integrating Security and Systems Engineering*. Wiley Software Patterns Series.

Büttnera, F., Gogollaa, M., & Richtersb, M. (2007). USE: A UML-Based Specification Environment for Validating UML and OCL. *Science of Computer Programming*, *69*(1-3), 27–34. doi:10.1016/j.scico.2007.01.013

Choi, B., Kim, H., & Yoon, S. (2009). Performance Testing based on Test-Driven Development for Mobile Applications. *Proceedings of the 3rd International Conference on Ubiquitous Information Management and Communication (ICUIMC'09)*.

Clarke, E., Emerson, A., Edmund, M., & Sistla, A. (1986). Automatic Verification of Finite-state Concurrent Systems using Temporal Logic Specifications. *ACM Transactions on Programming Languages and Systems*, *8*(2), 244–263. doi:10.1145/5397.5399

Dalal, S. R., Jain, A., Karunanithi, N., Leaton, J. M., Lott, C. M., Patton, G. C., & Horowitz, B. M. (1999). Model-based Testing in Practice. *Proceedings of the International Conference on Software Engineering (ICSE'99)*, 285-294.

Dong, J., Peng, T., & Zhao, Y. (2008). Verifying Behavioral Correctness of Design Pattern Implementation. In *Proceedings of the 20th International Conference on Software Engineering & Knowledge Engineering (SEKE'08)* (pp. 454-459). IEEE Computer Society.

Dong, J., Peng, T., & Zhao, Y. (2009). Automated Verification of Security Pattern Compositions. *Information and Software Technology, 52*(3), 274–295. doi:10.1016/j.infsof.2009.10.001

Felderer, M., Agreiter, B., Breu, R., & Armenteros, A. (2010). Security Testing by Telling TestStories. *Proceedings of the Conference on Modellierung*, 24-26.

Felderer, M., Zech, P., Breu, R., Büchler, M., & Pretschner, A. (2016). Model-Based Security Testing: A Taxonomy and Systematic Classification. *Journal of Software: Testing , Verification and Reliability, 26*(2), 119–148. doi:10.1002tvr.1580

Fernandez, E. B., Washizaki, H., & Yoshioka, N. (2016). Patterns for Secure Cloud IaaS. *Proceedings of the 5th Asian Conference on Pattern Languages of Programs (AsianPLoP 2016).*

Fernandez, E. B., Yoshioka, N., & Washizaki, H. (2008). Abstract security patterns. *Proceedings of the 2nd PLoP Workshop on Software Patterns and Quality (SPAQu'08).*

Fernandez, E. B., Yoshioka, N., & Washizaki, H. (2014). Patterns for cloud firewalls. *Proceedings of the 3rd Asian Conference on Pattern Language of Programs (AsianPLoP 2014).*

Fernandez, E. B., Yoshioka, N., & Washizaki, H. (2015a). Patterns for Security and Privacy in Cloud Ecosystems. *Proceedings of the 2nd International Workshop on Evolving Security and Privacy Requirements Engineering (ESPRE 2015).* 10.1109/ESPRE.2015.7330162

Fernandez, E. B., Yoshioka, N., & Washizaki, H. (2015b). Cloud Access Security Broker (CASB): A pattern for accessing secure cloud services. *Proceedings of the 4th Asian Conference on Pattern Languages of Programs (AsianPLoP 2015).*

Fernandez, E. B., Yoshioka, N., Washizaki, H., Jurjens, J., VanHilst, M., & Pernul, G. (2010). Using security patterns to develop secure systems. In *Software Engineering for Secure Systems.* IGI Global.

Fernandez, E.B., Yoshioka, N., Washizaki, H., & Syed, M.H. (2016). Modeling and Security in Cloud Ecosystems. *Future Internet, 13*(2), 1-15.

Fernandez, E. B., Yoshioka, N., Washizaki, H., & Yoder, J. (2014). Abstract security patterns for requirements and analysis of secure systems. *Proceedings of the 17th Workshop on Requirements Engineering (WER 2014)*.

Fernandez, E. B., Yoshioka, N., Washizaki, H., & Yoder, J. (2018). An Abstract Security Pattern for Authentication and a Derived Concrete Pattern, the Credential-based Authentication. *Proceedings of the 7th Asian Conference on Pattern Languages of Programs (AsianPLoP 2018)*.

Finkelstein, A., Honiden, S., & Yoshioka, N. (2004). Security Patterns: a Method for Constructing Secure and Efficient Inter-company Coordination Systems. *Proceedings of the 8th IEEE International Enterprise Distributed Object Computing Conference (EDOC'04)*, 84–97.

Hamid, B., Percebois, C., & Gouteux, D. (2012). Methodology for Integration of Patterns with Validation Purpose. *Proceedings of the European Conference on Pattern Language of Programs (EuroPLoP)*, 1–14.

Ito, Y., Washizaki, H., Yoshizawa, M., Fukazawa, Y., Okubo, T., Kaiya, H., ... Fernandez, E. B. (2015). Systematic Mapping of Security Patterns Research. *Proceedings of the 22nd Conference on Pattern Languages of Programs Conference 2015 (PLoP 2015)*.

Jiang, Y., & Liu, X. (2008). Formal Analysis for Network Security Properties on a Trace Semantics. *Proceedings of the 2008 International Conference on Advanced Computer Theory and Engineering (ICACTE'08)*. 10.1109/ICACTE.2008.31

Josang, A. (1995). *Security Protocol Verification using Spin*. Montreal, Canada: INRS-Telecommunications.

Jurjens, J. (2005). *Secure Systems Development with UML*. Springer.

Jurjens, J., Popp, G., & Wimmel, G. (2002). Towards using Security Patterns in Model-Based System Development. *Proceedings of the 9th Conference on Pattern Language of Programs (PLoP'02)*.

Kleppe, A., & Warmer, J. (1999). *The Object Constraint Language: Precise Modeling with UML*. Addison-Wesley Object Technology Series.

Kobashi, T., Yoshioka, N., Kaiya, H., Washizaki, H., Okubo, T., & Fukazawa, Y. (2014). Validating Security Design Pattern Applications by Testing Design Models. *International Journal of Secure Software Engineering*, 5(4), 1–30. doi:10.4018/ijsse.2014100101

Kobashi, T., Yoshioka, N., Okubo, T., Kaiya, H., Washizaki, H., & Fukazawa, Y. (2013). Validating Security Design Pattern Applications Using Model Testing. *Proceedings of the 8th International Conference on Availability, Reliability and Security (ARES2013)*. 10.1109/ARES.2013.13

Kobashi, T., Yoshizawa, M., Washizaki, H., Fukazawa, Y., Yoshioka, N., Kaiya, H., & Okubo, T. (2015). TESEM: A Tool for Verifying Security Design Pattern Applications by Model Testing. *Proceedings of the 8th IEEE International Conference on Software Testing, Verification, and Validation (ICST 2015)*. 10.1109/ICST.2015.7102633

Lai, R., Nagappan, R., & Steel, C. (2005). *Core Security Patterns: Best Practices and Strategies for J2EE, Web Services, and Identity Management*. Prentice Hall.

Mackman, A., & Maher, P. (2007). Web Application Security Frame. *Microsoft Patterns & Practices*. Retrieved from http://msdn.microsoft.com/en-us/library/ms978518

Maruyama, K., Washizaki, H., & Yoshioka, N. (2008). A Survey on Security Patterns. *Progress in Informatics, 5*, 35-47.

Munetoh, S., & Yoshioka, N. (2013). Model-Assisted Access Control Implementation for Code-centric Ruby-on-Rails Web Application Development. *Proceedings of the International Conference on Availability, Reliability and Security (ARES'13)*, 350–359. 10.1109/ARES.2013.47

Nhlabatsi, A., Bandara, A., Hayashi, S., Haley, C. B., Jurjens, J., Kaiya, H., ... Yu, Y. (2010). Security Patterns: Comparing Modeling Approaches. In *Software Engineering for Secure Systems*. IGI Global.

Okubo, T., Kaiya, H., & Yoshioka, N. (2012). Effective Security Impact Analysis with Patterns for Software Enhancement. In *Proceedings of the 2011 Sixth International Conference on Availability, Reliability and Security (ARES'12)*. IEEE Computer Society.

Okubo, T., Taguchi, K., & Yoshioka, N. (2009). Misuse Cases + Assets + Security Goals. In *Proceedings of the International Conference on Computational Science and Engineering (CSE'09)*. IEEE Computer Society.

Pilgrim, P. (2013). *Java EE 7 Developer Handbook*. Packt Publishing.

Priebe, T., Fernandez-Buglioni, E., Mehlau, J. I., & Pernul, G. (2004). A Pattern System for Access Control. In *Research Directions in Data and Applications Security XVIII* (Vol. 144). IFIP International Federation for Information Processing. doi:10.1007/1-4020-8128-6_16

Santos, R. (2017). *Microsoft Threat Modeling Tool mitigations*. Retrieved from https://docs.microsoft.com/en-ie/azure/security/azure-security-threat-modeling-tool-mitigations

Schieferdecker, I., Grossmann, J., & Schneider, M. (2012). Model-Based Security Testing. *Proceedings of the 7th Workshop on Model Based Testing*, 1-12.

Sonia & Singhal, A. (2011). Development of Agile Security Framework Using a Hybrid Technique for Requirements Elicitation. *Proceedings of the International Conference on Advances in Computing, Communication and Control (ICAC'11)*, 178–188.

Tretmans, J., & Brinksma, E. (2003). TorX: Automated Model-Based Testing. *Proceedings of the Conference on Model-Driven Software Engineering*, 11-12.

Washizaki, H. (2017). Security Patterns: Research Direction, Metamodel, Application and Verification. *Proceedings of the 2017 International Workshop on Big Data & Information Security (IWBIS)*. 10.1109/IWBIS.2017.8275094

Washizaki, H., Xia, T., Kamata, N., Fukazawa, Y., Kanuka, H., Yamaoto, D., ... Priyalakshmi, G. (2018). Taxonomy and Literature Survey of Security Pattern Research. *Proceedings of the IEEE Conference on Applications, Information and Network Security (AINS 2018)*.

Yoshizawa, M., Kobashi, T., Washizaki, H., Fukazawa, Y., Okubo, T., Kaiya, H., & Yoshioka, N. (2014). Verification of Implementing Security Design Patterns Using a Test Template. *Proceedings of the 9th International Conference on Availability, Reliability and Security (ARES2014)*.

Yoshizawa, M., Washizaki, H., Fukazawa, Y., Okubo, T., Kaiya, H., & Yoshioka, N. (2016). Implementation Support of Security Design Patterns Using Test Templates. *Information, 2*(34), 1-19.

ENDNOTES

[1]   Source code of the tool is open to the public at https://github.com/takanorioo/TESEM.

[2]   Note that these Ex-SDPs are selected at the current abstraction level. In further detail design and construction phases, additional Ex-SDPs may be additionally or alternatively applied upon considering the design and construction details. For example, the proper SQL statements (such as using prepared statements) and the input validation would prevent the "SQL Injection" threat.

Chapter 7
State Actor Model for Cloud–Based Online Auction

Yun Shu
Auckland University of Technology, New Zealand

Jian Yu
Auckland University of Technology, New Zealand

Wei Qi Yan
Auckland University of Technology, New Zealand

ABSTRACT

In recent decades, internet auctions have become the most significant e-commerce business model worldwide. With the rapid rise of cloud computing over the last few years, the legacy online auction platform is gradually being replaced using service-oriented cloud computing in real time. This chapter describes the design and implementation of a state and high-performance online auction system over cloud and proposes the methodology to provide persistent state records during the auction process so that we are able to ensure the reliability of submitted bid price and guarantee the security of price message in the delivery process. The authors employ actor-based applications to achieve stateful, parallel, and distributed architecture. Meanwhile, utilizing distributed databases provides secure and efficient data storage. To the best of the authors' knowledge, this is the first time that the actor framework has been applied to the online auction. The preliminary result is for implementation of high-performance and real-time bidding online auction.

DOI: 10.4018/978-1-5225-6313-6.ch007

INTRODUCTION

Cloud computing is becoming increasingly attractive to firms and developers nowadays. Compared with traditional Internet service provider, the legacy service providers are grouped into infrastructure vendors and service providers. The infrastructure providers (Platform as a Service) include Microsoft Azure, Amazon Web Services (AWS), and Google App Engine shown as Figure 1. The services provide impressive, reliable, and cost-efficient cloud-based platforms and lease these platform to the service providers who rent resources from infrastructure providers to serve end clients (Armbrust, 2010). Moreover, those developers who worked for the service providers have significant opportunities to transform their innovative ideas into highly scalable Internet services. We also call them Software as a Service (SaaS). These services can be easily expanded to a large scale to handle the expeditious increase in service demands (Armbrust, 2009).

Because of these features, we, therefore, have the opportunity to deploy actor-based applications in parallel and distributed system on cloud to overcome the bottlenecks of traditional client / server framework of the online auction. The actor model (Hewitt, P. Bishop, and R. Steiger, 1973) adopts an abstract concept to describe concurrency of the program that is centred on the actor unit which performs distributed computations and communicates through asynchronous information exchange. Thus, the actor is suitable for developing large-scale parallel programs. However, the concurrency of actors is limited by hardware resources and capability of logical computations (Agha, 1985). As the rapid progression and innovation of cloud technology in recent years, hardware constraints gradually weakened. The actor model is increasingly being applied to highly concurrent applications on SaaS, such as Microsoft Orleans and JVM Akka.

The main technical bottleneck of traditional online auction systems is that it is hard to handle significant amounts of data from different regions in a highly concurrent and parallel environment. More specifically, when an online auction system receives quotes from all over the world, traditional tree-tired architecture shown as Figure 4 will place cache area between middle tire and physical storage for improving I/O performance (Power and Li, 2010). Unfortunately, usage of the cache will directly lose the concurrency. The cache manager or application must adopt concurrency control policy to avoid deviations resulting from concurrent updates to a cached object (Strangers, 2005). Hence, the traditional architecture has to face major issues that come from traffic reliability and massive data processing within a short period. With or without the cache, this pattern cannot fulfil the requirement of conformity on a cache with rapid reaction for interactive access (Bernstein, et

Figure 1. Architecture of legacy web applications

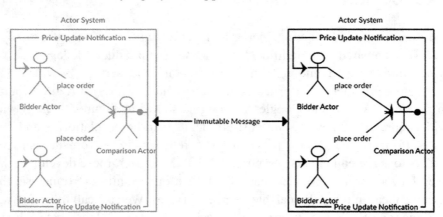

al., 2014). Eventually, these problems will result in excessive use of CPU resources and physical memory depletion. On the other hand, traditional relational database that is commonly utilised in a concurrently read or write scenario cannot provide reliable data concurrency and consistency.

In this chapter, we discuss a methodology that can be implemented to convert the structure of traditional English online auction into actor architecture so that we can guarantee data consistency and integrity in the high-performed environment of the online auction. We utilise the mechanism of safe message delivery which ensures security of bid data from end to end. Moreover, internal state of the actor offers reliability of persistent state records during the auction process. Finally, fair scheduling, location transparency and mobility move burden of assuring data integrality and consistency to the actor model (Strangers, 2005) resulting in offering high-concurrency and low-latency online auction service. To the best of our knowledge, this is the first time that the actor framework is applied to the online auction.

The remaining part of this chapter is organised as follows. Section II will present related work, the current actor framework will be illustrated in Section III, the system design will be introduced in Section IV; the distributed database will be described in Section V. In Section VI we will detail the implementation and testing; in Section VII, we will conclude this chapter and present directions of future work.

RELATED WORK

Traffic Reliability in Online Auction

Traditional client/server architecture faces a severe problem of traffic reliability in an online auction. The server is responsible for processing all clients' bid data regarding each round in a live online auction system. Because of network delay, the clients' request could be late to arrive the server side. Thus, the data from clients' side will be dropped that will result in packet loss. This is one of the main reasons why online auction systems cannot be trusted. Bidders never know whether their bid has arrived safely on the server side or not.

A proposed solution to solve this problem is active protocol filters (Liu, Wang and Fei, 2003). This protocol has a capability of filtering out low-bid data in the process of price delivery before they reach the server side. Then the active filters will reject the appropriate clients. Meanwhile, sending rejection notices to clients is for the sake of improving loading balance of the server side. Other online auctioneers use semi-enclosed auctions, which can lengthen the auction cycle. For example, eBay or Amazon provides non-real-time online auction method so that there is no need to control network delays of the online auction system. Obviously, performance and stability of the communications between online auction systems, such as cost, fairness, response time, traffic reliability and packets loss, have become the major concern for all parties involved in the online auctions (McAdam, 2001). Another mode (Liu, Wang and T. Fei, 2003) is for multicast-based online auctions. Although the multicast model can enhance the capability of packet delays and traffic rates, the issue of packet loss still cannot be resolved.

Auction Model

In general, most e-commercial auction services launched are based on disclosed method, like English auction or reverse auction. eBay in USA, Alibaba from China, or Trademe in New Zealand are very good examples. These auction methods are developed and used in B2C, C2C and B2B domains. C2C-based English auction is the dominant mechanism in e-commerce marketplace (Karmani, Shali and Agha, 2009).

With globalisation of Internet-based cloud services, the online auction platform is reshaping the market by providing a professional service. A key aspect of this shift is the provision of many services, especially professional services, which are no longer limited by the common location of buyers and sellers (Ackerberg, Hirano and Shahriar, 2006). The research outcome Krasnokutskaya, et al. (Krasnokutskaya,

Terwiesch and Tiererova, 2016) indicates that 80% of online transactions are carried out by participants (both buyers and sellers) from foreign countries and regions.

Under these conditions, it is difficult for us to track the status of all bidders in the clustering of trade to ensure the fairness and reliability of online auctions. English auction has set an excellent example which is the most widely used methodology on the Internet. Meanwhile, this type of transaction has a very high demand for concurrency and responsiveness of a system. In a very short period, the system needs to complete the price comparisons, price updates, and real-time notifications of all bidders shown as Figure 2.

Two important principles should be emphasised on cloud-based online auction: price priority and time priority. Bidding keeps increasing before the close time, and finally the bidder holding the highest offer will win absolutely. Also, an English auction provides a given period to all interested bidders in each round. This ensures that buyers have enough time to think over and give their final responses shown as Figure 5. However, we must take into account that the network delay can quite easily lead to several buyers in a few milliseconds of time to place the same price. For traditional online auction system, all quotes must be stochastically posted back to the main server for price and time comparison. Moreover, the system achieves the highest offer to the database in each round. If several buyers place the same highest offer, the system will compare the timestamps to choose the earliest bidder.

English Auction allows sellers to set a start price, a reserve price, and bid increment. Reserve price (Kekre and Bharadi, 2010) provides an insurance mechanism against low closing prices which means that if the final bidding cannot reach the reserve price, all bidders will be failed. Moreover, bid increment also plays a pivotal role in

Figure 2. The workflow of real-time bidding

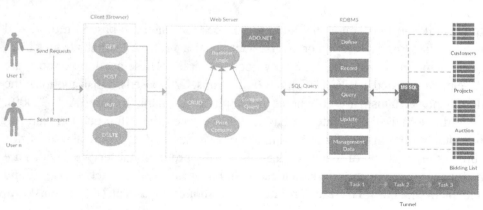

English auction outcomes. Although high bidding increment pushes bidding price up quickly (Karmani, Shali and Agha, 009)), it will result in reducing the participations.

Most of the online English auctions offer proxy bid service. It allows the buyers to place the maximum bid price via the service. Moreover, bidding will keep increasing until it reaches the proxy bid price (Chan, Ho and Lee, 2001).

The biggest challenge for applying this trading model to an online trading platform is whether we distribute the comparisons of the highest price and the timestamp to the other clusters. Also, it is tough to guarantee that the security of information exchange between clusters. Because of features of the distribution of clustering, information exchange on the Internet will be riskier than we expected. The existing technology of signature verification has been quite effective for online message protection (Philip and Bharadi, 2016). For example, modified digital difference analyser algorithm is the best case in this point. It is used to capture dynamic characteristics of a signature in discrete values so that we are able to identify whether the variables in messages have been modified (Kekre and Bharadi, 2010). Most of these solutions of security for a "live" online auction is too heavily. The encryption and decryption process will undoubtedly affect efficiency of online auction systems. We are still looking for a more lightweight solution to solve the issue of information exchange, like actor model. This is also the main reason why we introduce the actor model to the online auction platform. The technology is also widely used in big data deployment and data mining to guarantee the efficiency of data processing (Estrada and Ruiz, 2016).

ACTOR FRAMEWORKS

Five key features are demonstrated (Karmani, Shali and Agha, 2009) for comparing those existing actor frameworks: safe message delivery, mobility, state persistence, location transparency and fair scheduling. There are now three main actor frameworks: Erlang, Akka, and Orleans.

Erlang

Erlang is a functional programming language (Armstrong, Virding, Wikström and Williams, 1993). The actor in Erlang is called process. Compared with Orleans, actors in Erlang are created explicitly (Orleans uses virtual actors). So once the actor is created, its location cannot be changed anymore (Armstrong, 2007). Meanwhile, Erlang uses the link to handle the erratic propagation. The problem is that if the processes are not linked together, the process will die silently. Moreover, Erlang utilises the Open Telecom Platform (OTP) to expand performance and capabilities from distribution, fault tolerance, and concurrency. OTP provides supervisor tree for unexpected error handling (Vinoski, 2007), but it will kill all its children and recreates them once one of them dead. Otherwise, the developer needs to control the process of lifecycle manually. By contract, Orleans and Akka create and garbage collect their actors on runtime automatically.

Akka

Akka is an actor-based framework, which is available for Java, Scala, and C#. The main features are almost as same as Orleans. For instance, each actor is single threaded, the private state is able to access through the reference. The difference is that the actor in Akka is named by the path that illustrates the hierarchy structure from the supervisor to children.

Orleans

Orleans is the latest actor framework from Microsoft. It blends several technologies from previous actor frameworks, such as Erlang and Akka. For example, it fully supports immutable message delivery, state persistence, efficient and fair scheduling for actors of sharing CPU, location transparency. Meanwhile, Orleans also supports weak mobility - the actor can be moved from one machine to another in the idle state (Bernstein, et al., 2014).

The main features of an actor, namely, an event-based asynchronous thread, protected internal states mailbox mechanism, transparent location, make it scale out from clusters and scale up to multi-core processors (Koster, et al., 2013). An actor is regarded as a container for behaviour, internal state, children, and supervisor strategy as shown in Figure 3.

The mailbox is utilised to store and deal with immutable messages that are sent from other actors who are in or out of the actor system (Hewitt, 2010). The behaviour of the actor defines the actions that are responsible for the matched messages. States in actor reflect the possible statuses that could be business logic, a set of listeners, the situation of HTTP requests, and so on. The state data is significant for actors. Thus, actors encapsulate the internal state's data and only share them with other actors through immutable messages (Haller, 2012). Each actor will split tasks into sub-tasks and delivery to its generated children shown as Figure 3. Meanwhile, it will automatically handle failures (also called supervisor strategy) from these children for the sake of providing an environment of highly fault-tolerant systems shown as Figure 3.

Figure 3. Understanding of an actor

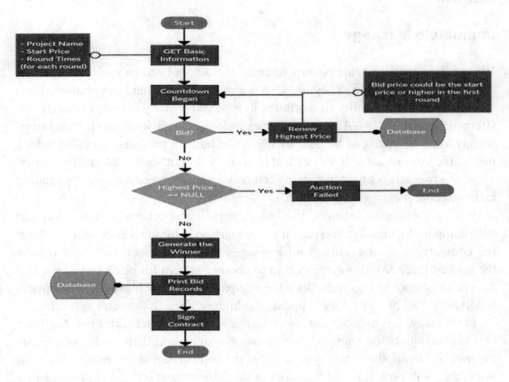

Figure 4. A supervisor and its children in a graph

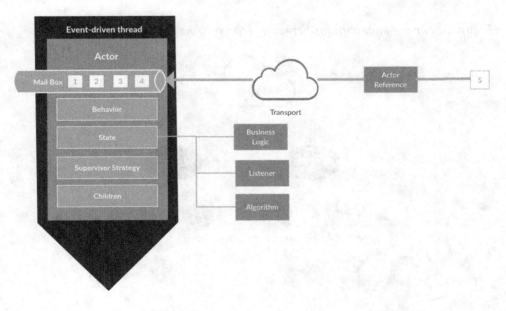

DESIGN

Immutable Message

When we instantiate actor pattern in code, the actors become essential building blocks of an application. They are also a unit of isolation and distribution. Each actor has its unique identity consisting of its type and primary key (a 128-bit GUID) (Bernstein, et al., 2014). An actor will encapsulate its behaviours and internal state. Meanwhile, the state can be held by using the built-in persistence facility which means the core of actor is isolated, that is, they do not share state and memory. Thus, the two actors or actor systems can only interact asynchronously by sending an immutable message (Gupta, 2012).

With regarding to features, the bidder actor encapsulates its quotation and timestamp in the message and pass it to comparison actor in its actor system. After the comparison actor evaluates all messages from bidder actors, it will deliver the highest price from its actor system to another system for price and timestamp estimation shown as Figure 6. Once the comparison actor achieves the final price, it will notice all bidder actors to update the highest price in the actor system.

In this way, figuring out the highest offer will be hierarchical. First, the filter of a highest quotation starts from each actor system, and then gradually spreads the message to another actor system. After the comparison actors receive the final price, they will push it to bidder actors in the actor system instead of broadcasting

Figure 5. The communications between actor systems

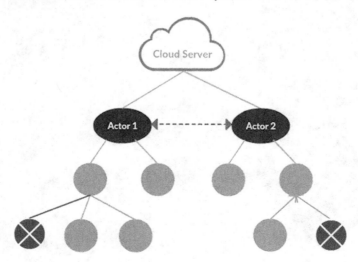

the result to all clients. Due to the hierarchical feature, this pattern improves the network load balancing efficiently.

Shown as Figure 5 when bidders place their offers, they must require the timestamp for server side first. The bidder actor will send a request to Server Time Sync Actor through timestamp message. There are three parts of information in one message: project ID, bidder ID, and timestamp. When a message arrived the Server Time Sync Actor, this actor will generate a new timestamp and update its state, which will be stored in the document database. This information will be an intense connection between actors.

A Comparison Actor also communicates with the Bidder Actor through BidderMessage as shown in Figure 6. The difference is that the Comparison Actor will set up an Observer Pattern to keep tracking the messages from Bidder Actor in real time. The Comparison Actor has the capability to subscript several actors' messages at the same time so that the messages from various actors in different regions are able to be handled immediately.

Figure 6. A bidder actor and its behaviors

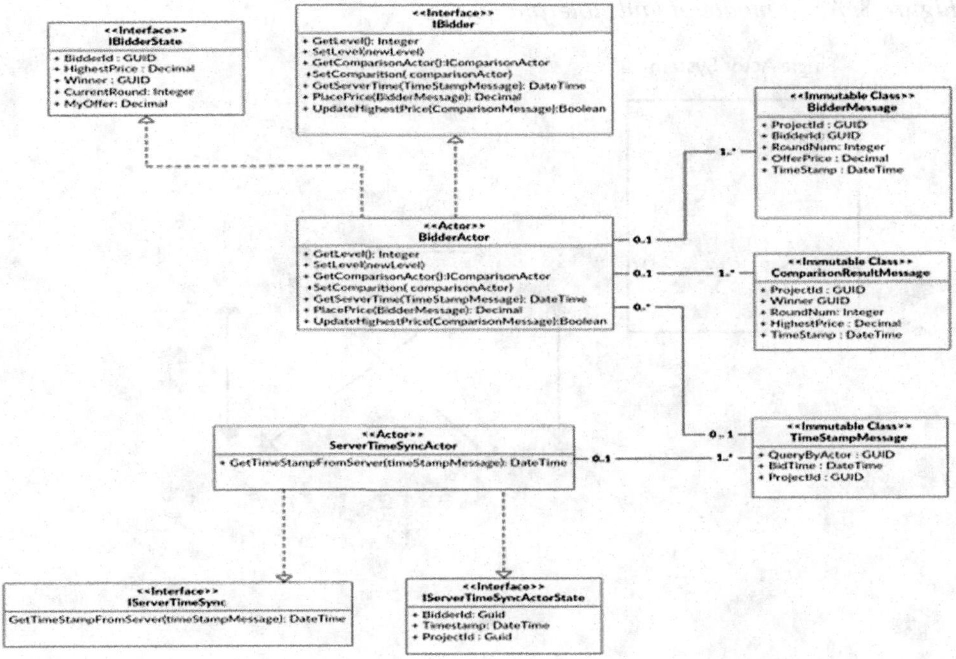

Figure 7. A diagram of the comparison actor

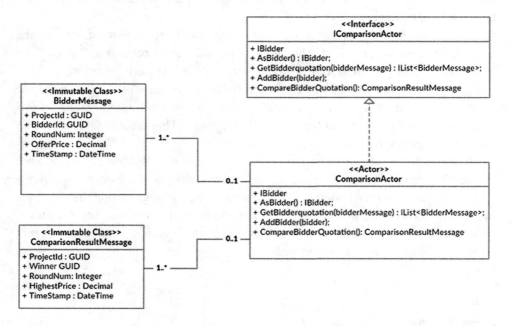

Figure 8. Actor model of fault-tolerant

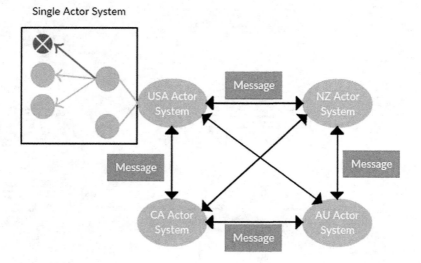

Fault-Tolerant

The fault-tolerant mechanism notoriously is hard to implement correctly the distributed systems that include actor model applications and distributed databases (Stutsman, Lee and Ousterhout, 2015). The reason is that the nodes may crash before finishing its computing or database server may crash and result in losing all data and replicas shown as Figure 7.

The actor models commonly employ hierarchies of supervisor strategy to establish an intensive supervisor – children relationships to achieve an efficient solution of fault-tolerance (K. Lu *et al.*, 2016). When the failure occurs in nodes, the error message will propagate upwards to the root node. If the error node cannot be activated, the root node will force to restart the node and recover its state and message box (Armstrong, et al. 1993).

Location Transparency

Location transparency allows actors and actor systems to easily talk to each other without knowing physical locations. The actor is designed to extend out to a significant number of dedicated servers and to allow this actor instantiated at different places (Thurau, 2012). There is nearly no physical address for the actors. They may exist in the purely virtual memory. In this way, the actor model can easily relocate some actors to a different host server, so that we can scale out our web applications (Bernstein, et al., 2014). Significantly, the actors no longer heavily rely on the Web API for the actual remoting layer.

State Persistence in Actor Model

There are two options for persistent in actor model. Firstly, we load state from the external relational database, or system information, such as bidder's user ID, level, and project ID from the authentication token. Moreover, we populate the variables of the actor. Another option is that we can choose the distributed document database on cloud, like Document DB on Azure or Mongo DB on AWS. Both document databases provide the shard mechanism. Specifically, the document can be spread with reading and writing transactions across more infrastructures with a high throughput. Technically, the storage that is used to store the state data on the cloud can scale out unlimited shown as Figure 9.

The document has a unique ID and a partition key for collection shard. Documents are stored in a collection. Meanwhile, the collection can be shard between different servers in various locations. Even if some data fragments are lost, document database can recover them by using replicas.

Figure 9. State persistence for bidding

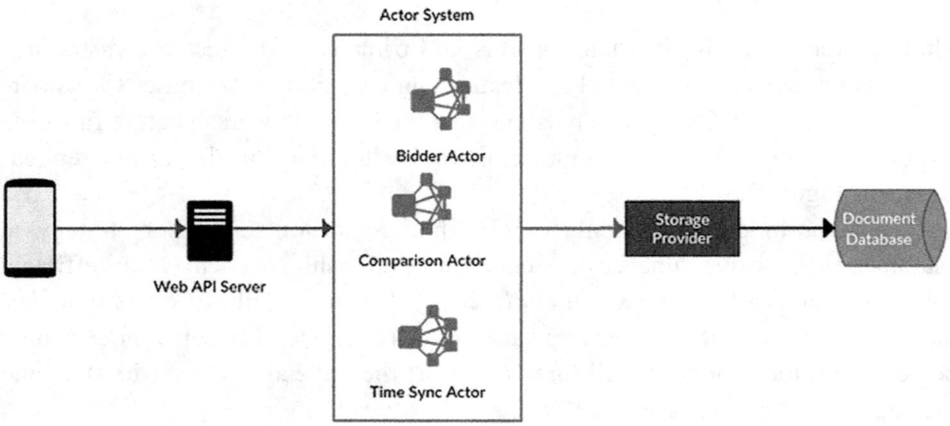

DISTRIBUTED DATABASES

Traditional relational database has difficulties to fulfil the requirements of the high-concurrent applications. As we all know, the biggest problem is that it is hard to deal with the exponential growth of data collection (Tauro, Aravindh and Shreeharsha, 2012). If we need to track and record the status of all bidders, the process will generate a plenty of associated data. Additionally, complex relationship like many to many relationships between tables, which enables data query, has become tough in a relational database. For instance, some of the queries need to cross several tables for retrieving many related data. In this stage, relational databases must join tons of table together and traverse all data pace by pace.

High-Performance Read and Write

To achieve the best performance of an actor model, the databases that are served must be distributed and extendable. Meanwhile, they are also demanded to fulfil the requirement of high performance of reading and writing with high concurrency and low latency (Han, et al., 2011). Most of the document databases, like MongoDB, offer the capability of massively-parallel data processing (Moniruzzaman and Hossain, 2013). Owing to the dependence on relationship between the tables, the document database is schemaless. We deposit complex data types with BSON or JSON document so that we are able to significantly speed up the access to mass data. The access to Mongo DB is at ten times faster than relational database such as MySQL (Castro and Liskov, 1999).

Fault-Tolerance

Generally, most of the NoSQL databases take use of replication and sharding to provide the fault-tolerant design.

- Replication allows database scale horizontally. It is also called Master-Slave Replication. In the pattern, only the Master database responds to write request, slaves respond to read requests from clients.
- Sharding machinimas allow us to store separated replication sets into each shard, and results in offering high availability and data consistency.

Additionally, another replication algorithm (Byzantine faults tolerate BFT) from MIT can provide highly available service without interruptions like system bugs, accidental operation and malicious attacks (Castro and Liskov, 1999).

IMPLEMENTATION AND TESTING

The actor framework we proposed is Orleans from Microsoft. The latest version of Orleans combined most of the actor models from Erlang and Akka. We implement three grains (bidder actor, time sync actor and comparison actor) in an actor system. We implement a single SiloHost server on the local server and calling actors from another laptop. We find that the advanced features of the actor are stronger than the legacy client / server framework as shown in Table 1.

In Table 1, we find that the actor is stateful. Each actor shares its inner state through immutable message. We are able to see the state tracking on the server side. When a bidder actor tries to get the timestamp from the ServerTimeSync actor, its behaviours or states will be stored in a database on Azure. The messages passing through the actors are in pairs. Each actor has a unique GUID code so that every behaviour of the actor is trackable. The state persistence ensures the data concurrency and consistency.

In order to observe the price notification between bidder actors, we set up three bidder robots to bid the price randomly in one hundred rounds. Specifically, every time a bidder bids the highest price, the asynchronous notification will be triggered. The Comparison Actor will send the notifications to all bidders (except winner itself) through winner message. The advantage of the asynchronous notification is that the winner actor will not be noticed, which means that the server side will not broadcast to all clients, they only update bidders' state. In this way, we improve the loading balance of this network. In addition, the document database is schemaless. The data with different structures are able to be saved in the same collection. To

Table 1. A comparison with features of the actor framework and the client-server architecture

#	Actor Framework	Client-Server
1	Tracking the state changes to clients immediately	Needing to request state changes to clients from the server every time.
2	Providing safe message delivery	Utilising SSL protocol and digital signature technique to guarantees the message security.
3	Distributed to different server	Only implemented on one server
4	At-least-once model guarantees no data packets loss	Packet loss in heavy network traffic
5	Supervison strategy and internal state provide data fault tolerant	No fault tolerant support
6	Location transparency	Physical address requirements
7	Capability of nodes generation	Do not support children management.
8	Using NoSQL database to tracking persistent state (record states' changes every time)	Support NoSQL or Relational database to store the final result (winner only)

be more specific, we store the bidder actor, compare actor and server time async actor's states in the same collection though the data structures is entirely different. The benefit of the schemaless is that we do not need to join or transaction data in various tables resulting in providing high-performance reading, writing, updating and deleting.

For example, the document database, such as MongoDB, that we used in the implementation provides high speed of reading, creating, and updating. When the bidder robots get the system timestamp, we track the ServerTimeSync actor's state changes. We set up two different databases (SQL Server and MongoDB) as the data record providers. In the process of inserting the first 5000 data, it's hard for us to distinguish who is faster. However, when the amount of data written gradually increased to 15000, the SQL database writing speed is almost ten times slower than MongoDB shown as Figure 10.

The state of bidder and comparison is a complex data structure. For instance, states of the comparison actor include bidder actors' states in each round of competition. So, we need to join two or three tables together to query the data in SQL Server. However, the database only nests the relevant information in a document. For complex data queries, we are not surprised that MongoDB is still faster. When the query data is higher than 15000, SQL takes 16 seconds, and MongoDB takes approximately 5 seconds shown as Figure 11.

Figure 10. Insert ServerTimeSync status into database

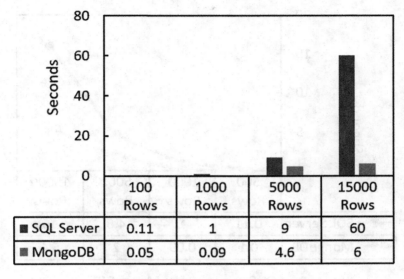

	100 Rows	1000 Rows	5000 Rows	15000 Rows
■ SQL Server	0.11	1	9	60
■ MongoDB	0.05	0.09	4.6	6

■ SQL Server   ■ MongoDB

CONCLUSION AND FUTURE WORK

The online auction platform is to transfer the market by providing reliable and professional services. A key aspect of this shift is the accommodation of clustering services. These services are no longer limited by the interconnected location of buyers and sellers (Ackerberg, Hirano and Shahriar, 2006). 80% of online participants (both buyers and sellers) are from different countries or regions.

In this situation, the traditional client-server architecture does not have enough capability to manage all bidders in the distinct clustering of trading to ensure the fairness and reliability of online auctions. The English Auction is an excellent case at point. It has a very high demand for system concurrency and responsiveness because the system needs to complete the price delivery, comparison, and notification in very short time period.

Thus, the actor framework is employed to provide the data consistency and integrity during the high-performance network environment. To the best of our knowledge, this is the first time that the actor framework is applied to the online auction. The main contribution of this chapter is as follows. (1) Using the actor framework to improve the packet loss and traffic rates for our cloud online auction model. The message is wrapped in the web stock, we cannot guarantee that any messages can be received or dispatched each time successfully. Thus, the additional implementation must be taken to actor mode like at-least-once in Orleans. It requires retry when

Figure 11. Query state from comparison actor and bidder actor

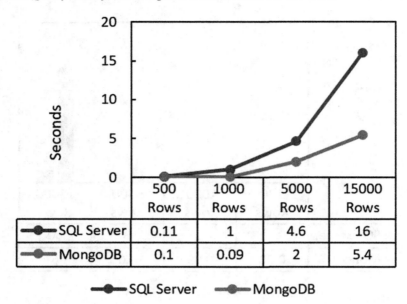

	500 Rows	1000 Rows	5000 Rows	15000 Rows
●—SQL Server	0.11	1	4.6	16
●—MongoDB	0.1	0.09	2	5.4

●—SQL Server   ●—MongoDB

transport losses. (2) Implementation of the mechanism of safe message delivery ensures our bid price cannot be tempered during the data passing from end to end. (3) Recording all actors' state persistently in document database so that we are able to approve the data persistence, which is a highly difficult task in the latency database like SQL database.

Although immutable message guarantees data security within the delivery process, we cannot stop online fraud by using actor model. In future, we will set a REST API server to test the performance in another different network environment.

REFERENCES

Ackerberg, D., Hirano, K., & Shahriar, Q. (2006). *The buy-it-now option, risk aversion, and impatience in an empirical model of eBay bidding*. University of Arizona.

Agha, G. (1985). *Actors: A model of concurrent computation in distributed systems*. DTIC Document.

Armbrust, M. (2009). *Above the clouds: A berkeley view of cloud computing*. Tech. Rep. UCB/EECS-2009-28, EECS Department, U.C. Berkeley.

Armbrust, M., Stoica, I., Zaharia, M., Fox, A., Griffith, R., Joseph, A. D., ... Rabkin, A. (2010). A view of cloud computing. *Communications of the ACM*, *53*(4), 50–58. doi:10.1145/1721654.1721672

Armstrong, J. (2007). *Programming Erlang: software for a concurrent world*. Pragmatic Bookshelf.

Armstrong, J., Virding, R., Wikström, C., & Williams, M. (1993). *Concurrent programming in ERLANG*. Academic Press.

Bernstein, P., Bykov, S., Geller, A., Kliot, G., & Thelin, J. (2014). *Orleans: Distributed virtual actors for programmability and scalability*. MSR-TR-2014–41.

Castro, M., & Liskov, B. (1999). *Practical Byzantine fault tolerance* (Vol. 99). OSDI.

Chan, H., Ho, I., & Lee, R. (2001) Design and implementation of a mobile agent-based auction system, *IEEE Pacific Rim Conference on Communications, Computers and signal Processing*, 2, 740-743. 10.1109/PACRIM.2001.953738

De Koster, J., Marr, S., D'Hondt, T., & Van Cutsem, T. (2013). Tanks: multiple reader, single writer actors. The workshop on Programming based on actors, agents, and decentralized control, 61-68. doi:10.1145/2541329.2541331

Estrada, R., & Ruiz, I. (2016). *Big Data SMACK*. Apress. doi:10.1007/978-1-4842-2175-4

Gupta, M. (2012). *Akka essentials*. Packt Publishing Ltd.

Haller, P. (2012). On the integration of the actor model in mainstream technologies: the scala perspective. In *Proceedings of Programming systems, languages and applications based on actors, agents, and decentralized control abstractions* (pp. 1–6). ACM. doi:10.1145/2414639.2414641

Han, J., Haihong, E., Le, G., & Du, J. (2011). Survey on NoSQL database. *International Conference on Pervasive computing and applications (ICPCA)*, 363-366.

Hewitt, C. (2010). *Actor model of computation: scalable robust information systems*. arXiv preprint arXiv:1008.1459

Hewitt, C., Bishop, P., & Steiger, R. (1973). A Universal Modular ACTOR Formalism for Artificial Intelligence. *Advance Papers of the Conference*, *3*, 235.

Karmani, R., Shali, A., & Agha, G. (2009). Actor frameworks for the JVM platform: a comparative analysis. In *International Conference on Principles and Practice of Programming in Java* (pp. 11–20). ACM.

Kekre, H., & Bharadi, V. (2010). Dynamic signature pre-processing by modified digital difference analyzer algorithm. In *Thinkquest 2010* (pp. 67–73). Springer.

Krasnokutskaya, E., Terwiesch, C., & Tiererova, L. (2016). Trading across Borders in Online Auctions. In *Meeting Papers, no. 1537*. Society for Economic Dynamics.

Liu, H., Wang, S., & Fei, T. (2003). Multicast-based online auctions: A performance perspective, *Benchmarking. International Journal (Toronto, Ont.), 10*(1), 54–64.

Lu, K., Yahyapour, R., Wieder, P., Yaqub, E., Abdullah, M., Schloer, B., & Kotsokalis, C. (2016). Fault-tolerant Service Level Agreement lifecycle management in clouds using actor system. *Future Generation Computer Systems, 54*, 247–259. doi:10.1016/j.future.2015.03.016

McAdam, R. (2001). Fragmenting the function-process interface: The role of process benchmarking, *Benchmarking. International Journal (Toronto, Ont.), 8*(4), 332–349.

Moniruzzaman, A., & Hossain, S. (2013). *Nosql database: New era of databases for big data analytics-classification, characteristics and comparison.* arXiv preprint arXiv:1307.0191

Philip, J., & Bharadi, V. (2016) Online Signature Verification in Banking Application: Biometrics SaaS Implementation. *Proceedings on International Conference on Communication Computing and Virtualization, 306*, 28-33.

Power, R., & Li, J. (2010) Building fast, distributed programs with partitioned tables. *9th USENIX Symposium on Operating Systems Design and Implementation.*

Strangers, C. (2005). *Programming in E as Plan Coordination.* Springer-Verlag Berlin Heidelberg.

Stutsman, R., Lee, C., & Ousterhout, J. (2015). Experience with Rules-Based Programming for Distributed, Concurrent, Fault-Tolerant Code. *USENIX Annual Technical Conference*, 17-30.

Tauro, C., Aravindh, S., & Shreeharsha, A. (2012). Comparative study of the new generation, agile, scalable, high performance NOSQL databases. *International Journal of Computers and Applications, 48*(20), 1–4. doi:10.5120/7461-0336

Thurau, M. (2012). *Akka framework.* University of Lübeck.

Chapter 8
Blockchain for Security of Cloud–Based Online Auction

Yun Shu
Auckland University of Technology, New Zealand

Jian Yu
Auckland University of Technology, New Zealand

Wei Qi Yan
Auckland University of Technology, New Zealand

ABSTRACT

Online auction is one of the most successful internet business models. However, auction fraud has become the highest threat and hazard to the future of this business model. The blockchain provides a new perspective to resolve this problem. It can be used for current financial services, certificates, remittances, and online payments; meanwhile it also provides several crucial services such as smart contract, smart property, trust system, and security services. This chapter discusses how to apply blockchain to a cloud-based online auction and the principle of operation. The purpose is to fundamentally solve the problem of online fraud caused by information asymmetry of electronic transactions. To the best of the authors' knowledge, this is the first time that the blockchain has been applied to authentication of online auction. The preliminary contribution is for preventing auction fraud from the aspects of smart properties and smart contract.

DOI: 10.4018/978-1-5225-6313-6.ch008

INTRODUCTION

As one of the most significant electronic markets, online auction transfers the collectables business and e-commercial business to a global billion-dollar market (Grazioli and Jarvenpaa, 2000; Peters, et al., 2015; Corcoran, 1999). With the idea of frictionless economy, online auction is considered to be rapid and efficient platform to eliminate geographic boundaries and establish the accurate price based on supply and demand (Ba, et al., 2003). Alibaba, Amazon, and E-Bay are the exemplar cases in this area. These platforms offer low cost, excellent technical support, and massive data analysis so that traditional sales begin to transition to e-business model increasingly. The usage of online auction sites ranges from individuals to firms; however, the market fraud is rising. According to the Internet fraud operated by the National Consumers Union, online auctions were still the primary source of Internet fraud (Alanezi, 2016).

For this reason, a growing number of institutions, such as Alibaba, Samsung, Louis Vuitton, Internet Fraud Watch (www.fraud.org) and the Internet Fraud Complaint Center (www.ifccfbi.gov), are jointly developing new mechanism to combat this challenge (Chua and Wareham, 2004). Simultaneously, Alibaba and a myriad of financial institutions to propose a new solution - giant distributed database "block chain." The blockchain is secured by Byzantine fault tolerance (BFT). This database is used to maintain a continuous growth of blocks. As shown in Figure 1, the design of blockchain is to prevent data modification. Once the data are recorded, it cannot be altered reversely anymore.

In blockchain, each block consists of block hash link, timestamp, and valuable data as shown in Figure 2 The blocks can be transferred from one blockchain to another. This technology has approved that it can eliminate the double-spending problem (Pilkington, 2015).

Thus, it can be utilised to various scenarios, such as financial services and medical record (Peters and Panayi, 2016). The blockchain might become the most critical online promising technology for Internet interaction (Zheng, 2016). This database is more magic than we expected. It could be the final solution to online auction fraud.

Based on the distributed blockchain technology, we create a broad range of distributed applications. The revolutionary methodology in this area is the Etherum platform, which includes a complete programable framework (English, 2016). This framework is utilised to implement smart contract. Moreover, the blockchain infrastructure facilitates virtual currency, such as Bitcoin, trust and contract applications. The most significant feature is that the linked data are decentralised so that we do not need to be dependent on central server anymore.

Figure 1. The diagram of blockchains

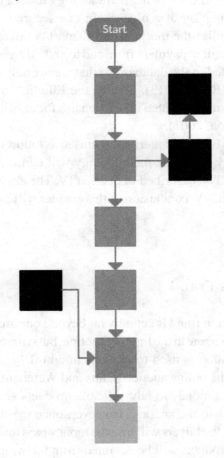

Figure 2. Bitcoin network (resource from bitcoin)

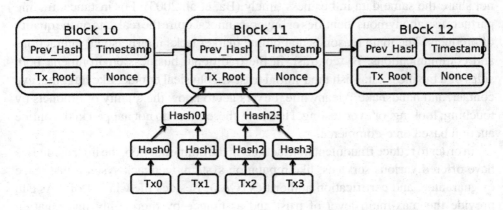

In this chapter, we will discuss the methodology that can prevent online fraud actively. The implementation of a blockchain can secure the currency transition of online action. We utilise the mechanism of smart contract and link data which ensures the security of online payment from end to end. Moreover, final transactions are permanently recorded in the database so that we are able to provide permanent records for all clients (Black, 2013). Finally, the Elliptic Curve Digital Signature Algorithm (ECDSA) is implemented in blockchains for offering trusted handshakes between blocks (Johnson, 2001).

The remaining parts of this chapter are organised as follows. In Section II, we will present the related work while the methodology will be introduced in Section III, the results database will be described in Section IV. The analysis and comparisons will be detailed in Section V, conclusion of this chapter will be stated in Section VI.

RELATED WORK

Type of the Online Fraud

The seriousness of auction fraud is actually far beyond our imagination. Victims do not actually have to participate in the Internet auction, but will suffer the consequences of fraud. The triangulation is used to implement an offline fraud via a merchant sells the product from the online auction (Chua and Wareham, 2004). For example, when a thief uses stolen money to buy valuable products and put them online for auction, anyone could win the auction. However, once the fraudulent purchase is restricted and confined, the buyers will lose the money paid for these stolen products. Meanwhile all stolen products will be detained from the winners.

Information asymmetry has been recognized as the major issues that result in cheating easily over the Internet (Macaulay, 1963). This results that two parties do not share the same data in business timely (Ba, et al. 2003). For instance, trading partners use anonymous identities or buyers cannot acquire the real data on the quality of products. The main reason is that online market lacks interpersonal interactions and communications. By contrast, in the traditional business environment, both sides of a business establish their initial trust via physical contact like hugging, eye contact, and handshake. Meanwhile, buyers get to know the quality of products by touching, looking, or even tasting. However, these cases do not happen in the online auction based on e-commerce.

In order to reduce fraudulent transactions in the online auction, the intermediaries have offered various services, like reputation system, feedback system, insurance or guarantee, and certification authorities (CAs). Besides the Class 4 of CAs can provide the maximum level of trust and assurance by thoroughly investigating companies and individuals, most of the anti-fraud mechanisms are passive defense (Froomkin, 1996). Literatures have shown that trading partners heavily rely on their reputations in the traditional business. Specifically, individual's reputation can act as a "hostage". The disrepute always spreads quickly in the business community. The social pressure or lost trusts caused by bad reputations might be more effective than legislations in this online community (Macaulay, 1963). Because the online auction sites rarely provide the strong authentication at present. Thus, those disrepute traders may renew the identity by re-registering a new user ID (Ba, et al. 2003) to get the new reputation.

Table 1 provides several frauds of online auctions, the triangulation is just one of them (Chua and Wareham, 2002). Moreover, there are variations of online frauds. For instance, Escrow Services fraud is a variant of failure to ship. The escrow services are provided by the trusted third party, like Alipay, which are responsible to hold transaction funds from the buyers before the deal is successfully accomplished. However, the cheaters are able to set up a fake escrow service after receiving the funds. In order to prevent this type of fraud, auction houses establish a reputation system to mark each trader, like Alibaba, Amazon, and E-bay.

Bidders not only can view the reputation score itself, but also can find the number of positive, neutral or dissatisfied transactions as well as the comments (Ba, et al., 2002). However, the reputation score is rarely computed based on the high-priced consumable market like artwork auction even if the seller really hardly tells the fakes from originals.

With globalisation of Internet-based cloud services, the online auction platform is reshaping the market by providing a professional service platform. A key aspect of this shift is the provision of multiple services, especially professional services, which are no longer limited by the location of buyers and sellers. The research outcome (Krasnokutskaya, Terwiesch and Tiererova, 2016) indicates that 80% of online transactions were joined by participants (both buyers and sellers) from different countries and regions.

Under these conditions, information asymmetry illustrates a specific situation that two parties do not share with the same information; it has been regarded as the majority of issues in the electronic markets (Akerlof, 1970). There are two most important aspects related to online frauds: one is the anonymous trading; the other is the unwarranted products or uncertain quality of goods (Choi, Stahl and Whinston, 1997).

Blockchain

Blockchains are considered as one of the most promising technologies in the next generation of Internet transaction systems. It can be used not only for current

Table 1. Type of online fraud

#	Fraud Type	Description
1	Failure to ship	Never ship the product after payment.
2	Failure to pay	Buyers do not send the money to seller.
3	Misrepresentation	Seller describes items incorrectly that do not match real items
4	Loss or damage claims	Buyer claim the loss or damage services to retrieve money back.
5	Shilling	Seller uses another account to bids on own stuff to push up the prices.
6	Triangulation Fraud	Sell stolen items online.
8	Buy and switch	Buyer switches the original sound with inferior one and return it to seller.
9	Shell auction	Seller set up a fake auction to store the credit card information from buyer.
10	Bid shielding	Two or three bidders collude on an auction.
11	Fee stacking	Seller asks the buyer to pay extra fees after auction ends.

financial services such as digital asset management, deposit certificates, remittances and online payment systems, but also for smart contracts, Internet of Things (IoT), reputation systems and security services (Peters, Panayi and Chapelle, 2015), etc. In order to provide a secure environment for virtual currency transactions, Bitcoins (BTC) utilise blockchain to reinforce its cryptocurrency.

Specifically, blockchain facilitates the elastic and distributed ledger for storing a significant amount of transactions, attributing them to a block in the network and ordering these blocks in real time (English, Auer and Domingue, 2016). As the number of blocks grows rapidly, generating new blocks requires significant resources. So many private organisations join the competing with each other for utilising dedicated high-power computers to run ASICs for real-time process of Bitcoin networks (Kroll, Davey and Felten, 2013). This process is also called "mining" as shown in Figure 3. Once the miner successfully finds a new valid block on the longest branch of the branching tree, a new transaction will be added into the log and its nonce is selected. Meanwhile, invalid blocks will be ignored. This mechanism is called proof-of-work (POW), which is considered difficult to be performed, but the result is easy to be verified (Becker, et al., 2013).

Blockchains work in a decentralised and untrusted environment through the integration of encryption hash, consensus mechanism, and digital signatures (based on asymmetric encryption). Fig 4 shows the details of a branch of blockchain. In the blockchain, each client fully participates in all operations, such as initiating new transactions, receiving transactions, validating transactions, and the generation of new blocks.

Figure 3. An example of mining process in the blockchain

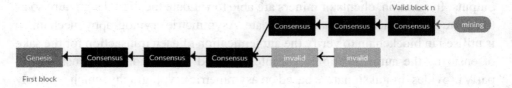

Figure 4. The details of a branch of blockchain

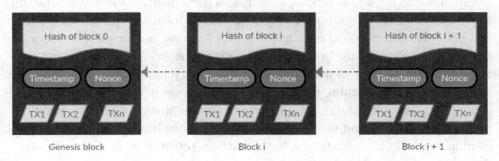

Block

To prevent online fraud, such as double spending, all clients must participate in a peer-to-peer protocol that implements a distributed timestamp service, and provide a fully-serialized log which contains the details of all transactions. The transactions in the log are formulated into blocks that contain block version, serial numbers, timestamps, encrypted hashes, a nonce, metadata, and a set of valid records of transaction. A single block structure is shown in Figure 5, which is presented by JavaScript Object Notation.

Specifically, a header of the blockchain illustrates which block validation rule should be followed. The previous block is a 256-bit encrypted hash number. The difficulty is utilised to indicate the coefficient of difficulty for mining the new block. The timestamp is a big integer that shows the current time stamp for the world UTC time since 1970. A nonce number is a 4-byte field. This field usually begins from zero, and each time the block is hashed, this field is incremented. The maximum amount of transactions, which are stored in the single block, totally depend on the size of the blocks and the size of each record.

The block body contains the amount of transaction records and the set of transaction logs. A credible record of transaction is consisted of two mainly components: output and input. The identity section of records of transaction inputs is a significant reference to the unspent transaction outputs (UTXO) of the sender while the sender must have to designate the destination address and numbers in outputs. In addition, clients or miners are able to validate the digital signature so as to ensure the transaction is entirely validate. Asymmetric cryptography mechanism is utilised in blockchain to verify the authentication of each transaction for the sake of ensuring the authentication, data integrity, and repudiation. The trusted third party provides digital signature based on asymmetric cryptography which is widely utilised in an online market (Christidis and Devetsikiotis, 2016).

In online auctions, massive individuals participate in transactions. This situation makes it tough to bind an identity to a participant. Obviously, blockchain facilitates to solve this problem easily. The absence of interpersonal interactions and communications based authentication in electronic markets is another issue that leads to online frauds. In a traditional business, buyers and sales have got used to face-to-face business at the same place. Customers and vendors establish their basic trust via conversation, handshake, facial expression, eye contacts, etc. (Ba, et al. 2003). The in-kind transactions provide opportunities to know the quality of products by viewing and touching. Thus, due to the existing problems in online auction, we will demonstrate how the blockchain solves these problems by using decentralise framework, reputation system and smart contract.

Figure 5. A block in blockchain that is represented by JSON (javascript object notation)

```
{
    "hash": "893a09b5a19838027b60f8007876bcf4333d4904",
    "prev_block": "90f8b1f196c97b60c760f2d18601bc29bc5fe23a",
    "time": 1491973298603,
    "difficulty": 3343090408,
    "nonce": 2504324516,
    "tx": [{"hash ":"YXNkZmFzMjM0",
            "in": [{
                "prev_out": {
                    "hash": "000..."
                }
            }],
            "out": [{
                "value": "74.76710074",
                "scriptPubKey": "36a1..."
            }]
        },
        ...
    ]
}
```

Figure 6. Digital signature in blockchain technology

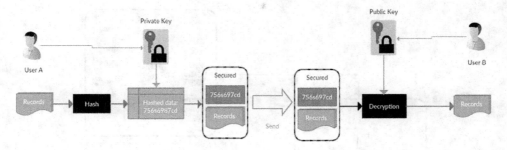

Decentralized Framework

Once the records of transaction or block are generated, the validation mechanism will be triggered immediately. The new node needs to be verified by the network. However, as shown in Figure 7, there may be highly distrusted network of blockchain, because each branch may have a view which is different from the entire network state. Thus, a decentralised network is needed to diminish the branches in blockchain.

In a distributed blockchain database, one of the most challenging issues is how to reach consensus block on a transaction among the invalid blocks. Each miner communicates with the blockchain database through a dedicated node in which a client is implemented. Many blocks across the network form a decentralised network. Once a block receives transaction record from another customer, it is going to verify the authentication of the block first. And then, the result of validation will be broadcasted to every valid block connected to it. Thus, the valid block will be rapidly spread throughout the whole network. The advantage of the decentralised systems is the independency, which is able to save the cost of enterprise. However, the decentralised network also increases the difficulty in verifying the transaction record in the untrusted environment.

Smart Contract and Smart Property

From the very beginning, the smart contract and smart property in Blockchain 2.0 are mainly utilised to solve the critical issue from generic identification and authorization. Whereas, the Blockchain 1.0 focuses on virtual money transaction, the Blockchain 2.0 is for decentralising the market generally, and the implementation of a blockchain beyond the currency (Kosba, et al., 2016). Specifically, the technologies from Blockchain 2.0, such as smart contract, smart property, decentralized applications (Dapps) and decentralized autonomous organizations (DAOs), are implemented on the application layer that provides to the software developer a tightly integrated

Figure 7. Decentralize network

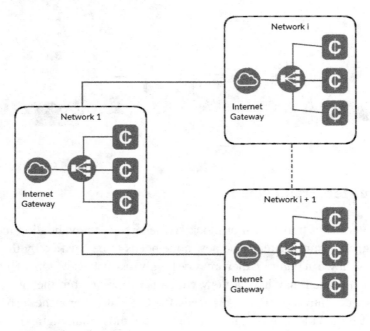

end-to-end platform, such as Ethereum (Altcoin project), for building blockchain-based software (Wood, 2014).

The key functionality of decentralised transaction ledger in the Blockchain 2.0 is utilised to register, approve, and execute all types of contracts and properties. Table II illustrated the properties, the contracts could be transferred with the blockchain.

Any forms of assets can be registered in blockchain database, once these properties are encoded into blockchain, they become smart properties, such as public records, private records, identification, digital documents, financial reports, and intangible assets, like stock shares, copyrights of music and books. The key idea of smart property is controlled by the owner who has the private key (Swan, 2015). By using the smart contract, the ownership of smart property is able to be transferred automatically to another owner after all payments are made. The execution of this smart contract is totally automatic, there is no need to be interacted by human operations when authentication and verification are successfully processed.

Tradenet

With the rapid development of Bitcoin, we gradually realise that the practical value of blockchain is far more than the electronic money system, especially in the

Table 2. Example of blockchain applications in version 2.0

#	Category	Properties
1	Public records	Land and properties title, death certification, business registration data, and vehicle registration data.
2	Private records	Personal contracts, digital signature, individual loans and marriage certifications.
3	Identification	Passport, ID cards, driver license.
4	Documents	Notarized documents, property ownership Certifications, and proof of insurance documents
5	Financial records	Deposit, bank statement, private equities, stock records, bonds, pensions.
6	Intangible assets	Copyrights, intellectual property, domain names, and reservations.

auction market. All deals are able to be automatically transacted based on specific permissions and contract (Swan, 2016). The Real-time Bidding (RTB) networks are the best case in existing examples of automatic markets.

With the rise of online auctions in future, the blockchain is applied to restrict the order and plan transactions for resource allocation of our real world. An advanced concept is that the self-operation system (integrated with blockchain) will be implemented for the management of those self-owned assets like house, private stock, and self-owning car. Once these assets are registered into blockchain, they will become self-directed assets (smart properties). These properties are able to employ themselves for automatically trading based on continuously connected to the Internet so that they can query significant data and search for the potential transferee (Pagliery, 2014). If the conditions of potential customers meet the requirement of smart properties, they are going to execute the smart contracts to finish the transaction. This is a significant step of the distributed online auction.

Challenges of Blockchain

Blockchain has great capacity for establishing future Internet interaction systems, but it has to face technical challenges. To be more specific, there are further needs to be considered in the current blockchain for the sake of meeting the requirement of real-time processing of billions of transactions. Additionally, there is a need to propose a new mechanism to avoid selfish miners in blockchain (Eyal and Sirer, 2014). Meanwhile, before the blockchain is widely applied to various Internet interactions, other challenges also need to be addressed, such as the lack of privacy and current consensus algorithms (Kosba, et al., 2016).

METHODOLOGY

Elliptic Curve Cryptography

Elliptic Curve Digital Signature Algorithm (ECDSA) was used to implement in online transaction based on blockchain. Elliptic curve for cryptography (ECC) is utilised to the establishment of open key encryption algorithm (Koblitz, 1987; Miller, 1985). Compared to the RSA algorithm, the advantage of using ECC is that it has shorter keys to achieve the same effectiveness of security[27]. Elliptic Curve cryptography is based on eq.(1).

$$Y^2 = \left(X^3 + aX + b\right) \bmod p \qquad (1)$$

where the possible value of Y^2 should between 0 to p^{-1}, we thus have the modulo p.

There is a significant rule that is called chord-and-tangent rule. For example, let $p = 23$ and the elliptic curve E: $Y^2 = X^3 - 4X + 0$ where $a = -4$ and $b = 0$. We have two distinct points on an elliptic curve **E**: **P** = (x_1, y_1), **Q** = (x_2, y_2). If we draw

Figure 8. The addition of two distinct elliptic curve points: **P + Q = R**

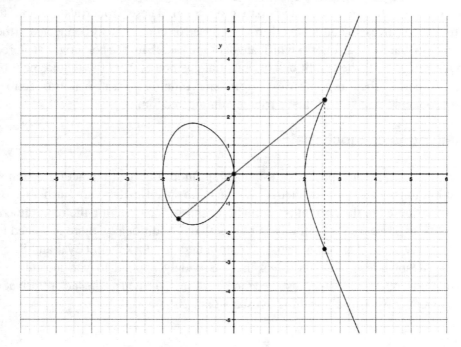

Figure 9. The doubling of an elliptic curve point

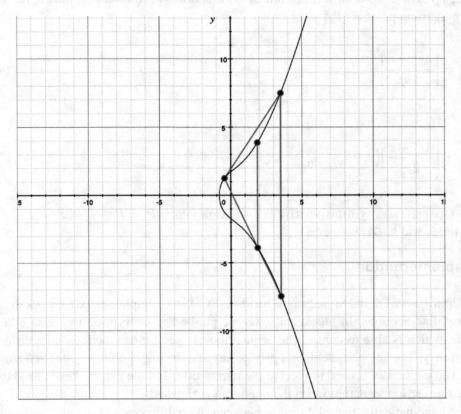

a line through **P** and **Q**, there must be an intersection point **R** on the elliptic curve. Then the reflection point (x_3, y_3) of **R** is the sum of **P** and **Q**.

$$x_3 = \left(\frac{y_2 - y_1}{x_2 - x_1} \right) - x_1 - x_2 \tag{2}$$

$$y_3 = \left(\frac{y_2 - y_1}{x_2 - x_1} \right)(x, -x_3) - y_1 \tag{3}$$

In the same way, we have a point $\mathbf{P}(x_1, y_1)$ on the elliptic curve $\mathbf{E}: y^2 = x^3 + 3x + 3$ where $P \neq -P$, and $a = b = 3$. We are able to draw a tangent line at point **P**, it will intersect with the **E** at the third point, and its reflection point will be at 2**P** =

(x_2, y_2). Thus, we draw a line from $2P$ to P and it will intersect on the curve, the symmetrical point is $3P$,

$$x_2 = \left(\frac{3x_1^2 + a}{2y_1}\right)^2 - 2x_1 \tag{4}$$

$$y_2 = \left(\frac{3x_1^2 + a}{2y_1}\right)(x, -x_2) - y_1 \tag{5}$$

One particularity of this point is that if we have a point: $kP = P + P + P + ... + P$ (k times and $k \in Z^+$ is integer)

Implementation

Elliptic Curve Digital Signature Algorithm (ECDSA) is implemented to Blockchain for online auctions. In blockchain, we use public key encryption to create a key pair, which is able to control the acquisition of specific transactions, like virtual currency. The key pair includes a private key and the only public key derived from it. The public key is used to receive the transaction, and the private key is used for the transaction signature when the operation is finished.

Mathematically, the relationship between the public key and the private key is that the private key is able to be utilised for the signature of a particular message. This signature is able to be used to verify the public key. Meanwhile we do not need to disclose our private key.

When the transaction is finished, current owner of the virtual currency needs to submit its public key and signature in the transaction (the signatures of each operation are different, but they are generated from the same private key). All traders in online auction using the blockchain are able to be verified by the submitted public key and signature for the sake of validity of the transaction.

In online auction, the whole process uses ECDSA with secp256k1 curve. We will demonstrate that the above procedure includes three phases: key generation, signature, and verification (Zyskind and Nathan, 2015). To be more specific, the key pair of an entity is associated with a specific set of EC domain parameters (Johnson, Menezes and Vanstone, 2001), $= \left(q, FR, a, b, G, n, h\right)$.

The key pairs are generated as follows:

Step 1: Select a random integer d in $[1, n\text{-}1]$
Step 2: $Q = dP$ (**P** is a point of prime order n in the E)
Step 3: Public key is **Q**, while the d is private key.

Signature massage are as follows:

Step 1: Select a random or pseudorandom number k in the interval $[1, n\text{-}1]$.
Step 2: Compute $k\mathbf{P} = x_1, y_1$ and $r = x_1 \bmod n$ (where x_1 is regarded as an integer between 0 and $q\text{-}1$). If $r = 0$, then go to **Step 1**.
Step 3: Compute $(k\text{-}1) \bmod n$.
Step 4: Compute $s = (k\text{-}1)[h(m) + d_r] \bmod n$, where h is the Secure Hash Algorithm (SHA-1). If $s = 0$, then go to step 1.
Step 5: The signature for the message m is the pair of integers (r, s)

Verification is following the steps:

Step 1: Verify that r and s are integers in the interval $[1, n\text{-}1]$.
Step 2: Compute $w = (s\text{-}1) \bmod n$ and $h(m)$
Step 3: Compute $u_1 = h(m)w \bmod n$ and $u_2 = r_w \bmod n$.
Step 4: Compute $u_1\mathbf{P} + u_2\mathbf{Q} = (x_0, y_0)$ and $v = x_0 \bmod n$.
Step 5: Accept the signature if and only if $v = r$.

RESULTS

We now used the design algorithms for testing. Our example was from a prototype of an online auction which we have developed. Compared with the most of online auction systems, we embedded the blockchain into our auction platform. Meanwhile, we utilize standard cryptographic building blocks in this platform: keys generator, digital signature and verification are employed by using the ECDSA prime256v1 curve. First, the SHA-256 result is shown along with the private and public set of keys.

```
Input: "37F01AC0-66D5-49DA-AE14-E5F369225C5E",
SHA -256 Hash
Output:
0d13ba7e63ee5faa77214fde9541e4cc4ec70cc22b5341e415a85ad955b6d46c
```

We utilise the SHA-256 hash to reproduce the hash code that is stored in the header of each block. The hash code of this new block is hashed by its parent's hash code, GUID and timestamp. So, each block is tightly linked together by the chain. The most significant thing is that the hash is irreversible. This prevents the block from being deleted and changed. Thus, we can easily retrieve the history of transaction. These features are critical to prevent the online auction fraud. For example, we register a diamond and its certification is based on the blockchain for auction. Before the diamond becomes smart property, the specific data of the diamond, such as brand, colour, size, certification number, and price will be broadcasted for verification. These broadcast messages are signed by private key so other networks can easily verify these messages by using public key. This process will be described in the coming section. If the data is verified, the blockchain is able to generate a new node to save the data.

The next step is to generate the paired keys. According to the algebraic description over F_p, the p is a prime number. In our cryptographic applications p must be a huge random prime number.

Key Pair Generation: 256-bit random private key and corresponding public key. We use the NIST standard curve (P-256) to implementation of EC cryptography.

The modulus p is:

```
11579208921035624876269744694940757353008614341529031419553
3631308867097853951
```

The order n:

```
11579208921035624876269744694940757352999695522413576034242
2259061068512044369
```

The domain parameter seed is:

```
c49d3608 86e70493 6a6678e1 139d26b7 819f7e90
```

According to the P-256 standard, we can generate the paired keys:

```
-----BEGIN EC PRIVATE KEY-----
MHcCAQEEIKz8GGNNeWs79SyS7oKiceneJ97VZ/oHbLwl1TU+qKYloAoGCCqGSM4
9AwEHoUQDQgAEDzylCotL5r+Tmr8eDRBk3mJ0rZbQwlpbBVo4P3BZx4JC/66YCs
93DNEvM09v40zS+DamySjZbpCQ8r0SDUb7UA==
-----END EC PRIVATE KEY-----
-----BEGIN PUBLIC KEY-----
```

MFkwEwYHKoZIzj0CAQYIKoZIzj0DAQcDQgAEDzylCotL5r+Tmr8eDRBk3mJ0rZb
QwlpbBVo4P3BZx4JC/66YCs93DNEvM09v40zS+DamySjZbpCQ8r0SDUb7UA==
-----END PUBLIC KEY-----

Signature

We utilise the private key to generate signature (r, s) on a file as shown in Fig 12, where

```
r=0xB1CC56C49D15D43065D6C33856CCA8B0267C8808E4F585DEFC5B6A1007
40870E
s=0xDD37897025A9BA67192604B68BA3EF43AC3BBAC6335AC3966E03C38457
FD2B6B
```

Proof of Verification

We have already known the *r* and *s* in the signature (r, s) on the transaction file, so the easiest method to prove the verification is to utilize the OpenSSL. We save the private key into the file: *ec_private_key.pem*, and then store the public key into the file: *ec_public_key.pem*. The signature transaction file is deposited in *ec_signature. der*. Meanwhile, the transaction file is kept in *transaction.json* file. We only need to run and execute the command line: openssl dgst -sha256 -verify ec_pub_key.pem -signature ec_signature.der transaction.json

Figure 10. Blockchain hash code example

```
{
    "hash" : "00000000569b85207a17444f19fb54aa21870cb4c47a914121870cb4c47a9141",
    "confirmations" : 308321,
    "size" : 285,
    "height" : 0,
    "version" : 1,
    "merkleroot" : "dd29ecf524b030a65261e3059c48ab9e1ecb258548ab9e1ecb258548ab9e1",
    "tx" : [
        "3492cdeab6fbf14cab4cbcb0be831c23dc772bf6831c23dc772bf6831c23dc772bf6"
    ],
    "time" : 1498049926399,
    "nonce" : 20832332434,
    "bits" : "1d00ffff",
    "difficulty" : 1.00000000,
    "nextblockhash" : "00000000569b85207a17444f19fb54aa21870cb4c47a914121870cb4c47a9145"
}
```

Figure 11. Private key and Public key in Hexadecimal

```
priv:
    00:ac:fc:18:63:4d:79:6b:3b:f5:2c:92:ee:82:a2:
    71:e9:de:27:de:d5:67:fa:07:6c:bc:25:d5:35:3e:
    a8:a6:25
pub:
    04:0f:3c:a5:0a:8b:4b:e6:bf:93:9a:bf:1e:0d:10:
    64:de:62:74:ad:96:d0:c2:5a:5b:05:5a:38:3f:70:
    59:c7:82:42:ff:ae:98:0a:cf:77:0c:d1:2f:33:4f:
    6f:e3:4c:d2:f8:36:a6:c9:28:d9:6e:90:90:f2:bd:
    12:0d:46:fb:50
ASN1 OID: prime256v1
NIST CURVE: P-256
```

Figure 12. The transaction file needs to be signed by private key

```
{
    "confirmations": 308421,
    "size": 285,
    "height": 0,
    "version": 1,
    "merkleroot": "4a5e1e4baab89f3a32518a88c31bc87f618f76673e2cc77ab2127b7afdeda33b",
    "tx": [
        "4a5e1e4baab89f3a32518a88c31bc87f618f76673e2cc77ab2127b7afdeda33b"
    ],
    "time": 1497454344469,
    "nonce": 2083235593,
    "bits": "1d00ffff",
    "difficulty": 1.00000000
}
```

We should emphasise that this example involves extremely modest-size integer numbers for the sake of explanation of basic principle of ECDSA. In blockchain applications, these integers are typically 256 bits long. For example, the hash code in the header of the block is actually hashed twice by the SHA256 algorithm. Thus, this process will result in dramatically increasing the cost of operations. However, the process also dramatically enhances the cost of hacking. In other words, it is impossible to restore the private key from the public key.

The experiment result demonstrates the fact that the implementation of blockchain in online auction system is able to prevent the online fraud issue. Because of the ECDSA is employed, every key link needs to be signed and verified. So, we are able to easily retrieve the critical information about transaction records, like traders' identities, authenticity of goods or trading history of trading items. We do not need to predict the potential fraud through analysing behaviour pattern of transaction of sellers.

TRANSACTION VERIFICATION IN BLOCKCHAIN

The ECDSA is the essence of blockchain applications. This system is a point-to-point (P2P) network whose primary purpose is to propagate transactions that need to be validated to all participants (Antonopoulos, 2014). Generally, the registration of smart properties or the transaction of payment is validated through replicated execution of the nodes that receive this signification information. For example, we register a house on blockchain for online auction. The house's registration data, such as real estate license, land certificate, holder history information, etc. will be signed by our private key and broadcasted to other networks (the third part organization) for verification. When these messages arrive at other institutions' network, their verification server is able to decrypt these messages by using our public key. They will know where the verification request comes from. It is an excellent idea to ensure the authenticity of the data.

The land certificate data is able to be verified by government department, who will decrypt verification request and then check whether our information of land certification is entirely match their database; the historical records of housing transaction are able to be verified by banks. They can retrieve all transaction records of the house in their database to compare our data of trading history. The potential auction price will also be circulated over the community for price comparisons. Validation data contain transaction records of similar model of units and nearby locations. So, other auction organisations will inform us that whether our price is reasonable or not. The whole process of verification is covered by ECDSA algorism so that verification request and response are impossible to be tempered. Meanwhile, the verification response with digital signature is generally issued by trusted hosting organizations. Thus, these processes are quite useful for providing high degree of credibility under the untrusted environment.

The properties are able to be registered or the payments are able to be finished successfully if and only if the validation process is valid. This is a huge difference from the most popular algorithm of fraud detection which utilises data mining to optimise the fraudulent behavioural patterns from social networks or reputation systems. By contract, the blockchain only stores the solid data for transactions. It is easier to authenticate the transaction data are fake or not.

CONCLUSION AND FUTURE WORK

The online auctions promote the global market by providing reliable and professional service. A key aspect of this shift is the accommodation of clustering services. These services are no longer limited by interconnected location of buyers and sellers (Ackerberg, Hirano and Shahriar, 2006). 80% of online participants (both buyers and sellers) are from different countries or regions.

Online fraud detection is extremely hard to be implemented. The traditional methodology does not have enough capability to prevent online fraud in the distinct clustering of trade to ensure the fairness and reliability of online auctions. Blockchain 2.0 and 3.0 provide the fundamental solution for these issues. English auction is an excellent case in point. It has a very high demand for protecting transactions under untrusted environment. Blockchain provides a complete set of secure trading mechanisms, from certification, smart property to smart contract.

Thus, blockchain is offered to the confidential transaction in the untrusted environment. Once the subject is registered into blockchain, it will automatically become a smart property. All relevant data of the subject will be stored in the distributed blockchain and are not able be deleted and modified. In each of online auction transactions, all relevant data about the subject has been verified through broadcast the information to all distributed blockchain databases for verifications, such as house ownership certification. When the online auction transactions are finished, the smart contract will be automatically verified and the transaction is completed.

REFERENCES

Ackerberg, D., Hirano, K., & Shahriar, Q. (2006). *The buy-it-now option, risk aversion, and impatience in an empirical model of eBay bidding*. University of Arizona.

Akerlof. (1970). *The market for "lemons": quality uncertainty and the market mechanism*. Academic Press.

Alanezi, F. (2016). *Perceptions of online fraud and the impact on the countermeasures for the control of online fraud in Saudi Arabian financial institutions*. Brunel University London.

Antonopoulos. (2014). *Mastering Bitcoin: unlocking digital cryptocurrencies*. O'Reilly Media, Inc.

Ba, S., & Pavlou, P. A. (2002). Evidence of the effect of trust building technology in electronic markets: Price premiums and buyer behavior. *Management Information Systems Quarterly, 26*(3), 243–268. doi:10.2307/4132332

Ba, S., Whinston, A. B., & Zhang, H. (2003). Building trust in online auction markets through an economic incentive mechanism. *Decision Support Systems, 35*(3), 273–286. doi:10.1016/S0167-9236(02)00074-X

Becker, J., Breuker, D., Heide, T., Holler, J., Rauer, H. P., & Böhme, R. (2013). Can we afford integrity by proof-of-work? Scenarios inspired by the Bitcoin currency. In *The Economics of Information Security and Privacy* (pp. 135–156). Springer. doi:10.1007/978-3-642-39498-0_7

Black, J., Hashimzade, N., & Myles, G. (2013). *Committee on Payment and Settlement Systems*. Oxford University Press.

Choi, S.-Y., Stahl, D. O., & Whinston, A. B. (1997). *The economics of electronic commerce*. Macmillan Technical Publishing.

Christidis, K., & Devetsikiotis, M. (2016). Blockchains and Smart Contracts for the Internet of Things. *IEEE Access: Practical Innovations, Open Solutions, 4,* 2292–2303. doi:10.1109/ACCESS.2016.2566339

Chua, C. E. H., & Wareham, J. (2004). Fighting internet auction fraud: An assessment and proposal. *Computer, 37*(10), 31–37. doi:10.1109/MC.2004.165

Chua & Wareham. (2002). Self-regulation for online auctions: An analysis. *Self, 12,* 31.

Corcoran. (1999). The auction economy. *Red Herring,* 69.

English, M., Auer, S., & Domingue, J. (2016). *Block Chain Technologies & The Semantic Web: A Framework for Symbiotic Development. Technical report.* University of Bonn.

Eyal, I., & Sirer, E. G. (2014) Majority is not enough: Bitcoin mining is vulnerable. *International Conference on Financial Cryptography and Data Security,* 436–454.

Froomkin. (1996). *Essential Role of Trusted Third Parties in Electronic Commerce.* Academic Press. doi:10.1007/978-3-662-45472-5_28

Grazioli, S., & Jarvenpaa, S. L. (2000). Perils of Internet fraud: An empirical investigation of deception and trust with experienced Internet consumers. *IEEE Transactions on Systems, Man, and Cybernetics. Part A, Systems and Humans, 30*(4), 395–410. doi:10.1109/3468.852434

Johnson, D., Menezes, A., & Vanstone, S. (2001). The elliptic curve digital signature algorithm (ECDSA). *International Journal of Information Security, 1*(1), 36–63. doi:10.1007102070100002

Koblitz, N. (1987). Elliptic curve cryptosystems. *Mathematics of Computation, 48*(177), 203–209. doi:10.1090/S0025-5718-1987-0866109-5

Kosba, A., Miller, A., Shi, E., Wen, Z., & Papamanthou, C. (2016). Hawk: The blockchain model of cryptography and privacy-preserving smart contracts. *IEEE Symposium on Security and Privacy (SP)*, 839-858. 10.1109/SP.2016.55

Krasnokutskaya, Terwiesch, & Tiererova. (2016). *Trading across Borders in Online Auctions*. Society for Economic Dynamics (no. 1537).

Kroll, J. A., Davey, I. C., & Felten, E. W. (2013) The economics of Bitcoin mining, or Bitcoin in the presence of adversaries. *Proceedings of WEIS*.

Macaulay, S. (1963). Non-contractual relations in business: A preliminary study. *American Sociological Review, 28*(1), 55–67. doi:10.2307/2090458

Miller, V. S. (1985). Use of elliptic curves in cryptography. *Conference on the Theory and Application of Cryptographic Techniques*, 417-426.

Pagliery. (2014). *Bitcoin: And the Future of Money*. Triumph Books.

Peters, G. W., & Panayi, E. (2016). Understanding Modern Banking Ledgers through Blockchain Technologies: Future of Transaction Processing and Smart Contracts on the Internet of Money. In *Banking Beyond Banks and Money* (pp. 239–278). Springer. doi:10.1007/978-3-319-42448-4_13

Peters, Panayi, & Chapelle. (2015). *Trends in crypto-currencies and blockchain technologies: A monetary theory and regulation perspective*. Academic Press.

Pilkington, M. (2015). *Blockchain technology: principles and applications*. Browser Download This Paper.

Swan. (2015). *Blockchain: Blueprint for a new economy*. O'Reilly Media, Inc.

Wood. (2014). *Ethereum: A secure decentralised generalised transaction ledger*. Ethereum Project Yellow Paper 151.

Zheng, Z., Xie, S., Dai, H.-N., & Wang, H. (2016). Blockchain Challenges and Opportunities. *Survey (London, England)*.

Zyskind, G., & Nathan, O. (2015). Decentralizing privacy: Using blockchain to protect personal data. In *Security and Privacy Workshops* (pp. 180–184). SPW. doi:10.1109/SPW.2015.27

Chapter 9
Performing Security on Digital Images

Abdallah Soualmi

https://orcid.org/0000-0003-2107-8598
Ferhat Abbas University, Algeria

Lamri Laouamer
Qassim University, Saudi Arabia

Adel Alti
Ferhat Abbas University, Algeria

ABSTRACT

In image watermarking, information is embedded in the original image for many reasons, such as ownership proofing, alteration detection, and/or fingerprinting, but it can also be used for real-time services such as e-payment, broadcast monitoring, and surveillance systems. For these, the data embedded must be extractable even if the image is manipulated intentionally or unintentionally. In contrast, robust techniques are the kind of watermarking that could assure the authenticity and protect the copyright. Many robust image watermarking approaches have been proposed in the last few years, and the purpose of this chapter is to provide a survey about recent relevant robust image watermarking methods existing in the literature.

DOI: 10.4018/978-1-5225-6313-6.ch009

INTRODUCTION

The emergence of high-throughput applications in multimedia networks has a great interest after the research community, this applications is characterized by an important and voluminous amount of data compared to the traditional applications, consequently it becomes an integral part of several areas of life (military, health, education ...etc.) (Poljicak, 2011; Islam et al, 2014; Shao et al, 2016;Thilagavathi et al, 2015). However, the data security turn into a fundamental and necessary requirement which necessitates the development of new strategies; that takes into account the specific characteristics of this kinds of applications (Wang et al, 2016; Kandi et al, 2017; Jawad et al, 2013).

There are various techniques that help to develop secure architecture and software systems especially for multimedia databases systems. These techniques make it difficult for hackers to influence credibility and effectiveness of the software. Software architecture and design are very important in order to create secure software, especially also in the context of multimedia databases. A security domain is the list of objects a subject is allowed to access. More broadly defined, domains are groups of subjects and objects with similar security requirements such integrity, authenticity and confidentiality of multimedia (images, sounds and videos) in that type of systems.

Cryptography was the first solution in that direction. It is about making the content of the document unreadable and unnecessary for an unauthorized user. But it protects the document only during its transmission, which means that once a document is decoded we cannot prevent its modification or illegal reproduction (Saini, 2015; Hsu et al, 2013).

The watermarking technique has emerged as an alternative that can complement cryptography. It consist of embedding the data information into a host image (Su et al, 2013; Benoraira et al, 2015) to enhance cryptographic integrity, protect the benefits of the document and prohibit the illegal reproduction (Rahmani ete al, 2010; Liu et al, 2016; Wang et al, 2016; Arsalan et al, 2017). In the other hand, the watermarked image may face obstacles, and in some applications even the smoothest distortion in the host image is intolerable (Verma et al, 2016; Amri et al, 2016; Khan et al, 2014); for example, in the field of medical imagery, if an image is slightly modified; this may change the interpretation of the medicine, which can cause disastrous consequences. In contrast, the watermark should be resistant to the alteration introduced during either normal use (unintentional attacks), or intentional modification which used to break or remove the watermark (malicious attacks) (Tao et al, 2014; Islam et al, 2014). So, there is a strong need to employ a robust watermarking which allows full resistant to the embedded data against the majority of attacks, this type of watermarking is gaining more attention for the last few years because of its increasing uses in many applications (Jose et al, 2012)

Several robust watermarking algorithms have been proposed in this decade, a number of new techniques or improved versions of the latest approaches have been developed .This gave rise to the appearance of new surveys. Tao et al. (2014) reported a review about robust image watermarking techniques. They present the basics requirements and discuss the techniques existing; however, they cover very limited area and discuss only few works. Mousavi et al (2014) introduced a survey about watermarking techniques used in medical image. But few of works are analyzed and compared.

In this survey, we aim to collect and present all of the literature currently available in the field of robust watermarking and review in detail with a deep analysis of the topic (using block-diagrams, tabular-comparisons) the newly emerging approaches.

PRELIMINARIES

The watermark data could be independent from the host image (extern) or a part of the cover image (informed or zero watermarking), and this data may be embedded in the spatial domain or transform domain (Das, et al, 2014) for the first, the data is embedded directly in the host image by modifying the image pixels intensity (Su et al, 2013), while in the second, it encrusted in a transformed of the original image (Daraee et al, 2014).

In addition, different types of watermarking technique are reported in the literature; namely: robust, fragile, and semi-fragile (Arsalan et al, 2017; Prasad et al, 2016; Kamran et al, 2014). In robust watermarking, the watermark is designed to resist after any operation used to alter the image (Wang et al, 2017; Ghosal et al, 2014), while, in semi-fragile, the watermark needs to survive minor manipulation (Preda et al, 2013). In fragile watermarking, the watermark collapse or degraded if the watermarked image undergoes any kind of alteration (Urvi et al, 2015). These types of watermarking approaches have different applications, and they are employed according to the purpose of the watermarking system, for example, the robust schemes could be used in order to prove the ownership and copyright protection, while fragile and semi-fragile are used for image authentication and data integrity checking (Radharani et al, 2010). But, the majority of the existing watermarking techniques are semi-fragile or fragile.

Furthermore, in terms of the watermark extraction process, the watermarking schemes are regrouped into three categories, blind, semi-blind and non-blind schemes (Lagzian et al, 2011; Agarwal et al, 2014). For the first class, the watermark extraction process does neither require the original image nor and the watermark (Das et al,

2014). For the second class, the watermark is required (Mohamadi et al, 2015) and the extraction operation necessitates the presence of the original image (Jane et al, 2014). Figure 1, recapitulates the important classes of watermarking approaches.

The watermarking schemes have five important proprieties (Saini et al, 2015; Tao et al, 2014) imperceptibility, embedding capacity, complexity, security and robustness. Imperceptibility means the similarity degree between the original and the watermarked images. Embedding capacity means the maximum amount of data that could be hidden in the host image without degrading the image quality. Complexity expresses the amount of time needed both for watermark embedding and extracting. Security refers to the security of the embedded and the extracted data; it means that no one could remove or extract the watermark without knowing the key used in the embedding process. While robustness design the degrees of resistance against any kind of illegal manipulation. Figure 2 shows the proprieties requirement schemes of any watermarking framework.

Based on the used images, the watermark sensitivity must contain a trade-off between the five proprieties cited bellow.

Figure 1. Classification of watermarking approaches.

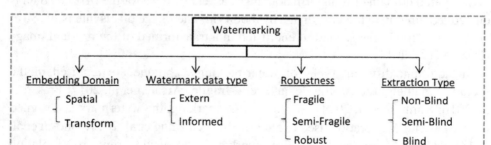

Figure 2. Watermarking schemes proprieties requirements.

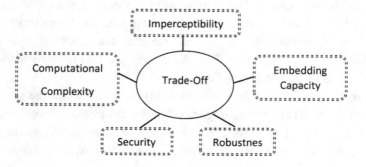

MALICIOUS ATTACKS AND QUALITY MEASURES

The imperceptibility and robustness degrees are measured in term of the quality between the watermarked and the extracted watermark after applying attacks. In this section we present the most famous malicious attacks and quality measures used to analyze the imperceptibility and robustness.

Malicious Attacks

Several intentional attacks are cited in the literature, its common objective, is to attempt to remove the watermark or confuse the authentication (Khalifa et al, 2012). These attacks are regrouped into two principal groups namely: signal processing attacks and geometric attacks.

Signal Processing Attacks

Called also image processing attacks. These types infect directly the signal of the image in order to remove the watermark (Tao et al, 2014). Among the attacks of this category we cite:

JPEG Compression

This attack decreases the image size by deleting the redundant information's, and consequently affect the watermark data's (Parah et al, 2016).

Noising

The basic idea of this attack is to add noise (white, salt & pepper, Gaussian...) to the watermarked image in order to degrade the watermark quality and increase the difficulty of the extraction (Singh et al, 2016; Raghavender et al, 2016). The value of noise degree is in [0, 1].

Filtering

Filtering attack is a signal processing operation which's used to reduce noise and enhance smoothness (P. S. et al, 2017; Singh et al, 2016). Several filtering-based attacks are mentioned in literature, but the most famous are: mean filtering, median filtering and Weiner filtering. Mean filtering replace each sample of the watermarked image with the average value of neighboring pixels. Median filtering modifies the center pixel value with the middle value of the sorted pixel. While Weiner filtering estimate the watermark data in order to generate the watermark embedded. This attack require the basic knowledge of the embedding operation (Roy et al, 2016; Roy et al, 2017).

Dithering

The mean idea of this attack is to use a set of black and white points to represent the same number of image pixels and keep their integrated intensity. This makes the watermark distortion degree very significant (Ming et al, 2010).

Histogram Equalization

The mean role of this attack is to modify some intensity of the histogram. This attack could even eliminate completely the watermark information (Roy et al, 2016).

Gamma Correction

This attack has a goal to adjust the image quality with power low transformation in order to cause high distortion to the watermark (Roy et al, 2017).

Blurring

This attack is a kind of distortion which could be caused for example from the long time of the capture process or simply from a scattered light distortion (Khalifa et al, 2012).

Geometric Attacks

The mean purpose of this kind of attacks is to destroy the synchronization of detection in order to make difficult the extraction process and even impossible (Yang et al, 2010). The most geometric attacks used are rotation, cropping, scaling and translation.

Rotation

The idea of this attack is to rotate the watermarked image from 0° to 360° in order to affect the watermark data (P.S. et al, 2017; Roy et al, 2016).

Cropping

The essential principle of this attack is removing the borders of the uniform color in order to destabilize the extraction operation (Raghavender et al, 2014)

Scaling

Is the resizing of the watermarked image in order to increase the complexity of the extracting operation (Roy et al, 2016).

Translation

The principle of this attack is to move the image pixels to a different location within the image size (P.S. et al, 2017).

Quality Measures

Imperceptibility and robustness of any watermarking method must be proved. To this end, the quality of the watermarked image and the extracted one is analyzed using several statistical measures.

Mean Square Error (MSE)

The MSE is the average squared error between two images (I1, I2) of sizes NxM. It is calculated as follow:

$$MSE = \frac{1}{N \times M} \sum_{j=0}^{N-1} \sum_{k=0}^{M-1} \left(I1(j,k) - I2(j,k) \right) \tag{1}$$

Peak Signal Noise Ratio (PSNR)

This metric is used to evaluate the imperceptibility performance. A higher PSNR value indicates higher imperceptibility (Al-Nahbani et al, 2015). The PSNR is based on MSE and calculated as follow:

$$PSNR(dB) = 10 \log_{10} \left(\frac{255^2}{MSE} \right) \tag{2}$$

Normalized Correlation (NC)

This metric is used to compare the original watermark with the extracted one (Cetinel et al, 2016). A higher NC value means a good robustness of the watermarking method.

$$NC = \sum_{j=0}^{WN-1} \sum_{k=0}^{WM-1} \left(W1\left(j,k\right) - W2\left(j,k\right) \right) \tag{3}$$

where WNxWM are the watermark size and W1, W2 are the original watermark and the extracted one respectively.

Correlation coefficient (CRC)

CRC is used to quantify the linear relation between two images (I1, I2) of sizes NxM (Pal et al, 2017). These images could be the host image and the watermarked one. In this case, the purpose is to measure the imperceptibility degree or it could be the inserted watermark and the extracted one. CRC is measured as follow.

$$CRC = \frac{\sum_{j=0}^{N-1} \sum_{k=0}^{M-1} I1\left(j,k\right) I2\left(j,k\right)}{\sqrt{\sum_{j=0}^{N-1} \sum_{k=0}^{M-1} I1\left(j,k\right)^2 * \sum_{j=0}^{N-1} \sum_{k=0}^{M-1} I2\left(j,k\right)^2}} \tag{4}$$

Bit Error Rate (BER)

The BER shows the probability of watermark binary data that are received incorrectly (Kandi et al, 2017). The lower BER value indicates the better performance of the watermarking system.

$$BER = 100 * \frac{CB}{AB} \tag{5}$$

where CB is the corrupted bits number of the watermark and AB is the number watermark bits.

Bit Correct Rate (BCR)

BCR calculate the probability of the correct bit of the extracted watermark.

$$BCR = \overline{BER} \tag{6}$$

Structural Similarity (SSIM)

SSIM is used to measure the quality of the watermarked image or the watermark. It conducts a visual quality assessment similar to the Human Visual System (HVS) (Mousavi et al, 2014). SSIM expressed as:

$$SSIM = \frac{\left(2\mu 1\mu 2 + c1\right)\left(2\sigma j + c2\right)}{\left(\mu 1^2 + \mu 2^2 + c1\right)\left(\sigma 1^2 + \sigma 2^2 + c2\right)} \tag{7}$$

where μ1, μ2, σ1, σ2, σj are the average of the host image, the average of the watermarked image, the variance of the host image, the variance of the watermarked image and the covariance of the watermarked images. c1 and c2 are two constant used to avoid the zero dominators.

ROBUST WATERMARKING APPROACHES

In this section, we review the new relevant robust approaches and categorizing them in terms of extraction types into three groups namely: non-blind, semi-blind and blind approaches. The third group contains more approaches; the reason is that the blind methods are more practicable and present a challenge for some applications. To this end, more techniques are discussed and compared.

Non-Blind Methods

Authors in (Dogan et al, 2011), presented a robust technique in the spatial domain based on Singular Value Decomposition (SVD). The main idea is to decompose the host image with SVD, then add the watermark to the singular value's matrix. Experimental results prove the good robustness against geometrical attacks. It offers also a high imperceptibility. However, the false positive problem was not avoided and the security of the watermark during embedding/extracting is not assured. Also the scheme offers low embedding capacity.

Jose et al. (2012) proposed a robust watermarking scheme based on Discrete Cosine Transform (DCT), Discrete Wavelet Transform (DWT) and SVD. The host image is reordered and transformed by DCT succeeded by DWT. After that, SVD is applied to LH and HL sub-bands, and the singular values of the watermark are embedded into the singular values computed of the host image. (Figure 3). Simulation results show that this approach can survive attacks like rotation, cropping, noising and JPEG compression. However, it is tested only with few attacks and introduces low security degree for the watermark.

Ali et al. (2014) presented a combined technique based on DCT, SVD and Differential Evolution (DE). The main idea is to partition the host image into blocks, then perform DCT on each block. After that, an approximation image is obtained by collecting the DC coefficients, and the SVD is performed on this image. The scrambled watermark is embedded in the singular values computed bellow. The DE is used to identify the best multiple scaling factors; in order to achieve the best performance in terms of robustness and imperceptibility. Figure 4 summarizes the embedding operation. This approach shows a good imperceptibility, security

Figure 3. Embedding process

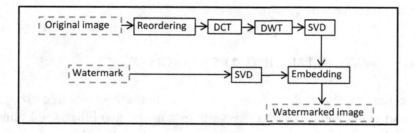

Figure 4. Embedding process.

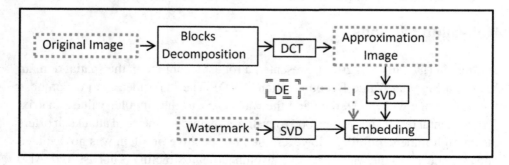

and robustness against many attacks non including rotation, cropping and gamma correction (the PSNR values were less than 20 dB). Also, the proposed approach requires an important computational complexity.

In (Loukhaoukha et al, 2014) authors proposed a non-blind approach based on Lifting Wavelet Transform (LWT), SVD and Multi−Objective Particle Swarm Optimization (MOPSO). The original image is decomposed up by LWT and the SVD is performed to a chosen sub−band. After that, the singular values are modified by multiple scaling factors (MSF) to embed the singular values of the watermark. The MOPSO is employed to achieve a highest possible robustness and imperceptibility by optimizing MSF (Figure 5). The disadvantage of this approach is the important computational complexity. Except that, the scheme offers good performance in terms of security, imperceptibility and robustness.

A non-blind scheme based on Steerable Pyramid Transform is presented in (El Hossani et al, 2014). The main idea consists to apply the Steerable Pyramid Transform on both the watermark and the original images by adding the watermark bands to the host image bands (Figure 6). As shown in Figure 6, the proposed approach is

Figure 5. Embedding process.

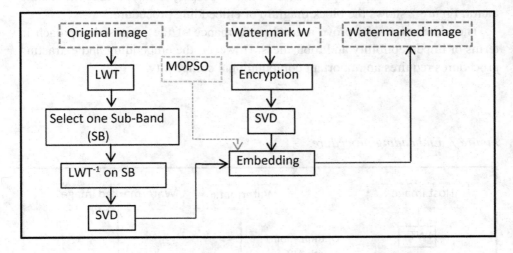

Figure 6. Embedding operation

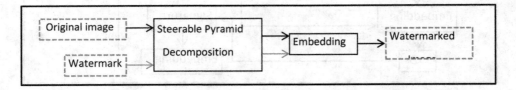

robust against many attacks, except rotation (NC= 0.7580). However, it provides low security degree for the watermark, and the value of scaling factors wasn't optimized and this provides a scope for improvement in terms of imperceptibility and robustness.

Authors in (Singh et al, 2015) introduced a multiple watermarking method for medical image based on DWT, DCT and SVD. In the embedding process, the cover image is decomposed up with DWT. After that, DCT and SVD are performed on the watermark and the LL band of the host image. The singular values of the watermark are embedded in the singular values of the host image. In addition, the second watermark is embedded in HH band. The watermark is encrypted before the embedding process in order to enhance the security. The experimental results show a good performance of the scheme in terms of robustness, embedding capacity and security. However, the imperceptibility is not much improved with the used image (PSNR value=33dB for ct-scanning image). Also the scheme require an important computational complexity.

Ansari et al. (2012) proposed a robust technique in integer wavelet transformation (IWT) based on SVD and Artificial Bee Colony (ABC). The watermark is embedded into the singular values of IWT bands of the original image. More, digital signature is encrusted in the LL band to avoid the false positive error. In order to improve the robustness and imperceptibility, the ABC is employed to optimize the scaling factor. Figure 7 shows the block diagram of embedding procedure.

The obtained results prove a good performance of the proposed approach in terms of imperceptibility and robustness. However, the embedding and extracting procedures requires an important computational complexity.

Figure 7. Embedding procedure.

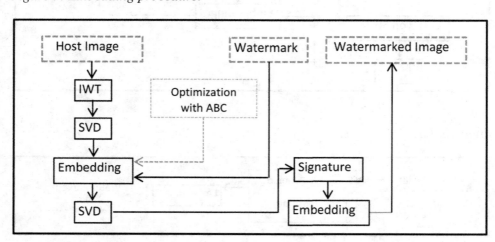

Kabra et al. (2016) introduced a robust watermarking scheme based on LWT and SVD. The main idea is to decompose the host image using LWT with three resolution levels and performing SVD on all the sub-bands. After that, the watermark is divided into four blocks and the SVD is applied on each of them. Finally, the singular values of the watermark is added to the singular values of the cover image. Figure 8 recapitulates the embedding operation.

The scheme proves good performance in terms of imperceptibility and robustness with the attacks used in experimentation, except histogram equalization, cropping, dithering and gamma correction (CRC values < 0.8). Also the watermark data are not secured.

Authors in (Cetinel et al, 2016), introduced a hybrid technique based on Redundant Discrete Wavelet Transform (RDWT) and SVD. The SVD after applying RDWT is performed on the host image and the scrambled watermark. Then, the singular values of the watermark are embedded into the singular values of the host image. The Experimental results prove a good performance of the scheme in terms of security, imperceptibility and robustness. However, it requires an important execution time in embedding/extracting operations. Also, it uses multiple scaling factors, and it became very difficult to get a good trade-off between imperceptibility and robustness without using an optimization algorithm for the scaling factors.

Singh et al. (2017), developed a robust framework using non-linear chaotic map. The main idea is to use chaotic map to generate keys to be used in the embedding process. Generating keys is proposed firstly followed by the embedding process. Finally a robust extraction process is proposed to verify the presence of watermark. Simulation results prove the robustness of the proposed framework. Except that, the scheme was tested only with few attacks. Imperceptibility was not much improved (PSNR values were between 31dB and 33 dB for gray scale images) and the embedding/extracting processes require an important computational complexity.

Figure 8. Embedding operation.

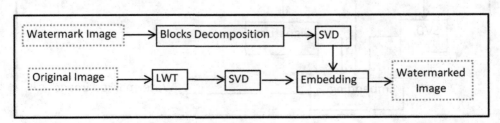

Semi-Blind Methods

Gupta et al. (2012), introduced a robust technique based on DWT and SVD. SVD is performed on the watermark, and then a data signature is generated from the U and V matrices. This is used to avoid the false positive problem. After that, the host image is decomposed up with DWT, and the SVD is performed on the HH sub-band. The singular values of the watermark and the signature generated bellow are inserted in the singular values of the host image. (Figure 9).

The hybridization of DWT and SVD give a good results in terms of imperceptibility and robustness. However, beside the important computational complexity, the scheme is not much robust against Gaussian noise attack (var=0.01) (CRC=0.4772), salt & pepper noise attack (var=0.01) (CRC=0.4986) and scaling attack (512>>256>>512) (CRC=0.4418).

In (Han et al, 2013), authors presented a combined zero-watermarking technique for 3D medical images based on Discrete Fourier Transform (DFT), DWT, DCT and Hermite chaotic neural network. The main idea is to perform the three-dimensional DWT and DFT on the host image. Then, selecting low and intermediate frequency coefficients as medical volume data features. These are used to structure the zero-watermark. The watermark is scrambled using Hermite chaotic neural network and encrusted in the DCT coefficients of the original image. Figure 10 shows the embedding operation steps. This technique gets good trade-off between robustness, security and imperceptibility. The approach was tested only with few attacks requiring an important computational complexity.

Figure 9. Embedding process.

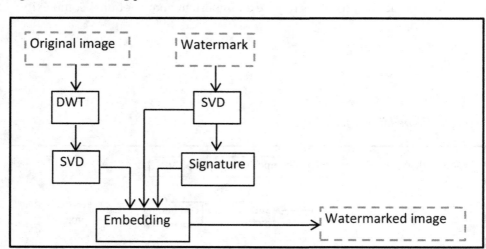

Figure 10. Encrusting operation.

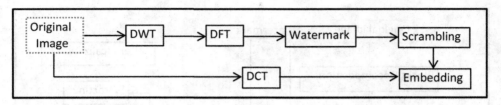

Figure 11. Embedding process block diagram.

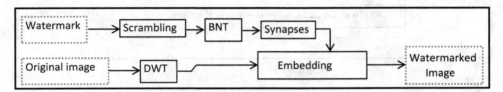

In (Rani et al, 2013), authors proposed a semi blind technique based on DWT, Balanced Neural Tree (BNT) and SVD. The main idea is to perform DWT on the host image. Then, applying the SVD on the LL sub-bands by training the BNT to learn the watermark. For the embedding, the synapses (optimal weights) of the trained BNT are scrambled and encrusted in the singular values computed bellow (Figure 11). The algorithm gives good results in terms of security, imperceptibility and robustness. Except that, it requires an important execution time for embedding/ extracting.

The authors in (Laouamer et al, 2015) presented a semi-blind technique for sensitive text images based on DCT and YUV transform. The main idea is to perform the YUV transform on the original and watermark images. Then, perform DCT on Y blocks and divide each matrix's coefficients with matrix quantization to obtain quantized matrices. For the embedding, the watermark quantized matrix is encrusted in the original image quantized matrix. Experimentation results and attacks analysis prove the advantages of the scheme in terms of imperceptibility and robustness. However, it requires an important execution time for embedding/ extracting processes and the security metric is not assured.

Authors in (Ali et al, 2014) introduced a robust zero-watermarking approach based on weber law. The main idea is to decompose the host image on blocks. After that, employ the weber differential excitation to define the zero-watermark and embed its intensity in the center pixel of each block (Figure 12).

The scheme offers good robustness and imperceptibility and allows the possibility to localize the altered zones. However, the security of the watermark is not assured.

Figure 12. Embedding and extraction processes.

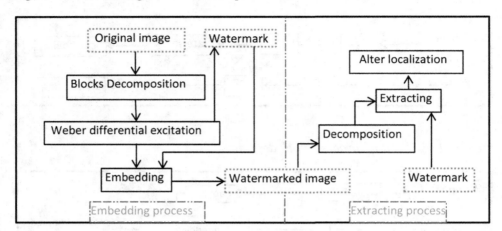

The authors in (Ghadi et al, 2016) proposed a semi-blind technique based on Frequent Pattern Mining (FPM) and Appriori algorithm. The idea is to decompose the host image into blocks, then represent these blocks in a Boolean database using some thresholds. After that, the A priori algorithm is employed to extract the maximal patterns which are the most robust blocks. These are used as an embedding location. Simulation results and attack analysis show the efficiency of this scheme in terms of imperceptibility and robustness. However, beside the low degrees of the security metric, the embedding capacity is limited by the blocks number.

Mansoori et al (2016) presented a novel method based on Ordered Hadamard transform (OHT). The basic idea is to decompose the host image and the watermark into blocks and perform OHT on each block. After that, high frequency coefficients of the host image are substituted with the watermark coefficients without using any scaling factor, this guarantees the extraction of watermark with primary quality.

This method offers several advantages of imperceptibility, computational complexity and embedding capacity. However, beside the low security degree, the scheme is vulnerable with some attacks like: JPEG compression (PSNR=16.73dB and NC=0.79) and salt & pepper noise (PSNR=11.17dB NC=0.75).

The authors in (P. S. et al, 2017) present a method combined DWT, Countourlet transforms (CT), Schur Decomposition, SVD and Arnold transform to enhance the imperceptibility, security and robustness (Figure 13).

Experimental results show that the scheme is not much robust against salt & pepper noise(0.2) (PSNR in dB), Gaussian noise(0.1) (PSNR in dB). Also, a high computational complexity is required for embedding and extracting operations (Wang et al, 2016; Wang et al, 2017; Roy et al, 2017).

Figure 13. Embedding process.

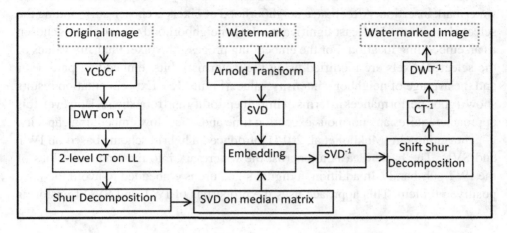

Figure 14. Embedding and extracting process.

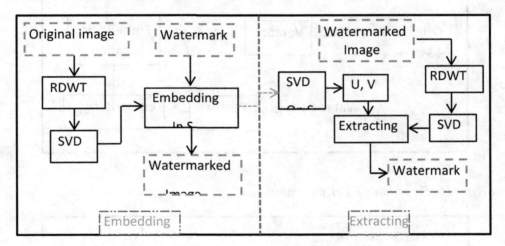

Blind Methods

Makbol et al. (2013) introduced a blind method combine RDWT and SVD. The gray scale image watermark is embedded directly into the singular values of the host image RDWT sub-bands. (Figure 14). This approach benefited from the good robustness of RDWT and the high stability of the SVD transform. However, the principal disadvantage is its low security degree for the watermark.

Moghaddam et al (2013) presented a novel method in the spatial domain using Imperialist Competitive Algorithm (ICA). The host image and the watermark are converted into vectors. Then, the ICA is used to identify the best's locations for the watermark insertion. After that, a neighborhood of pixels is chosen surrounding the selected locations. And least significant color in neighborhood of each pixel is chosen as an embedding location. For the embedding process, the pixel intensity values of the selected pixels are modified using the watermark bits, embedding parameter and the average of neighbor's intensity value. (Figure 15). Experimentation results show a good performances in terms of imperceptibility and robustness. However, this approach requires an enormous execution time and offers low embedding capacity.

The authors in (Makbol et al, 2014) introduced a hybrid scheme based on IWT and SVD. The basic idea is to encrust the watermark into the singular values of the IWT sub-bands. In addition, a digital signature is embedded to avoid the false positive problem. This approach uses the properties of IWT and SVD transforms

Figure 15. Embedding algorithm.

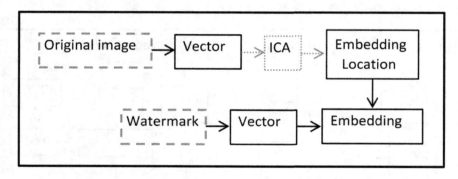

Figure 16. Embedding block diagram.

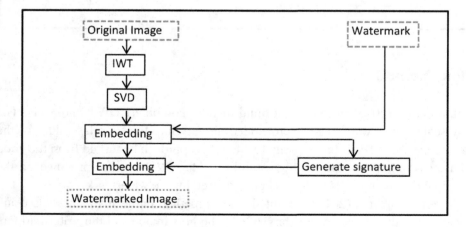

to achieve the performance requirements, which are the good stability of the SVD and the ability of the IWT to preserve a good reconstruction (Figure 16). The disadvantages of this approach, is the important computational complexity, and the scaling factors value wasn't optimized and this provides a scope for improvement in imperceptibility and robustness.

Zhao et al. (2015) presented a new technique in the Non-sub Sampled Contourlet Transform (NSCT) domain. The NSCT is performed on the host image and the largest energy sub-band is selected for embedding the watermark. The watermark is embedded into the scale invariant feature transform (SIFT) regions. The algorithm offers good imperceptibility, robustness and embedding capacity. However, it offers also low security and requires an enormous computational complexity.

A novel IWT-based is proposed in (Behlou et al, 2014). The SURF decoder is used to extract the interest points, and the non-overlapping blocks around each point are selected. The watermark is embedded into the IWT coefficients of points selected bellow. The simulation results show a good trade-off between imperceptibility and robustness. However, the scheme offers low security degree for the watermark, and the embedding/ extracting processes require an important execution time.

Authors in (Al-Nabhani et a, 2015) presented a robust technique using DWT and Probabilistic Neural Network (PNN). In the embedding, the watermark binary blocks are embedded in the coefficients blocks after applying DWT with Haar filter. In the extraction process, the coefficients blocks after on DWT coefficients are used as an input to the trained PNN to obtain the watermark. Simulation results of the method prove the good performance in terms of embedding capacity, imperceptibility and robustness. However, the quality of the watermark extracted after JPEG compression attack is much degraded (NC value< 0.75 for compression intensity <= 50).

Thanh et al (2015) proposed a hybrid technique based on DWT, SVD and Quantization Index Modulation (QIM). Firstly, a new frequency domain called q-LFD is proposed. The main idea is the composition of the classical frequency domain such as DWT and SVD, with the q-logarithm function and its inverse the q-exponential function. After that, a scheme based on q-LFD and QIM is introduced. The principle is to embed the watermark in the low-frequency of q-LFD using QIM technique.

This approach achieves good performance in terms of robustness, security and imperceptibility. However, the watermark is collapsed after some attacks such histogram equalization (0.46<NC<0.57) and average filtering (0.49<NC<0.57).

Hu et al. (2016) introduced a new method using DCT and Partly Sign-Altered (PSA). Firstly, the original image is decomposed into blocks and the DCT is performed on each block. After that, the PSA is obtained by changing the signs of selected DCT coefficients and taking there's average. The watermark embedding is carried out by manipulating the PSA mean and taking into account the HVS

Figure 17. Embedding process.

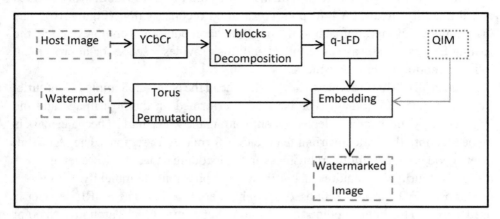

Figure 18. Block diagram of embedding operation.

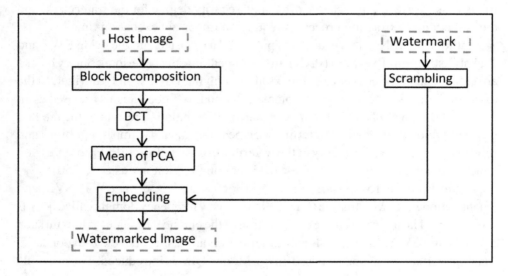

characteristic (Figure 18). The scheme resists very well with many attacks and offers high imperceptibility. However, it require an important complexity and the watermark was not secured, also the watermark is vulnerable with Gaussian noise attack (V=0.01 and 0.1) (BER > 45%).

Authors in (Roy et al, 2016) proposed a blind approach combining RDWT, DCT, Repetition Code (RC) and Arnold chaotic map. The host image is decomposed up into blocks, and the RDWT succeed by DCT are applied on each blocks. After that, as an embedding location, a number of Middle Band coefficients are selected according to the zigzag order (Figure 19). The watermark is scrambled using Arnold chaotic map to assure high security, and the RC is used to reinforce the resistance of the watermark. Experimentation results and attacks analysis proves the good performance in terms of robustness, security and imperceptibility. However, beside the important computational complexity, the scheme offers low embedding capacity. Also the watermark was corrupted with some signal processing attacks like: median filter(3,3) (NC < 0.78 and BER > 25%), Weiner filter(3,3) (NC < 0.78 and BER > 24%), speckle noise(var=0.01) (NC<0.8 and BER>20%), dithering (NC < 0.75 and BER > 27%).

A robust technique based on DCT and Inter-block Coefficient Differencing is proposed in (Parah et al, 2016). First, the difference between two DCT coefficients of the adjacent blocks at the same position is calculated. Then, the difference is modified according to the watermark bit by modifying one of the two DCT coefficients. The amount of modification of a DCT coefficient depends upon the scaling factor, DC coefficient and the median of zigzag ordered coefficients (Figure 19). Figure 20 summarizes the embedding operation of this approach. The experimentation results prove that this approach resist very well against many attacks, except salt & pepper noise(v=0.01) (BER=14.18% and NC=0.87). However, the watermark data wasn't secured.

Authors in (Abdelhakim et al, 2017), presented a blind method based on DCT and ABC. First, the DCT is performed on each block of the host image. Then, the coefficients positions are selected from two groups of predetermined locations. In the embedding step, the absolute difference value between the two coefficients is checked if it is enough to provide robustness. More, a new fitness function based on ABC is proposed for searching the optimum scaling factor. Simulation results show the good robustness degree of this approach. However, the execution time is

Figure 19. Zigzag selection illustration.

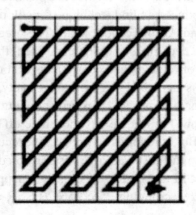

Figure 20. Embedding process.

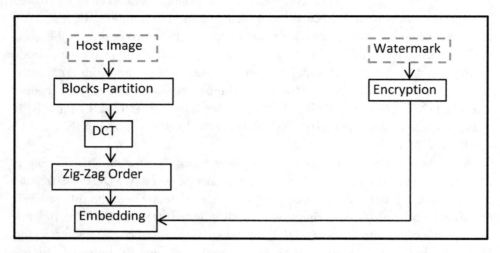

important and the approach doesn't employ any security technique for the watermark. Also, the watermark extracted after some attacks was almost readable, such Gaussian noise attack (BCR < 64%), rotation(0.5° and 0.75°) (BCR < 62%), average filter(7x7 and 9x9) (BCR<65%), median filter(9x9) (BCR<53%).

Varghese et al. (2016) presented a hybrid scheme based on DFT, SVD and a proposed decomposition algorithm called onion peel decomposition (OPD). The OPD is a circular traversal starts from the upper left corner and ends at the center of the image (Figure 21). The mean idea of the scheme is to use The OPD to decompose the Fourier transformed image into four blocks. Then, perform the SVD on each block. Finally, the singular values of watermark are added to the singular values of the host image (Figure 22). The scheme introduces good imperceptibility and robustness. However, it requires an important time for the embedding /extracting process, the security metric is unfound and the false positive problem wasn't avoided.

Roy et al. (2017) introduced a blind technique for colored image based on DCT, Repetition Code (RC) and Arnold chaotic map. The green and blue components of the original image are decomposed on blocks. Then, the DCT is performed on each of them. A number of middle band coefficients according to the zigzag order (Figure 19) are selected as an embedding location. Finally, the two watermarks are scrambled with Arnold chaotic map, and the corresponding bit of RC is embedded in the locations selected bellow. The scheme gets good trade-off between imperceptibility, robustness and security. But, it requires an important execution time and offers low embedding capacity. Also the first watermark is corrupted with some attacks, like Gaussian noise: (PSNR < 21 and BER > 10%), salt & pepper noise(density=0.03): (PSNR~25 and BER=12%), cropping(256×256): (PSNR<12 and BER>12.8%).

Figure 21. Illustration of OPD algorithm proposed in

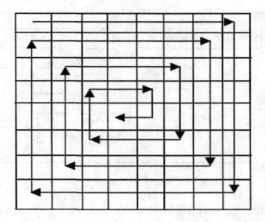

Figure 22. Block diagram of embedding Process.

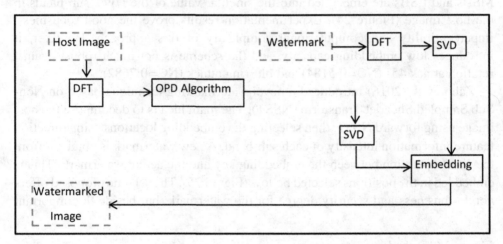

A robust watermarking approach in Contourlet Domain based on Schur decomposition and QIM technique In (Wang et al, 2016) is proposed. The idea is to perform the Countourlet transform on the host image. Then, perform DCT succeed by Schur decomposition on the low frequency coefficients blocks. The binary watermark is embedded using the quantization step of QIM. The embedding locations is chosen from each couples (DC, DC') where the distance between DC and DC' is greater than a predetermined threshold (Figure 23). The scheme combines the advantages of the three famous methods. But it requires an enormous computational complexity and the security degree is very low.

Figure 23. Embedding operation.

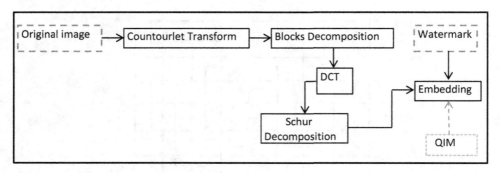

A hybrid technique based on DWT, SVD and DCT is presented in (Singh et al, 2016). The basic idea is to split the watermark into two parts using four bits MSBs and four bits LSBs of each pixel. Then, the scrambled DCT coefficients of these MSBs and LSBs are embedded into the singular value of the DWT sub-bands in the host image (Figure 24). Experimentation results prove the good robustness, imperceptibility and computational complexity of this approach. However, it introduces low embedding capacity, and the scheme is not much robust against rotation attack 45° (NC=0.5184) and blurring attack (NC=0.7682).

Zaho et al. (2016) introduced a novel watermarking technique based on Non-Sub Sampled Shearlet Transform (NSST). The main idea is to decompose the host image using forward NSST, then selecting the embedding locations using direction feature information intensity of each sub-band. A new watermark is obtained from the XOR operation between the embedding key and the actual watermark. This is embedded in the positions selected bellow (Figure 25). The scheme proposed offers good robustness and security degree for the watermark, but beside the important

Figure 24. Embedding process.

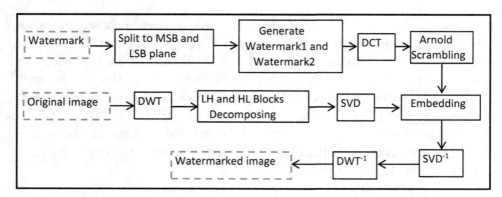

Figure 25. Embedding process.

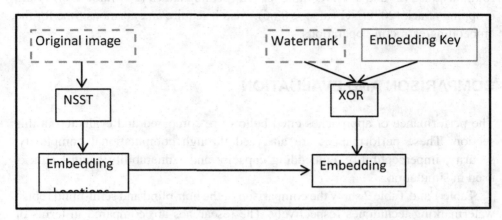

computational complexity, the watermark quality is degraded very much after some signal processing attacks such: Gaussian noise(where v > 0.001) (SSIM < 48%) and salt & pepper noise(v=0.05 and v=0.1) (SSIM < 41%).

Dong et al. (2016) Presented a robust technique for medical image based on DWT and DCT. Firstly, the host image is encrypted using DWT, DCT and logistic sequence to encrypt the host image. Then, the watermark is scrambled and embedded in the feature vector of the host image extracted from the DWT and DCT coefficients. Figure 26 summarizes the embedding operation. This approach offers good performance in terms of security and robustness. However, the approach is not much robust against

Figure 26. Embedding operation.

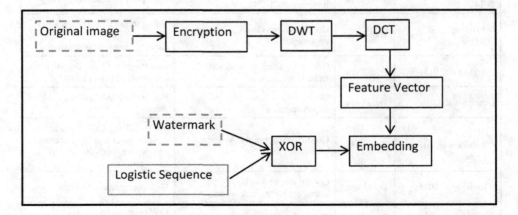

rotation attack (2° and 4°) (NC value < 0.76), scaling attack (NC value < 0.71) and cropping attack (20°) (NC value < 0.66). Also it require an enormous time for the embedding/extracting operations.

COMPARISON AND EVALUATION

The performance of approaches cited bellow are compared and evaluated in this section. These performances are analyzed through computational complexity, security, imperceptibility, embedding capacity and vulnerability against attacks used in simulation.

Table 1 and Table 2 show the comparison of the non-blind and semi-blind robust watermarking techniques respectively. The researches are compared in terms of embedding domain (E.D), Strength points and drawbacks remarked. In all of these

Table 1. Comparison of robust non-blind works.

Works	E.D	Strength Points	Drawbacks
(Dongan et al, 2011)	Spatial	Good robustness with many geometrical attacks, high imperceptibility, Average Computational complexity.	Low security and embedding capacity, the presence of the false positive menace.
(Jose et al, 2012)	Transform	Robustness with the attacks used in simulation, good imperceptibility.	Low security degree. High computational complexity.
(Ali et al, 2014)	Transform	Good security and imperceptibility. Average robustness.	Vulnerability with rotation, cropping and gamma correction attack. Require an important execution time.
(Loukhaoukha et al, 2014)	Transform	Good robustness, security and imperceptibility.	High computational complexity.
(El Hossani et al, 2014)	Transform	Good robustness and imperceptibility.	Vulnerability with rotation attack, low security degree, the scaling factor value wasn't optimized.
(Singh et al, 2015)	Transform	Good robustness, security and embedding capacity.	Low imperceptibility degree. High computational complexity.
(Ansari et al, 2016)	Transform	Good robustness, security and imperceptibility.	Require an important execution time.
(Radhika et al, 2016)	Transform	Good imperceptibility, Average robustness.	Vulnerability with histogram equalization, cropping, dithering and gamma correction attacks. Low security.
(Cetinel et al, 2016)	Transform	Good robustness and imperceptibility, High security.	High computational complexity.
(Pal Singh et al, 2017)	Spatial	Good robustness and security.	Low imperceptibility, high computational complexity.

Table 2. Comparison of robust semi-blind works

Works	E.D	Strength Points	Drawbacks
(Gupta et al, 2014)	Transform	Good security and imperceptibility, Average robustness.	High computational complexity. Vulnerability with Gaussian noise, salt & pepper noise and scaling attacks.
(Han et al, 2013)	Transform	Good robustness and security.	The method was tested only with few attacks. High computational complexity.
(Kahn et al, 2014)	Transform	Good trade-off between security, imperceptibility and robustness.	High computational complexity.
(Laouamer et al, 2015)	Transform	Good robustness and imperceptibility.	Important computational complexity, low security.
(Laouamer et al, 2015)	Spatial	Good robustness and imperceptibility, alter detection and localization.	Low security.
(Ghadi et al, 2016)	Spatial	Good robustness and imperceptibility.	Limited embedding capacity, low security.
(Mansori et al, 2016)	Transform	Good trade-off between robustness, security and computational complexity.	Low security, vulnerability with JPEG compression and salt & pepper noise.
(P. S. et al, 2017)	Transform	Good imperceptibility, security and robustness.	High computational complexity, vulnerability with salt & pepper noise and Gaussian noise.

works, the watermark type is extern, except the works in (Han et al, 2013; Laouamer et al, 2015) in Table 2 which is informed.

In table 3, the blind based watermarking techniques are compared and evaluated, the works are compared in terms of strength points and drawbacks remarked. In this entire works, the embedding is effectuated in the transform domain except for the works presented in (Moghaddam et al, 2013; Al-Nabhani et al, 2015), also the watermark type is extern for all the works.

Some of our finding related to robust watermarking methods:

1. Non-blind extracting methods are less computationally complex and more robust against signal processing attacks.
2. Semi-blind methods reduce the size of auxiliary data and consequently they help in increasing the embedding capacity. Also they improve good imperceptibility especially in the case of zero-watermarking.
3. Blind methods are more computationally complex and require more space for embedding the auxiliary data. However this kinds of schemes are more imperceptible and effective.

Table 3. Comparison of different robust blind works

Works	Strength Points	Drawbacks
(Makbol et al, 2013)	Good robustness and imperceptibility.	Low security degree.
(Moghaddam et al, 2013)	Good imperceptibility and robustness.	Require an enormous computational complexity. Offers low embedding capacity.
(Ye et al, 2014)	Good robustness, security and embedding capacity.	High computational complexity and the imperceptibility degree wasn't indicated.
(Makbol et al, 2014)	Good robustness.	The scaling factor value wasn't optimized. Require high computational complexity.
(Zhao et al, 2015)	Good trade-off between imperceptibility, embedding capacity and robustness.	Low security and require high computational complexity.
(Behloul et al, 2014)	Good imperceptibility and robustness.	Low security and require an important computational complexity
(Al-Nabhani et al, 2015)	Good imperceptibility, embedding capacity and robustness.	Low security and vulnerability with JPEG compression attack.
(Thanh et al, 2015)	Good imperceptibility, robustness and security.	Vulnerability with histogram equalization and average filtering attacks. High computational complexity.
(Hu et al, 2016)	Good robustness. High imperceptibility.	Low security, require high computational complexity, vulnerable with Gaussian noise attack.
(Roy et al, 2016)	Good trade-off between Robustness, security and imperceptibility.	Require high computational complexity, vulnerable with median filter (3x3), Weiner filter (3x3) and dithering attacks. Low embedding capacity.
(Parah et al, 2016)	Good robustness, average computational complexity, good imperceptibility.	Vulnerability with salt and pepper noise, low security.
(Abdelhakim et al, 2017)	Good imperceptibility and Average robustness.	High computational complexity, low security degree, vulnerability with Gaussian noise, rotation (0.5° and 0.75°), average filter(7x7 and 9x9) and median filter(9x9) attacks.
(Varghese et al, 2016)	Good imperceptibility and robustness.	High computational complexity, low security.
(Roy et al, 2016)	Good trade-off between security, imperceptibility and robustness.	Low embedding capacity. Important computational complexity. Vulnerability with cropping (256x256), salt & pepper noise and Gaussian noise attacks.
(Wang et al, 2016)	Good imperceptibility and robustness.	High computational complexity and low security.
(Singh et al, 2016)	Good trade-off between robustness, imperceptibility and security.	Vulnerability with rotation (45°) and blurring attacks. High computational complexity.
(Zhao et al, 2016)	Good robustness and security.	Important computational complexity, vulnerability with Gaussian noise and salt & pepper noise attacks. Imperceptibility degree wasn't indicated.
(Dong et al, 2016)	Good security and average robustness.	High computational complexity, vulnerability with rotation (2° and 4°), cropping (20°) and scaling attacks.

We have observed that almost of the transform-based robust approaches are based on SVD, even that these techniques add more robustness. It may introduce another problem who could affect the performance; which is the false positive problem. Many relevant schemes avoid this problem with the embedding of a data signature with the watermark, in contrast, this could increase the space required for the watermark embedding, and consequently it reduce the embedding capacity. Another solution is to use the SVD only on the host image, but these also decrease the embedding capacity. Finally we suggest that robustness and embedding capacity could be assured with the hybridization in transform domain. Extra security can be assured with the encryption of the watermark and the good imperceptibility could be assured using zero watermarking.

CONCLUSION

With the appearance of new technologies, preserving security and authenticity of images becomes a fundamental and necessary requirement. Over previous years, various robust watermarking algorithms have been proposed by a number of different researchers, but each method has a number of associated advantages as well as drawbacks. In this chapter, we have presented many robust watermarking methods with explanations and comparisons between them. The methods are categorized into three major categories; non-blind, semi-blind and blind approaches. The performance of these approaches is analyzed through computational complexity, embedding capacity, security, imperceptibility and vulnerability against some attacks. Our future focus will be redirected towards the robust zero-watermarking techniques for medical image with tamper detection and localization.

REFERENCES

Abdelhakim, A., Saleh, H., & Nassar, A. (2017). A quality guaranteed robust image watermarking optimization with Artificial Bee Colony. *Expert Systems with Applications, 72,* 317–326. doi:10.1016/j.eswa.2016.10.056

Agarwal, H., Raman, B., & Venkat, I. (2014). Blind reliable invisible watermarking method in wavelet domain for face image watermark. *Multimedia Tools and Applications, 74*(17), 6897–6935. doi:10.100711042-014-1934-1

Al-Nabhani, Jalab, Wahid, & Noor. (2015). Robust watermarking algorithm for digital images using discrete wavelet and probabilistic neural network. *Journal of King Saud University - Computer and Information Sciences, 27*(4), 393-401.

Ali, M., Ahn, C., & Pant, M. (2014). A robust image watermarking technique using SVD and differential evolution in DCT domain. *Optik - International Journal for Light and Electron Optics, 125*(1), 428-434. doi:10.1016/j.ijleo.2013.06.082

Amri, H., Khalfallah, A., Gargouri, M., Nebhani, N., Lapayre, J., & Bouhlel, M. (2016). Medical Image Compression Approach Based on Image Resizing, Digital Watermarking and Lossless Compression. *Journal of Signal Processing Systems for Signal, Image, and Video Technology.*

Ansari, I., Pant, M., & Ahn, C. (2016). Robust and false positive free watermarking in IWT domain using SVD and ABC. *Engineering Applications of Artificial Intelligence, 49*, 114–125. doi:10.1016/j.engappai.2015.12.004

Arsalan, M., Qureshi, A., Khan, A., & Rajarajan, M. (2017). Protection of medical images and patient related information in healthcare: Using an intelligent and reversible watermarking technique. *Applied Soft Computing, 51*, 168–179. doi:10.1016/j.asoc.2016.11.044

Behloul, A. (2014). A blind robust image watermarking using interest points and IWT. *Proceedings of the 6th International Conference on Management of Emergent Digital EcoSystems 'MEDES'*, 139-145. 10.1145/2668260.2668305

Benoraira, A., Benmahammed, K., & Boucenna, N. (2015). Blind image watermarking technique based on differential embedding in DWT and DCT domains. *EURASIP Journal on Advances in Signal Processing, 2015*(1), 55. doi:10.118613634-015-0239-5

Çetinel, G., & Çerkezi, L. (2016). Robust Chaotic Digital Image Watermarking Scheme based on RDWT and SVD. *International Journal of Image, Graphics and Signal Processing, 8*(8), 58–67. doi:10.5815/ijigsp.2016.08.08

Daraee, F., & Mozaffari, S. (2014). Watermarking in binary document images using fractal codes. *Pattern Recognition Letters, 35*, 120–129. doi:10.1016/j.patrec.2013.04.022

Das, C., Panigrahi, S., Sharma, V., & Mahapatra, K. (2014). A novel blind robust image watermarking in DCT domain using inter-block coefficient correlation. *AEÜ. International Journal of Electronics and Communications, 68*(3), 244–253. doi:10.1016/j.aeue.2013.08.018

Dogan, S., Tuncer, T., Avci, E., & Gulten, A. (2011). A robust color image watermarking with Singular Value Decomposition method. *Advances in Engineering Software, 42*(6), 336–346. doi:10.1016/j.advengsoft.2011.02.012

Dong, Li, Duan, & Guo. (2016). A Robust Zero-Watermarking Algorithm for Encrypted Medical Images in the DWT-DCT Encrypted Domain. *International Journal of Simulation Systems, Science & Technology, 17*(43), 1-7.

El Hossaini, A., El Aroussi, M., Jamali, K., Mbarki, S., & Wahbi, M. (2014). A robust watermarking scheme based on steerable pyramid and singular value decomposition. *Applied Mathematical Sciences, 8*, 2997–3008. doi:10.12988/ams.2014.4126

Ghadi, M., Laouamer, L., Nana, L., & Pascu, A. (2016). A Robust Associative Watermarking Technique based on Frequent Pattern Mining and Texture Analysis. *Proceedings of the 8th International Conference on Management of Digital EcoSystems*, 73-81. 10.1145/3012071.3012101

Ghosal, S., & Mandal, J. (2014). Binomial transform based fragile watermarking for image authentication. *Journal of Information Security and Applications, 19*(4-5), 272–281. doi:10.1016/j.jisa.2014.07.004

Gupta, A. K., & Raval, M. S. (2012). A robust and secure watermarking scheme based on singular values replacement. *Sadhana, 37*(4), 425–440. doi:10.100712046-012-0089-x

Han, B., Li, J., & Zong, L. (2013). A New Robust Zero-watermarking Algorithm for Medical Volume Data. *International Journal of Signal Processing, Image Processing and Pattern Recognition, 6*(6), 245–258. doi:10.14257/ijsip.2013.6.6.23

Hoang Ngan Le, T., Hung Nguyen, K., & Bac Le, H. (2010). Literature Survey on Image Watermarking Tools, Watermark Attacks, and Benchmarking Tools. *Proceeding of the Second International Conferences on Advances in Multimedia (MMEDIA)*, 67-73.

Hsu, F., Wu, M., Wang, S., & Huang, C. (2013). Reversibility of image with balanced fidelity and capacity upon pixels differencing expansion. *The Journal of Supercomputing, 66*(2), 812–828. doi:10.100711227-013-0896-9

Hu, H., Chang, J., & Hsu, L. (2016). Robust blind image watermarking by modulating the mean of partly sign-altered DCT coefficients guided by human visual perception. *AEÜ. International Journal of Electronics and Communications, 70*(10), 1374–1381. doi:10.1016/j.aeue.2016.07.011

Islam, M., & Chong, U. (2014). A Digital Image Watermarking Algorithm Based on DWT DCT and SVD. *International Journal of Computer and Communication Engineering, 3*(5), 356–360. doi:10.7763/IJCCE.2014.V3.349

Jane, O., Elbaşi, E., & İlk, H. (2014). Hybrid Non-Blind Watermarking Based on DWT and SVD. *Journal of Applied Research and Technology, 12*(4), 750–761. doi:10.1016/S1665-6423(14)70091-4

Jawad, K., & Khan, A. (2013). Genetic algorithm and difference expansion based reversible watermarking for relational databases. *Journal of Systems and Software, 86*(11), 2742–2753. doi:10.1016/j.jss.2013.06.023

Jose, S., Cherian Roy, R., & Nambiar, S. S. (2012). Robust Image Watermarking based on DCT-DWT-SVD Method. *International Journal of Computers and Applications, 58*(21), 12–16. doi:10.5120/9406-3798

Kabra, R. G., & Agrawal, S. S. (2016). Robust Embedding of Image Watermark using LWT and SVD. *Proceeding of the International Conference on Communication and Signal Processing*, 1968-1972. 10.1109/ICCSP.2016.7754516

Kamran, A. K., & Malik, S. (2014). A high capacity reversible watermarking approach for authenticating images: Exploiting down-sampling, histogram processing, and block selection. *Information Sciences, 256,* 162–183. doi:10.1016/j.ins.2013.07.035

Kandi, H., Mishra, D., & Gorthi, S. (2017). Exploring the learning capabilities of convolutional neural networks for robust image watermarking. *Computers & Security, 65,* 247–268. doi:10.1016/j.cose.2016.11.016

Khalifa, Yusof, Abdalla, & Olanrewaju. (2012). State-Of-The-Art Digital Watermarking Attacks. *Proceeding of the International Conference on Computer and Communication Engineering (ICCCE)*, 744-750.

Khan, A., Siddiqa, A., Munib, S., & Malik, S. (2014). A recent survey of reversible watermarking techniques. *Information Sciences, 279,* 251–272. doi:10.1016/j.ins.2014.03.118

Lagzian, S., Soryani, M., & Fathi, M. (2011). A New Robust Watermarking Scheme Based on RDWT-SVD. *International Journal of Intelligent Information Processing, 2*(1), 22–29. doi:10.4156/ijiip.vol2.issue1.3

Lakshmi Prasad, K., Malleswara Rao, T., & Kannan, V. (2016). A Novel and Hybrid Secure Digital Image Watermarking Framework Through sc-LWT-SVD. *Indian Journal of Science and Technology, 9*(23), 1–10. doi:10.17485/ijst/2016/v9i23/95273

Laouamer, L., AlShaikh, M., Nana, L., & Pascu, A. (2015). Robust watermarking scheme and tamper detection based on threshold versus intensity. *Journal of Innovation in Digital Ecosystems, 2*(1-2), 1–12. doi:10.1016/j.jides.2015.10.001

Laouamer, L., & Tayan, O. (2015). A Semi-Blind Robust DCT Watermarking Approach for Sensitive Text Images. *Arabian Journal for Science and Engineering*, *40*(4), 1097–1109. doi:10.100713369-015-1596-y

Liu, H., Xiao, D., Zhang, R., Zhang, Y., & Bai, S. (2016). Robust and hierarchical watermarking of encrypted images based on Compressive Sensing. *Signal Processing Image Communication*, *45*, 41–51. doi:10.1016/j.image.2016.04.002

Loukhaoukha, K., Nabti, M., & Zebbiche, K. (2014). A robust SVD-based image watermarking using a multi-objective particle swarm optimization. *Opto-Electronics Review*, *22*(1), 45–54. doi:10.247811772-014-0177-z

Makbol, N., & Khoo, B. (2013). Robust blind image watermarking scheme based on Redundant Discrete Wavelet Transform and Singular Value Decomposition. *AEÜ. International Journal of Electronics and Communications*, *67*(2), 102–112. doi:10.1016/j.aeue.2012.06.008

Makbol, N., & Khoo, B. (2014). A new robust and secure digital image watermarking scheme based on the integer wavelet transform and singular value decomposition. *Digital Signal Processing*, *33*, 134–147. doi:10.1016/j.dsp.2014.06.012

Mansoori, E., & Soltani, S. (2016). A new semi-blind watermarking algorithm using ordered Hadamard transform. *Imaging Science Journal*, *64*(4), 204–214. doi:10.1 080/13682199.2016.1159816

Ming, M., Zhiguang, Q., & Fang, L. (2010). A Digital Watermarking Algorithm against Dithering Attack Based on Watson Perceptual Pattern. *Proceeding of the second International Conference on Signal Processing Systems (ICSPS)*, *3*, 306-309. 10.1109/ICSPS.2010.5555803

Moghaddam, M., & Nemati, N. (2013). A robust color image watermarking technique using modified Imperialist Competitive Algorithm. *Forensic Science International*, *233*(1-3), 193–200. doi:10.1016/j.forsciint.2013.09.005 PMID:24314520

Mohammadi, S. (2015). A semi blind watermarking algorithm for color image using chaotic map. *Proceeding of the second International Conference on Knowledge-Based Engineering and Innovation (KBEI)*, 106-110. 10.1109/KBEI.2015.7436030

Mousavi, S., Naghsh, A., & Abu-Bakar, S. (2014). Watermarking Techniques used in Medical Images: A Survey. *Journal of Digital Imaging*, *27*(6), 714–729. doi:10.100710278-014-9700-5 PMID:24871349

P. S. & C. P. V. S. S. R. (2017). A robust semi-blind watermarking for color images based on multiple decompositions. *Multimedia Tools and Applications*.

Pal Singh, S., & Bhatnagar, G. (2017). A Novel Chaos Based Robust Watermarking Framework. *Proceedings of the International Conference on Computer Vision and Image Processing, Advances in Intelligent Systems and Computing*, 439-447. 10.1007/978-981-10-2107-7_40

Parah, S., Sheikh, J., Loan, N., & Bhat, G. (2016). Robust and blind watermarking technique in DCT domain using inter-block coefficient differencing. *Digital Signal Processing, 53*, 11–24. doi:10.1016/j.dsp.2016.02.005

Poljicak, A. (2011). Discrete Fourier transform–based watermarking method with an optimal implementation radius. *Journal of Electronic Imaging, 20*(3), 033008. doi:10.1117/1.3609010

Preda, R. (2013). Semi-fragile watermarking for image authentication with sensitive tamper localization in the wavelet domain. *Measurement, 46*(1), 367–373. doi:10.1016/j.measurement.2012.07.010

Radharani, S., & Valarmathi, D. (2010). A Study on Watermarking Schemes for Image Authentication. *International Journal of Computers and Applications, 2*(4), 24–32. doi:10.5120/658-925

Raghavender Rao, Y., & Nagabhooshanam, E. (2014). A novel image zero-watermarking scheme based on DWT-BN-SVD. *International Conference on Information Communication and Embedded Systems (ICICES)*, 1-6.

Rahmani, H., Mortezaei, R., & Ebrahimi Moghaddam, M. (2010). A New Robust Watermarking Scheme to Increase Image Security. *EURASIP Journal on Advances in Signal Processing, 2010*(1), 428183. doi:10.1155/2010/428183

Rani, A., Raman, B., & Kumar, S. (2013). A robust watermarking scheme exploiting balanced neural tree for rightful ownership protection. *Multimedia Tools and Applications, 72*(3), 2225–2248. doi:10.100711042-013-1528-3

Roy, S., & Pal, A. (2016). A robust blind hybrid image watermarking scheme in RDWT-DCT domain using Arnold scrambling. *Multimedia Tools and Applications, 76*(3), 3577–3616. doi:10.100711042-016-3902-4

Roy, S., & Pal, A. (2017). A blind DCT based color watermarking algorithm for embedding multiple watermarks. *AEÜ. International Journal of Electronics and Communications, 72*, 149–161. doi:10.1016/j.aeue.2016.12.003

Saini, S. (2015). A survey on watermarking web contents for protecting copyright. *IEEE second International Conference on Innovations in Information Embedded and Communication Systems ICIIECS*, 1-4. 10.1109/ICIIECS.2015.7193239

Shao, Z., Shang, Y., Zeng, R., Shu, H., Coatrieux, G., & Wu, J. (2016). Robust watermarking scheme for color image based on quaternion-type moment invariants and visual cryptography. *Signal Processing Image Communication*, *48*, 12–21. doi:10.1016/j.image.2016.09.001

Singh, A., Dave, M., & Mohan, A. (2015). Hybrid technique for robust and imperceptible multiple watermarking using medical images. *Multimedia Tools and Applications*, *75*(14), 8381–8401. doi:10.100711042-015-2754-7

Singh, D., & Singh, S. (2016). DWT-SVD and DCT based robust and blind watermarking scheme for copyright protection. *Multimedia Tools and Applications*.

Su, Q., Niu, Y., Wang, Q., & Sheng, G. (2013). A blind color image watermarking based on DC component in the spatial domain. Optik - International Journal for Light and Electron Optics, 124(23), 6255-6260. doi:10.1016/j.ijleo.2013.05.013

Tao, H., Chongmin, L., Mohamad Zain, J., & Abdalla, A. (2014). Robust Image Watermarking Theories and Techniques: A Review. *Journal of Applied Research and Technology*, *12*(1), 122–138. doi:10.1016/S1665-6423(14)71612-8

Thanh, T., & Tanaka, K. (2015). The novel and robust watermarking method based on q-logarithm frequency domain. *Multimedia Tools and Applications*, *75*(18), 11097–11125. doi:10.100711042-015-2836-6

Thilagavathi, N., Saravanan, D., Kumarakrishnan, S., Sakthivel, P., Amudhavel, J., & Prabu, U. (2015). A Survey of Reversible Watermarking Techniques, Application and Attacks. *Proceedings of the International Conference on Advanced Research in Computer Science Engineering & Technology (ICARCSET)*. 10.1145/2743065.2743102

Urvi, H., Panchal, R. & Srivastava. (2015). A Comprehensive Survey on Digital Image Watermarking Techniques. *Proceeding of the Fifth International Conference on Communication Systems and Network Technologies (CSNT)*, 591-595.

Varghese, J., Subash, S., Bin Hussain, O., Nallaperumal, K., Ramadan Saady, M., & Samiulla Khan, M. (2016). An improved digital image watermarking scheme using the discrete Fourier transform and singular value decomposition. *Turkish Journal of Electrical Engineering and Computer Sciences*, *24*, 3432–3447. doi:10.3906/elk-1409-12

Verma, G., Gawande, S., Bhura, M., & Koolagudi, S. (2016). Polygonal Meshes Predicated Watermarking Algorithm to Avert Misinterpretation of ATM Cards. *Procedia Computer Science*, *89*, 587–596. doi:10.1016/j.procs.2016.06.018

Wang, C., Wang, X., Zhang, C., & Xia, Z. (2017). Geometric correction based color image watermarking using fuzzy least squares support vector machine and Bessel K form distribution. *Signal Processing, 134,* 197–208. doi:10.1016/j.sigpro.2016.12.010

Wang, J., & Liu, Y. (2016). Schur Decomposition Based Robust Watermarking Algorithm in Contourlet Domain. *Proceeding of the International Conference on Cloud Computing and Security (ICCCS),* 114-124.

Wang, X., Liu, Y., Xu, H., Wang, A., & Yang, H. (2016). Blind optimum detector for robust image watermarking in nonsubsampled shearlet Domain. *Information Sciences, 372,* 634–654. doi:10.1016/j.ins.2016.08.076

Yang, S., Song, Z., Fang, Z., & Yang, J. (2010). A novel affine attack robust blind watermarking algorithm. *Procedia Engineering, 7,* 239–246. doi:10.1016/j.proeng.2010.11.038

Ye, X., Chen, X., Deng, M., Hui, S., & Wang, Y. (2014). A Multiple-Level DCT Based Robust DWT-SVD Watermark Method. *Proceeding of the Tenth International Conference on Computational Intelligence and Security,* 479-483. 10.1109/CIS.2014.28

Zhao, J., Xu, W., Zhang, S., Fan, S., & Zhang, W. (2016). A Strong Robust Zero-Watermarking Scheme Based on Shearlets High Ability for Capturing Directional Features. *Mathematical Problems in Engineering, 2016,* 1–11.

Zhao, J., Zhang, N., Jia, J., & Wang, H. (2015). Digital watermarking algorithm based on scale-invariant feature regions in non-subsampled contourlet transform domain. *Journal of Systems Engineering and Electronics, 26*(6), 1309–1314. doi:10.1109/JSEE.2015.00143

Chapter 10
A Framework for Image Encryption on Frequency Domain

Zhe Liu
Auckland University of Technology, New Zealand

Mee Loong Yang
Auckland University of Technology, New Zealand

Wei Qi Yan
Auckland University of Technology, New Zealand

ABSTRACT

In this chapter, the authors propose an improved image encryption algorithm based on digital watermarking. The algorithm combines discrete wavelet transform (DWT), discrete cosine transform (DCT), and singular value decomposition (SVD) together in a DWT-DCT-SVD framework to improve the robust watermarking technique. The secret image is embedded into both high-frequency and low-frequency sub-bands of the host image; this makes it difficult to be attacked in all the sub-bands. To reduce the size of a secret key, the authors use a logistic map to generate random images so as to replace the host images. They tested the algorithm by using five types of attacks and the results indicate that the proposed algorithm has higher robustness than traditional chaotic scrambling method and the DRPE method. It shows strong resilience against the five types of attacks as well as statistical attacks.

DOI: 10.4018/978-1-5225-6313-6.ch010

INTRODUCTION

Image encryption techniques can be divided into two groups. One group operates in spatial domain while the other in frequency domain. Earlier encryption methods work typically using chaotic logistic maps which require large amount of computations.

Generally, in these methods, discrete cosine transform (DCT) and discrete wavelet transform (DWT) are widely adopted because DCT avoids complex calculation compared with traditional discrete Fourier transform (DFT) (Ahmed, Natarajan, & Rao, 1974), and DWT can obtain good properties of input image in both spatial and frequency domain (Burrus, Gopinath, & Guo, 1998). They provide convenience for image encryption based on spatial and frequency domain.

We are aware that digital watermarking in frequency domain has high robustness. The basic workflow of digital watermarking is similar to image encryption and decryption processes. In this book chapter, we propose a new encryption method based on watermarking techniques, the encrypted and decrypted processes are designed by using a robust watermarking scheme which is called DWT-DCT-SVD framework. We also extend our method using chaotic map to generate the encryption/decryption images and reduce the size of the secret key. We carried out a series of experiments and found that the proposed method has higher robustness than DRPE method using DFT and DCT.

BACKGROUND

Since mainstream methods for image encryption and digital watermarking focus on frequency domain, we will outline these methods in this section. In 2017, three optical encryption schemes based on DRPE by using DWT were proposed (Mohamed, Samrah & Allah, 2017). These schemes were based on DRPE by using DWT and chaotic maps; one of them used DWT instead of fast Fourier Transform (FFT) in traditional DRPE. Another used DWT and steganography combined technique, and the last one utilized fractional fast Fourier transform (FRFFT), DWT and steganography together. The results were compared with three traditional techniques. From the performance metrics, the proposed three methods based on DWT achieved better performance and robustness versus conventional ones.

DCT has strong energy concentration characteristics in the low-frequency part. DCT is widely used in image processing such as image compression and image encryption. Compared with DFT, the computations of DCT are in real domain. Thus, DCT can resist geometric attack effectively. Because of these advantages, DCT has outstanding performance in the field of image encryption. In 2010, an image encryption algorithm was proposed based on Arnold transform and DCT

(Liu, et al., 2011). In 2011, an image encryption algorithm using DCT and Secure Hash Algorithm-1 (SHA-1) was proposed (Yuen and Wong, 2011).

A watermarking algorithm for digital images based on DWT-DCT-SVD framework was proposed (Yuan and Zhou, 2011)(Wang, et al., 2009) where a four-layer DWT was applied to a secret image. Firstly, the low-frequency subband and three high-frequency subbands of the fourth layer were chosen. Similarly, the same operation was applied to the watermarking image. By using DCT and SVD, the four subbands obtained from the watermarking image were embedded into the host image adaptively. Finally, the watermarked image is obtained after the inverse SVD, DCT and DWT. Compared with the methods by using DCT-SVD and DWT-SVD frameworks, the experiments show that this method is more robust against geometric attacks.

Different from the existing methods for image encryption and image watermarking, we combine DCT, DWT and SVD together and form an image encryption scheme. Our method is robust to resist several kinds of attacks.

METHODOLOGY

Basic Workflow

In this book chapter, we will apply a similar idea of image watermarking to image encryption so as to hide the secret image as the watermark inside the host image. The watermarking algorithm can be treated as the encryption process of image encryption. In the process of watermark extraction, the host image is needed and it can be treated as the secret key for encryption. The process of watermark extraction can be treated as the image decryption. The basic workflow for this proposed encryption method based on watermark technique is illustrated in Figure 1.

Figure 1. The workflow of our proposed method

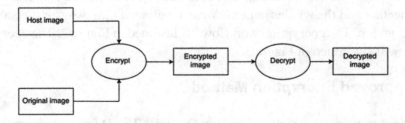

Figure 2. The encryption process of the proposed method

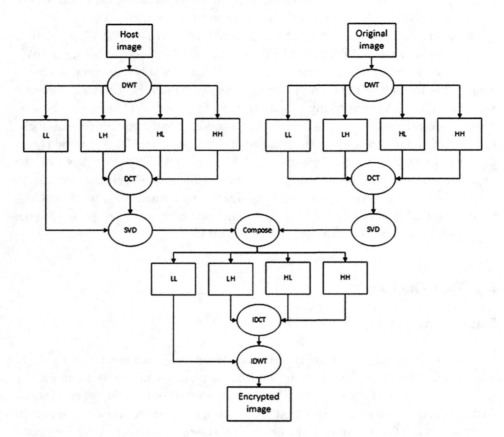

The DWT-DCT-SVD Framework

The proposed encryption method is designed based on a watermarking technique which has high stability (Chakraborty, et al., 2017). It combines DWT, DCT and SVD together and the whole framework can be divided into two parts: encryption and decryption. The encryption workflow is illustrated in Figure 2. The decryption workflow is illustrated in Figure 3.

The Improved Encryption Method

The proposed encryption method based on DWT-DCTSVD framework requires the host image to be the secret key which is too large and inconvenient for transmission. As an improvement, we use the logistic map (Pareek, Patidar, & Sud, 2006) to generate the random image being used as the host image.

The initial value x_0 and parameter μ to generate the random image can be utilized as secret keys, reducing the key size. For this method, we need 11 secret keys which are the initial value x_0, parameterμ, 8 singular matrices of the decomposed secret image as well as the selection of the wavelet basis function.

RESULTS

In our experiments, the proposed DWT-DCT-SVD method as well as the improved method were tested by using the four sample images as shown in Fig. 4. We applied five types of attacks to the encrypted images by using Gaussian noise, salt-and-pepper noise, average filtering, image cropping and image rotating. Given the secret image and its size W×H, we use five metrics to evaluate the encrypted images: Mean Square Error (MSE), Peak Signal-to-Noise Ratio (PSNR), Normalization

Figure 3. The decryption process of the proposed method

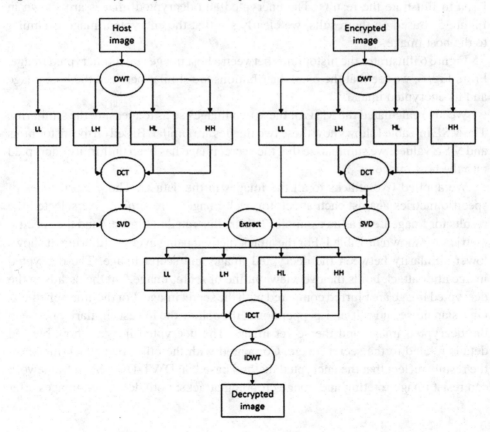

Figure 4. The test images with the resolution 512×512: (a) Airplane (b) Lake (c) Lena (d) Pepper

Cross Correlation (NCC), Number of Pixels Change Rate (NPCR), and Structure Similarity Index (SSIM).

Method-I: Encryption Method Based on DWT-DCT-SVD Framework

We used four secret images in the dataset to test our method and chose the image Lena to illustrate the results. The encrypted and decrypted images are shown in Figure 5. Based on the results, we clearly see that the encrypted image is similar to the host image.

Figure 6 illustrates the histograms between a host image and its encrypted image. From Fig. 6, we see that the pixel distributions are similar between the host image and its encrypted image.

We also calculated the MSE of these two images so as to measure the similarity. The MSE in Table I shows how these two images are similar. Based on the histograms and MSE values, we summarize that the secret image has been uniformly encrypted into the host image.

We applied five attacks to all the images in the dataset. The performances of specific metrics against each attack for each image were similar. We selected the results for image Lena as an example. This is illustrated in Figure 7 and the specific metrics are shown in Table I. For the attack method using average filtering, it shows lower similarity between the decrypted image and secret image. The decrypted image after attack holds the overview outline of secret image, but the details in the decrypted image are blurred compared with the secret image. For the attack methods Gaussian noise and salt-and-pepper noise, they show the lowest similarity between the decrypted image and the secret image. The decrypted images show blurred details related to the secret image. Compared with the other two attack methods, the results reflect that the encrypted method based on DWT-DCT-SVD framework can resist image rotating and image cropping attacks; both decrypted images after

Figure 5. The secret, encrypted, and decrypted images using Method-I.

Figure 6. Pixel distributions of (a) the host image, (b) the encrypted image

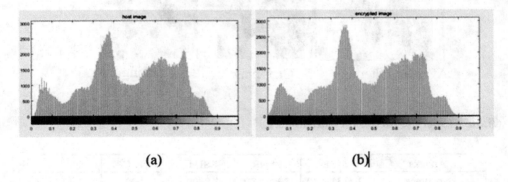

these two attacks hold not only the outline of the secret image but also the details of secret image.

Method-II: Improved Method Based on DWT-DCT-SVD by Using Chaotic Mapping

We used the same four original images in the dataset to verify the encryption algorithm and we chose the image Lena as an example in Fig. 8. From these figures, we see that the encrypted image is obviously similar to the host image and the decrypted image resembles the information of original image clearly. Figure 9 (a) and (b) are

Figure 7. The decrypted images after attacks using Method-I

No Attacks	Gaussian Noise	Salt & Pepper Noise

Average Filtering	Cropping	Rotating

Table 1. Specific Metrics for Methods-I

Attacks	MSE	PSNR	SSIM	NCC	NPCR
No attack	2.3131E-30	296.3580	1.0000	1.0000	0
Gaussian noise	0.0291	15.3633	0.3005	0.9526	0.9854
Salt & pepper noise	0.0469	13.2906	0.2370	0.9282	0.9883
Average filter 7*7	0.0013	28.7080	0.8308	0.9976	0.9317
Crop 100*100 pixels	5.2916E-04	32.7642	0.9930	0.9990	0.9192
Rotate 5 degree	0.0048	23.1647	0,9070	0.9916	0.9802

Figure 8. The original, encrypted and decrypted images using Method-II

the histograms for the original and encrypted images, respectively. We see that the pixel distribution in the host image is random whereas it is a normal distribution in the encrypted image. We applied five attacks to all the images in the dataset, the performance of specific metrics against five attacks for each image is similar as illustrated using the image Lena. We selected the image Lena as the sample for evaluation which is illustrated in Fig.10. The specific metrics are given in Table II.

Figure 9. Pixel distributions of (a) the host image (b) the encrypted image

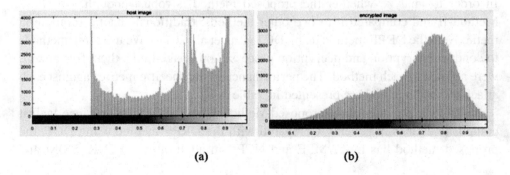

Figure 10. The decrypted images after attacks using Method-II

| No attack | Gaussian Noise | Salt&Pepper Noise |

| Average Filtering | Cropping | Rotating |

Table 2. Specific Metrics for Method II

Attacks	MSE	PSNR	SSIM	NCC	NPCR
No attack	9.8689E-31	300.0573	1.0000	1.0000	0
Gaussian noise	0.0011	29.7285	0.8622	0.9981	0.9414
Salt & pepper noise	0.0022	26.5336	0.7638	0.9960	0.9587
Average filter 7*7	0.1122	9.4984	-0.0765	0.8066	0.9941
Crop 100*100 pixels	0.0041	23.8938	0.9378	0.9926	0.9760
Rotate 5 degree	0.0067	21.7112	0.6898	0.9890	0.9813

Analysis

In order to analyze whether the proposed method is robust enough, we chose Method-II and compared it to two other methods: traditional chaotic scrambling method and the DRPE method using DCT (Liu, et al., 2011). We use three methods to conduct encryption and decryption processes on image Lena; then, five attacks were applied to each method. The performance of the specific metrics against each attack for each method are presented in Table 3.

In Table 3, we find that the proposed Method-II has the best performance against composite attacks in general. Compared with the DRPE method using DCT, the proposed method has lower MSE and NCPR in addition, the PSNR, SSIM and

Table 3. Specific Metrics for the three encrytopn

Attacks	Methods	MSE	PSNR	SSIM	NCC	NCPR
Gaussian noise	Scrambling	0.010	20.078	0.263	0.982	0.984
	DRPE	1.575E+05	-5.197E+01	5.257E-09	1.313E-04	1.000E+00
	Method 2	0.0011	29.7285	0.8622	0.9981	0.9414
Salt & pepper noise	Scrambling	0.014	18.392	0.328	0.974	0.051
	DRPE	6.564E+05	-5.817E+01	3.498E-09	-1.272E-04	1.000E+00
	Method 2	0.0022	26.5336	0.7638	0.9960	0.9587
Average filter 7*7	Scrambling	0.035	14.557	0.330	0.933	0.992
	DRPE	9.734E+05	-5.988E+01	-1.570E-08	3.872E-03	1.000E+00
	Method 2	0.1122	9.4984	-0.0765	0.8066	0.9941
Crop 100*100 pixels	Scrambling	0.010	19.860	0.436	0.981	0.038
	DRPE	6.982E+08	-8.844E+01	-4.756E-13	3.043E-03	1.000E+00
	Method 2	0.0041	23.8938	0.9378	0.9926	0.9760
Rotate 5 degree	Scrambling	0.079	11.049	0.020	0.853	0.993
	DRPE	4.781E+09	-9.680E+01	2.075E-11	-1.747E-02	1.000E+00
	Method 2	0.0067	21.7112	0.6898	0.9890	0.9813

NCC of proposed method are significantly higher than the DRPE method against all attacks. Compared with traditional chaotic scrambling method, the proposed method has higher PSNR, SSIM and NCC as well as lower MSE and NCPR for all of the attacks except the averaging 7×7 filter. The traditional chaotic scrambling method shows better performances against the average filtering attack; in particular, the chaotic scrambling method has larger PSNR, SSIM and NCC values. The MSE and NCPR values are also smaller than the proposed method. From these comparative measurements, it is clear that the proposed method has a better performance compared to the traditional chaotic scrambling method except average filtering attack. Compared with the DRPE method using DCT, the performance for the proposed method is much better. It is obvious that the proposed method has achieved higher robustness over that of chaotic scrambling and DRPE method against composite attacks.

CONCLUSION

In this book chapter, we introduced image encryption on frequency domain; then, we describe a new method based on DWT-DCT-SVD framework and proposed an improved method using chaotic map to generate a random image for use as the host image. We provided the analysis for these two methods and compared the results with the traditional chaotic scrambling method and the DRPE method using DCT.

The proposed method overcomes the shortcomings of those methods and has a higher robustness. The experimental results along with the attack resistance were analyzed in details.

Our future work will be on image encryption using robust ways and apply image reconstruction techniques to remove the image artifacts from composite attacks by using the methods from artificial neural networks and artificial intelligence so that the robustness of selected method may be further improved.

REFERENCES

Ahmed, N., Natarajan, T., & Rao, K. R. (1974). Discrete Cosine Transform. *IEEE Transactions on Computers*, *100*(1), 90–93. doi:10.1109/T-C.1974.223784

Burrus, C. S., Gopinath, R. A., & Guo, H. (1998). *Introduction to Wavelets and Wavelet Transforms: A Primer*. Prentice-Hall, Inc.

Chakraborty, S., Chatterjee, S., Dey, N., Ashour, A. S., & Hassanien, A. E. (2017). *Comparative approach between singular value decomposition and randomized singular value decomposition-based watermarking. In Intelligent Techniques in Signal Processing for Multimedia Security* (pp. 133–149). Springer International Publishing.

Liu, Z., Xu, L., Liu, T., Chen, H., Li, P., Lin, C., & Liu, S. (2011). Color image encryption by using Arnold transform and color-blend operation in discrete cosine transform domains. *Optics Communications*, *284*(1), 123–128. doi:10.1016/j.optcom.2010.09.013

Mohamed, M. A., Samrah, A. S., & Fath Allah, M. I. (2017). DWT vs WP based optical color image encryption robust to composite attacks. Advances in OptoElectronics.

Pareek, N. K., Patidar, V., & Sud, K. K. (2006). Image encryption using chaotic logistic map. *Image and Vision Computing*, *24*(9), 926–934. doi:10.1016/j.imavis.2006.02.021

Wang, B., Ding, J., Wen, Q., Liao, X., & Liu, C. (2009). An image watermarking algorithm based on DWT, DCT and SVD. *IEEE International Conference on Network Infrastructure and Digital Content*, 1034–1038. 10.1109/ICNIDC.2009.5360866

Yan, W. (2017). *Introduction to intelligent surveillance*. London: Springer. doi:10.1007/978-3-319-60228-8

Yuan, X. G., & Zhou, Z. (2011). A novel robust watermarking algorithm based on DWT-DCT-SVD. *Computer Engineering and Science*, *1*, 27.

Yuen, C. H., & Wong, K. W. (2011). A chaos-based joint image compression and encryption scheme using DCT and SHA-1. *Applied Soft Computing*, *11*(8), 5092–5098. doi:10.1016/j.asoc.2011.05.050

Chapter 11
Measuring Developers' Software Security Skills, Usage, and Training Needs

Tosin Daniel Oyetoyan
Western Norway University of Applied Sciences, Norway

Martin Gilje Gilje Jaatun
SINTEF Digital, Norway

Daniela Soares Cruzes
SINTEF Digital, Norway

ABSTRACT

Software security does not emerge fully formed by divine intervention in deserving software development organizations; it requires that developers have the required theoretical background and practical skills to enable them to write secure software, and that the software security activities are actually performed, not just documented procedures that sit gathering dust on a shelf. In this chapter, the authors present a survey instrument that can be used to investigate software security usage, competence, and training needs in agile organizations. They present results of using this instrument in two organizations. They find that regardless of cost or benefit, skill drives the kind of activities that are performed, and secure design may be the most important training need.

DOI: 10.4018/978-1-5225-6313-6.ch011

INTRODUCTION

Traditional security engineering processes are often associated with additional development efforts and are likely to be unpopular among agile development teams (ben Othmane et al., 2014; Beznosov & Kruchten, 2004). A software security approach tailored to the agile mind-set thus seems necessary.

Some approaches have been proposed to integrate security activities into agile development, e.g., the Microsoft SDL for Agile (Microsoft, 2012). However, these approaches have been criticised for looking too similar to the traditional versions in terms of workload (e.g., performing a long list of security verification and validation tasks) (ben Othmane et al., 2014). As a result, "agile" organizations have approached software security in a way that better fits their process and practices. Thus, regardless of whether agile is perceived to be incompatible with any particular secure software development lifecycle, the major discussion we should have is how to improve security within the agile context (Bartsch, 2011). Previous studies (Ayalew et al., 2013; Baca & Carlsson, 2011) have investigated which security activities are practiced in different organizations, and which are compatible with agile practices from cost and benefit perspectives. Using a survey of software security activities among software practitioners, they identify and recommend certain security activities that are compatible with agile practices.

While these activities could be argued to be beneficial and cost effective to integrate, there are still gaps between what is "adequate" security (Allen, 2005), and what is currently practiced within several organizations. According to Allen (2005), adequate security is defined as *"The condition where the protection and sustainability strategies for an organization's critical assets and business processes are commensurate with the organization's tolerance for risk"*.

BACKGROUND

Software security has existed as a distinct field of research for over a decade, and reached prominence with the publication of the book "Software Security" (Gary McGraw, 2006).

The studies by Ayalew et al. (2013), Baca and Carlsson (2011), and Morrison et al. (2017) have investigated security activities from cost and benefit dimensions to advise on frameworks and selection of security activities that can be integrated to agile software development. Jaatun et al. (2015) have used BSIMM to measure security practices but with focus on security maturity at an organisational level. Other studies not directly related to our work have looked into market skills relevant for cybersecurity jobs. For example, Potter and Vickers (2015) used a questionnaire to answer and address the question of what skills does a security professional need in the current information technology environment, and they explored this question by looking at the current state of the Australian industry. Fontenele (Fontenele, 2017) developed a conceptual model and an ontological methodology to aid a robust discovery of the fittest expertise driven by the specific needs of cyber security projects, as well as benchmarking expertise shortages.

Our work differs from these studies as we have measured developers' skills and training needs along software security activities.

Secure Software Development Lifecycles

A number of Secure Software Development Lifecycles (SSDLs) have been proposed, in the following we briefly introduce to most important ones as they relate to this paper.

OWASP CLASP

The Comprehensive, Lightweight Application Security Process (CLASP) (OWASP, 2006) was a project under the Open Web Application Security Project (OWASP). A high-level overview of CLASP is given in Figure 1. CLASP was based on seven best practices:

1. Institute awareness programs
2. Perform application assessments
3. Capture security requirements
4. Implement secure development practices
5. Build vulnerability remediation procedures
6. Define and monitor metrics
7. Publish operational security guidelines

CLASP has not been updated since 2006, and is currently considered abandoned. However, some of the CLASP activities can still be considered useful by themselves.

Microsoft SDL for Agile

The Microsoft Security Development Lifecycle for Agile Development (SDL-Agile) (Microsoft, 2012) is the agile version of the traditional Microsoft SDL (Howard & Lipner, 2006). SDL-Agile is split into three types of activities (see Table 1);

Figure 1. CLASP Overview

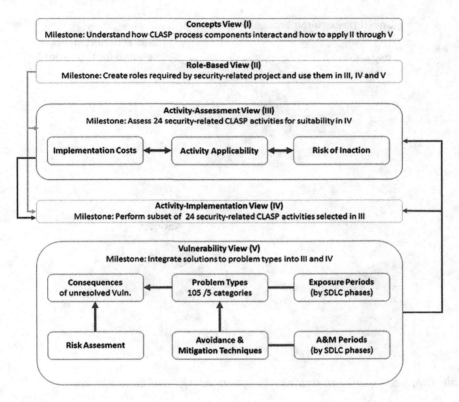

- **"Every-Sprint Requirements" (S):** These activities should be performed in every iteration
- **"Bucket Requirements" (B):** These activities must be performed on a regular basis during the development lifecycle; there are three types of such requirements defined (each type referred to as a bucket) and typically one is picked from each bucket in each sprint
- **"One-Time Requirements" (O):** These activities typically only need to be performed once at the beginning of the project.

Cigital Touchpoints

The Cigital Touchpoints (Gary McGraw, 2004; Gary McGraw, 2005) (de Win et al., 2009) were introduced as a lightweight way of distilling the essence of practical software security. They have been presented slightly different over the years, but the essence is as illustrated in Figure 3.

Figure 2. The SDL-agile one-time and bucket requirements illustrated

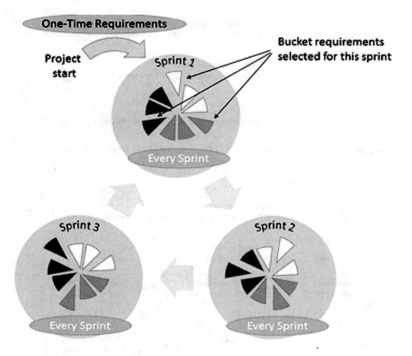

Table 1. MS SDL-agile activities – (o)ne-time, (s)print, and (b)ucket

1. Training	2. Requirement	3. Design	4. Implementation	5. Verification	6. Release	7. Response
	2. Establish Security Requirements (O)	5. Establish Design Requirements (O)	8. Use Approved Tools (S)	11. Perform Dynamic Analysis (B)	14. Create an Incident Response Plan (O)	
1. Core Security Training	3. Create Quality Bug Bars (B)	6. Perform Attack Surface Analysis/ Reduction (O)	9. Deprecate Unsafe Functions (S)	12. Perform Fuzz Testing (B)	15. Conduct Final Security Review (S)	17. Execute Incident Response Plan
	4. Perform Security and Privacy Risk Assessments (O)	7. Use Threat Modeling (S)	10. Perform Static Analysis (S)	13. Conduct Attack Surface Review (B)	16. Certify Release and Archive (S)	

Figure 3. The cigital touchpoints

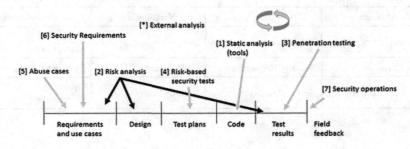

In order of effectiveness, the 7 touchpoints are:

1. Code review
2. Architectural risk analysis
3. Penetration testing
4. Risk-based security tests
5. Abuse cases
6. Security requirements
7. Security operations

ISO/IEC Application Security Standard

In 2011, the International Standards Organization published an application security standard as part of its 27000-series (ISO/IEC, 2011). We have not seen this standard in use in any of the organizations we have worked with, but it may prove relevant in the future.

Measuring Software Security Activities

Measuring software security is difficult (Jaatun, 2012), and therefore second-order metrics are often employed, i.e., measuring what kind of software security activities are performed when developing the software.

OpenSAMM

The OWASP Software Assurance Maturity Model (SAMM or OpenSAMM) (OWASP, 2016) is an open software security framework divided into four business functions: Governance, Construction, Verification and Deployment. Each business function is composed of three security practices, as shown in Table 2.

Table 2. The OpenSAMM software security framework

Governance	Construction	Verification	Deployment
Strategy and Metrics	Threat Assessment	Design Review	Vulnerability Management
Policy & Compliance	Security Requirements	Code Review	Environment Hardening
Education & Guidance	Secure Architecture	Security Testing	Operational Enablement

Each practice is assessed at a maturity level from 1 to 3 (plus 0 for "no maturity"), and for each maturity level there is an objective and two activities that have to be fulfilled to achieve that level. OpenSAMM is "prescriptive", in the sense that it advocates that all the specified activities must be performed in order to be a high-maturity organisation.

BSIMM

The Building Security In Maturity Model (BSIMM) first saw the light of day in 2009, based on a study of 9 software development organizations. BSIMM is structured around a Software Security Framework of four domains, each divided into three practices, as illustrated in Table 3. As is evident from the table, BSIMM shares origins with the OpenSAMM framework described above. The latest version of the BSIMM report (Gary McGraw et al., 2018) features results from 120 companies, measuring 116 different software security activities.

Although BSIMM also ranks software security activities in three maturity levels, it purports to be descriptive rather than prescriptive, and there is no implicit expectation that all organizations should do all 116 activities. Due to the large number of software security activities, BSIMM can said to be more specific than OpenSAMM. New BSIMM activities are added as they are observed in the field,

Table 3. The BSIMM software security framework

Governance	Intelligence	SSDL Touchpoints	Deployment
Strategy and Metrics	Attack Models	Architecture Analysis	Penetration Testing
Compliance and Policy	Security Features and Design	Code Review	Software Environment
Training	Standards and Requirements	Security Testing	Configuration Management and Vulnerability Management)

and activities that fall out of use are removed. The maturity level of a given activity can also be changed from one version of the study to the next.

BSIMM has also been used to measure security practices in different organizations. Jaatun et al. (2015) used a questionnaire based on the BSIMM activities to measure the security maturity of Norwegian public organizations. They found that there is a need for improvements in metrics, penetration testing and training developers in secure development. BSIMM is useful for measuring the software security maturity of an organization and helping them formulate overall security strategy (Gary McGraw et al., 2018). However, it is not perceived as a lightweight measurement tool to directly measure developers' skill or usage of software security activities within a development team.

Common Criteria

The Common Criteria (ISO/IEC, 2009) (CC) emerged toward the end of the previous century as an amalgamation of the US DoD Trusted Computer Systems Evaluation Criteria (TCSEC, a.k.a. "the Orange Book"), the European ITSEC and the Canadian CTCPEC. CC is used in the security evaluation of computer-based systems, typically for military or critical infrastructure use. A fundamental concept of CC is that a Protection Profile containing functional security requirements and security assurance requirements is established. A security assurance requirement is intended to help achieve a certain level of confidence that the claimed (functional) security requirements are fulfilled, and typically relate to *how* the system is developed. There are sets of predefined security assurance requirements which are referred to as Evaluation Assurance Levels (EAL1-7). The manufacturer will create a Security Target document which elaborates how the requirements of the Protection Profile are met, and finally an external evaluator will perform an evaluation to confirm or reject the claims.

CC is essentially a long list of requirements, and it is totally up to the Protection Profile which requirements are considered for a given product. Some of the assurance requirements are effectively software security activities.

The Top 10 Software Security Design Flaws

The IEEE Center for Secure Design has published a document (Arce et al., 2014) explaining how to avoid the ten most common software security design flaws. The recommendations are as follows:

1. Earn or Give, but Never Assume, Trust
2. Use an Authentication Mechanism that Cannot be Bypassed or Tampered With

3.   Authorize after You Authenticate
4.   Strictly Separate Data and Control Instructions, and Never Process Control Instructions Received from Untrusted Sources
5.   Define an Approach that Ensures all Data are Explicitly Validated
6.   Use Cryptography Correctly
7.   Identify Sensitive Data and How They Should Be Handled
8.   Always Consider the Users
9.   Understand How Integrating External Components Changes Your Attack Surface
10.   Be Flexible When Considering Future Changes to Objects and Actors

RESEARCH METHODOLOGY AND STUDY DESIGN

The research presented here is motivated based on the perceived knowledge gaps in software security in agile software development organizations in Norway (Jaatun et al., 2015). In order to address these gaps, management must first understand the current status of software security practices and capability within their organization. We used our survey instrument in a study carried out in 2 organizations (in the following referred to as "Org-1" and "Org-2"), that develop software in telecommunication and transportation, respectively. The case study is described in more detail in our previous work (Oyetoyan et al., 2016; Oyetoyan et al., 2017) investigating existing practice, skills, and training needs within agile teams. The survey instrument is intended to shed light on the training needs and understand the relationships between skills and usage of security activities among teams and across roles. The findings are important to guide management decisions towards improving security within their organization.

The sections below describe the research questions, hypotheses, data collection procedure that we used in our case studies, the instruments used, and the type of data analysis performed.

Research Questions

We make the following assumptions that:

- Developers have relatively different skills in software security, regardless of the organization where they currently work.
- Agile organizations have different usage patterns with software security activities. An agile team is mostly autonomous and self-confident (Robinson & Sharp, 2004), and thus makes decisions that the team members think best

contribute to customer satisfaction and product quality. Since activities are chosen in a voluntary manner in agile settings, we believe that organizations would use activities that best fit their process and business needs.

- Based on conventional wisdom, using an activity requires certain level of know-how. Hence, teams would use activities where they have competence.
- Experienced developers would most probably have taken security related decisions during their development career, and thus have knowledge and experience in software security.

Our instrument is suitable for investigating whether the skills, usage and training needs in software security activities in several organizations are similar or different. Understanding the similarities and differences between organizations also help during replications and adoptions of software security activities and programs across different organizations.

The research questions that could be addressed include:

- Which software security activities are most used within the organization?
- Which training needs are important to the organization?
- How are security experience and the perceived need for software security training influenced by years of developer of experience?
- What is the relationship between usage of, and skill in software security activities?

Data Collection

The method of choice for the project is Action Research (Greenwood & Levin, 2006). Action research is an appropriate research methodology for this investigation for several reasons. First, the study's combination of scientific and practical objectives is a good match with the basic tenet of action research, which is to merge theory and practice in a way that real-world problems are solved by theoretically informed actions in collaboration between researchers and practitioners (Greenwood & Levin, 2006). Therefore, the design of the instruments had to take in consideration the usefulness of the results for the companies and for research.

In addition, for the interpretation and discussion of the results, answers from the survey should be complemented by document analysis of project artifacts, observations of meetings, and discussions with different stakeholders in the companies. Other focused interviews on specific topics, and the feedback from the survey results, should be compared with the collected information about the organizational contexts and documents.

Survey Questionnaire

The questionnaire was designed in phases, getting feedback from the companies and experts for getting to the final version. The first version of the questionnaire contained questions on different software security activities from OWASP CLASP, Microsoft SDL for Agile, Common Criteria, and Cigital Touchpoints that have been used in previous studies (Ayalew et al., 2013; Baca & Carlsson, 2011). The table also includes additional practices such as "pair programming" and "drawing a countermeasure graph" considered in these studies; both are common security activities used in agile settings, e.g., when security experts rotate through programming pairs (Bartsch, 2011; Wäyrynen et al., 2004).

The instrument has been jointly reviewed by the authors, a security professional, a security champion and a project manager. The activities are classified differently than in the traditional software development lifecycle (SDLC), but they do, however, fit into each development lifecycle. The rationale is to invoke a different way of perceiving these activities than from a traditional viewpoint. This could make it possible to spot some assumptions such as for instance, whereas secure design involves many activities from "Threat modelling and risk management", we can argue that software designers could make assumptions about secure design when they include, e.g., authentication mechanisms (Arce et al., 2014). However, performing a comprehensive threat analysis could reveal an insecure design, e.g., a possibility to bypass an authentication or authorization mechanism by directly navigating to an obscure webpage or resource.

Similarly, we have considered software security tools separately in order to identify strong and weak areas of usage and skills. Findings from the survey can trigger further questions, e.g., why certain implemented tools are not used within the organization, and this could lead to useful actions. These activities are divided into: Inception, threat modelling and risk management, secure design and coding, security tools, security testing, and release. Table 5 shows the software security activities. In addition, we provided a short explanation of each term we have used in the survey for the respondents. We have used a scale for the skill level as shown in Table 4; the respondents were instructed to use this scale when assessing their own skill level.

For the software activities listed in Table 5, we asked the following 3 questions:

Q1: What is your skill level in this activity or tool?
Q2: Do you currently use this activity or tool? (Check box for yes)
Q3: Do you want to have training in this activity or tool? (Check box for yes)

In addition, we asked 2 questions about security and development experience:

Q4: Do you have security experience? (Yes or no)
Q5: Number of years with software development.

We have designed both an online questionnaire and a paper-based version. We further refined the instrument by running a test on our industrial contacts, an independent architect and a post-doctoral fellow in software engineering. The target response time was 10-12 minutes. In our experience, administering the questionnaire manually to the development teams on site will increase the response rate, and provide the opportunity to clarify questions that respondents might have.

The final questionnaire can be found in the original paper (Oyetoyan et al., 2017), and is also provided in Appendix A in this chapter. The skills are listed in Table 5, and additional explanations are further provided in Appendix A.

Comparing with the software security activities defined in BSIMM (Gary McGraw et al., 2018), we find that most of the activities in Table 5 are fully or partly covered by BSIMM, except "Countermeasure techniques", "Pair programming", and "Use of threat modelling tool". Threat modelling is equivalent to what BSIMM calls "Architecture Analysis", but this practice does not mention using a tool.

RESULTS

We used our survey instrument on two local companies (Oyetoyan et al., 2017), and in the following we briefly present some results of the survey and analysis conducted among the two organizations, discussing each research question in turn.

Table 4. Scale for skill level

Novice [1]	Basic [2]	Moderate [3]	High [4]	Expert [5]
Have no experience working in this area	You have the level of experience gained in a classroom and/ or experimental scenarios or as a trainee on-the-job. You are expected to need help when performing in this area	You are able to successfully complete tasks in this area as requested. Help from an expert may be required from time to time, but you can usually perform the skill independently	You can perform the actions associated in this area without assistance. You are certainly recognized within your immediate organization as "a person to ask" when difficult questions arise regarding this area	You are known as an expert in this area. You can provide guidance, troubleshoot and answer questions related to this area of expertise and the field where the skill is used

Table 5. Mapping of software security activities

	CLASP	MS-SDL	CT	CC	Others	BSIMM Activities
Inception						
Functioning as project security officer/champion	*	*				SM1.2, SM2.3, T2.5, T2.7, T3.1, T3.5
Gathering security requirements	*	*	*	*		Partly covered by SR1.3 (Maybe whole practice SR)
Writing abuse stories/cases	*		*			AM2.1, ST3.5
Threat Modeling and Risk Management						
Threat modeling	*	*				Practice AM
Attack surface analysis	*	*				Partly covered by Practice AM
Countermeasure techniques	*	*				-
Asset analysis				*		Partly covered by AM1.2, CP2.1
Risk analysis	*		*	*		AA2.1
Role matrix identification	*					SM1.1
Secure Design and Coding						
Secure design	*	*	*			SFD1.2, SFD2.1, SFD2.2, SFD3.3
Secure coding	*	*	*			SR2.6, CR3.5
Pair programming					*	-
Static code analysis	*	*	*			Practice CR
Use of Security Tools						
Use of threat modeling tool					*	-
Use of dynamic code analysis tool					*	Partly covered by practice PT
Use of static code analysis tool					*	Partly covered by CR1.4
Use of code review tool					*	CR1.4, CR2.5, CR2.6, CR3.4
Security Testing						
Vulnerability assessment						Partly covered by practice AM
Penetration testing			*			Practice PT
Red team testing						PT1.1, PT1.3, PT3.1
Fuzz testing			*			ST2.6
Dynamic testing	*					Partly covered by Practice CR and ST
Risk-based testing			*			Practice ST
Security code review	*		*			Practice CR
Release						
Incident response management	*	*				CMVM1.1, CMVM2.1, CMVM3.3

Which Activities Are Most Used Within the Organizations?

Research performed by Microsoft (Adams, 2012) indicates that only 36% of developers are confident to write secure software. Our small sample indicates that this situation still persists. Our results show that the three most commonly used activities were:

- Use of code review tool
- Static code analysis
- Pair programming.

Note that none of these are necessarily pure software security activities, and may indeed be used without improving software security at all.

Which Training Needs Are Important to the Organizations?

In our study, secure design was indicated as the single most important training need expressed by teams in both organizations. There is thus a need to focus on how to address and assist agile teams in the area of secure design. Architectural-related challenges such as lack of time, motivation to consider design choices, and unknown domain and untried solutions have been shown to affect agile development teams (Babar, 2009).

How Are Security Experience and the Perceived Need for Software Security Training Influenced by Years of Developer Experience?

We can infer that training needs may or may not be influenced by years of development experience. Factors such as an organization's working culture, teams' distribution, teams' interactions, security experience, and how new employees are integrated could be responsible for training needs perceptions across different years of experience.

Zhu et al. (2013) argued that only a small fraction of developers are well trained in secure software development. This is because most Computer Science (CS) and Software Engineering (SE) curricula train students in programming and application development, but not secure software development. As a result, CS and SE graduates are not trained in programming techniques to reduce security bugs and vulnerabilities and would unintentionally introduce avoidable security bugs in the application. While this result is not surprising, we believe it should be a call to integrate software security education in the curriculum for the next generation of CS and SE graduates.

Figure 4. % of Training Needs across all roles compared between the 2 organizations

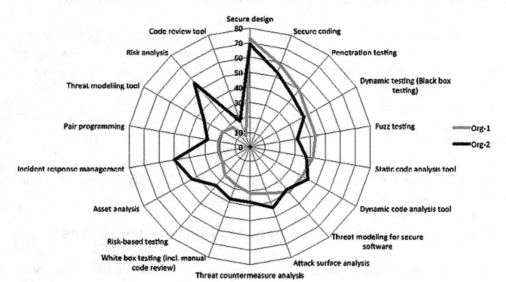

What Is the Relationship Between Usage of, and Skill in Software Security Activities?

Correlation analysis between indicated skill levels and usage of activities shows that skill drives usage of activities. In both organizations, the correlation result is very high at more than 0.9 and statistically significant at 95% confidence interval. Regardless of the cost of activity, we found that teams do well in activities where they indicate high level of skills. The studies by Baca & Carlsson (2011) and Ayaew et al. (2013) report code review to be detrimental in cost and benefit and pair programming to have marginal benefit and detrimental in cost to agile. However, our findings reveal that code review and pair programming are well practiced in both organizations and are areas where respondents indicate high skill levels.

Pair programming is an important practice in eXtreme Programming (XP) and by itself includes the art of code review (Beck, 1999). In addition, peer code review is claimed to catch about 60% of the defects (Boehm & Basili, 2005). These could explain the reasons both organizations have adopted these practices. The work of Dybå et al. (2004) that investigated the factors affecting software developer acceptance and utilization of Electronic Process Guides (EPG) corroborates this finding. Their results suggest that software developers are mainly concerned about the usefulness of the EPG regardless of whether it is easy to use, how much support they receive, or how much they are influenced by others.

On the other hand, we could hypothesize that management can increase usage in certain software security activity if they invest into increasing the team's skill in this area.

DISCUSSION

A brief summary of our research questions and results (Oyetoyan et al., 2017) is presented in Table 6. Note that despite the interpretation by Rindell et al. (Rindell et al., 2017), our contribution is not intended as another secure software development lifecycle.

Through interviews we discovered that certain security relevant tools (e.g. static analysis tools) are not used for finding security defects. This implies that simply making tools available will not improve security, unless the tools are actually used with security in mind.

Although both organizations deliver solutions for critical infrastructures, Org-1 has a higher level of security awareness, which is driven by the security expert group. This context is important in order to understand why this organization's usage is higher than the other. We need to further investigate the drivers for increase in software security adoption in an organization, such as research efforts, government funding and policies, education, and commitments by management to security.

Furthermore, the results from our survey show gaps in secure software development and opportunity for improvement. Among the development team, secure coding is practiced by less than half of the developers in both organizations. Invariably, over 50% of the developers are not paying attention to secure coding. The main question is whether this number is an acceptable risk for the management. Similarly, secure design is practiced by less than 40% of architects in both organizations. The high

Table 6. Summary of results per research question

RQs	Conclusion
1. Which software security activities are most used within the organizations?	Use of code review tool, static code analysis, and pair programming
2. Which training needs are important to the organizations?	The organizations agree on secure design and secure coding, and additionally they identify training need in penetration testing and risk analysis
3. How are security experience and the perceived need for software security training influenced by years of developer of experience?	Security experience increases with development experience, but perceived need for software security varies between organizations
4. What is the relationship between usage of, and skill in software security activities?	Usage increases for activities where teams have a high level of skill

level of individual and team autonomy in agile settings requires a careful balance with respect to software security integration. While different approaches to integrate software security into agile teams have been proposed (Baca et al., 2015; Bartsch, 2011; ben Othmane et al., 2014), there are still many challenges about how to achieve it. The cost and benefit in terms of additional activity such as in ben Othmane et al. (2014) and additional security personnel, as in Baca et al. (2015) need to be acceptable to the agile team and management.

An important result from our survey is that secure design is the highest training need expressed by all roles in both organizations. We believe that this is not accidental. The need for secure design is corroborated in Arce et al. (2014). Critics of agile software development have argued that the lack of attention to design and architectural issues is a serious limitation of the agile approach (Dybå & Dingsøyr, 2008; Rosenberg & Stephens, 2003). About 60% of defects in a system is introduced during design (Bernstein & Yuhas, 2005), and fixing defects after release is a hundred times costlier than fixing it during requirement or design (Boehm & Basili, 2005). In terms of security defects in design, the strongest statement comes from a group of software security professionals (Arce et al., 2014): *While a system may always have implementation defects, we have found that the security of many systems is breached due to design flaws.* In agile development, the lack of a complete overview of the system leaves room for unidentified risks during design.

Our impression is that none of the top 10 security design flaws (Arce et al., 2014) are particularly well known among developers, but many fall into the trap of equating authentication mechanisms with software security. Thus, this aspect is often implicitly covered, when good-practice standard authentication solutions are employed.

Clearly, there is a need for more practice-oriented research efforts to find an acceptable approach that can help agile organization move towards their "adequate" level of security. We argue that security loopholes could be created by any team or individual within the organization with weak approaches to security. There are two major points to ponder in this result regarding software security adoption: 1) How can skill be increased in specific software security areas relevant to the development team and the goal of the organization? and 2) How can we create an environment that make replication of software security successes possible among teams? Creating a learning environment is central to point 1. Although agile development and learning are highly related (Aniche & de Azevedo Silveira, 2011), building a learning environment for security is not that easy. Differences in technologies and team autonomy are just two of the challenges to consider.

CONCLUSION

We have presented an instrument for measuring the current usage, team competencies and training needs in software security activities in agile organizations. Our survey instrument complements maturity models such as BSIMM and OpenSAMM by focusing on the individuals rather than on organizations.

We have found that the individuals in our small sample of organizations were similar in terms of employing certain activities such as use of code review tool, pair programming, and use of static code analysis/tool, but since these activities may or may not be used specifically for security, particular focus on software security is necessary for these to have an impact on software security. Furthermore, skill drives the usage of activities, and we found that secure design may be the topmost area where there is a need for training.

We have identified learning and knowledge transfer as important to increase software security usage among teams.

ACKNOWLEDGMENT

The work in this chapter was supported by the Research Council of Norway through the project SoS-Agile: Science of Security in Agile Software Development (grant number 247678). We are grateful to our industrial partners and the survey respondents.

REFERENCES

Adams, E. (2012). *The Biggest Information Security Mistakes that Organizations Make and How to Avoid Making Them*. Retrieved from https://web.securityinnovation.com/the-biggest-information-security-mistakes-that-organizations-make

Allen, J. (2005). *Governing for enterprise security* (CMU/SEI-2005-TN-023). Retrieved from http://resources.sei.cmu.edu/library/asset-view.cfm?assetid=7453

Aniche, M. F., & de Azevedo Silveira, G. (2011). *Increasing learning in an agile environment: Lessons learned in an agile team*. Paper presented at the Agile Conference (AGILE), 2011. 10.1109/AGILE.2011.13

Arce, I., Clark-Fisher, K., Daswani, N., DelGrosso, J., Dhillon, D., Kern, C., . . . West, J. (2014). *Avoiding The Top 10 Software Security Design Flaws*. Retrieved from https://www.computer.org/cms/CYBSI/docs/Top-10-Flaws.pdf

Ayalew, T., Kidane, T., & Carlsson, B. (2013). *Identification and Evaluation of Security Activities in Agile Projects. In Secure IT Systems* (pp. 139–153). Springer.

Babar, M. A. (2009). *An exploratory study of architectural practices and challenges in using agile software development approaches.* Paper presented at the 2009 Joint Working IEEE/IFIP Conference on Software Architecture & European Conference on Software Architecture. 10.1109/WICSA.2009.5290794

Baca, D., Boldt, M., Carlsson, B., & Jacobsson, A. (2015). *A Novel Security-Enhanced Agile Software Development Process Applied in an Industrial Setting.* Paper presented at the Availability, Reliability and Security (ARES), 2015 10th International Conference on. 10.1109/ARES.2015.45

Baca, D., & Carlsson, B. (2011). Agile development with security engineering activities. *Proceedings of the 2011 International Conference on Software and Systems Process.*

Bartsch, S. (2011). *Practitioners' perspectives on security in agile development.* Paper presented at the Availability, Reliability and Security (ARES), 2011 Sixth International Conference on. 10.1109/ARES.2011.82

Beck, K. (1999). Embracing change with extreme programming. *Computer, 32*(10), 70–77. doi:10.1109/2.796139

ben Othmane, L., Angin, P., Weffers, H., & Bhargava, B. (2014). Extending the agile development process to develop acceptably secure software. *IEEE Transactions on Dependable and Secure Computing, 11*(6), 497-509.

Bernstein, L., & Yuhas, C. M. (2005). *Trustworthy systems through quantitative software engineering* (Vol. 1). John Wiley & Sons. doi:10.1002/0471750336

Beznosov, K., & Kruchten, P. (2004). Towards agile security assurance. *Proceedings of the 2004 workshop on New security paradigms.*

Boehm, B., & Basili, V. R. (2005). *Software defect reduction top 10 list. In Foundations of empirical software engineering: the legacy of Victor R* (Vol. 426). Basili. doi:10.1007/3-540-27662-9

de Win, B., Scandariato, R., Buyens, K., Grégoire, J., & Joosen, W. (2009). On the secure software development process: CLASP, SDL and Touchpoints compared. *Information and Software Technology, 51*(7), 1152–1171. doi:10.1016/j.infsof.2008.01.010

Dybå, T., & Dingsøyr, T. (2008). Empirical studies of agile software development: A systematic review. *Information and Software Technology*, *50*(9), 833–859. doi:10.1016/j.infsof.2008.01.006

Dybå, T., Moe, N. B., & Mikkelsen, E. M. (2004). An empirical investigation on factors affecting software developer acceptance and utilization of electronic process guides. *Software Metrics, 2004. Proceedings. 10th International Symposium on.* 10.1109/METRIC.2004.1357905

Fontenele, M. P. (2017). *Designing a method for discovering expertise in cyber security communities: an ontological approach.* University of Reading.

Greenwood, D. J., & Levin, M. (2006). *Introduction to action research: Social research for social change.* SAGE Publications.

Howard, M., & Lipner, S. (2006). *The Security Development Lifecycle.* Microsoft Press.

ISO/IEC. (2009). Information technology -- Security techniques -- Evaluation criteria for IT security -- Part 1: Introduction and general model: ISO/IEC 15408-1:2009.

ISO/IEC. (2011). Information technology -- Security techniques -- Application security -- Part 1: Overview and concepts: ISO/IEC 27034-1:2011.

Jaatun, M. G. (2012). Hunting for Aardvarks: Can Software Security be Measured? In G. Quirchmayr, J. Basl, I. You, L. Xu, & E. Weippl (Eds.), *Multidisciplinary Research and Practice for Information Systems* (pp. 85–92). Springer Berlin Heidelberg. doi:10.1007/978-3-642-32498-7_7

Jaatun, M. G., Cruzes, D. S., Bernsmed, K., Tøndel, I. A., & Røstad, L. (2015). *Software Security Maturity in Public Organisations.* Paper presented at the Information Security: 18th International Conference, ISC 2015, Trondheim, Norway. 10.1007/978-3-319-23318-5_7

McGraw, G. (2004). Software Security. *IEEE Security and Privacy*, *2*(2), 80–83. doi:10.1109/MSECP.2004.1281254

McGraw, G. (2005). The 7 Touchpoints of Secure Software. *Dr. Dobb's Journal.*

McGraw, G. (2006). Software Security: Building Security In. Addison-Wesley Professional.

McGraw, G., Migues, S., & West, J. (2018). *Building Security In Maturity Model (BSIMM 9).* Academic Press.

Microsoft. (2012). *Security Development Lifecycle for Agile Development*. Retrieved from https://msdn.microsoft.com/en-us/library/windows/desktop/ee790621.aspx

Morrison, P., Smith, B. H., & Williams, L. (2017). *Surveying security practice adherence in software development*. Paper presented at the Hot Topics in Science of Security: Symposium and Bootcamp. 10.1145/3055305.3055312

OWASP. (2006). *CLASP concepts*. Retrieved from https://www.owasp.org/index.php/CLASP_Concepts

OWASP. (2016). *Software Assurance Maturity Model*. Retrieved from http://www.opensamm.org/

Oyetoyan, T. D., Cruzes, D. S., & Jaatun, M. G. (2016). *An Empirical Study on the Relationship between Software Security Skills, Usage and Training Needs in Agile Settings*. Paper presented at the Availability, Reliability and Security (ARES), 2016 11th International Conference on. 10.1109/ARES.2016.103

Oyetoyan, T. D., Jaatun, M. G., & Cruzes, D. S. (2017). A Lightweight Measurement of Software Security Skills, Usage and Training Needs in Agile Teams. *International Journal of Secure Software Engineering, 8*(1), 27. doi:10.4018/IJSSE.2017010101

Potter, L. E., & Vickers, G. (2015). What skills do you need to work in cyber security?: A look at the Australian market. *Proceedings of the 2015 ACM SIGMIS Conference on Computers and People Research*. 10.1145/2751957.2751967

Rindell, K., Hyrynsalmi, S., & Leppänen, V. (2017). Busting a Myth: Review of Agile Security Engineering Methods. *Proceedings of the 12th International Conference on Availability, Reliability and Security*. 10.1145/3098954.3103170

Robinson, H., & Sharp, H. (2004). Extreme Programming and Agile Processes in Software Engineering. *5th International Conference, XP 2004 Proceedings*. 10.1007/978-3-540-24853-8_16

Rosenberg, D., & Stephens, M. (2003). *Extreme programming refactored: the case against XP*. Apress.

Wäyrynen, J., Bodén, M., & Boström, G. (2004). *Security engineering and eXtreme programming: An impossible marriage? In Extreme programming and agile methods-XP/Agile Universe 2004* (pp. 117–128). Springer. doi:10.1007/978-3-540-27777-4_12

Zhu, J., Lipford, H. R., & Chu, B. (2013). Interactive support for secure programming education. *Proceeding of the 44th ACM technical symposium on Computer science education*. 10.1145/2445196.2445396

APPENDIX

SURVEY INSTRUMENT AND EXPLANATION OF TERMS

Software Security Activities in Agile Software Development Team

Instructions: Please mark the options that best fit your responses to these questions.

Section A: General Information

(Multiple answers are possible, see Table 7)

Section B: Capability and Interest

See Tables 8 and 9.

Table 7.

	Developer	Tester	Architect	Project Manager	Product Owner	Others (Please indicate)		
What is your role(s) in the agile team?								
	Scrum	Extreme Programming (XP)	Feature Driven Development (FDD)	Lean Software Development	Crystal Methods	Kanban	Agile Unified Process (AUP)	Dynamic Systems Development Method (DSDM)	Others
Which Agile Method-ologies do you use?									
	Yes	No							
Do you have software security experience?									
No of years with software development:									
Name of product:									
Type of product (e.g. web, mobile, network, control system, e-commerce, etc.):									

Table 8.

Novice [1]	Basic [2]	Moderate [3]	High [4]	Expert [5]
Have no experience working in this area	You have the level of experience gained in a classroom and/ or experimental scenarios or as a trainee on-the-job. You are expected to need help when performing in this area	You are able to successfully complete tasks in this area as requested. Help from an expert may be required from time to time, but you can usually perform the skill independently	You can perform the actions associated in this area without assistance. You are certainly recognized within your immediate organization as "a person to ask" when difficult questions arise regarding this area.	You are known as an expert in this area. You can provide guidance, troubleshoot and answer questions related to this area of expertise and the field where the skill is used.

Section C: Training

Instruction: Please tick the activities you would like to receive training on (see Table 10).

Comment/Feedback

Please provide any comment or feedback in the space below.

Explanation of Terms in Questionnaire

See Table 11.

Table 9.

	Currently Do/Use It	What Is Your Skill Level in This Activity?						What Is Your Level Of Interest in This Activity?				
		Novice 1	2	3	4	Expert 5	Don't know	Not Interested	Slightly Interested	Moderately Interested	Very Interested	Don't Know
Security code review												
Secure design												
Secure coding												
Static code analysis tool												
Dynamic code analysis tool												
Code review tool												
Threat modeling tool												
Static code analysis												
Dynamic code analysis												
Vulnerability assessment												
Penetration testing												
Red team testing												
Fuzz testing												
Dynamic testing												
Risk-based testing												
Threat modelling												
Attack surface analysis												
Risk analysis												
Role matrix identification												
Asset analysis												
Countermeasure techniques												
Pair programming												
Functioning as project security officer/ Champion												
Writing abuse stories/cases												
Gathering security requirements												
Incident Response Management												

Table 10.

	I want to have training in this activity/tool
Threat and Risk Management	
Threat modeling for secure software	
Attack surface analysis	
Threat countermeasure analysis	
Asset analysis	
Risk analysis	
Secure design & coding activities	
Secure coding	
Pair programming	
Secure design (e.g. attack surface reduction, secure defaults)	
Security tools	
Static code analysis tool	
Dynamic code analysis tool	
Code review tool	
Threat modeling tool	
Security Testing (Note that several techniques exist for security testing and some of these techniques may be overlapping)	
Penetration testing	
Dynamic testing (Black box testing)	
Fuzz testing	
White box testing (Including manual code review)	
Risk-based testing	
Release Activity	
Incident Response Management	

Table 11.

I	Term	Definition	Examples
A	Abuse stories	Brief and informal stories that identify how attackers may abuse the system and jeopardize stakeholders' assets	
	Attack surface	All different points where an attacker could get into a system and get data out of the system	• user interface forms & fields • HTTP headers and cookies • APIs • Files • Databases • etc.
	Asset analysis	Identifying both physical and abstract assets of the organization. Assets are threat target. For example, an asset of an application might be a list of clients and their personal information; this is a physical asset. An abstract asset might be the reputation of an organization. Analysis may include identifying the trust levels (i.e. The level of access required to access the entry point is documented here)	
C	Code signing	Providing the stakeholder with a way to validate the origin and integrity of the system	
	Countermeasure	Action taken in order to protect an asset against threats	• Threat – Tampering with data • Countermeasures – appropriate authorization, hashes, digital signatures, etc.
D	Dynamic analysis tools	Automated runtime testing tools	• Penetration testing tools (e.g. ZAP, IBM AppScan, etc)
	Dynamic testing	Run-time verification of software programs	• memory corruption • user privilege issues • etc.
F	Final security review	A deliberate examination of all the security activities performed on a software application prior to release	
	Fuzz testing	Dynamic testing used to induce system failure by deliberately introducing malformed or random data to an application	
I	Incident response plan	A set of written instructions for detecting, responding to and limiting the effects of an information security event	
P	Pair programming	Two people create code where one writes the code while the other reviews each line of code as it is typed.	
	Penetration testing	Proactive and authorized attempt to evaluate the security of a system, by finding and exploiting vulnerabilities, technical flaws, or weaknesses to compromise the system	
Q	Quality gates/ bug bars	Minimum acceptable levels of security and privacy quality before the code goes into production	• All SQL statements must be parameterized before deployment • All API classes must be reviewed before deployment • Mandatory check for known vulnerabilities of all 3rd party libraries • All critical security bugs must be resolved
R	Red team testing	Simulate real-world attacks against an organization, challenging its defenses against electronic, physical and social exploits	Red team – an external[1] team with the goal to hack the system
	Risk analysis	An approach of gathering requisite data to make informed decision based on knowledge about asset, vulnerability, threat, impact, countermeasures and probability	
	Risk-based testing	Test approach that takes a risk into account by identifying and analyzing the risks related to the system	
	Role matrix	Identifying all possible user roles and their access levels to the system	

continued on following page

Table 11. Continued

I	Term	Definition	Examples
S	Secure coding	Development practices that assure secure software	• Input validation • parameterized SQL • etc.
	Secure design	Design practices that assure secure software	• reducing attack surface during design • placement of security checks before input processing • etc.
	Security code review	Manual review of source code for finding security bugs	
	Security metrics	Metrics that measure organization's defense against attacks	• Defect density • Windows of exposure (how long a security defect is open) • #Vulnerability • etc.
	Security patterns	A well understood solution to security problems	
	Security testing	An activity to assess a system for security bugs (technical flaws, vulnerabilities or weaknesses)	• Vulnerability assessment • Penetration testing • Dynamic testing (black box testing) • Code review (white box testing) • Automated analysis (dynamic and static)
	Static code analysis	Verification of source code	
	Static code analysis tools	Automated code review tools	• IDE vulnerability rule checker • Anti-XSS library • etc.
T	Threat modeling	An approach to identify, quantify, and address the security risks associated with a system	• identifying external dependencies • entry points • assets • trust levels • data flow diagrams • Categorize threats (attacker goals) e.g. Spoofing • Determine countermeasures (e.g. security controls) • etc.
U	UMLSec	Extension of Unified Modeling Language that allows to express security-relevant information within the diagrams in a system specification	
V	Vulnerability assessment	Scanning for security issues using a combination of automated tools and manual assessment techniques. The goal is to confirm the presence of a vulnerability without actually exploiting it	

Chapter 12
Challenges in Agile
Security Engineering:
A Case Study

Kalle Rindell
University of Turku, Finland

Sami Hyrynsalmi
Tampere University of Technology, Finland

Ville Leppänen
University of Turku, Finland

ABSTRACT

This chapter describes a case of a large ICT service provider building a secure identity management system for a government customer. Security concerns are a guiding factor in the design of software-intensive products and services. They also affect the processes of their development. In regulated environments, development of products requires special security for the development processes, product release, maintenance and hosting, and also require security-oriented management and governance. Integrating the security engineering processes into an agile development model is argued to have the effect of mitigating the agile methods' intended benefits. The project case was an effort of multi-team, multi-site, security engineering, and development work, executed using the Scrum framework and regulated by governmental security standards and guidelines. In this case research, the experiences in combining security engineering with agile development are reported, challenges discussed, and certain security enhancements to Scrum are proposed.

DOI: 10.4018/978-1-5225-6313-6.ch012

1. INTRODUCTION

Security regulations are an important driver in various aspects of software development and information systems and services. Even in the cases when formal security standards or guidelines are not strictly required the drive for security still guides the selection of design patterns and technological components, as well as the design and development work. Increasing diversity in development methods, technology, and the environments where the systems are used, have prompted organizations to follow various security standards, as well as created the need to establish new ones to guarantee adequate security assurance. In 2001, the government of Finland begun to issue a set of security regulations, called VAHTI instructions[1]. Compliance with the instructions is now mandatory for all government agencies and the regulation is also applied to any information system and data connected to a VAHTI-classified system.

While the importance and use of security regulations has increased, the use of lightweight software development processes and methods, i.e., *agile development*, has become the *de facto* standard in the industry (VersionOne, 2016). While there exists a series of suggested methods how to conduct security engineering activities in an agile project (see e.g. Baca & Carlsson, 2011; Beznosov & Kruchten, 2004; Fitzgerald, Stol & Sullivan, 2013; Ge, Paige, Polack & Brooke, 2007; Pietikäinen & Röning, 2014; Rindell, Hyrynsalmi & Leppänen, 2015:1), the empiric evidence is still largely anecdotal and the cases reported specific to an industry or a single company. The study reported in this paper is exploratory, and thus the research, by its nature, explorative. This study reports the experiences in agile development in a security-regulated environment. The research objective (RO) is:

RO: Identify advantages, best practices and the possible disadvantages of using agile software development methodologies in security engineering.

The results contribute to the on-going discussion by being a result of a deep analysis of combining security engineering with an agile method in an industry setting. Furthermore, the result of this study pave the way for further work deepening our understanding on the benefits and drawbacks of using agile software development methodologies in security sensitive development work.

In the case examined, a Scrum project was conducted with the objective of building an IDM system for information systems compliant with the security regulations. This included building a secure compliant server platform to host the IDM; the same platform would be utilized also to host the client's other information systems. Also software development projects' infrastructure would be hosted on the same platform, although with certain (unrelated) dispensations from the client's security regulations.

The project was executed from 2014 to 2015, spanning over 12 months. Depending on the tasks in each sprint, the team was split into two to three geographically dispersed groups. The client, a government agency that initiated the building of the platform, mandated the project to be managed by unmodified "textbook version" of Scrum. This called for strict adherence to fixed-length sprints, well-communicated product and sprint backlogs and daily progress monitoring by the Product Owner, and the steering group watching over all the ongoing projects. The project was under strict control of the Project Management Office, and schedules of related infrastructure and software development projects were depending on the results of this project. Compliance with the government regulation, VAHTI, was a central objective of the project. In addition to VAHTI, the client agency had also their own additional security demands, as well as recommendations from other government agencies, most importantly the National Cyber Security Centre's (NCSA-FI)[2] security instructions. The server platform to be built was to be acceptable for use for all government agencies, as well as private companies or organizations requiring similar level of VAHTI compliance.

This paper presents how Scrum was applied for the security-related work required in the project, the challenges that were met, and how the project was overall conducted. As observed, not all the objectives of using "pure" Scrum were not met; therefore, suggestions are made to improve the efficiency of the development work by e.g. introducing rudimentary security engineering extensions to the Scrum framework. These extensions include a new role for a security developer. In addition, use of specific security sprints and other security-oriented additions are suggested. We also discuss how the introduction of the security engineering activities into the project affect cost, efficiency and the conduct of the project.

Chapter 2 will present the related work and standards, as well as clarify the motivation for the study. The Scrum process and some useful security augmentations to it are presented in Chapter 3. This is followed by an explanation of the research process, and the description of the case. In Chapter 6, an analysis is presented, and the last two chapters conclude the study with discussion and proposals for future work.

2. BACKGROUND AND MOTIVATION

A software development process model depicts how development work is divided into smaller parts and how those are managed. In addition, the method may define different artefacts, tools, ceremonies and practices that should be used. Currently, agile software development methods form the current state of the art in software development projects, whereas the security standards regulating software development processes, such as ISO/IEC 21817 (2008) and ISO/IEC 27002 (2013) originate in the time preceding the agile methods.

Based on the literature, the typical approach to agile security engineering is to simply start using the methodology at hand without formal adjustments – the observations made in this particular case follow this same pattern. In the literature, notable exceptions of thorough and formal approach to security engineering are described e.g. by Baca & Carlsson (2011) and Fitzgerald & al. (2013). There are even well documented cases of attempts to achieve formal ISO/IEC capability maturity level incorporating agile methods, such as Diaz, Garbajosa & Calvo-Manzano (2009). Unfortunately, the findings and suggestions made in these studies were not directly applicable in a project that was not strictly restricted to software development.

Instead, a more *ad hoc* approach was used by the project team of this case study. In this approach, the security-related tasks are treated simply as any other items in the backlog: the security requirements are converted to tasks, given story points, and completed among the other items as best seen fit. In cases when security items could not reasonably be time-boxed, because of the inherent uncertainties in the work estimate – or the inexperience of the team – they were separated from the Scrum sprint cycle and completed in non-time-boxed spikes. This was a common pattern throughout the project, and a notable motivation to examine if the project could have benefited from the ´divide and conquer' approach enforced by restricting the tasks to the length of a sprint. Although technically spikes conform to the Scrum methodology, this can also be seen as a partial abandonment of agile methods when performing the crucial security tasks of the project.

While the ad hoc method may succeed in achieving "minimum viable security" by complying with the formal requirements, it is hardly the most effective way to achieve the goals, nor does it necessarily provide the best security assurance for the product. Producing proper security assurance is possible with careful planning, hindered by a lack of proper security requirement management and security task pre-planning. Absence of these elements in the project management methodology tend to lead to inefficiencies and consequently delays, as well as increased development costs. Lack of proper security assurance may also increase the amount and severity of the residual security risk during the software system's life span.

Our argument is that by adjusting the Scrum methodology to better align with the goals of security engineering, the security cost overhead can be reduced while the security of the end product is enhanced, compared to traditional sequential security engineering practices. This is achieved by incorporating the security processes into Scrum activities, as opposed to treating them merely as items in the backlog, by introducing new security-oriented roles into the development team. By incorporating the security engineering activities into the development method, the full benefit of incremental agile methods can be utilized to achieve better efficiency ratio and, arguably, better software products.

The next subsections provide more information about the used governmental security standard, VAHTI, and the use of Scrum methodology in development projects requiring security standards compliance as well as the related work. Notable similarities in the software security and safety regulations, and the ways they are enforced, prompt a suggestion that similar methodologies are applicable to both fields of requirement.

2.1. Related Work

To the best of the authors' knowledge, this work is among the first empirical explorations on an industrial setting where security engineering project has been handled with an agile method. While, e.g., Boström et al. (2006) studied empirically on the applicability of secure enhanced XP method, they used students in their controlled experiments. However, due to the simulative nature of the student cases as well as limitations and imbalance of students' skills, the applicability and generalizability of results are limited, at the best.

Despite the lack of empirical evidence, a series of different methods and adaptions to the existing processes have been presented. In 2004, only a few years after the agile manifesto, Wäyrynen et al. (2004) discussed on the applicability of and needed improvements to XP development method to a security engineering project. Kongsli (2011) presented an approach to integrate security mechanisms into the agile methods. Chivers, Paige and Ge (2005) propose the use of iterative security architecture for achieving agile security. They continued the work in Ge et al (2007) by proposing security practices for XP.

While this research concentrates more on the overview of the issues faced in a project including a considerable amount of security work, also more detailed descriptions of security work have been created. Villamizar et al. (2018) have conducted a systematic mapping of security requirements engineering in agile development. They identify several approaches to meet these security requirements. Among them are process adjustments, introducing new security-related artefacts and guidelines to handle security issues – all of which were also observed in the project reported in this article. Cruzes et al. (2017) provide detailed empiric reports on security testing in agile development, suggesting further awareness on security issues to improve the effectiveness and coverage of security testing. Morrison et al. (2017) have studied how well development teams adhere to security procedures, also measuring the security engineering based on the time spent on security during development. Their findings are partially consistent with the observations in this study, particularly on the strong negative experienced effect of security tooling and security reviews on the work schedule. Contrary to this, security documentation of the technical stack was experienced positively in the study of Morrison et al., whereas our experience reports indicated a clearly negative impact of the extensive documentation requirements.

Achieving software security is a goal separate from software security, although it is achieved by very similar means. Kasauli et al. (2018) have conducted a mapping study of agile development of safety-critical systems, listing also the challenges found in industry projects. Their findings have a strong resemblance to our observations: waterfall mindset, strong focus on documentation and reported *lack of trust in agile methods* were all evident in our project as well; in practice, the waterfall mindset resulted in abandonment of iterative workflow, a key component of agile methods, in crucial project tasks. Heeager et al. (2018) have completed a systematic literature review of agile development in safety-critical context. They identify four "problem areas" in the research field: documentation, requirements, lifecycle and testing. Although their focus is more on the quality assurance issues, the literature analysis suggests that these areas are interdependent. In security, similarly to safety, the security requirements do not change; however, if agile development models are abandoned because of this, the quality improvement and other benefits of agile methods are lost altogether, adversely affecting the implementation of requirements that *do* change.

Recent works by Othmane et al. (2014), Sonia, Singhal and Banati (2014) as well as by Rindell, Hyrynsalmi, and Leppänen (2015:2) have aimed to more complete approach. For example, Rindell et al. (2015:2) presented an applied version of Scrum method that fulfills the national security development requirements. Yet, their study is also lacking an empirical evidence on the applicability of the presented method. Thus, this study aims to explore a real-world industrial case in order to provide first evidence on the actual applicability of agile methods in security engineering. In the following, we will present Scrum and some of its security enhancements as it was used by our case study team.

3. SECURITY-AUGMENTED SCRUM

Scrum is a generic agile framework, originally intended to manage software development projects with small co-located teams. Scrum suggests that the product to be completed is divided into smaller components, or features, based on the customer requirements. These requirements are represented by user stories, which are then translated into product features by the development team. Features are then further divided into work packages or items, which are compiled into a product backlog. Items in the product backlog are completed in an incremental and iterative manner during short-term development sprints. The team, consisting of the Scrum Master, the Developers, and the Product Owner as customer's representative, determines the items to be completed during the next 2-4 weeks sprint, consisting of daily scrums. After the sprint, the work is demonstrated, and optionally the team performs self-assessment of the past sprint in a retrospect event.

In this representation, the Scrum process is augmented by three major extensions, presented in Figure 1.

1. The role of a *security developer*. The security developer, or developers, focus on the security of the product, and typically create or review the documentation required to pass the security audits.

2. Security assurance provided by creating *security artefacts*, mostly security-related documentation. They consist of security training certificates required from the project team, but most importantly the architecture documentation, risk management plans, test plans, test reports, system's log files and other evidence required by the security auditor. The audits also produce reports, which are part of the security assurance provided for the customer.

3. Anticipation of and planning for *security-related tasks*. To better illustrate this aspect of security work, security engineering activities are presented as iterative tasks in the sprint cycle in addition to the daily scrum. It should be noted that not all sprints may have all the security tasks, and if the organization decides to perform security-oriented security sprints, the daily scrum may entirely consist of security activities.

Figure 1. Security-oriented Scrum process and roles
(adapted from Rindell, Hyrynsalmi & Leppänen (2015:2).

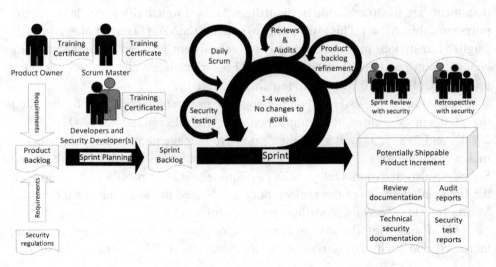

In a project using unmodified Scrum, such as the one used in this case, the security testing, reviews and audits are viewed as normal stories in the sprint backlog and executed as part of the daily scrum. In this view, the security tests and audits are part of the product, as compliance with security standards and regulations is mandatory during development time. The main shortcoming is the difficulty or outright inability to estimate the amount of work involved in the security activities, which merits for giving them special treatment. By emphasizing the importance and special role of the security stories, compared to treating them as overhead and extra burden, is prospected to produce better results with higher efficiency. In effect, this will reduce the cost of the development work.

VAHTI is an open and free collection of the Finnish government's security guidelines, published on the Internet since 2001. The aim of this regulatory framework is to promote and enforce organizational information security, risk management and overall security competence of various government agencies, and harmonize security practices throughout the organizations. As of spring 2016, the collection comprises of 52 documents. The following VAHTI instructions were found to be relevant for this project:

- VAHTI 2/2009 "Provisions for ICT service interruptions and emergencies", VAHTI (2009:2)
- VAHTI 2b/2012 "Requirements for ICT Contingency Planning", VAHTI (2012:2b)
- VAHTI 3/2012 "Instructions for Technical Environment Security", VAHTI (2012:3)

Of these, only the document 2b/2012 is available in English. The other relevant documents are made available in Finnish, and their English titles translated for the purpose of this chapter. This also applies to much of the VAHTI terminology: official English translations may not exist, may be inconsistent between documents or may change over time. Even the name of VAHTI board itself has changed at least twice after 2015, although the acronym remains unaltered.

In addition to the VAHTI requirements, the company responsible for building the platform is audited for compliance with ISO/IEC standards 9001, 27001, 27002, and 21817, as well as its own extensive management framework, which it makes available for its clients for review. The company has functions in the United States, so also Sarbanes-Oxley (SOX) act applied. SOX is mostly concerned with the financial elements of the project, but still affected the work load of the Scrum Master by adding certain reporting responsibilities.

VAHTI classifies the information systems into three security levels: basic, increased and high. The server platform, where the IDM system was installed, was built for the increased security level. Information contained in the systems is classified into levels from IV to I, level IV being the lowest. Information contained in a system audited for increased security level may contain clear-text information up to level III. In this case, however, all data stored on the platform is always encrypted despite the official classification level.

According to Hope, McGraw & Anton (2004), software security is an emergent property, not a feature or set of features of the software. The term 'security engineering' used in this chapter comprises all security-related *software* engineering tasks within a software-intensive product's life cycle. In current standardization, these activities are categorized into three main process areas: risk, engineering and assurance processes, as presented in ISO/IEC 21817:

S*ecurity risk process* assesses the risk and aims in minimizing it by assessing threats and vulnerabilities, and the impact they have, producing risk information.

Security engineering process uses this information with other security-related input to define security needs and provides solutions to fill them.

Security assurance process collects and produces evidence of security's existence, and aims in its verification and validation.

The ultimate goal of these processes is to identify and mitigate security threats, and define the impact and actions to be taken when the residual or unrecognized risk is realized: what will happen if, and when, the security becomes compromised.

In the Scrum development process both functional (business) requirements and the non-functional (quality, architecture, environment) requirements are transformed into a working software product. Security is typically classified as a non-functional requirement: these are noted to receive lessened attention in the agile methods (see e.g. Ramesh, Cao & Baskerville, 2010). However, in the case of *regulated security*, the distinction between functional and non-functional requirements becomes irrelevant, as incorporation of security requirements is an absolute acceptance criterion for the product. The security requirements were given as strict list of processes to put in place, functionality to implement and artefacts (security assurance) to produce. These requirements were all evaluated, and assigned story points in a iteration planning event; however, as shown in the case description (Chapter 5), this process failed with certain types of security tasks, as they could not be fitted into the rigidly time-boxed iterations. This happened at least partially because the security experts were used to work in a more traditional way, and where the work units (tasks) are considerably larger and, in this case, apparently indivisible. Despite not being part of sprints, the performers of security-related items were still adhering to the Scrum practices, and their work was monitored in daily meetings. In the team's experience, Scrum provided clear and consistent improvement to the security engineering work also in this sense.

4. RESEARCH PROCESS

This study follows a case study design method by Yin (2003), and a qualitative research approach by Cresswell (2003). The research approach is exploratory as there are only little empirical evidence prior this study, and acts as a research effort towards revealing some of the mechanisms for future inquiries. For the study, a development project utilizing agile methods in compliance with security regulations or standards was sought out. VAHTI regulations, as a national security standard in Finland, provided this context readily in Finland. In addition, a project either already finished or near its ending was favored in order to provide quick access to the challenges and solutions, and to a chance to evaluate the success of the model used in the project. Finally, the selected case should be a representative candidate as well as be able to produce rich information about the phenomenon under study.

In the project case an identity management and verification service was ordered by a governmental client, who also required the use of VAHTI security instructions; also, their acquisition guidelines mandated use of Scrum, providing an ideal target for research. The development work in the project was done by following a modified version of Scrum software development method. As Scrum is currently one of the most used development methods, the findings from this case study can be held representative of industry practices.

The project was executed by a well-known software product development and consultancy company in Finland. The company has a long history of and is experienced on both agile methods as well as producing information systems for the government. By the wish of the company, the client and the interviewees, all participants to the project shall remain anonymous.

A post-implementation group interview for the key personnel of the selected project was held. Semi-structured interview approach was used, where time was given to the interviewees to elaborate their thoughts about the phenomenon under study. The general questions concerned the scope and size of the project, amount of the personnel involved, and the daily routines of the team.

Additionally, the security standards that were applied to the project were gathered. The security mechanisms developed to implement the requirements were charted, along with how they were presented to the client and auditors. Finally, the amount of extra work caused by the security requirements was discussed and roughly estimated, and the interviewees recounted their views of the lessons learned in the project. The interview session also acted as a retrospective for the whole project, where the participants were able to express their views of positive and negative aspects of the project and the effect the security requirements had. The results of the interview were then analyzed by the researchers and the key observations were emphasized.

There were two interviewees: the Scrum Master and the head architect of the project; the latter was also responsible for the design of the technical stack, including the security features. In practice, the architect assumed a new role in the implementation team dubbed *security developer*. Both of the interviewees were essential to the project's implementation, and the one most capable of providing insight to the project background and its execution, as well as to evaluate its results and level of success. The interviewees were also the only team members that consistently participated in all of the sprints in the project, and were involved in the project for its whole duration.

The questions posed before the interviewees were divided into three groups. First three questions concerned the project background (Q1-Q3); following five questions concentrated on the project process, security standards, and feedback on the Scrum and security (Q4-Q8); and the final two questions canvassed the interviewees' views on the project results and success factors (Q9-Q10).

The questions asked in the interview were as follows:

Q1: Project subject and scope?

Q2: Project resources, budget, and duration?

Q3: Personnel locations, multi-site teams?

Q4: What VAHTI standards were followed?

Q5: What other security standards and regulation were included?

Q6: Other restrictions (safety, privacy, agency specific regulations)?

Q7: What *types* of steps were taken to enforce them?

Q8: How was the security assurance verified (audited) and audit trail maintained?

Q9: Did the budget and schedule hold, and what was the amount of extra work caused by security?

Q10: What were the lessons learned?

After the interview, some complementary questions were asked via emails to confirm certain details, but otherwise the initial interview session was deemed sufficient for the purpose of this study. Access to exact budget or workload figures, or system logs or other technical documentation was not made available for research: the security classification of the platform prevented using this data even for verification. Instead, the interviewees relied on their personal experience and notes made during the project, and provided best estimates on the matters in a general level accepted for publication.

5. CASE DESCRIPTION

The client agency required a VAHTI compliant IDM platform for their information systems, and for users and system administration and management purposes. The platform was to be built using off-the-shelf components, installed on common open source operating systems, and deployed onto a large scalable array of virtual servers. A similar IDM platform was built also to authenticate and manage the identities of the administrators who manage other VAHTI compliant servers and services, and is to be separately instantiated for regular office users as well based on the experience and solutions gained in this project.

The IDM was deemed a critical service in respect of agency's security, privacy and business requirements. Whereas the agency had 650 internal users connecting to 450 separate server-side computer systems, they also manage a sizable array of contractors with up to 12,000 users. The building project was conducted at the same time the server platform itself was being built, which added to the challenge in such way that all the requirements of VAHTI were to be met by a novel implementation.

Nearly all the design and definition work was to be completed in this project. To add to the challenge, the work was to be performed using Scrum, mainly to ensure steering group's visibility to the project's progress, and to enable reacting to any unexpected obstacles or hindrances met during the project execution. Unfortunately, for the project team, the client also saw use of Scrum as a method to change the project's scope during its execution by adding items to the product backlog, or removing them from there, which caused certain degree of confusion among the team and forced it to abandon some work already completed. These aspects of Scrum projects, however, are not a security issue but of a more generic field of project management, and therefore are not further discussed.

The development work consists of distinct phases, which were completed during one or more iterations:

1. **Definition:** Synthesis of the requirements, component candidate selection, risk assessment and analysis.
2. **Design:** Architecture design, definition of interfaces, component hardening plans.
3. **Development:** Component research, modification (especially hardening the operating systems and software), and installation.
4. **Testing, Reviews, Audits and Acceptance:** Security testing, external audits and formal acceptance of the product to be a part of the agency's system portfolio. In effect, security assurance processes.

As there were no formal milestones preset at the beginning of the project, the security gates, such as audits, were passed flexibly whenever each feature was considered mature enough. This removed certain amount of unnecessary overhead, as a traditional fixed milestone dates may call for the team to work overtime, which may get costly due to pay compensations and cause delays to other projects due to resource shortage.

5.1. Project Organization

The project involved an average of nine persons at any given time: Scrum Master, dedicated Product Owner, Security Architect (who, during sprints, was completing tasks in the role of a developer), and the developers split into their production teams based on location and occupation.

The service provider in charge of the project is a devout follower of ITIL[3], a well-established and recognized set of industry standard best practices for IT service management. As is typical for an ITIL-oriented organization, the infrastructure production teams reside in their respective "silos", with very little communication with other teams. Production teams were divided by their specialization. The platform teams involved in the project were "Storage and Backup", "Server Hardware", "Windows Operating Systems", "Linux Operating Systems", "UNIX Operating Systems", "Databases" and "Networks". The IDM application specialists came from their own team, a separate unit within the corporation.

This Scrum project brought together the specialists from these various teams at least for the daily 15-minute stand-up meeting – albeit most of the time virtually. Due to teams' multiple physically separated locations, the meetings were without exception held as telephone conferences.

The developers participating to the project in its different phases were so diverse that only the Scrum Master, security developer (i.e., the architect) and the Product Owner participated in each sprint throughout the project. The developers were part of a larger resource pool and drawn into the sprints or spikes in various phases of the project whenever their expertise was required.

Much of the work related to VAHTI regulations was done in the planning phase: it turned out that in addition to VAHTI, the client agency had compiled their own list of requirements, which was based on VAHTI but had new security elements added to the public requirements. The client viewed this to be necessary to compensate the dropping the specific requirements for VAHTI compliant application development (VAHTI, 2013:1) in the beginning of the project.

The project extended over a period of 12 months, from planning phase to accepted delivery of final sprint. The amount of work was measured in story points, and the average velocity of each sprint was 43 points. Divided with the average number of the developers (9) and the length of the sprint (15 workdays) gives a rough estimate of a story point equaling three workdays. As an overall measure, the story points give an impression of the size of the tasks. This sort of conversion may not be meaningful in general and outside of the scope of a single project, as the story points are primarily used to compare the features (or stories) to each other within a single project. For purposes of this study, the fact that largest single units of security work, the hardenings, were not performed in sprints and therefore not measured in story points, makes pinpointing the cost of security work much harder. In this case, the interviewees' estimates were the only source of the amount of workload, and although trusted to be reliable, exact figures would have been preferred.

5.2. Project Execution

From the beginning, the team's approach to the security tasks was pragmatic, although in terms of Scrum, rudimentary: stories that were found difficult to time-box at the time of their implementation were taken out of the sprint cycle and completed as spikes. Prime examples of such tasks were operating system hardenings, a task essential for the platform security: the project team allocated resources to these tasks, and just ran them as long as the tasks took. This resulted in a project structure presented in Figure 2, where there were major sidetracks to the main sprint cycle. As tasks such as these were in the very core of the project goals, it would have been beneficial to go through the trouble or even adjust the Scrum structure to better accommodate these items.

The sprints are represented as the main story line. The parallel lines represent the spikes that were executed outside the main sprint structure. Their results (deliverables) were demonstrated at a sprint demo after the spike had run its course, although they were executed independently without time-boxing. There were three distinct task types outside the sprint structure:

Figure 2. Project structure and spikes.

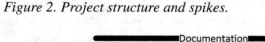
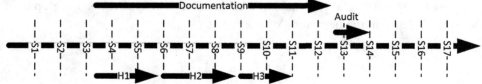

1. *System hardenings*, performed for each tier or environment of the system under development: Development, Quality Assurance (QA), and Production environments. The results obtained in the Development phase were not directly usable for the upper environments, whereas the QA environment was built to be production-like. As a result, the work done at QA phase was partly reusable at Production phase. Despite the technical similarities, the ITIL-guided maintenance models of these two environments were so great that the team proceeded in executing the Production environment hardenings as a spike as well.

2. *Documentation* was a ubiquitous process during the development. This included risk management, technical architecture and technical component documentation, test plans and reports. Documentation comprised most of the security assurance. Complete list of VAHTI requirements for documentation are presented in Appendix 3 of the VAHTI instruction 3/2012[4]. In this document, there are 224 mandatory requirements listed for the increased security level information systems. Almost all of these requirements call for some type of written evidence to be verified and reviewed, although most of the documentation artefacts are created in other than the development phase of the information system's life cycle.

3. *Reviews and audit* were performed based on the documentation and included physical testing of implementation.

The demand for increased security (literally, the "increased level" on VAHTI security classification) also stated how the systems were deployed: to maintain audit trail, all changes to the production environment, including all server and hardware installations during its buildup, were performed following ITIL processes. These processes added extra levels of bureaucracy, and the team reported getting acceptance from the Change Advisory Board (CAB) for all changes to be made in the production environment had a very adverse effect on the deployment schedules. Combined with the policy of role separation between developers and maintenance personnel, this caused the building and installation of the production environment to be document-driven, bureaucratic and slow. The policy of separating the roles of developers and maintenance effectively prevents the DevOps type of continuous delivery maintenance model, and would require e.g. a form of "continuous security" model, such as presented by Fitzgerald & Stol (2014).

In this project, the continuous delivery model was used with the lower environments, speeding the rate of delivery significantly. When building the production environment, the flow of work assumed in previous sprints was disrupted, which caused unnecessary slowness and cost overhead. Documentation necessary for the maintenance personnel was to be created before the handover, and as such did not necessarily contain all the required information and details. Mandatory use of ITIL processes when building the production environment was one of the main schedule hindrances of the project according to the interviewees.

Depending on the items in the current sprint backlog, the team was divided in two or three geographically separated locations during the whole length of the project. The organizational separation of the developers resulted in situation, where even the persons based on the same location did not necessarily sit near each other or communicate with other team members directly. The central location for the project, and the physical location of the server platform was Helsinki, Finland, but the team members were divided on several sites. The Scrum Master performed most of her duties remotely, without being in direct contact with the developers except rarely. As usual in large ICT service companies, almost all developers were also involved in other projects at the same time. The overall experience of the team was deemed very high, although in infrastructure work the use of agile methods is not very common, and is customer dependent at best. As per this fact, most personnel was mostly inexperienced with Scrum, although they received basic Scrum training before and during the project. Use of Scrum was reflected by the use of collaboration and project management tools, most importantly Atlassian JIRA[5] specifically customized for the agency's use. The Scrum Master promoted and demanded the use of JIRA as reflecting the work performed in daily sprints. The Product Owner's most visible role was following the project's progress based on what team members reported on this tool. In general, the team was reported to be happy or at least content with Scrum, at least up until the production environment-building phase where ITIL processes broke the team's workflow.

The requirements called primarily for well-documented software quality and component and process security. Most of the additional work was directly security related, and creating its documentation. The platform also had strict and formal requirements for availability and reliability. Outside the security domain, the main source of regulation-related work was duplication of all infrastructure into the service provider's second data center. The data centers themselves, as well as the personnel administering the system and its infrastructure were subject to meticulous security screening. Proper level of access control was enforced, the server rooms' CCTV system extended to cover the new servers, and remote connection practices were reviewed. All personnel involved with the client was to be security checked by the national Finnish Security Intelligence Service[6]. Data itself must reside within the country's borders and even the infrastructure's configuration data and work tickets in the Configuration Management Database (CMDB) were to be made inaccessible for personnel who are not security checked.

As an infrastructure project, the main technical obstacle was securing the hardware, operating systems, middleware and the application (the IDM system) against security threats. The bulk of this work was performed by one of the interviewees, the security developer. Hardening in this case covered analyzing and removal, or blocking, of hardware and software features, and testing against the threats. The purpose is to reduce the attack surface of the platform under construction and protect it from both internal and external threats, as well as minimize the components where potential future vulnerabilities may emerge.

On hardware level, hardening means controlling the network interfaces and the surrounding local area network, routing and traffic rules. It also covers all hardware maintenance interfaces, typically accessible through the network. On operating system and software level, the operating system's or software manufacturers, such as Microsoft, provide their own hardening instructions, which were used as a baseline. These were combined with the best practices of the consultant company's own experiences and policies, and the explicit instructions and requirements given by the client organization. These included uninstalling a large number of modules and services, disabling a number user accounts and policies, and enforcing a number of others, and restricting access and privileges throughout the system. The same principles were applied to each software component installed on the server platform.

By definition, all access rules and user validations had to be applied to the infrastructure services provided for the server platform; these include software and hardware patching, network access, malware protection, hardware and application monitoring, and backups. The inherent uncertainty of security testing, together with the inter-dependency of the components affected by the removal and alteration of the services and restriction of rights made predictable time-boxing of these tasks so unreliable that the team decided to execute them as spikes.

5.3. Cost of Security Work

The Scrum Master estimated that the extra work caused by the regulations was approximately 25 to 50% of the project's total workload and, in practice, the duration of the project. As accurate billing information was not made available for the researchers, this was accepted as the best estimate of the real cost of the security work. Most of the overhead comprises from the documentation of the solutions. Security-related documentation was created by all team members: project manager and the security developer (architect) created most of the documentation, and the Product Owner as the client's representative made sure that the correct regulations were applied.

Developers were burdened by creating appropriate level of security-oriented technical documentation of all their work, especially related to operating system and application hardening procedures. The hardening process itself lasted for four months, presenting the largest tasks in the project. Changes to the production environment were further complicated by ITIL's requirement of strict Change Advisory Board processing of each change that was made.

6. ANALYSIS

The research objective for this study is to identify best practices as well as hindrances of using agile software development. This case provides a good view how unmodified Scrum lent itself to a situation, where a large amount of regulations caused extra work with uncertainties in work estimates. Due to these uncertainties, or the large amount of presumably indivisible work included in some of these tasks, the team was simply not able to fit certain features into the sprint structure. Additionally, in contradiction to traditional security view, iterative and incremental approach to development and building forced the project team, steering group and the client to rethink how the product's and its management's security assurance was to be provided. In a sequential waterfall model, the security deliverables and tasks were tied into the predetermined milestones, without the flexibility provided by Scrum. As presented in Figure 2, the project was in practice executed partly following a "waterfall" model, yet without milestones fixed in advance; these waterfall processes ran alongside the main project, and their deliverables were then included in the project outcomes.

Based on the above, in the strictest sense the project organization failed utilizing Scrum methodology to create the product, although the superficial requirements were fulfilled – the client was mostly interested in progress reports and the timely delivery of the complete and standard compliant product. The failures were partly due to inflexibilities on both the company developing the system, and the client demanding a formal and fixed approach to Scrum. Sprint planning for tasks, for example, called for features to be completed during the sprint. When this was already known to be extremely unlikely, these features were agreed to be performed as spikes. In retrospect, this was most likely caused by the thinking that security features were perceived as *overhead* and not actual features in the product, while in reality the security features were essential to the product itself. The resulting implementation model is partially waterfall-like.

Even without applying any formal modifications to Scrum, at least one of the "secure Scrum" features, presented in Section 3 and

Figure 1, was taken into use, as the project architect assumed the role of security developer. In practice, most of the physical work triggered by security requirements was done in spikes outside the sprints. When the work is done in a non-iterative way, just letting them run along the project, the benefits of Scrum are lost. Based on the project manager's estimate of cost increase factor was 1.5-2x, caused by the security features, and thus there exists a large saving potential in rearranging the security work. Attempting a new approach and restructuring the work into iterations is recommendable in future projects. Initial spikes are acceptable, but in this case, the team failed to utilize the experience gained from them, and continued to implement similar security features as spikes even after the first one. This is represented in Figure 2 by the OS hardening spikes H1, H2 and H3. During the spikes, there was very little activity in the actual sprints, as also documentation was done as a spike.

The team defended their selected approach by stressing the inherent differences in the physical environment and management practices of the development, quality assurance and production environments, but also from the undertones of the developer's interview, it was perceivable that the attitude towards using Scrum in this kind of project was negative to start with. Time-boxing the uncertain tasks to three-week sprints, having to perform the demonstrations after each sprint, and other Scrum routines were perceived to some degree as distractions from the main work. This mentality seemed to affect some members of the team despite the personnel was trained in the Scrum method and the tools necessary.

During the interview, the team was uniform on the key success factors of the project. They emphasized the importance of document management, and very strict requirement management. The amount of overlapping and sometimes outright conflicting security requirements even within the VAHTI requirements increased the Scrum Master's workload substantially. Use of Scrum was deemed to have overwhelmingly positive effect, by enabling faster reaction to changes in the requirements and directness of the client feedback. In addition, the team praised frequent sprint planning for the effect of keeping the team focused, especially in contrast to the very long spikes run during the project. In retrospect, the team regretted not utilizing the Product Owner more already in the beginning, as direct channels to the client were viewed to be very valuable during the implementation. Furthermore, the client's key personnel were not always present at sprint demos, which caused unnecessary questions and insecurity on the client's side, despite the features were already completed and already once comprehensively demonstrated.

The effect of Scrum to the efficiency of the work was estimated very positive. The extra cost of the security was partly compensated by the fact that rigorous testing and documentation of the technical solutions had also a positive impact on the quality of the work, improving the system's reliability and availability. It can also be argued that the cost of security work is lower when it is done proactively rather than repairing an old system or trying to recover a breached one.

7. DISCUSSION

There are three key findings in this study:

- First, an agile development method works in a security-regulated environment. This study showed that is possible to develop a system with set governmental security regulations by utilizing an agile method (Scrum). While the evidence is based on a single case, when combined with other evidence it shows that the oft-repeated belief of agile methods being unsuitable for security engineering (cf. Rindell, Hyrynsalmi, and Leppänen 2017) seems not to hold.
- Second, Scrum as a method appears highly applicable for the software security engineering projects. In this case, only little modifications were needed to the method for meeting the security regulation restrictions. Yet, the team constantly faced "surprises", and were forced to adopt new techniques and models in order to avoid pitfalls. While this is not a hoped approach, the adoption to surprising changes is in the hearth of agile software development methods and the Scum's empirical software process improvement principle.
- Third, the interviewees reported that required security routines and their documentation took up to 25-50% of the project's total budget. The time reports were not made available for researchers, yet this was the estimate given by the project manager.

This study has presented a case of building an infrastructure and setting up an identity management software platform for a governmental client. The client agency had a definitive set of security regulation and requirements: the VAHTI instructions. In addition to the government requirements, the service provider contracted to build the system was committed to several international ISO/IEC standards, as well as to their own management frameworks. Additionally, the project management was burdened with complex financial reporting tools and rules. Both the agency and the service provider's project management offices required employing the Scrum methodology as the project management framework. The research was conducted as post-project semi-structural interviews, and the information was gathered based on interviewees' experiences and personal notes of the project. The parties involved are anonymized, and only publicly available information about the project and the regulations involved was to be disclosed.

Scrum was initially applied in its standard form, with no formal security extensions. Security engineering activities were integrated into the product backlog, and performed within sprints whenever possible. During the project, the team adapted to the security work by creating a *de facto* security developer role, and many of the security engineering tasks ended to be performed outside of the regular sprint structure. Typically, security assurance is based on evidence gained through security testing, which also in this case had an adverse effect on the team's ability to schedule and time-box the items that were subject to these tests; these were performed as spikes instead. The same technique was also applied to documentation, which was performed outside the main sprints, and audits and reviews, which were separately scheduled one-time tasks. The results of these spikes were still presented in sprint demos among the other artefacts and results. The reported issues at product deployment in production environment prompt for developing and applying a delivery model that provides the required security assurance without the interruption to iterative development.

The team viewed the use of Scrum as a positive factor to project cost and quality, although arguably Scrum was not utilized to the maximum extent: important parts of the work were done in spikes outside of the main sprint flow, without attempts to utilize the experience gained from them to time-box the future tasks. This was seen to benefit the project, although an iterative and more exploratory approach to those tasks might have proved more benefits in the long term, and it is still a possibility that the experience gained in this project can be utilized in similar future projects. The project team still regarded the security engineering activities and providing the required security assurance to compose a significant amount of extra work: at final stages, the workload effectively doubled. The initial approach in this project was more or less an unmodified textbook example of the Scrum method, but the team applied naturally certain security extensions. Conducting weekly product backlog refinement sessions was deemed essential for the project's success.

This project was a model case of two large entities that have decided to fit their organizations to work according to an agile framework. The nature of work itself has not changed, although the introduction of growing amount of security engineering and increasing regulation put an additional strain on the project's requirement management. Agile methods have inherent preference to produce working solutions instead of spending time documenting them; in contradiction to this goal, the documentation of the solutions is a key deliverable in the field of security. Scrum will continue to be used by both organizations. As the team's experience grows, we also expect the cost of the secure systems development to drop, while their quality and security gets better.

Based on the experiences gained in this case, Scrum has shown the potential to be suitable for security-oriented development work. With certain additions and modifications, it can be used to provide the security assurance required by the regulators in the ICT and software industry. Especially when applied by an organization capable to adjust itself to fully utilize the flexibility of incremental agile frameworks, instead of partially reverting to sequential mode of operations. We are yet to observe a pure agile project where security standards are in a central role: truly integrating security engineering processes and security assurance activities without losing the agile values and benefits gained by the use of those methods is still a work in progress.

Naturally, this study has its limitations. First, the analysis is based on a single case and overgeneralization of the results should be avoided. As study is by its design explorative, restricting to a single case is understandable. However, further work are needed to verify the results with new cases. Furthermore, case studies should be extended to cover also other agile methodologies used in software security engineering than Scrum. While Scrum is among the most popular development methods nowadays, it still present only a handful of different methods, tools and techniques developed inside the agile community.

Second, due to the nature of the project, non-disclosure agreements and security classifications, the researchers could not access the project documentation and verify the project team's interpretations. Thus, no proper data triangulation with written documentation could have been done.

Third, the study presents a case where software security engineering succeeded well with a selected agile method. However, as the project faced only small disturbances that were able overcome with simple modifications, complete view on the methods suitability for complex security project cannot be assessed. A comparative study with, e.g., student teams handling a complex security project with agile, as well as traditional method will reveal more insights into this issue.

Finally, this study opens further avenues for research. Our study reported that the development team and manager estimated that almost half of the project's budget was spent on the security related tasks. Regardless of the exact amount, this finding calls for further development work on revealing the real cost of security as well as methods and tools to reduce time spent on security issues.

In addition, while Scrum was shown to cope with security development, it is clearly not perfect fit for the work. Thus, future work should be focused on developing, testing and validating tools, techniques and models to extend Scrum or other methods to be more suitable for security development projects.

8. CONCLUSION

This chapter presented an exploratory case study on a security development project regarding a governmental information system with strictly regulations. The aim was to explore whether agile was a successful approach for the development work or not. The result shows that agile development, performed using the Scrum method, is suitable also for security engineering work. While drawing too far-reaching conclusions from a single case study would be ill advised, this case still clearly contradicts the criticism against agile methods' suitability for security engineering. Among the key factors to success were Scum's iterative approach, enhancing the management of client's strict security requirements. Use of Scrum processes, artifacts and roles also improved communication both within the team and towards the client.

In contrast, the observations also reveal certain negative issues in the Scrum method, and the way agile values and principles are affecting the security development. The findings of this study suggest the requirement for new tools, techniques and models to solve the challenges and alleviate the issues in agile software security engineering. The solutions include security training for all the project participants, improved mechanisms to manage security requirements, and techniques to the security tasks into iterative process.

ACKNOWLEDGMENT

The authors gratefully acknowledge TEKES, the Finnish Funding Agency for Innovation, DIMECC Oy, and the Cyber Trust research program for their support.

REFERENCES

Baca, D., & Carlsson, B. (2011). Agile development with security engineering activities. In *Proceedings of the 2011 International Conference on Software and Systems Process, ICSSP '11* (pp. 149-158). ACM.

Beznosov, K., & Kruchten, P. (2004). Towards agile security assurance. *NSPW '04 Proceedings of the 2004 workshop on New security paradigms*, 47-54.

Boström, G., Wäyrynen, J., Bodén, M., Beznosov, K., & Kruchten, P. (2006). Extending XP Practices to Support Security Requirements Engineering. In *Proceedings of the 2006 International Workshop on Software Engineering for Secure Systems* (pp. 11-18). New York, NY: ACM. 10.1145/1137627.1137631

Chivers, H., Paige, R., & Ge, X. (2005). Agile security using an incremental security architecture. *Proceedings of the 6th international conference on Extreme Programming and Agile Processes in Software Engineering*. 10.1007/11499053_7

Creswell, J. W. (2003). *Research Design: Qualitative and Quantitative and Mixed Methods Approaches* (2nd ed.). Thousand Oaks, CA: SAGE Publications, Inc.

Cruzes, D. S., Felderer, M., Oyetoyan, T. D., Gander, M., & Pekaric, I. (2017). How is security testing done in agile teams? a cross-case analysis of four software teams. In H. Baumeister, H. Lichter, & M. Riebisch (Eds.), *Agile Processes in Software Engineering and Extreme Programming* (pp. 201–216). Cham: Springer International Publishing. doi:10.1007/978-3-319-57633-6_13

Diaz, J., Garbajosa, J., & Calvo-Manzano, J. A. (2009). Mapping CMMI Level 2 to Scrum Practices: An Experience Report. Software Process Improvement. Comm. in Computer and Information Science, 42, 93-104.

Fitzgerald, B., & Stol, K.-J. (2014). Continuous software engineering and beyond: Trends and challenges. In *Proceedings of the 1st International Workshop on Rapid Continuous Software Engineering, RCoSE 2014* (pp. 1-9). New York: ACM. 10.1145/2593812.2593813

Fitzgerald, B., Stol, K.-J., O'Sullivan, R., & O'Brien, D. (2013). Scaling agile methods to regulated environments: An industry case study. *Proc. of International Conference on Software Engineering, ICSE '13*, 863-872. 10.1109/ICSE.2013.6606635

Ge, X., Paige, R. F., Polack, F., & Brooke, P. (2007). Extreme programming security practices. Agile Processes in Software Engineering and Extreme Programming, 226-230. doi:10.1007/978-3-540-73101-6_42

Heeager, L., & Nielsen, P. (2018). A conceptual model of agile software development in a safety-critical context: A systematic literature review. *Information and Software Technology, 103*, 22-39.

Hope, P., McGraw, G., & Anton, A. I. (2004). Misuse and abuse cases: Getting past the positive. *IEEE Security and Privacy, 2*(3), 90–92. doi:10.1109/MSP.2004.17

ISO/IEC. (2008). Information Technology - Security Techniques - Systems Security Engineering - Capability Maturity Model (SSE-CMM) ISO/IEC 21817:2008.

ISO/IEC, (2013). Information Technology - Security Techniques - Code of Practice for Information Security Controls. ISO/IEC 27002:2013.

Kasauli, R., Knauss, E., Kanagwa, B., Nilsson, A., & Calikli, G. (2018). Safety-Critical Systems and Agile Development: A Mapping Study. Euromicro Conf. on Software Engineering and Advanced Applications 2018, Prague, Czech Republic.

Kongsli, V. (2006). Towards agile security in web applications. Companion to the 21st ACM SIGPLAN symposium on Object-oriented programming systems, languages, and applications, Portland, OR. 10.1145/1176617.1176727

Morrison, P., Smith, B., & Williams, L. (2017). Surveying Security Practice Adherence in Software Development. In *Proceedings of the Hot Topics in Science of Security: Symposium and Bootcamp (HoTSoS)*. ACM. DOI: 10.1145/3055305.3055312

Othmane, L., Angin, P., Weffers, H., & Bhargava, B. (2014). Extending the Agile Development Process to Develop Acceptably Secure Software. *IEEE Transactions on Dependable and Secure Computing*, *11*(6), 497–509. doi:10.1109/TDSC.2014.2298011

Pietikäinen, P., & Röning, J. (2014). *Handbook of the Secure Agile Software Development Life Cycle*. Univ. of Oulu.

Ramesh, B., Cao, L., & Baskerville, R. (2010). Agile requirements engineering practices and challenges: An empirical study. *Information Systems Journal*, *20*(5), 449–480. doi:10.1111/j.1365-2575.2007.00259.x

Rindell, K., Hyrynsalmi, S., & Leppänen, V. (2015a). A comparison of security assurance support of agile software development methods. In *Proceedings of Proceedings of the 15th International Conference on Computer Systems and Technologies* (pp. 61-68). ACM. 10.1145/2812428.2812431

Rindell, K., Hyrynsalmi, S., & Leppänen, V. (2015b). Securing Scrum for VAHTI. CEUR Workshop Proceedings, 1525, 236-250.

Rindell, K., Hyrynsalmi, S., & Leppänen, V. (2017). Busting a Myth: Review of Agile Security Engineering Methods. In *Proceedings of the 12th International Conference on Availability, Reliability and Security* (pp. 74:1-74:10). ACM. 10.1145/3098954.3103170

Sonia, Singhal, A., & Banati, H. (2014). FISA-XP: An agile-based integration of security activities with extreme programming. *Software Engineering Notes*, *39*(3), 1–14. doi:10.1145/2597716.2597728

VAHTI. (2009). *ICT-toiminnan varautuminen häiriö- ja erityistilanteisiin*. Retrieved from https://www.vahtiohje.fi/web/guest/2/2009-ict-toiminnan-varautuminen-hairio-ja-erityistilanteisiin

VAHTI. (2012a). *Requirements for ICT Contingency Planning*. Retrieved from https://www.vahtiohje.fi/web/guest/2b/2012-requirements-for-ict-contingency-planning

VAHTI. (2012b). *Teknisen ympäristön tietoturvataso-ohje*. Retrieved from https://www.vahtiohje.fi/web/guest/3/2012-teknisen-ympariston-tietoturvataso-ohje

VAHTI. (2013). *Sovelluskehityksen tietoturvaohje*. Retrieved from https://www.vahtiohje.fi/web/guest/vahti-1/2013-sovelluskehityksen-tietoturvaohje

VersionOne. (2017). *11th annual state of agile survey*. Retrieved from https://explore.versionone.com/state-of-agile/versionone-11th-annual-state-of-agile-report-2 Retrieved 15/08/2017

Villamizar, H., Kalinowski, M., Viana, M., & Méndez Fernández, D. (2018). A Systematic Mapping Study on Security in Agile Requirements Engineering. *Euromicro Conference on Software Engineering and Advanced Applications 2018*. 10.1109/SEAA.2018.00080

Wäyrynen, J., Bodén, M., & Boström, G. (2004). Security Engineering and eXtreme Programming: An Impossible Marriage? Springer Berlin Heidelberg.

Yin, R. K. (2003). *Case Study Research: Design and Methods* (3rd ed.). SAGE Publications, Inc.

ENDNOTES

[1] https://www.vahtiohje.fi/web/guest/home
[2] https://www.viestintavirasto.fi/en/cybersecurity/ficorasinformationsecurityservices/ncsa-fi.html
[3] http://www.itil.org.uk/
[4] https://www.vahtiohje.fi/web/guest/708 (available in Finnish only)
[5] https://www.atlassian.com/software/jira/agile
[6] http://www.supo.fi/security_clearances

Compilation of References

Abdelhakim, A., Saleh, H., & Nassar, A. (2017). A quality guaranteed robust image watermarking optimization with Artificial Bee Colony. *Expert Systems with Applications*, *72*, 317–326. doi:10.1016/j.eswa.2016.10.056

Abdulrazeg, A. A., Norwawi, N. M., & Basir, N. (2017). RiskSRP: Prioritizing Security Requirements Based on Total Risk Avoidance. *Advanced Science Letters*, *23*(5), 4596–4600. doi:10.1166/asl.2017.8901

Abrahamsson, P., Warsta, J., Siponen, M. T., & Ronkainen, J. (2003). New directions on agile methods: A comparative analysis. In *Proceedings of the 25th International Conference on Software Engineering* (pp. 244–254). Washington, DC: IEEE Computer Society.

Abrahamsson, P., Salo, O., Ronkainen, J., & Warsta, J. (2002). *Agile software development methods*. VTT Publications.

Abramov, J., Shoval, P., & Sturm, A. (2009). Validating and Implementing Security Patterns for Database Applications. *Proceedings of the 3rd International Workshop on Software Patterns and Quality (SPAQu'09)*.

Abrial, J. R. (1996). *The B Book*. Cambridge University Press. doi:10.1017/CBO9780511624162

Ackerberg, D., Hirano, K., & Shahriar, Q. (2006). *The buy-it-now option, risk aversion, and impatience in an empirical model of eBay bidding*. University of Arizona.

Adams, E. (2012). *The Biggest Information Security Mistakes that Organizations Make and How to Avoid Making Them*. Retrieved from https://web.securityinnovation.com/the-biggest-information-security-mistakes-that-organizations-make

Adelyar, S. H., & Horta, A. (2016). Towards a Secure Agile Software Development Process. In *2016 10th International Conference on the Quality of Information and Communications Technology* (pp. 101-106). IEEE. 10.1109/QUATIC.2016.028

Adelyar, S. H. (2018). *Secure Agile Agent-Oriented Software Development*. Tallinna University of Technology, Dissertations in Natural Sciences No. 51.

Agarwal, H., Raman, B., & Venkat, I. (2014). Blind reliable invisible watermarking method in wavelet domain for face image watermark. *Multimedia Tools and Applications, 74*(17), 6897–6935. doi:10.100711042-014-1934-1

Agha, G. (1985). *Actors: A model of concurrent computation in distributed systems.* DTIC Document.

Agreement, T. (2009). *Common criteria for information technology security evaluation part 1: Introduction and general model july 2009 revision 3 final foreword.* NIST.

Ahmed, N., Natarajan, T., & Rao, K. R. (1974). Discrete Cosine Transform. *IEEE Transactions on Computers, 100*(1), 90–93. doi:10.1109/T-C.1974.223784

Ahn, G. J., & Hu, H. (2007, June). Towards realizing a formal RBAC model in real systems. *Proc. of the 12th ACM symposium on Access control models and technologies,* 215-224. 10.1145/1266840.1266875

Akerlof. (1970). *The market for "lemons": quality uncertainty and the market mechanism.* Academic Press.

Alanezi, F. (2016). *Perceptions of online fraud and the impact on the countermeasures for the control of online fraud in Saudi Arabian financial institutions.* Brunel University London.

Alberts, C., Dorofee, A., Stevens, J., & Woody, C. (2003). *Introduction to the OCTAVE Approach.* Retrieved from http://www.dtic.mil/docs/citations/ADA634134

Al-Hadhrami, N., Aziz, B., & Othmane, L. (2016). An Incremental B-Model for RBAC-Controlled Electronic Marking System. *International Journal of Secure Software Engineering, 7*(2), 37–64. doi:10.4018/IJSSE.2016040103

Ali, M., Ahn, C., & Pant, M. (2014). A robust image watermarking technique using SVD and differential evolution in DCT domain. Optik - International Journal for Light and Electron Optics, 125(1), 428-434. doi:10.1016/j.ijleo.2013.06.082

Allen, J. (2005). *Governing for enterprise security* (CMU/SEI-2005-TN-023). Retrieved from http://resources.sei.cmu.edu/library/asset-view.cfm?assetid=7453

Al-Nabhani, Jalab, Wahid, & Noor. (2015). Robust watermarking algorithm for digital images using discrete wavelet and probabilistic neural network. *Journal of King Saud University - Computer and Information Sciences, 27*(4), 393-401.

Alnatheer, A., Gravell, A., & Argles, D. (2010). Agile security issues: A research study. *Proceedings of the 5th International Doctoral Symposium on Empirical Software Engineering.*

Amri, H., Khalfallah, A., Gargouri, M., Nebhani, N., Lapayre, J., & Bouhlel, M. (2016). Medical Image Compression Approach Based on Image Resizing, Digital Watermarking and Lossless Compression. *Journal of Signal Processing Systems for Signal, Image, and Video Technology.*

Compilation of References

Anderson, R. J. (2010). *Security engineering: a guide to building dependable distributed systems*. John Wiley & Sons.

Andreas, L., & Sindre, G. (2000). Eliciting Security Requirements by Misuse Cases. In *Proceedings of the 37th International Conference on Technology of Object-Oriented Languages and Systems (TOOLS-Pacific 2000)*. IEEE Computer Society.

Aniche, M. F., & de Azevedo Silveira, G. (2011). *Increasing learning in an agile environment: Lessons learned in an agile team*. Paper presented at the Agile Conference (AGILE), 2011. 10.1109/AGILE.2011.13

Ansari, I., Pant, M., & Ahn, C. (2016). Robust and false positive free watermarking in IWT domain using SVD and ABC. *Engineering Applications of Artificial Intelligence, 49*, 114–125. doi:10.1016/j.engappai.2015.12.004

Antonopoulos. (2014). *Mastering Bitcoin: unlocking digital cryptocurrencies*. O'Reilly Media, Inc.

Arce, I., Clark-Fisher, K., Daswani, N., DelGrosso, J., Dhillon, D., Kern, C., . . . West, J. (2014). *Avoiding The Top 10 Software Security Design Flaws*. Retrieved from https://www.computer.org/cms/CYBSI/docs/Top-10-Flaws.pdf

Armbrust, M. (2009). *Above the clouds: A berkeley view of cloud computing*. Tech. Rep. UCB/EECS-2009-28, EECS Department, U.C. Berkeley.

Armbrust, M., Stoica, I., Zaharia, M., Fox, A., Griffith, R., Joseph, A. D., ... Rabkin, A. (2010). A view of cloud computing. *Communications of the ACM, 53*(4), 50–58. doi:10.1145/1721654.1721672

Armstrong, J., Virding, R., Wikström, C., & Williams, M. (1993). *Concurrent programming in ERLANG*. Academic Press.

Armstrong, J. (2007). *Programming Erlang: software for a concurrent world*. Pragmatic Bookshelf.

Arsalan, M., Qureshi, A., Khan, A., & Rajarajan, M. (2017). Protection of medical images and patient related information in healthcare: Using an intelligent and reversible watermarking technique. *Applied Soft Computing, 51*, 168–179. doi:10.1016/j.asoc.2016.11.044

Assal, H., & Chiasson, S. (2018). Security in the software development lifecycle. In *Fourteenth symposium on usable privacy and security (SOUPS 2018)* (pp. 281-296). Academic Press.

Astels, D., Beck, K., Boehm, B., Fraser, S., McGregor, J., Newkirk, J., & Poole, C. (2003). Discipline and Practices of TDD (test driven development). *Companion of the 18th annual ACM SIGPLAN conference on Object-oriented programming, systems, languages, and applications (OOPSLA'03)*.

Attiogbe, C. (2009). Tool-Assisted Multi-Facet Analysis of Formal Specifications (Using Alelier-B and ProB). *Proc. IASTED Conf. on Software Engineering*, 85-90.

Ayalew, T., Kidane, T., & Carlsson, B. (2013) Identification and Evaluation of Security Activities in Agile Projects. Springer. doi:10.1007/978-3-642-41488-6_10

Ayalew, T., Kidane, T., & Carlsson, B. (2013). *Identification and Evaluation of Security Activities in Agile Projects. In Secure IT Systems* (pp. 139–153). Springer.

Babar, M. A. (2009). *An exploratory study of architectural practices and challenges in using agile software development approaches.* Paper presented at the 2009 Joint Working IEEE/IFIP Conference on Software Architecture & European Conference on Software Architecture. 10.1109/WICSA.2009.5290794

Baca, D., Boldt, M., Carlsson, B., & Jacobsson, A. (2015). *A Novel Security-Enhanced Agile Software Development Process Applied in an Industrial Setting.* Paper presented at the Availability, Reliability and Security (ARES), 2015 10th International Conference on. 10.1109/ARES.2015.45

Baca, D., & Carlsson, B. (2011). Agile development with security engineering activities. In *Proceedings of the 2011 International Conference on Software and Systems Process, ICSSP '11* (pp. 149–158). New York: ACM.

Baca, D., & Carlsson, B. (2011). Agile development with security engineering activities. *Proceedings of the 2011 International Conference on Software and Systems Process.*

Barber, B., & Davey, J. (1992). The use of the CCTA risk analysis and management methodology CRAMM in health information systems. In *7th International Congress on Medical Informatics.* (pp. 1589-1593). North-Holland.

Bartsch, S. (2011). *Practitioners' perspectives on security in agile development.* Paper presented at the Availability, Reliability and Security (ARES), 2011 Sixth International Conference on. 10.1109/ARES.2011.82

Ba, S., & Pavlou, P. A. (2002). Evidence of the effect of trust building technology in electronic markets: Price premiums and buyer behavior. *Management Information Systems Quarterly, 26*(3), 243–268. doi:10.2307/4132332

Ba, S., Whinston, A. B., & Zhang, H. (2003). Building trust in online auction markets through an economic incentive mechanism. *Decision Support Systems, 35*(3), 273–286. doi:10.1016/S0167-9236(02)00074-X

Basin, D., Doser, J., & Loddersted, T. (2002). SecureUML: A UML-Based Modeling Language for Model-Driven Security. *Proceedings of the 5th International Conference Model Engineering, Concepts, and Tools (UML'02).*

Beck, K. (1999). Embracing change with extreme programming. *IEEE Computer, 32.*

Beck, K., Beedle, M., Van Bennekum, A., Cockburn, A., Cunningham, W., Fowler, M., . . . Thomas, D. (2001). *Manifesto for agile software development.* Retrieved from http://agilemanifesto.org/

Becker, J., Breuker, D., Heide, T., Holler, J., Rauer, H. P., & Böhme, R. (2013). Can we afford integrity by proof-of-work? Scenarios inspired by the Bitcoin currency. In *The Economics of Information Security and Privacy* (pp. 135–156). Springer. doi:10.1007/978-3-642-39498-0_7

Beck, K. (1999). Embracing change with extreme programming. *Computer*, *32*(10), 70–77. doi:10.1109/2.796139

Behloul, A. (2014). A blind robust image watermarking using interest points and IWT. *Proceedings of the 6th International Conference on Management of Emergent Digital EcoSystems 'MEDES'*, 139-145. 10.1145/2668260.2668305

ben Othmane, L., Angin, P., Weffers, H., & Bhargava, B. (2014). Extending the agile development process to develop acceptably secure software. *IEEE Transactions on Dependable and Secure Computing*, *11*(6), 497-509.

Benoraira, A., Benmahammed, K., & Boucenna, N. (2015). Blind image watermarking technique based on differential embedding in DWT and DCT domains. *EURASIP Journal on Advances in Signal Processing*, *2015*(1), 55. doi:10.118613634-015-0239-5

Bernstein, P., Bykov, S., Geller, A., Kliot, G., & Thelin, J. (2014). *Orleans: Distributed virtual actors for programmability and scalability*. MSR-TR-2014–41.

Bernstein, L., & Yuhas, C. M. (2005). *Trustworthy systems through quantitative software engineering* (Vol. 1). John Wiley & Sons. doi:10.1002/0471750336

Beznosov, K., & Kruchten, P. (2004). Towards agile security assurance. *NSPW '04 Proceedings of the 2004 workshop on New security paradigms*, 47-54.

Beznosov, K., & Kruchten, P. (2004). Towards agile security assurance. *NSPW '04 Proceedings of the 2004 workshop on New security paradigms*, 47–54.

Beznosov, K., & Kruchten, P. (2004). Towards agile security assurance. *Proceedings of the 2004 workshop on New security paradigms*.

bin Othmane, L., Angin, P., Weffers, H., & Bhargava, B. (2014). Extending the Agile Development Process to Develop Acceptably Secure Software. *IEEE Transactions on Dependable and Secure Computing*, *11*(6), 497-509.

Bischop, M. (2002). *The Art and Science of Computer Security*. Addison-Wesley Longman Publishing Co., Inc.

Black, J., Hashimzade, N., & Myles, G. (2013). *Committee on Payment and Settlement Systems*. Oxford University Press.

Boehm, B., & Basili, V. R. (2005). *Software defect reduction top 10 list. In Foundations of empirical software engineering: the legacy of Victor R* (Vol. 426). Basili. doi:10.1007/3-540-27662-9

Bondareva, K., & Milutinovich, J. (2014). *Unified Modeling Language*. Retrieved September 10, 2014, from http://www.omg.org/gettingstarted/what_is_uml.htm

Boström, G., Wäyrynen, J., Bodén, M., Beznosov, K., & Kruchten, P. (2006). Extending XP practices to support security requirements engineering. *Proceedings of the 2006 International Workshop on Software Engineering for Secure Systems, SESS '06*. 10.1145/1137627.1137631

Boulanger, J. (2012). *Industrial Use of Formal Methods: Formal Verification*. London, UK: ISTE Ltd and John Wiley & Sons, Inc. doi:10.1002/9781118561829

Bulut, E., Khadraoui, D., & Marquet, B. (2007). Multi-agent based security assurance monitoring system for telecommunication infrastructures. In *Proceedings of the Fourth IASTED International Conference on Communication, Network and Information Security* (pp. 90-95). ACTA Press.

Burrus, C. S., Gopinath, R. A., & Guo, H. (1998). *Introduction to Wavelets and Wavelet Transforms: A Primer*. Prentice-Hall, Inc.

Buschmann, F., Fernandez-Buglioni, E., Schumacher, M., Sommerlad, P., & Hybertson, D. (2006). *Security Patterns: Integrating Security and Systems Engineering*. Wiley Software Patterns Series.

Büttnera, F., Gogollaa, M., & Richtersb, M. (2007). USE: A UML-Based Specification Environment for Validating UML and OCL. *Science of Computer Programming*, 69(1-3), 27–34. doi:10.1016/j.scico.2007.01.013

Caldiera, V. R.-G., & Rombach, H. D. (1994). Goal question metric paradigm. Encyclopedia of software engineering, 528-532.

Camacho, C. R., Marczak, S., & Cruzes, D. S. (2016, Aug). Agile team members perceptions on non-functional testing: Influencing factors from an empirical study. In *2016 11th international conference on availability, reliability and security (ARES)* (p. 582-589). Academic Press. doi: 10.1109/ARES.2016.98

Cansell, D., & Méry, D. (2012). Foundations of the B method. Computing and Informatics, 22(3-4), 221-256.

Castro, M., & Liskov, B. (1999). *Practical Byzantine fault tolerance* (Vol. 99). OSDI.

Çetinel, G., & Çerkezi, L. (2016). Robust Chaotic Digital Image Watermarking Scheme based on RDWT and SVD. *International Journal of Image, Graphics and Signal Processing*, 8(8), 58–67. doi:10.5815/ijigsp.2016.08.08

Chae, J. H., & Shiri, N. (2007). Formalization of RBAC policy with object class hierarchy. *Proc. Information Security Practice and Experience,* 162-176.

Chakraborty, S., Chatterjee, S., Dey, N., Ashour, A. S., & Hassanien, A. E. (2017). *Comparative approach between singular value decomposition and randomized singular value decomposition-based watermarking. In Intelligent Techniques in Signal Processing for Multimedia Security* (pp. 133–149). Springer International Publishing.

Chan, H., Ho, I., & Lee, R. (2001) Design and implementation of a mobile agent-based auction system, *IEEE Pacific Rim Conference on Communications, Computers and signal Processing*, 2, 740-743. 10.1109/PACRIM.2001.953738

Chivers, H., Paige, R. F., & Ge, X. (2005) Agile security using an incremental security architecture. *Proceedings of the 6th international conference on Extreme Programming and Agile Processes in Software Engineering*. 10.1007/11499053_7

Choi, B., Kim, H., & Yoon, S. (2009). Performance Testing based on Test-Driven Development for Mobile Applications. *Proceedings of the 3rd International Conference on Ubiquitous Information Management and Communication (ICUIMC'09)*.

Choi, S.-Y., Stahl, D. O., & Whinston, A. B. (1997). *The economics of electronic commerce*. Macmillan Technical Publishing.

Christidis, K., & Devetsikiotis, M. (2016). Blockchains and Smart Contracts for the Internet of Things. *IEEE Access: Practical Innovations, Open Solutions, 4*, 2292–2303. doi:10.1109/ACCESS.2016.2566339

Chua & Wareham. (2002). Self-regulation for online auctions: An analysis. *Self, 12*, 31.

Chua, C. E. H., & Wareham, J. (2004). Fighting internet auction fraud: An assessment and proposal. *Computer, 37*(10), 31–37. doi:10.1109/MC.2004.165

Clarke, E. M., & Wing, J. M. (1996). Formal methods: State of the art and future directions. *ACM Computing Surveys, 28*(4), 626–643. doi:10.1145/242223.242257

Clarke, E., Emerson, A., Edmund, M., & Sistla, A. (1986). Automatic Verification of Finite-state Concurrent Systems using Temporal Logic Specifications. *ACM Transactions on Programming Languages and Systems, 8*(2), 244–263. doi:10.1145/5397.5399

Conklin, L. (2014). *CRV2 AppThreatModeling*. Retrieved from https://www.owasp.org/index.php/CRV2AppThreatModeling

CORAS. (2018). *The CORAS Tool*. Retrieved from http://coras.sourceforge.net/coras_tool.html

Corcoran. (1999). The auction economy. *Red Herring, 69*.

Creswell, J. W. (2003). *Research Design: Qualitative and Quantitative and Mixed Methods Approaches* (2nd ed.). Thousand Oaks, CA: SAGE Publications, Inc.

Cruzes, D. S., Felderer, M., Oyetoyan, T. D., Gander, M., & Pekaric, I. (2017). How is security testing done in agile teams? a cross-case analysis of four software teams. In H. Baumeister, H. Lichter, & M. Riebisch (Eds.), *Agile Processes in Software Engineering and Extreme Programming* (pp. 201–216). Cham: Springer International Publishing. doi:10.1007/978-3-319-57633-6_13

Cruzes, D. S., Jaatun, M. G., Bernsmed, K., & Tøndel, I. A. (2018). Challenges and Experiences with Applying Microsoft Threat Modeling in Agile Development Projects. *Proceedings of the 25th Australasian Software Engineering Conference (ASWEC)*.

Dalal, S. R., Jain, A., Karunanithi, N., Leaton, J. M., Lott, C. M., Patton, G. C., & Horowitz, B. M. (1999). Model-based Testing in Practice. *Proceedings of the International Conference on Software Engineering (ICSE'99)*, 285-294.

Daraee, F., & Mozaffari, S. (2014). Watermarking in binary document images using fractal codes. *Pattern Recognition Letters, 35*, 120–129. doi:10.1016/j.patrec.2013.04.022

Das, C., Panigrahi, S., Sharma, V., & Mahapatra, K. (2014). A novel blind robust image watermarking in DCT domain using inter-block coefficient correlation. *AEÜ. International Journal of Electronics and Communications*, 68(3), 244–253. doi:10.1016/j.aeue.2013.08.018

Davison, R., Martinsons, M. G., & Kock, N. (2004). Principles of canonical action research. *Information Systems Journal*, 14(1), 65–86. doi:10.1111/j.1365-2575.2004.00162.x

De Koster, J., Marr, S., D'Hondt, T., & Van Cutsem, T. (2013). Tanks: multiple reader, single writer actors. The workshop on Programming based on actors, agents, and decentralized control, 61-68. doi:10.1145/2541329.2541331

De Win, B., Scandariato, R., Buyens, K., Grégoire, J., & Joosen, W. (2009). On the secure software development process: CLASP, SDL and Touchpoints compared. *Information and Software Technology*, 51(7), 1152–1171. doi:10.1016/j.infsof.2008.01.010

Dhillon, D. (2011, July). Developer-driven threat modeling: Lessons learned in the trenches. *IEEE Security and Privacy*, 9(4), 41–47. doi:10.1109/MSP.2011.47

Diaz, J., Garbajosa, J., & Calvo-Manzano, J. A. (2009). Mapping CMMI Level 2 to Scrum Practices: An Experience Report. Software Process Improvement. Comm. in Computer and Information Science, 42, 93-104.

Dogan, S., Tuncer, T., Avci, E., & Gulten, A. (2011). A robust color image watermarking with Singular Value Decomposition method. *Advances in Engineering Software*, 42(6), 336–346. doi:10.1016/j.advengsoft.2011.02.012

Dong, Li, Duan, & Guo. (2016). A Robust Zero-Watermarking Algorithm for Encrypted Medical Images in the DWT-DCT Encrypted Domain. *International Journal of Simulation Systems, Science & Technology, 17*(43), 1-7.

Dong, J., Peng, T., & Zhao, Y. (2008). Verifying Behavioral Correctness of Design Pattern Implementation. In *Proceedings of the 20th International Conference on Software Engineering & Knowledge Engineering (SEKE'08)* (pp. 454-459). IEEE Computer Society.

Dong, J., Peng, T., & Zhao, Y. (2009). Automated Verification of Security Pattern Compositions. *Information and Software Technology*, 52(3), 274–295. doi:10.1016/j.infsof.2009.10.001

Drouineaud, M., Bortin, M., Torrini, P., & Sohr, K. (Sep. 2004). A First Step Towards Formal Verification of Security Policy Properties for RBAC. *Proc. of the 4th IEEE International Conference on Quality Software*, 60-67. 10.1109/QSIC.2004.1357945

Dybå, T., Moe, N. B., & Mikkelsen, E. M. (2004). An empirical investigation on factors affecting software developer acceptance and utilization of electronic process guides. *Software Metrics, 2004. Proceedings. 10th International Symposium on.* 10.1109/METRIC.2004.1357905

Dybå, T., & Dingsøyr, T. (2008). Empirical studies of agile software development: A systematic review. *Information and Software Technology*, 50(9), 833–859. doi:10.1016/j.infsof.2008.01.006

Eclipse. (2018). Retrieved from https://www.eclipse.org/

El Hossaini, A., El Aroussi, M., Jamali, K., Mbarki, S., & Wahbi, M. (2014). A robust watermarking scheme based on steerable pyramid and singular value decomposition. *Applied Mathematical Sciences*, *8*, 2997–3008. doi:10.12988/ams.2014.4126

English, M., Auer, S., & Domingue, J. (2016). *Block Chain Technologies & The Semantic Web: A Framework for Symbiotic Development. Technical report.* University of Bonn.

Erdogan, G., Li, Y., Runde, R. K., Seehusen, F., & Stølen, K. (2014). Approaches for the combined use of risk analysis and testing: A systematic literature review. *International Journal of Software Tools for Technology Transfer*, *16*(5), 627–642. doi:10.100710009-014-0330-5

Estrada, R., & Ruiz, I. (2016). *Big Data SMACK.* Apress. doi:10.1007/978-1-4842-2175-4

Eyal, I., & Sirer, E. G. (2014) Majority is not enough: Bitcoin mining is vulnerable. *International Conference on Financial Cryptography and Data Security*, 436-454.

Felderer, M., Grossmann, J., & Schieferdecker, I. (2018). *Recent Results on Classifying Risk-Based Testing Approaches.* Computing Research Repository, arXiv:1801.06812

Felderer, M., Agreiter, B., Breu, R., & Armenteros, A. (2010). Security Testing by Telling TestStories. *Proceedings of the Conference on Modellierung*, 24-26.

Felderer, M., Buchler, M., Johns, M., Brucker, A. D., Breu, R., & Pretschner, A. (2016). Security testing: A survey. In *Advances in Computers* (pp. 1–51). Elsevier.

Felderer, M., & Ramler, R. (2016). Risk orientation in software testing processes of small and medium enterprises: An exploratory and comparative study. *Software Quality Journal*, *24*(3), 519–548. doi:10.100711219-015-9289-z

Felderer, M., & Schieferdecker, I. (2014). A taxonomy of risk-based testing. *International Journal of Software Tools for Technology Transfer*, *16*(5), 559–568. doi:10.100710009-014-0332-3

Felderer, M., Zech, P., Breu, R., Büchler, M., & Pretschner, A. (2016). Model-based security testing: A taxonomy and systematic classification. *Software Testing, Verification & Reliability*, *26*(2), 119–148. doi:10.1002tvr.1580

Fernandez, E. B., Washizaki, H., & Yoshioka, N. (2016). Patterns for Secure Cloud IaaS. *Proceedings of the 5th Asian Conference on Pattern Languages of Programs (AsianPLoP 2016).*

Fernandez, E. B., Yoshioka, N., & Washizaki, H. (2014). Patterns for cloud firewalls. *Proceedings of the 3rd Asian Conference on Pattern Language of Programs (AsianPLoP 2014).*

Fernandez, E. B., Yoshioka, N., & Washizaki, H. (2015b). Cloud Access Security Broker (CASB): A pattern for accessing secure cloud services. *Proceedings of the 4th Asian Conference on Pattern Languages of Programs (AsianPLoP 2015).*

Fernandez, E. B., Yoshioka, N., Washizaki, H., & Yoder, J. (2018). An Abstract Security Pattern for Authentication and a Derived Concrete Pattern, the Credential-based Authentication. *Proceedings of the 7th Asian Conference on Pattern Languages of Programs (AsianPLoP 2018).*

Fernandez, E.B., Yoshioka, N., Washizaki, H., & Syed, M.H. (2016). Modeling and Security in Cloud Ecosystems. *Future Internet, 13*(2), 1-15.

Fernandez, E. B., Yoshioka, N., & Washizaki, H. (2008). Abstract security patterns. *Proceedings of the 2nd PLoP Workshop on Software Patterns and Quality (SPAQu'08).*

Fernandez, E. B., Yoshioka, N., & Washizaki, H. (2015a). Patterns for Security and Privacy in Cloud Ecosystems. *Proceedings of the 2nd International Workshop on Evolving Security and Privacy Requirements Engineering (ESPRE 2015).* 10.1109/ESPRE.2015.7330162

Fernandez, E. B., Yoshioka, N., Washizaki, H., Jurjens, J., VanHilst, M., & Pernul, G. (2010). Using security patterns to develop secure systems. In *Software Engineering for Secure Systems.* IGI Global.

Fernandez, E. B., Yoshioka, N., Washizaki, H., & Yoder, J. (2014). Abstract security patterns for requirements and analysis of secure systems. *Proceedings of the 17th Workshop on Requirements Engineering (WER 2014).*

Ferraiolo, D., Cugini, J., & Kuhn, D. R. (1995, December). Role-based access control (RBAC): Features and motivations. *Proceedings of 11th annual computer security application conference,* 241-48.

Finkelstein, A., Honiden, S., & Yoshioka, N. (2004). Security Patterns: a Method for Constructing Secure and Efficient Inter-company Coordination Systems. *Proceedings of the 8th IEEE International Enterprise Distributed Object Computing Conference (EDOC'04),* 84–97.

Fitzgerald, B., & Stol, K.-J. (2014). Continuous software engineering and beyond: Trends and challenges. In *Proceedings of the 1st International Workshop on Rapid Continuous Software Engineering* (pp. 1–9). New York: ACM. 10.1145/2593812.2593813

Fitzgerald, B., Stol, K.-J., O'Sullivan, R., & O'Brien, D. (2013). Scaling agile methods to regulated environments: An industry case study. *Proceedings of the 2013 International Conference on Software Engineering, ICSE '13,* 863–872. 10.1109/ICSE.2013.6606635

FMoF (2013). *Sovelluskehityksen tietoturvaohje.* FMoF.

Fontenele, M. P. (2017). *Designing a method for discovering expertise in cyber security communities: an ontological approach.* University of Reading.

Fraser, M. D., Kumar, K., & Vaishnavi, V. K. (1994). Strategies for incorporating formal specifications in software development. *Communications of the ACM, 37*(10), 74–87. doi:10.1145/194313.194399

Froomkin. (1996). *Essential Role of Trusted Third Parties in Electronic Commerce.* Academic Press. doi:10.1007/978-3-662-45472-5_28

Ge, X., Paige, R., Polack, F., & Brooke, P. (2007). Extreme programming security practices. In *Agile Processes in Software Engineering and Extreme Programming*, volume 4536 of *Lecture Notes in Computer Science* (pp. 226–230). Springer Berlin Heidelberg. doi:10.1007/978-3-540-73101-6_42

Ghadi, M., Laouamer, L., Nana, L., & Pascu, A. (2016). A Robust Associative Watermarking Technique based on Frequent Pattern Mining and Texture Analysis. *Proceedings of the 8th International Conference on Management of Digital EcoSystems*, 73-81. 10.1145/3012071.3012101

Ghosal, S., & Mandal, J. (2014). Binomial transform based fragile watermarking for image authentication. *Journal of Information Security and Applications*, *19*(4-5), 272–281. doi:10.1016/j.jisa.2014.07.004

Goertzel, K. M., Winograd, T., McKinley, H. L., Oh, L. J., Colon, M., McGibbon, T., & Vienneau, R. (2007). *Software security assurance: a State-of-Art Report (SAR). In Information Assurance Technology Analysis Center (IATAC)*. Academic Press. doi:10.21236/ADA472363

Google. (2018). *Chrome*. Retrieved from http://www.google.com/chrome/

Grazioli, S., & Jarvenpaa, S. L. (2000). Perils of Internet fraud: An empirical investigation of deception and trust with experienced Internet consumers. *IEEE Transactions on Systems, Man, and Cybernetics. Part A, Systems and Humans*, *30*(4), 395–410. doi:10.1109/3468.852434

Greenwood, D., & Levin, M. (1998). *Introduction to action research: Social research for social change*. SAGE Publications. Retrieved from https://books.google.no/books?id=nipHAAAAMAAJ

Greenwood, D. J., & Levin, M. (2006). *Introduction to action research: Social research for social change*. SAGE Publications.

Gritzalis, D., Iseppi, G., Mylonas, A., & Stavrou, V. (2018). Exiting the Risk Assessment Maze: A Meta-Survey. *ACM Computing Surveys*, *51*(1), 1–30. doi:10.1145/3145905

Großmann, J., Berger, M., & Viehmann, J. (2014). A trace management platform for risk-based security testing. In *Proceedings of the International Workshop on Risk Assessment and Risk-driven Testing* (pp. 120-135): Springer.

Großmann, J., Schneider, M., Viehmann, J., & Wendland, M.-F. (2014). Combining risk analysis and security testing. In *Proceedings of the International Symposium On Leveraging Applications of Formal Methods, Verification and Validation* (pp. 322-336). Springer.

Großmann, J., & Seehusen, F. (2015). Combining Security Risk Assessment and Security Testing Based on Standards. In *Proceedings of the International Workshop on Risk Assessment and Risk-driven Testing* (pp. 18-33). Springer. 10.1007/978-3-319-26416-5_2

Gupta, A. K., & Raval, M. S. (2012). A robust and secure watermarking scheme based on singular values replacement. *Sadhana*, *37*(4), 425–440. doi:10.100712046-012-0089-x

Gupta, M. (2012). *Akka essentials*. Packt Publishing Ltd.

Haddad, S., Dubus, S., Hecker, A., Kanstren, T., Marquet, B., & Savola, R. (2011). Operational security assurance evaluation in open infrastructures. In *Risk and Security of Internet and Systems (CRiSIS), 2011 6th International Conference on* (pp. 1-6). IEEE.

Haller, P. (2012). On the integration of the actor model in mainstream technologies: the scala perspective. In *Proceedings of Programming systems, languages and applications based on actors, agents, and decentralized control abstractions* (pp. 1–6). ACM. doi:10.1145/2414639.2414641

Hallerstede, S. (2008, September). On the purpose of Event-B proof obligations. In *International Conference on Abstract State Machines, B and Z* (pp. 125-138). Springer.10.1007/978-3-540-87603-8_11

Hamid, B., Percebois, C., & Gouteux, D. (2012). Methodology for Integration of Patterns with Validation Purpose. *Proceedings of the European Conference on Pattern Language of Programs (EuroPLoP)*, 1–14.

Han, B., Li, J., & Zong, L. (2013). A New Robust Zero-watermarking Algorithm for Medical Volume Data. *International Journal of Signal Processing, Image Processing and Pattern Recognition, 6*(6), 245–258. doi:10.14257/ijsip.2013.6.6.23

Han, J., Haihong, E., Le, G., & Du, J. (2011). Survey on NoSQL database. *International Conference on Pervasive computing and applications (ICPCA)*, 363-366.

Hansen, D., & Leuschel, M. (2012, January). Translating TLA+ to B for Validation with ProB. In Integrated Formal Methods (pp. 24-38). Springer Berlin Heidelberg.

Heeager, L., & Nielsen, P. (2018). A conceptual model of agile software development in a safety-critical context: A systematic literature review. *Information and Software Technology, 103*, 22-39.

Hewitt, C. (2010). *Actor model of computation: scalable robust information systems*. arXiv preprint arXiv:1008.1459

Hewitt, C., Bishop, P., & Steiger, R. (1973). A Universal Modular ACTOR Formalism for Artificial Intelligence. *Advance Papers of the Conference, 3*, 235.

Hoang Ngan Le, T., Hung Nguyen, K., & Bac Le, H. (2010). Literature Survey on Image Watermarking Tools, Watermark Attacks, and Benchmarking Tools. *Proceeding of the Second International Conferences on Advances in Multimedia (MMEDIA)*, 67-73.

Hope, P., McGraw, G., & Anton, A. I. (2004). Misuse and abuse cases: Getting past the positive. *IEEE Security and Privacy, 2*(3), 90–92. doi:10.1109/MSP.2004.17

Howard, M., & Lipner, S. (2006). *The security development lifecycle*. Microsoft Press.

Howard, M., & Lipner, S. (2006). *The Security Development Lifecycle*. Microsoft Press.

Hsu, F., Wu, M., Wang, S., & Huang, C. (2013). Reversibility of image with balanced fidelity and capacity upon pixels differencing expansion. *The Journal of Supercomputing, 66*(2), 812–828. doi:10.100711227-013-0896-9

Hudic, A., Smith, P., & Weippl, E. R. (2017). Security assurance assessment methodology for hybrid clouds. *Computers & Security*, *70*, 723–743. doi:10.1016/j.cose.2017.03.009

Hu, H., & Ahn, G. (2008, June). Enabling verification and conformance testing for access control model. *Proc. of the 13th ACM symposium on Access control models and technologies*, 195-204. 10.1145/1377836.1377867

Hu, H., Chang, J., & Hsu, L. (2016). Robust blind image watermarking by modulating the mean of partly sign-altered DCT coefficients guided by human visual perception. *AEÜ. International Journal of Electronics and Communications*, *70*(10), 1374–1381. doi:10.1016/j.aeue.2016.07.011

IBM. (2018). *IBM Rational Software Architect*. Retrieved from http://www.ibm.com/developerworks/downloads/r/architect/index.html

Islam, M., & Chong, U. (2014). A Digital Image Watermarking Algorithm Based on DWT DCT and SVD. *International Journal of Computer and Communication Engineering*, *3*(5), 356–360. doi:10.7763/IJCCE.2014.V3.349

ISO. (2009). *ISO 31000: Risk Management - Principles and Guidelines*. Geneva: International Organization for Standardization.

ISO. (2013a). *ISO/IEC/IEEE 29119-1: 2013 (E) Software and systems engineering - Software testing - Part 1: Concepts and definitions*. Geneva: International Organization for Standardization.

ISO. (2013b). *ISO/IEC/IEEE 29119-2: 2013 (E) Software and systems engineering - Software testing - Part 2: Test process*. Geneva: International Organization for Standardization.

ISO/IEC (2013). Information technology - security techniques - code of practice for information security controls iso/IEC 27002:2013.

ISO/IEC 27005:2011 Information technology - Security techniques - Information security risk management. (2011). Retrieved from https://www.iso.org/standard/56742.html

ISO/IEC standard 21827 (2008). Information Technology – Security Techniques – Systems Security Engineering – Capability Maturity Model (SSE-CMM). ISO/IEC.

ISO/IEC, (2013). Information Technology - Security Techniques - Code of Practice for Information Security Controls. ISO/IEC 27002:2013.

ISO/IEC. (2008). Information Technology - Security Techniques - Systems Security Engineering - Capability Maturity Model (SSE-CMM) ISO/IEC 21817:2008.

ISO/IEC. (2009). Information technology -- Security techniques -- Evaluation criteria for IT security -- Part 1: Introduction and general model: ISO/IEC 15408-1:2009.

ISO/IEC. (2011). Information technology -- Security techniques -- Application security -- Part 1: Overview and concepts: ISO/IEC 27034-1:2011.

Ito, Y., Washizaki, H., Yoshizawa, M., Fukazawa, Y., Okubo, T., Kaiya, H., ... Fernandez, E. B. (2015). Systematic Mapping of Security Patterns Research. *Proceedings of the 22nd Conference on Pattern Languages of Programs Conference 2015 (PLoP 2015)*.

Jaatun, M. G., & Tøndel, I. A. (2008). Covering your assets in software engineering. In *The third international conference on availability, reliability and security (ARES 2008)* (pp. 1172-1179). Barcelona, Spain: ARES. 10.1109/ARES.2008.8

Jaatun, M. G., Cruzes, D. S., Bernsmed, K., Tøndel, I. A., & Røstad, L. (2015). *Software Security Maturity in Public Organisations*. Paper presented at the Information Security: 18th International Conference, ISC 2015, Trondheim, Norway. 10.1007/978-3-319-23318-5_7

Jaatun, M. G. (2012). Hunting for Aardvarks: Can Software Security be Measured? In G. Quirchmayr, J. Basl, I. You, L. Xu, & E. Weippl (Eds.), *Multidisciplinary Research and Practice for Information Systems* (pp. 85–92). Springer Berlin Heidelberg. doi:10.1007/978-3-642-32498-7_7

Jaatun, M. G., Jensen, J., Meland, P. H., & Tøndel, I. A. (2011). A Lightweight Approach to Secure Software Engineering. In *A Multidisciplinary Introduction to Information Security* (pp. 183–216). CRC Press.

Jane, O., Elbaşi, E., & İlk, H. (2014). Hybrid Non-Blind Watermarking Based on DWT and SVD. *Journal of Applied Research and Technology*, *12*(4), 750–761. doi:10.1016/S1665-6423(14)70091-4

Jansen, W. (2010). *Directions in security metrics research*. Diane Publishing.

Jawad, K., & Khan, A. (2013). Genetic algorithm and difference expansion based reversible watermarking for relational databases. *Journal of Systems and Software*, *86*(11), 2742–2753. doi:10.1016/j.jss.2013.06.023

Jeffries, C. (2012). *Threat modeling and agile development practices*. Retrieved from https://technet.microsoft.com/en-us/security/hh855044.aspx

Jha, S., Li, N., Tripunitara, M., Wang, Q., & Winsborough, W. (2008). Towards formal verification of role-based access control policies. *IEEE Transactions on Dependable and Secure Computing*, *5*(4), 242–255. doi:10.1109/TDSC.2007.70225

Jiang, Y., & Liu, X. (2008). Formal Analysis for Network Security Properties on a Trace Semantics. *Proceedings of the 2008 International Conference on Advanced Computer Theory and Engineering (ICACTE'08)*. 10.1109/ICACTE.2008.31

Jim, M. (2016). *Open Web Application Security Project*. OWASP. Retrieved from https://www.owasp.org/images/3/33/OWASP_Application_Security_Verification_Standard_3.0.1.pdf

Johnson, D., Menezes, A., & Vanstone, S. (2001). The elliptic curve digital signature algorithm (ECDSA). *International Journal of Information Security*, *1*(1), 36–63. doi:10.1007102070100002

Josang, A. (1995). *Security Protocol Verification using Spin*. Montreal, Canada: INRS-Telecommunications.

Jose, S., Cherian Roy, R., & Nambiar, S. S. (2012). Robust Image Watermarking based on DCT-DWT-SVD Method. *International Journal of Computers and Applications*, *58*(21), 12–16. doi:10.5120/9406-3798

Joshi, C., & Singh, U. K. (2017). Information security risks management framework--A step towards mitigating security risks in university network. *Journal of Information Security and Applications*, 128-137.

Jurjens, J. (2005). *Secure Systems Development with UML*. Springer.

Jurjens, J., Popp, G., & Wimmel, G. (2002). Towards using Security Patterns in Model-Based System Development. *Proceedings of the 9th Conference on Pattern Language of Programs (PLoP'02)*.

Kabra, R. G., & Agrawal, S. S. (2016). Robust Embedding of Image Watermark using LWT and SVD. *Proceeding of the International Conference on Communication and Signal Processing*, 1968-1972. 10.1109/ICCSP.2016.7754516

Kamran, A. K., & Malik, S. (2014). A high capacity reversible watermarking approach for authenticating images: Exploiting down-sampling, histogram processing, and block selection. *Information Sciences*, *256*, 162–183. doi:10.1016/j.ins.2013.07.035

Kandi, H., Mishra, D., & Gorthi, S. (2017). Exploring the learning capabilities of convolutional neural networks for robust image watermarking. *Computers & Security*, *65*, 247–268. doi:10.1016/j.cose.2016.11.016

Karmani, R., Shali, A., & Agha, G. (2009). Actor frameworks for the JVM platform: a comparative analysis. In *International Conference on Principles and Practice of Programming in Java* (pp. 11–20). ACM.

Kasauli, R., Knauss, E., Kanagwa, B., Nilsson, A., & Calikli, G. (2018). Safety-Critical Systems and Agile Development: A Mapping Study. Euromicro Conf. on Software Engineering and Advanced Applications 2018, Prague, Czech Republic.

Katt, B., & Prasher, N. (2018). Quantitative security assurance metrics: REST API case studies. In *Proceedings of the 12th European Conference on Software Architecture: Companion Proceedings*. ACM. 10.1145/3241403.3241464

Kekre, H., & Bharadi, V. (2010). Dynamic signature pre-processing by modified digital difference analyzer algorithm. In *Thinkquest 2010* (pp. 67–73). Springer.

Khajvand, M., & Tarokh, M. J. (2011). Estimating customer future value of different customer segments based on adapted rfm model in retail banking context. *Procedia Computer Science*, *3*, 1327–1332. doi:10.1016/j.procs.2011.01.011

Khalifa, Yusof, Abdalla, & Olanrewaju. (2012). State-Of-The-Art Digital Watermarking Attacks. *Proceeding of the International Conference on Computer and Communication Engineering (ICCCE)*, 744-750.

Khan, A., Siddiqa, A., Munib, S., & Malik, S. (2014). A recent survey of reversible watermarking techniques. *Information Sciences*, *279*, 251–272. doi:10.1016/j.ins.2014.03.118

Kissel, R. L. (2013). *Glossary of Key Information Security Terms*. NIST Pubs. doi:10.6028/NIST.IR.7298r2

Kitchenham, B., Linkman, S., & Law, D. (1997). Desmet: A methodology for evaluating software engineering methods and tools. *Computing & Control Engineering Journal*, *8*(3), 120–126. doi:10.1049/cce:19970304

Kleppe, A., & Warmer, J. (1999). *The Object Constraint Language: Precise Modeling with UML*. Addison-Wesley Object Technology Series.

Ko, A. J., DeLine, R., & Venolia, G. (2007). Information needs in collocated software development teams. In *Proceedings of the 29th International Conference on Software Engineering, ICSE '07*. IEEE Computer Society. 10.1109/ICSE.2007.45

Kobashi, T., Yoshioka, N., Kaiya, H., Washizaki, H., Okubo, T., & Fukazawa, Y. (2014). Validating Security Design Pattern Applications by Testing Design Models. *International Journal of Secure Software Engineering*, *5*(4), 1–30. doi:10.4018/ijsse.2014100101

Kobashi, T., Yoshioka, N., Okubo, T., Kaiya, H., Washizaki, H., & Fukazawa, Y. (2013). Validating Security Design Pattern Applications Using Model Testing. *Proceedings of the 8th International Conference on Availability, Reliability and Security (ARES2013)*. 10.1109/ARES.2013.13

Kobashi, T., Yoshizawa, M., Washizaki, H., Fukazawa, Y., Yoshioka, N., Kaiya, H., & Okubo, T. (2015). TESEM: A Tool for Verifying Security Design Pattern Applications by Model Testing. *Proceedings of the 8th IEEE International Conference on Software Testing, Verification, and Validation (ICST 2015)*. 10.1109/ICST.2015.7102633

Koblitz, N. (1987). Elliptic curve cryptosystems. *Mathematics of Computation*, *48*(177), 203–209. doi:10.1090/S0025-5718-1987-0866109-5

Kongsli, V. (2006). Towards agile security in web applications. Companion to the 21st ACM SIGPLAN symposium on Object-oriented programming systems, languages, and applications, Portland, OR. 10.1145/1176617.1176727

Kongsli, V. (2006). Towards agile security in web applications. In *Companion to the 21st ACM SIGPLAN symposium on Object-oriented programming systems, languages, and applications (OOPSLA'06)* (pp. 805-808). ACM.

Kosba, A., Miller, A., Shi, E., Wen, Z., & Papamanthou, C. (2016). Hawk: The blockchain model of cryptography and privacy-preserving smart contracts. *IEEE Symposium on Security and Privacy (SP)*, 839-858. 10.1109/SP.2016.55

Krasnokutskaya, Terwiesch, & Tiererova. (2016). *Trading across Borders in Online Auctions*. Society for Economic Dynamics (no. 1537).

Krasnokutskaya, E., Terwiesch, C., & Tiererova, L. (2016). Trading across Borders in Online Auctions. In *Meeting Papers, no. 1537*. Society for Economic Dynamics.

Kroll, J. A., Davey, I. C., & Felten, E. W. (2013) The economics of Bitcoin mining, or Bitcoin in the presence of adversaries. *Proceedings of WEIS*.

Kruchten, P. (2010) Software Architecture and Agile Software Development – A Clash of Two Cultures? In *Proceedings of the International Conference on Software Engineering, ICSE'10* (pp. 497-498). ACM.

Lagzian, S., Soryani, M., & Fathi, M. (2011). A New Robust Watermarking Scheme Based on RDWT-SVD. *International Journal of Intelligent Information Processing*, 2(1), 22–29. doi:10.4156/ijiip.vol2.issue1.3

Lai, R., Nagappan, R., & Steel, C. (2005). *Core Security Patterns: Best Practices and Strategies for J2EE, Web Services, and Identity Management*. Prentice Hall.

Lakshmi Prasad, K., Malleswara Rao, T., & Kannan, V. (2016). A Novel and Hybrid Secure Digital Image Watermarking Framework Through sc-LWT-SVD. *Indian Journal of Science and Technology*, 9(23), 1–10. doi:10.17485/ijst/2016/v9i23/95273

Laouamer, L., AlShaikh, M., Nana, L., & Pascu, A. (2015). Robust watermarking scheme and tamper detection based on threshold versus intensity. *Journal of Innovation in Digital Ecosystems*, 2(1-2), 1–12. doi:10.1016/j.jides.2015.10.001

Laouamer, L., & Tayan, O. (2015). A Semi-Blind Robust DCT Watermarking Approach for Sensitive Text Images. *Arabian Journal for Science and Engineering*, 40(4), 1097–1109. doi:10.100713369-015-1596-y

LaToza, T. D., Venolia, G., & DeLine, R. (2006). Maintaining mental models: A study of developer work habits. In *Proceedings of the 28th International Conference on Software Engineering, ICSE '06* (pp. 492–501). New York: ACM. 10.1145/1134285.1134355

Leuschel, M., & Butler, M. J. (2003). ProB: A Model Checker for B. *Lecture Notes in Computer Science, 2805*, 855–874. 10.1007/978-3-540-45236-2_46

Licorish, S. A., Holvitie, J., Hyrynsalmi, S., Leppänen, V., Spínola, R. O., Mendes, T. S., ... Buchan, J. (2016). Adoption and suitability of software development methods and practices. In *23rd Asia-Pacific Software Engineering Conference, APSEC 2016* (pp. 369–372). IEEE Computer Society. 10.1109/APSEC.2016.062

Liu, H., Wang, S., & Fei, T. (2003). Multicast-based online auctions: A performance perspective, *Benchmarking. International Journal (Toronto, Ont.)*, 10(1), 54–64.

Liu, H., Xiao, D., Zhang, R., Zhang, Y., & Bai, S. (2016). Robust and hierarchical watermarking of encrypted images based on Compressive Sensing. *Signal Processing Image Communication*, 45, 41–51. doi:10.1016/j.image.2016.04.002

Liu, Z., Xu, L., Liu, T., Chen, H., Li, P., Lin, C., & Liu, S. (2011). Color image encryption by using Arnold transform and color-blend operation in discrete cosine transform domains. *Optics Communications, 284*(1), 123–128. doi:10.1016/j.optcom.2010.09.013

Lockhart, J., Purdy, C., & Wilsey, P. A. (2017, June). The use of automated theorem proving for error analysis and removal in safety critical embedded system specifications. In *Aerospace and Electronics Conference (NAECON), 2017 IEEE National* (pp. 358-361). IEEE.10.1109/NAECON.2017.8268802

Loukhaoukha, K., Nabti, M., & Zebbiche, K. (2014). A robust SVD-based image watermarking using a multi-objective particle swarm optimization. *Opto-Electronics Review, 22*(1), 45–54. doi:10.247811772-014-0177-z

Lu, K., Yahyapour, R., Wieder, P., Yaqub, E., Abdullah, M., Schloer, B., & Kotsokalis, C. (2016). Fault-tolerant Service Level Agreement lifecycle management in clouds using actor system. *Future Generation Computer Systems, 54*, 247–259. doi:10.1016/j.future.2015.03.016

Lund, M. S., Solhaug, B., & Stølen, K. (2010). *Model-driven risk analysis: the CORAS approach*. Springer.

Macaulay, S. (1963). Non-contractual relations in business: A preliminary study. *American Sociological Review, 28*(1), 55–67. doi:10.2307/2090458

Mackman, A., & Maher, P. (2007). Web Application Security Frame. *Microsoft Patterns & Practices*. Retrieved from http://msdn.microsoft.com/en-us/library/ms978518

Makbol, N., & Khoo, B. (2013). Robust blind image watermarking scheme based on Redundant Discrete Wavelet Transform and Singular Value Decomposition. *AEÜ. International Journal of Electronics and Communications, 67*(2), 102–112. doi:10.1016/j.aeue.2012.06.008

Makbol, N., & Khoo, B. (2014). A new robust and secure digital image watermarking scheme based on the integer wavelet transform and singular value decomposition. *Digital Signal Processing, 33*, 134–147. doi:10.1016/j.dsp.2014.06.012

Mansoori, E., & Soltani, S. (2016). A new semi-blind watermarking algorithm using ordered Hadamard transform. *Imaging Science Journal, 64*(4), 204–214. doi:10.1080/13682199.2016.1159816

Maruyama, K., Washizaki, H., & Yoshioka, N. (2008). A Survey on Security Patterns. *Progress in Informatics, 5*, 35-47.

McAdam, R. (2001). Fragmenting the function-process interface: The role of process benchmarking, *Benchmarking. International Journal (Toronto, Ont.), 8*(4), 332–349.

McGraw, G. (2005). The 7 Touchpoints of Secure Software. *Dr. Dobb's Journal*.

McGraw, G. (2006). Software Security: Building Security In. Addison-Wesley Professional.

McGraw, G., Migues, S., & West, J. (2018). *Building Security In Maturity Model (BSIMM 9).* Academic Press.

McGraw, G. (2004). Software security. *Security & Privacy, IEEE, 2*(2), 80–83. doi:10.1109/MSECP.2004.1281254

Mentré, D., Marché, C., Filliâtre, J. C., & Asuka, M. (2012). Discharging proof obligations from Atelier B using multiple automated provers. *Proc. Third International Conference, ABZ,* 238-251. 10.1007/978-3-642-30885-7_17

Microsoft. (2012). *Microsoft security development lifecycle (SDL) process guidance - version 5.2.* Microsoft.

Microsoft. (2012). *Pre-SDL Requirements: Security Training.* Retrieved from https://msdn.microsoft.com/en-us/library/windows/desktop/cc307407.aspx

Microsoft. (2012). *Security Development Lifecycle for Agile Development.* Retrieved from https://msdn.microsoft.com/en-us/library/windows/desktop/ee790621.aspx

Miller, V. S. (1985). Use of elliptic curves in cryptography. *Conference on the Theory and Application of Cryptographic Techniques,* 417-426.

Ming, M., Zhiguang, Q., & Fang, L. (2010). A Digital Watermarking Algorithm against Dithering Attack Based on Watson Perceptual Pattern. *Proceeding of the second International Conference on Signal Processing Systems (ICSPS),* 3, 306-309. 10.1109/ICSPS.2010.5555803

Moghaddam, M., & Nemati, N. (2013). A robust color image watermarking technique using modified Imperialist Competitive Algorithm. *Forensic Science International, 233*(1-3), 193–200. doi:10.1016/j.forsciint.2013.09.005 PMID:24314520

Mohamed, M. A., Samrah, A. S., & Fath Allah, M. I. (2017). DWT vs WP based optical color image encryption robust to composite attacks. Advances in OptoElectronics.

Mohammadi, S. (2015). A semi blind watermarking algorithm for color image using chaotic map. *Proceeding of the second International Conference on Knowledge-Based Engineering and Innovation (KBEI),* 106-110. 10.1109/KBEI.2015.7436030

Moniruzzaman, A., & Hossain, S. (2013). *Nosql database: New era of databases for big data analytics-classification, characteristics and comparison.* arXiv preprint arXiv:1307.0191

Morrison, P., Smith, B. H., & Williams, L. (2017). *Surveying security practice adherence in software development.* Paper presented at the Hot Topics in Science of Security: Symposium and Bootcamp. 10.1145/3055305.3055312

Mousavi, S., Naghsh, A., & Abu-Bakar, S. (2014). Watermarking Techniques used in Medical Images: A Survey. *Journal of Digital Imaging, 27*(6), 714–729. doi:10.100710278-014-9700-5 PMID:24871349

Mozilla. (2018). *Firefox Web browser*. Retrieved from https://www.mozilla.org/en-US/firefox/desktop/

Munetoh, S., & Yoshioka, N. (2013). Model-Assisted Access Control Implementation for Code-centric Ruby-on-Rails Web Application Development. *Proceedings of the International Conference on Availability, Reliability and Security (ARES'13)*, 350–359. 10.1109/ARES.2013.47

Nhlabatsi, A., Bandara, A., Hayashi, S., Haley, C. B., Jurjens, J., Kaiya, H., ... Yu, Y. (2010). Security Patterns: Comparing Modeling Approaches. In *Software Engineering for Secure Systems*. IGI Global.

Nikitina, N., Kajko-Mattsson, M., & Stråle, M. (2012). From Scrum to Scrumban: A case study of a process transition. In *Proceedings of the International Conference on Software and System Process, ICSSP '12* (pp. 140–149). IEEE Press. 10.1109/ICSSP.2012.6225959

NIST. (2012). *NIST SP 800-30, Revision 1, Guide for Conducting Risk Assessments*. National Institute of Standards and Technology.

Okubo, T., Kaiya, H., & Yoshioka, N. (2012). Effective Security Impact Analysis with Patterns for Software Enhancement. In *Proceedings of the 2011 Sixth International Conference on Availability, Reliability and Security (ARES'12)*. IEEE Computer Society.

Okubo, T., Taguchi, K., & Yoshioka, N. (2009). Misuse Cases + Assets + Security Goals. In *Proceedings of the International Conference on Computational Science and Engineering (CSE'09)*. IEEE Computer Society.

Othmane, L., Angin, P., Weffers, H., & Bhargava, B. (2014). Extending the Agile Development Process to Develop Acceptably Secure Software. *IEEE Transactions on Dependable and Secure Computing*, *11*(6), 497–509. doi:10.1109/TDSC.2014.2298011

Ouedraogo, M., Kuo, C.-T., Tjoa, S., Preston, D., Dubois, E., Simoes, P., & Cruz, T. (2014). Keeping an eye on your security through assurance indicators. In *Security and Cryptography (SECRYPT), 2014 11th International Conference on* (pp. 1-8). IEEE.

Ouedraogo, M., Mouratidis, H., Khadraoui, D., Dubois, E., & Palmer-Brown, D. (2009). Current trends and advances in IT service infrastructures security assurance evaluation. *The School of Computing, Information Technology and Engineering, 4th Annual Conference*, 132-141.

OWASP. (2006). *CLASP concepts*. Retrieved from https://www.owasp.org/index.php/CLASP_Concepts

OWASP. (2016). *Software Assurance Maturity Model*. Retrieved from http://www.opensamm.org/

OWASP. (2018). *OWASP Zed Attack Proxy Project*. Retrieved from https://www.owasp.org/index.php/OWASP_Zed_Attack_Proxy_Project

Oyetoyan, T. D., Cruzes, D. S., & Jaatun, M. G. (2016). An Empirical Study on the Relationship between Software Security Skills, Usage and Training Needs in Agile Settings. In *2016 11th International Conference on Availability, Reliability and Security* (pp. 548—555). ACM.

Oyetoyan, T. D., Cruzes, D. S., & Jaatun, M. G. (2016). *An Empirical Study on the Relationship between Software Security Skills, Usage and Training Needs in Agile Settings.* Paper presented at the Availability, Reliability and Security (ARES), 2016 11th International Conference on. 10.1109/ARES.2016.103

Oyetoyan, T. D., Jaatun, M. G., & Cruzes, D. S. (2017). A lightweight measurement of software security skills, usage and training needs in agile teams. *International Journal of Secure Software Engineering, 8*(1), 1–27. doi:10.4018/IJSSE.2017010101

P. S. & C. P. V. S. S. R. (2017). A robust semi-blind watermarking for color images based on multiple decompositions. *Multimedia Tools and Applications.*

Pagliery. (2014). *Bitcoin: And the Future of Money.* Triumph Books.

Pal Singh, S., & Bhatnagar, G. (2017). A Novel Chaos Based Robust Watermarking Framework. *Proceedings of the International Conference on Computer Vision and Image Processing, Advances in Intelligent Systems and Computing,* 439-447. 10.1007/978-981-10-2107-7_40

Parah, S., Sheikh, J., Loan, N., & Bhat, G. (2016). Robust and blind watermarking technique in DCT domain using inter-block coefficient differencing. *Digital Signal Processing, 53,* 11–24. doi:10.1016/j.dsp.2016.02.005

Pareek, N. K., Patidar, V., & Sud, K. K. (2006). Image encryption using chaotic logistic map. *Image and Vision Computing, 24*(9), 926–934. doi:10.1016/j.imavis.2006.02.021

Pendleton, M., Garcia-Lebron, R., Cho, J.-H., & Xu, S. (2017). *A survey on systems security metrics. In ACM Computing Surveys* (pp. 1–35). CSUR.

Peters, Panayi, & Chapelle. (2015). *Trends in crypto-currencies and blockchain technologies: A monetary theory and regulation perspective.* Academic Press.

Peters, G. W., & Panayi, E. (2016). Understanding Modern Banking Ledgers through Blockchain Technologies: Future of Transaction Processing and Smart Contracts on the Internet of Money. In *Banking Beyond Banks and Money* (pp. 239–278). Springer. doi:10.1007/978-3-319-42448-4_13

Pham, N., Baud, L., Bellot, P., & Riguidel, M. (2008). A near real-time system for security assurance assessment. In *The third International Conference on Internet monitoring and protection* (pp. 152-160). IEEE.

Philip, J., & Bharadi, V. (2016) Online Signature Verification in Banking Application: Biometrics SaaS Implementation. *Proceedings on International Conference on Communication Computing and Virtualization, 306,* 28-33.

Pietikäinen, P., & Röning, J. (2014). *Handbook of the Secure Agile Software Development Life Cycle.* Univ. of Oulu.

Pilgrim, P. (2013). *Java EE 7 Developer Handbook.* Packt Publishing.

Pilkington, M. (2015). *Blockchain technology: principles and applications*. Browser Download This Paper.

Poljicak, A. (2011). Discrete Fourier transform–based watermarking method with an optimal implementation radius. *Journal of Electronic Imaging, 20*(3), 033008. doi:10.1117/1.3609010

Poniszewska-Maranda, A. (2005, June). *Role engineering of information system using extended RBAC model. In 14th IEEE International Workshops on Enabling Technologies* (pp. 154–159). Infrastructure for Collaborative Enterprise.

Port, D., & Wilf, J. (2017). A Decision-Theoretic Approach to Measuring Security. *Proceedings of the 50th Hawaii International Conference on System Sciences*. 10.24251/HICSS.2017.737

Portswigger. (2018). *Portswigger Burp Suite Free Edition*. Retrieved from http://portswigger. net/burp/download.html

Potter, L. E., & Vickers, G. (2015). What skills do you need to work in cyber security?: A look at the Australian market. *Proceedings of the 2015 ACM SIGMIS Conference on Computers and People Research*. 10.1145/2751957.2751967

Power, R., & Li, J. (2010) Building fast, distributed programs with partitioned tables. *9th USENIX Symposium on Operating Systems Design and Implementation*.

Preda, R. (2013). Semi-fragile watermarking for image authentication with sensitive tamper localization in the wavelet domain. *Measurement, 46*(1), 367–373. doi:10.1016/j. measurement.2012.07.010

Priebe, T., Fernandez-Buglioni, E., Mehlau, J. I., & Pernul, G. (2004). A Pattern System for Access Control. In *Research Directions in Data and Applications Security XVIII* (Vol. 144). IFIP International Federation for Information Processing. doi:10.1007/1-4020-8128-6_16

Project, O. W. (2016). *Application Security Verification Standard 3.0.1*. OWASP.

Radharani, S., & Valarmathi, D. (2010). A Study on Watermarking Schemes for Image Authentication. *International Journal of Computers and Applications, 2*(4), 24–32. doi:10.5120/658-925

Raghavender Rao, Y., & Nagabhooshanam, E. (2014). A novel image zero-watermarking scheme based on DWT-BN-SVD. *International Conference on Information Communication and Embedded Systems (ICICES)*, 1-6.

Rahmani, H., Mortezaei, R., & Ebrahimi Moghaddam, M. (2010). A New Robust Watermarking Scheme to Increase Image Security. *EURASIP Journal on Advances in Signal Processing, 2010*(1), 428183. doi:10.1155/2010/428183

Ramesh, B., Cao, L., & Baskerville, R. (2010). Agile requirements engineering practices and challenges: An empirical study. *Information Systems Journal, 20*(5), 449–480. doi:10.1111/j.1365-2575.2007.00259.x

Rani, A., Raman, B., & Kumar, S. (2013). A robust watermarking scheme exploiting balanced neural tree for rightful ownership protection. *Multimedia Tools and Applications*, 72(3), 2225–2248. doi:10.100711042-013-1528-3

Ray, I., Li, N., France, R., & Kim, D. K. (2004, June). Using UML to visualize role-based access control constraints. In *Proceedings of the ninth ACM symposium on Access control models and technologies* (pp. 115-124). ACM. 10.1145/990036.990054

Rindell, K., Hyrynsalmi, S., & Leppänen, V. (2015b). Securing Scrum for VAHTI. CEUR Workshop Proceedings, 1525, 236-250.

Rindell, K., Hyrynsalmi, S., & Leppänen, V. (2016). Case study of security development in an agile environment: building identity management for a government agency. In *Proceedings of 2016 11th International Conference on Availability, Reliability and Security (ARES)* (pp. 556-593). IEEE. 10.1109/ARES.2016.45

Rindell, K., Hyrynsalmi, S., & Leppänen, V. (2017b). Busting a Myth: Review of Agile Security Engineering Methods. In *Proceedings of the 12th International Conference on Availability, Reliability and Security (ARES'17)* (pp. 74:1-74:10). ACM. 10.1145/3098954.3103170

Rindell, K., Hyrynsalmi, S., & Leppänen, V. (2015) Securing Scrum for VAHTI. In *Proceedings of 14th Symposium on Programming Languages and Software Tools (SPLST)* (pp. 236-250). University of Tampere.

Rindell, K., Hyrynsalmi, S., & Leppänen, V. (2015a). A comparison of security assurance support of agile software development methods. In *Proceedings of Proceedings of the 15th International Conference on Computer Systems and Technologies* (pp. 61-68). ACM. 10.1145/2812428.2812431

Rindell, K., Hyrynsalmi, S., & Leppänen, V. (2017a). Case Study of Agile Security Engineering: Building Identity Management for a Government Agency. *International Journal of Secure Software Engineering*, 8(1), 43–57. doi:10.4018/IJSSE.2017010103

Robinson, H., & Sharp, H. (2004). Extreme Programming and Agile Processes in Software Engineering. *5th International Conference, XP 2004 Proceedings*. 10.1007/978-3-540-24853-8_16

Rosenberg, D., & Stephens, M. (2003). *Extreme programming refactored: the case against XP*. Apress.

Roy, S., & Pal, A. (2016). A robust blind hybrid image watermarking scheme in RDWT-DCT domain using Arnold scrambling. *Multimedia Tools and Applications*, 76(3), 3577–3616. doi:10.100711042-016-3902-4

Roy, S., & Pal, A. (2017). A blind DCT based color watermarking algorithm for embedding multiple watermarks. *AEÜ. International Journal of Electronics and Communications*, 72, 149–161. doi:10.1016/j.aeue.2016.12.003

Runeson, P., Host, M., Rainer, A., & Regnell, B. (2012). *Case study research in software engineering: Guidelines and examples*. John Wiley & Sons. doi:10.1002/9781118181034

SAFECode. (2012). *Practical security stories and security tasks for agile development environments*. Retrieved from http://www.safecode.org/publication/SAFECode_Agile_Dev_Security0712.pdf

Saini, S. (2015). A survey on watermarking web contents for protecting copyright. *IEEE second International Conference on Innovations in Information Embedded and Communication Systems ICIIECS*, 1-4. 10.1109/ICIIECS.2015.7193239

Sandhu, R. S., Coyne, E. J., Feinstein, H. L., & Youman, C. E. (1996). Role-based access control models. *Computer*, *29*(2), 38–47. doi:10.1109/2.485845

Santos, R. (2017). *Microsoft Threat Modeling Tool mitigations*. Retrieved from https://docs.microsoft.com/en-ie/azure/security/azure-security-threat-modeling-tool-mitigations

Savola, R. M. (2013). Quality of security metrics and measurement. *Computers & Security*, *37*, 78–90. doi:10.1016/j.cose.2013.05.002

Schieferdecker, I., Grossmann, J., & Schneider, M. (2012). Model-Based Security Testing. *Proceedings of the 7th Workshop on Model Based Testing*, 1-12.

Schneider, S. (2001). *The b-method: an Introduction*. Basingstoke, UK: Palgrave.

Schneidewind, N. F. (2007). Risk-driven software testing and reliability. *International Journal of Reliability Quality and Safety Engineering*, *14*(02), 99–132. doi:10.1142/S0218539307002532

Schneier, B. (1999). Attack trees. *Dr. Dobb's Journal*, *24*(12), 21–29.

Schwaber, K. (1995). Scrum development process. *Proceedings of the 10th Annual ACM Conference on Object Oriented Programming Systems, Languages, and Applications (OOPSLA)*, 117–134.

Schwaber, K. (2004). *Agile Project Management with Scrum*. Redmond, WA: Microsoft Press.

Seehusen, F. (2014). A technique for risk-based test procedure identification, prioritization and selection. In *Proceedings of the International Symposium On Leveraging Applications of Formal Methods, Verification and Validation* (pp. 277-291). Springer. 10.1007/978-3-662-45231-8_20

Selenium. (2018). *SeleniumHQ*. Retrieved from http://www.seleniumhq.org/

Shao, Z., Shang, Y., Zeng, R., Shu, H., Coatrieux, G., & Wu, J. (2016). Robust watermarking scheme for color image based on quaternion-type moment invariants and visual cryptography. *Signal Processing Image Communication*, *48*, 12–21. doi:10.1016/j.image.2016.09.001

Shostack, A. (2014a). Elevation of privilege: Drawing developers into threat modeling. *2014 USENIX summit on gaming, games, and gamification in security education (3GSE 14)*.

Shostack, A. (2014b). *Threat modeling: Designing for security*. Wiley.

Singh, A., Dave, M., & Mohan, A. (2015). Hybrid technique for robust and imperceptible multiple watermarking using medical images. *Multimedia Tools and Applications*, *75*(14), 8381–8401. doi:10.100711042-015-2754-7

Singh, D., & Singh, S. (2016). DWT-SVD and DCT based robust and blind watermarking scheme for copyright protection. *Multimedia Tools and Applications.*

Smartesting. (2018). *Smartesting CertifyIt.* Retrieved from http://www.smartesting.com/en/certifyit/

Smite, D., Moe, N. B., & Torkar, R. (2008). Pitfalls in remote team coordination: Lessons learned from a case study. In A. Jedlitschka & O. Salo (Eds.), *Product-focused software process improvement* (pp. 345–359). Berlin: Springer Berlin Heidelberg. doi:10.1007/978-3-540-69566-0_28

Sohr, K., Drouineaud, M., Ahn, G. J., & Gogolla, M. (2008). Analyzing and managing role-based access control policies. *Knowledge and Data Engineering. IEEE Transactions on, 20*(7), 924–939.

Sonia & Singhal, A. (2011). Development of Agile Security Framework Using a Hybrid Technique for Requirements Elicitation. *Proceedings of the International Conference on Advances in Computing, Communication and Control (ICAC'11)*, 178–188.

Sonia, S. A., & Banati, H. (2014). FISA-XP: An agile-based integration of security activities with extreme programming. *Software Engineering Notes, 39*(3), 1–14. doi:10.1145/2597716.2597728

Spears, J. L., Barki, H., & Barton, R. R. (2013). Theorizing the concept and role of assurance in information systems security. *Information & Management, 50*(7), 598–605. doi:10.1016/j.im.2013.08.004

Statistics-Norway. (2017). *StatBank API User Guide. Statistics Norway.* Statistics Norway. Retrieved from http://www.ssb.no/en/omssb/tjenester-og-verktoy/api/px-api/_attachment/248250?_ts=15b48207778

Strangers, C. (2005). *Programming in E as Plan Coordination.* Springer-Verlag Berlin Heidelberg.

Strembeck, M., & Neumann, G. (2004). An Integrated Approach to Engineer and Enforce Context Constraints in RBAC Environments. *Proc. of the 8th ACM Symposium on Access Control Models and Technologies (SACMAT 2003), 3*, 392–427. 10.1145/1015040.1015043

Stutsman, R., Lee, C., & Ousterhout, J. (2015). Experience with Rules-Based Programming for Distributed, Concurrent, Fault-Tolerant Code. *USENIX Annual Technical Conference*, 17-30.

Su, Q., Niu, Y., Wang, Q., & Sheng, G. (2013). A blind color image watermarking based on DC component in the spatial domain. Optik - International Journal for Light and Electron Optics, 124(23), 6255-6260. doi:10.1016/j.ijleo.2013.05.013

Such, J. M., Gouglidis, A., Knowles, W., Misra, G., & Rashid, A. (2016). Information assurance techniques: Perceived cost effectiveness. *Computers & Security, 60*, 117–133. doi:10.1016/j.cose.2016.03.009

Swan. (2015). *Blockchain: Blueprint for a new economy.* O'Reilly Media, Inc.

Tao, H., Chongmin, L., Mohamad Zain, J., & Abdalla, A. (2014). Robust Image Watermarking Theories and Techniques: A Review. *Journal of Applied Research and Technology, 12*(1), 122–138. doi:10.1016/S1665-6423(14)71612-8

Tauro, C., Aravindh, S., & Shreeharsha, A. (2012). Comparative study of the new generation, agile, scalable, high performance NOSQL databases. *International Journal of Computers and Applications, 48*(20), 1–4. doi:10.5120/7461-0336

Thakurta, R. (2013). A value-based approach to prioritise non-functional requirements during software project development. *International Journal of Business Information Systems, 12*(4), 363–382. doi:10.1504/IJBIS.2013.053213

Thanh, T., & Tanaka, K. (2015). The novel and robust watermarking method based on q-logarithm frequency domain. *Multimedia Tools and Applications, 75*(18), 11097–11125. doi:10.100711042-015-2836-6

Thilagavathi, N., Saravanan, D., Kumarakrishnan, S., Sakthivel, P., Amudhavel, J., & Prabu, U. (2015). A Survey of Reversible Watermarking Techniques, Application and Attacks. *Proceedings of the International Conference on Advanced Research in Computer Science Engineering & Technology (ICARCSET)*. 10.1145/2743065.2743102

Thurau, M. (2012). *Akka framework*. University of Lübeck.

Tretmans, J., & Brinksma, E. (2003). TorX: Automated Model-Based Testing. *Proceedings of the Conference on Model-Driven Software Engineering*, 11-12.

Tuma, K., Calikli, G., & Scandariato, R. (2018). Threat analysis of software systems: A systematic literature review. *Journal of Systems and Software, 144*.

Tung, Y.-H., Lo, S.-C., Shih, J.-F., & Lin, H.-F. (2016). An integrated security testing framework for Secure Software Development Life Cycle. In *Network Operations and Management Symposium (APNOMS), 2016 18th Asia-Pacific* (pp. 1-4). IEEE. 10.1109/APNOMS.2016.7737238

Urvi, H., Panchal, R. & Srivastava. (2015). A Comprehensive Survey on Digital Image Watermarking Techniques. *Proceeding of the Fifth International Conference on Communication Systems and Network Technologies (CSNT)*, 591-595.

Utting, M., Pretschner, A., & Legeard, B. (2012). A taxonomy of model-based testing approaches. *Software Testing, Verification & Reliability, 22*(5), 297–312. doi:10.1002tvr.456

VAHTI. (2001-2016). *VAHTI instructions*. Retrieved from https://www.vahtiohje.fi/web/guest/home

VAHTI. (2009). *ICT-toiminnan varautuminen häiriö- ja erityistilanteisiin*. Retrieved from https://www.vahtiohje.fi/web/guest/2/2009-ict-toiminnan-varautuminen-hairio-ja-erityistilanteisiin

VAHTI. (2012a). *Requirements for ICT Contingency Planning*. Retrieved from https://www.vahtiohje.fi/web/guest/2b/2012-requirements-for-ict-contingency-planning

VAHTI. (2012b). *Teknisen ympäristön tietoturvataso-ohje*. Retrieved from https://www.vahtiohje.fi/web/guest/3/2012-teknisen-ympariston-tietoturvataso-ohje

VAHTI. (2013). *Sovelluskehityksen tietoturvaohje*. Retrieved from https://www.vahtiohje.fi/web/guest/vahti-1/2013-sovelluskehityksen-tietoturvaohje

Varghese, J., Subash, S., Bin Hussain, O., Nallaperumal, K., Ramadan Saady, M., & Samiulla Khan, M. (2016). An improved digital image watermarking scheme using the discrete Fourier transform and singular value decomposition. *Turkish Journal of Electrical Engineering and Computer Sciences*, *24*, 3432–3447. doi:10.3906/elk-1409-12

Verma, G., Gawande, S., Bhura, M., & Koolagudi, S. (2016). Polygonal Meshes Predicated Watermarking Algorithm to Avert Misinterpretation of ATM Cards. *Procedia Computer Science*, *89*, 587–596. doi:10.1016/j.procs.2016.06.018

VersionOne, C. (2018). *12th Annual State of the Agile Survey*. Author.

VersionOne. (2013). *8th Annual State of Agile Survey*. Retrieved from http://www.versionone.com/pdf/2013-state-of-agile-survey.pdf

VersionOne. (2017). *11th annual state of agile survey*. Retrieved from https://explore.versionone.com/state-of-agile/versionone-11th-annual-state-of-agile-report-2 Retrieved 15/08/2017

Villamizar, H., Kalinowski, M., Viana, M., & Méndez Fernández, D. (2018). A Systematic Mapping Study on Security in Agile Requirements Engineering. *Euromicro Conference on Software Engineering and Advanced Applications 2018*. 10.1109/SEAA.2018.00080

Vuori, M. (2011). *Agile Development of Safety-Critical Software*. Tampere: Tampere University of Technology.

Wang, J., & Liu, Y. (2016). Schur Decomposition Based Robust Watermarking Algorithm in Contourlet Domain. *Proceeding of the International Conference on Cloud Computing and Security (ICCCS)*, 114-124.

Wang, B., Ding, J., Wen, Q., Liao, X., & Liu, C. (2009). An image watermarking algorithm based on DWT, DCT and SVD. *IEEE International Conference on Network Infrastructure and Digital Content*, 1034–1038. 10.1109/ICNIDC.2009.5360866

Wang, C., Wang, X., Zhang, C., & Xia, Z. (2017). Geometric correction based color image watermarking using fuzzy least squares support vector machine and Bessel K form distribution. *Signal Processing*, *134*, 197–208. doi:10.1016/j.sigpro.2016.12.010

Wang, X., Liu, Y., Xu, H., Wang, A., & Yang, H. (2016). Blind optimum detector for robust image watermarking in nonsubsampled shearlet Domain. *Information Sciences*, *372*, 634–654. doi:10.1016/j.ins.2016.08.076

Washizaki, H. (2017). Security Patterns: Research Direction, Metamodel, Application and Verification. *Proceedings of the 2017 International Workshop on Big Data & Information Security (IWBIS)*. 10.1109/IWBIS.2017.8275094

Washizaki, H., Xia, T., Kamata, N., Fukazawa, Y., Kanuka, H., Yamaoto, D., ... Priyalakshmi, G. (2018). Taxonomy and Literature Survey of Security Pattern Research. *Proceedings of the IEEE Conference on Applications, Information and Network Security (AINS 2018).*

Wäyrynen, J., Bodén, M., & Boström, G. (2004). Security Engineering and eXtreme Programming: An Impossible Marriage? Springer Berlin Heidelberg.

Wäyrynen, J., Bodén, M., & Boström, G. (2004). *Security engineering and eXtreme programming: An impossible marriage?* In Extreme programming and agile methods-XP/Agile Universe 2004 (pp. 117–128). Springer. doi:10.1007/978-3-540-27777-4_12

Weldehawaryat, G. K., & Katt, B. (2018). Towards a Quantitative Approach for Security Assurance Metrics. In *SECURWARE 2018: The Twelfth International Conference on Emerging Security Information, Systems and Technologies.* IARIA.

Wireshark. (2018). Retrieved from https://www.wireshark.org/

Wong, W. E., Qi, Y., & Cooper, K. (2005). Source code-based software risk assessing. In *Proceedings of the 2005 ACM symposium on Applied computing* (pp. 1485-1490). ACM. 10.1145/1066677.1067014

Wood. (2014). *Ethereum: A secure decentralised generalised transaction ledger.* Ethereum Project Yellow Paper 151.

Yang, S., Song, Z., Fang, Z., & Yang, J. (2010). A novel affine attack robust blind watermarking algorithm. *Procedia Engineering, 7*, 239–246. doi:10.1016/j.proeng.2010.11.038

Yan, W. (2017). *Introduction to intelligent surveillance.* London: Springer. doi:10.1007/978-3-319-60228-8

Ye, X., Chen, X., Deng, M., Hui, S., & Wang, Y. (2014). A Multiple-Level DCT Based Robust DWT-SVD Watermark Method. *Proceeding of the Tenth International Conference on Computational Intelligence and Security, 479-483.* 10.1109/CIS.2014.28

Yin, R. K. (2003). *Case Study Research: Design and Methods* (3rd ed.). SAGE Publications, Inc.

Yoo, S. G., Vaca, H. P., & Kim, J. (2017). Enhanced Misuse Cases for Prioritization of Security Requirements. *Proceedings of the 9th International Conference on Information Management and Engineering, 1-10.* 10.1145/3149572.3149580

Yoshizawa, M., Kobashi, T., Washizaki, H., Fukazawa, Y., Okubo, T., Kaiya, H., & Yoshioka, N. (2014). Verification of Implementing Security Design Patterns Using a Test Template. *Proceedings of the 9th International Conference on Availability, Reliability and Security (ARES2014).*

Yoshizawa, M., Washizaki, H., Fukazawa, Y., Okubo, T., Kaiya, H., & Yoshioka, N. (2016). Implementation Support of Security Design Patterns Using Test Templates. *Information, 2*(34), 1-19.

Compilation of References

Yuan, C., He, Y., He, J., & Zhou, Z. (2006). *A Verifiable Formal Specification for RBAC Model with Constraints of Separation of Duty.* Academic Press.

Yuan, X. G., & Zhou, Z. (2011). A novel robust watermarking algorithm based on DWT-DCT-SVD. *Computer Engineering and Science, 1*, 27.

Yuen, C. H., & Wong, K. W. (2011). A chaos-based joint image compression and encryption scheme using DCT and SHA-1. *Applied Soft Computing, 11*(8), 5092–5098. doi:10.1016/j.asoc.2011.05.050

Yu, S., & Brewster, J. (2012). Formal specification and implementation of RBAC model with SOD. *Journal of Software, 7*(4), 870–877. doi:10.4304/jsw.7.4.870-877

Zhao, J., Xu, W., Zhang, S., Fan, S., & Zhang, W. (2016). A Strong Robust Zero-Watermarking Scheme Based on Shearlets High Ability for Capturing Directional Features. *Mathematical Problems in Engineering, 2016*, 1–11.

Zhao, J., Zhang, N., Jia, J., & Wang, H. (2015). Digital watermarking algorithm based on scale-invariant feature regions in non-subsampled contourlet transform domain. *Journal of Systems Engineering and Electronics, 26*(6), 1309–1314. doi:10.1109/JSEE.2015.00143

Zheng, Z., Xie, S., Dai, H.-N., & Wang, H. (2016). Blockchain Challenges and Opportunities. *Survey (London, England).*

Zhu, J., Lipford, H. R., & Chu, B. (2013). Interactive support for secure programming education. *Proceeding of the 44th ACM technical symposium on Computer science education.* 10.1145/2445196.2445396

Zyskind, G., & Nathan, O. (2015). Decentralizing privacy: Using blockchain to protect personal data. In *Security and Privacy Workshops* (pp. 180–184). SPW. doi:10.1109/SPW.2015.27

About the Contributors

Michael Felderer is a professor in software engineering at the Department of Computer Science at the University of Innsbruck, Austria and a guest professor at the Blekinge Institute of Technology, Sweden. He holds a PhD and a habilitation degree in computer science. His research interests in software and security engineering include testing and quality assurance, risk management, requirements engineering, design and modeling, processes, measurement and analytics as well as empirical research methodology in general. He is author of more than 130 publications. Michael Felderer works in close collaboration with industry and transfers his research results into practice as a consultant and speaker on industrial conferences.

* * *

Jan Øyvind Aagedal holds a PhD in computer science from the University of Oslo. He is currently the Country Manager at Equatex Norway. Dr. Aagedal was a Senior Research Scientist at SINTEF for 14 years, with a research focus on quality of service specifications and model transformations. Dr. Aagedal joined Telenor for two years as Systems Architect after his research career, and then in 2009 he became the CTO in Accurate Equity. Dr. Aagedal was program co-chair of EDOC 2002 and has been member of numerous program committees for workshops and conferences.

Nasser Al-Mur Al-Hadhrami is an IT teacher at a basic education school in the Sultanate of Oman. He is currently doing his PhD in cyber security at the University of Aberdeen, UK. He Obtained his M.Sc. degree in 2014 in Computer and Information Security from the University of Portsmouth, UK, and the B.Sc. degree in Computer Science from Nizwa College of Education, Oman (2006). His research interests include computer security, formal methods and software verification, and currently is focusing (as part of his PhD studies) on reasoning approaches, in particular the use of argumentation theory, to reason about conflicts and inconsistencies in security policies.

Adel Alti obtained the Master degree from the University of Setif (UFAS), Algeria, in 1998. He obtained a Ph.D. degree in software engineering from UFAS university of Sétif, Algeria, 2011. Right now he is an associate professor, HDR at University of Sétif. He is a header of the Smart Semantic Context-aware Services research group LRSD. His area of interests includes Mobility; ambient, pervasive and ubiquitous computing, automated software engineering, mapping multimedia concepts into UML, semantic integration of architectural description into MDA platforms, context-aware quality software architectures and automated service management, Context and QoS. During his work he has published number of publications concerning these subjects.

Karin Bernsmed is a senior research scientist at SINTEF Digital. She has a Ph.D. from the Norwegian University of Science and Technology, where she also holds an Associate Assistant Professor position. Karin has a long experience in cyber security threat and risk assessment, requirements engineering and design of secure and robust ICT systems in a number of different domains, including aviation, maritime and the energy sector. She is a certified ISO/IEC 27001 Lead Implementer.

Daniela S. Cruzes is a senior scientist at SINTEF. Previously, she was adjunct associate professor at the Norwegian University of Science and Technology (NTNU). She worked as a research fellow at the University of Maryland and Fraunhofer Center for Experimental Software Engineering-Maryland. Dr. Daniela Cruzes is the project manager of the SoS-Agile (Science of Security for Agile software Development) project funded by the Research Council of Norway. Her interests are agile software development, software security, global software engineering, empirical research methods, theory development and synthesis of software engineering studies.

Gencer Erdogan, PhD, Research Scientist at SINTEF. He received his PhD in computer science from the University of Oslo in 2016 with the dissertation thesis "CORAL: A Model-Based Approach to Risk-Driven Security Testing". His research interests include information and system security, modelling, model-based security and cyber-risk analysis, and model-based risk-driven security testing. Gencer Erdogan has broad experience from national and international research projects within the field of model-based specification and risk assessment, and risk-based security testing, as well as industrial experience as a software developer and security tester.

Jon Hofstad is Senior Manager at PwC IT Risk, focusing on cybersecurity, Operational Risk and Enterprise Risk Management (ERM). He has more than 17 years' experience from cybersecurity and risk management. Prior to PwC, Jon Hofstad held the role as the Corporate Risk Manager at EVRY ASA where he was responsible for developing and maintaining EVRY's risk management efforts across the organization. Hofstad has broad experience within the field of software security in the industry and has held several positions within EVRY, such as Senior Security Consultant, Senior Security Architect, and Chief Security Officer.

Sami Hyrynsalmi, D.Sc. (tech), is a nerd who has always enjoyed working with programming and computers. After graduating as M.Sc. in software engineering from the University of Turku in 2009, he decided to focus on the real issues and started his doctoral dissertation work on mobile application ecosystems. After successfully defending his thesis in 2014, he has focused on various themes from software and its production to business ecosystems, software metrics as well as to computer games. Currently, he is working as an Assistant Professor (tenure track) of Software Product Management and Business in TTY Pori at Tampere University of Technology.

Martin Gilje Jaatun is a Senior Scientist at SINTEF Digital and an Adjunct Professor at the University of Stavanger. He graduated from the Norwegian Institute of Technology (NTH) in 1992, and received the Dr.Philos. degree from the University of Stavanger in 2015. Previous positions include scientist at the Norwegian Defence Research Establishment (FFI), and Senior Lecturer in information security at the Bodø Graduate School of Business. His research interests include software security, security in cloud computing, and security of critical information infrastructures. He is vice chairman of the Cloud Computing Association (cloudcom. org), vice chair of IEEE TCCLD, and a Senior Member of the IEEE. He is also an IEEE Cybersecurity ambassador, and Editor-in-Chief of the International Journal of Secure Software Engineering.

Basel Katt is an Associate Professor at the Norwegian University of Science and Technology (NTNU), the department of information security and communication technology. Basel Katt holds a M.Sc. degree in Computer Science from the University of Essen-Duisburg, Germany, and his PhD degree in Computer Science from the University of Innsbruck, Austria. His research interest lies in the areas of security engineering, security testing, model driven security, security education, access control, and anomaly detection.

Lamri Laouamer is an assistant Professor at the department of management information systems at Qassim University, KSA. He is also an associate researcher at Lab-STICC, Université de Bretagne Occidentale, Brest, France. He received his Ph.D in computer science, in the field of information security, from Université de Bretagne Occidentale, France, in 2012; his MSc in computer science and applied mathematics from the University of Quebec at Trois Rivieres, Canada, in 2006; and his B.Sc. in computer science from the University of Setif, Algeria, in 1999. His research interests include: multimedia watermarking, cryptology and information security. He is an associate editor of the journal of telecommunication systems from 2014-201, published by Springer.

Ville Leppänen is a professor in software engineering and software security at the University of Turku (UTU), Finland. He has 200 international conference and journal publications. His research interests are related broadly to software engineering and security, ranging from software engineering methodologies, project management practices, and tools to security and quality issues, and to programming languages, parallelism, and architectural design topics. Leppänen is currently leading seven research and development projects. He acts as the head of Software Engineering (UTU) and leader of Software Development Laboratory of Turku Centre for Computer Science.

Phu H. Nguyen is a Research Scientist at the Department of Software and Service Innovation, SINTEF, Norway. He obtained a PhD in Computer Science at the Interdisciplinary Research Centre for Security, Reliability and Trust, University of Luxembourg, Luxembourg, an MSc in Computer Science & Engineering from the Eindhoven University of Technology, the Netherlands, and a BSc in Computer Science from the Hanoi University of Science and Technology, Vietnam. Before joining SINTEF, he was a Postdoctoral Fellow at the Simula Research Lab, Norway. His research interests span Model-Driven Security, IoT Security, Security Design Patterns, Microservices, Model-Based Security Testing, and Systematic Reviews. He has experience with the EU research projects and the research projects with industry in Norway.

Tosin Daniel Oyetoyan is an adjunct professor at the Western Norway University of Applied Sciences. He received his PhD in software engineering at the department of Computer and Information Science, Norwegian University of Science and Technology. He has previously worked as a post doctoral fellow at SINTEF Digital, and before that as a software developer and analyst in the banking, healthcare and automation sectors. His research interests are in software quality and maintenance, software design, software refactoring, software metrics, empirical software engineering, software security, embedded systems, machine learning, and code analysis.

Nishu Prasher is currently working as an Information Security Consultant at Statistics Norway. Nishu Prasher holds a Master's degree in Information Security from the Norwegian University of Science and Technology, Gjøvik. Her research interest lies in the areas of security testing, security education and social engineering.

Kalle Rindell is a computer, Internet and security enthusiast with nearly two decades of working experience in programming, R&D and consulting. He is currently working for the CGI Group as a security consultant, and a Ph.D. student (tech) at University of Turku, Finland, researching software security and software engineering.

Fredrik Seehusen holds a PhD in computer science from the University of Oslo. Dr. Seehusen is one of the contributors to the CORAS approach to model-driven risk analysis. His research interests include risk assessment, security testing, and formal and semi-formal specification techniques and languages. Dr. Seehusen has broad experience from national and international research projects and has, amongst others, coordinated the European research project RASEN which addresses compositional risk assessment and security testing of networked systems.

Yun Shu is a Masters student of department of computer science, Auckland University of Technology, New Zealand. His research interests are online auction and blockchain.

Ketil Stølen holds a PhD in computer science from the University of Manchester. He is currently a Chief Scientist at SINTEF Digital and a Professor at the University of Oslo. Prof. Stølen led the development of the CORAS approach since the very beginning in 2001, and was a co-author of the CORAS-book published in 2011. In 2001 he co-authored a book on the Focus method with Prof. Manfred Broy. Prof. Stølen is currently managing several major Norwegian/European research projects focusing on issues related to risk analysis, modeling, security, and testing.

Inger Anne Tøndel is a research scientist at SINTEF Digital and PhD candidate at the Norwegian University of Science and Technology (NTNU). She has more than ten years of experience in research on cyber security and software security in different domains, including energy systems and health care. Her research interests include security requirements, risk management and cyber insurance.

Hironori Washizaki is director and professor at Global Software Engineering Laboratory, Waseda University, Japan. He also works at National Institute of Informatics as visiting professor, at System Information Co., Ltd. as outside director, and at eXmotion Co., Ltd. as outside director. He is a technical adviser of Gaio Technology Co., Ltd.

Wei Qi Yan is an Associate Professor with the Auckland University of Technology (AUT), his expertise is in digital security, surveillance and forensics, he is leading the Computer and Communication Security (CCS) Research Group at AUT. Dr. Yan was an exchange Computer Scientist between the Royal Society of New Zealand (RSNZ) and the Chinese Academy of Sciences (CAS) China, he is Chair of the ACM Multimedia Chapter of New Zealand, a Member of the ACM, a Senior Member of the IEEE, TC members of the IEEE. Dr. Yan is a guest (adjunct) Professor with PhD supervision of the State Key Laboratory of Information Security (SKLOIS) China. A visiting Professor of the University of Auckland, New Zealand and the National University of Singapore, Singapore in computer science.

Nobukazu Yoshioka is a researcher at the National Institute of Informatics, Japan. Dr. Nobukazu Yoshioka received his B.E degree in Electronic and Information Engineering from Toyama University in 1993. He received his M.E. and Ph.D. degrees in School of Information Science from Japan Advanced Institute of Science and Technology in 1995 and 1998, respectively. From 1998 to 2002, he was with Toshiba Corporation, Japan. From 2002 to 2004 he was a researcher, and since August 2004, he has been an associate professor, in National Institute of Informatics, Japan. His research interests include Security and Privacy Software Engineering, Cloud computing, Agent Technology, software engineering, and software evolution. He is a member of the Information Processing Society of Japan (IPSJ), the Institute of Electronics, information and Communication Engineers (IEICE) and Japan Society for Software Science and Technology (JSSST), the Japanese Society for Artificial Intelligence (JSAI) and IEEE CS. He has been a chair of IEEE CS Japan Chapter since 2017.

Jian Yu is a senior lecturer of computer science, Auckland University of Technology, New Zealand. His research interest is cloud computing and web systems.

Index

Ensure Quality Research is Introduced to the Academic Community

Become an IGI Global Reviewer for Authored Book Projects

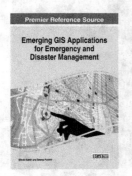

The overall success of an authored book project is dependent on quality and timely reviews.

In this competitive age of scholarly publishing, constructive and timely feedback significantly expedites the turnaround time of manuscripts from submission to acceptance, allowing the publication and discovery of forward-thinking research at a much more expeditious rate. Several IGI Global authored book projects are currently seeking highly qualified experts in the field to fill vacancies on their respective editorial review boards:

Applications may be sent to:
development@igi-global.com

Applicants must have a doctorate (or an equivalent degree) as well as publishing and reviewing experience. Reviewers are asked to write reviews in a timely, collegial, and constructive manner. All reviewers will begin their role on an ad-hoc basis for a period of one year, and upon successful completion of this term can be considered for full editorial review board status, with the potential for a subsequent promotion to Associate Editor.

If you have a colleague that may be interested in this opportunity, we encourage you to share this information with them.

Printed in the United States
By Bookmasters